MW00658421

INVENTED TRADITIONS IN
NORTH AND SOUTH KOREA

HAWAI'I STUDIES ON KOREA

Invented Traditions in North and South Korea

Edited by

ANDREW DAVID JACKSON
CODRUȚA SÎNTIONEAN
REMCO BREUKER
CEDARBOUGH SAEJI

University of Hawai'i Press, Honolulu
and
Center for Korean Studies, University of Hawai'i

27   26   25   24   23   22   6   5   4   3   2   1

Library of Congress Cataloging-in-Publication Data

Names: Jackson, Andrew David, editor. | Sîntionean, Codruța, editor. |
    Breuker, Remco E., editor. | Saeji, CedarBough, editor.
Title: Invented traditions in North and South Korea / edited by Andrew
    David Jackson, Codruța Sîntionean, Remco Breuker, CedarBough Saeji.
Other titles: Hawai'i studies on Korea.
Description: Honolulu : University of Hawai'i Press : Center for Korean
    Studies, University of Hawai'i, 2021. | Series: Hawai'i studies on Korea
    | Includes bibliographical references and index.
Identifiers: LCCN 2021015365 | ISBN 9780824890339 (hardback) | ISBN
    9780824890476 (adobe pdf) | ISBN 9780824890483 (epub) | ISBN
    9780824890490 (kindle edition)
Subjects: LCSH: Invented traditions—Korea (North) | Invented
    traditions—Korea (South) | Nationalism—Korea (North) |
    Nationalism—Korea (South) | Political culture—Korea (North) |
    Political culture—Korea (South)
Classification: LCC DS916.27 .I68 2021 | DDC 306.09519—dc23
LC record available at https://lccn.loc.gov/2021015365

 The Center for Korean Studies was established in 1972 to coordinate and develop resources for the study of Korea at the University of Hawai'i. Reflecting the diversity of the academic disciplines represented by affiliated members of the university faculty, the Center seeks especially to promote interdisciplinary and intercultural studies. Hawai'i Studies on Korea, published jointly by the Center and the University of Hawai'i Press, offers a forum for research in the social sciences and humanities pertaining to Korea and its people.

Cover photo: A small plastic Buddha nestles in a historic stone lantern at Chikjisa, near Kimchŏn in North Kyŏngsang Province, Korea. Photo by CedarBough Saeiji.

To
Wonae, Călin, Imke, Karjam

CONTENTS

PREFACE AND
ACKNOWLEDGMENTS

The original impetus for this collection came during the January 2016 Premodern Korean Studies in Europe Conference held in Paris where papers that focused on the revival of traditional cultural forms in modern-day South Korea generated some of the most compelling debates amongst the participants. The invention of tradition was a phrase that dominated the discussion and three of us—all premodernists by training—decided to put together a call for papers to investigate the revival of traditional cultural forms in modern-day Korea. In order to test the water and gauge the level of interest in the topic of invented traditions in the Korean context, in the summer of 2016, we put out a general call for contributions only to be inundated with responses from Koreanists from all over the world with ideas for the project. We decided to expand the field beyond historians with an interest in the political use of monumental invented traditions and invite anthropologists and ethno-musicologists who could bring to our collection the benefit of their insight into the performativity and creativity of culture. Our only regret was that we were unable to include all of the wonderful proposals that were sent to us, and we thank again all of those scholars who took so much of their valuable time to contribute ideas to this project.

The editors wish to thank Masako Ikeda, Cheryl Loe, and everyone at the University of Hawaiʻi Press for bringing this volume to press, but special thanks goes to Christopher Bae who provided invaluable support and great patience throughout this project. Thanks also go to Wendy Bolton, the eight peer reviewers, Suzanne Wertheim, Perry Iles, Gregory

S. Kailian, and Roald Maliangkay, whose feedback greatly improved the work and also to Robert Winstanley-Chesters. Elspeth McVey did a wonderful job of making the map under great pressure. The map in figure 2.1 created by Elspeth McVey uses modified data sourced from the World Bank (CC-BY 4.0); map data copyrighted OpenStreetMap contributors and available from https://www.openstreetmap.org. Thanks also to Isabelle Sancho whose conference provided the spark that lit the fire that keeps on burning.

A NOTE ON ROMANIZATION

We have used McCune-Reischauer to romanize Korean, Hepburn for Japanese, and Pinyin (without diacritics) for Chinese except in the case of commonly accepted alternative spellings of places like Pyongyang and Seoul and other words like taekwondo and hangul. We have used the Korean order of names with surname first and given names hyphenated as in Ch'oe Nam-sŏn. The exception is in the case of well-known names like Park Chung Hee and Syngman Rhee.

CHRONOLOGY

On the use of historical dates for kingdoms and dynasties, we have used the commonly purported dates throughout. This chronology includes the kingdoms, dynasties, and leaders most commonly featured in this volume.

HISTORICAL CHRONOLOGY OF KOREA

Old Chosŏn 古朝鮮	(Trad.) 2333 BCE–108 BCE
Tan'gun Chosŏn 檀君朝鮮	(Trad.) 2333 BCE–1295 BCE
Kija Chosŏn 箕子朝鮮	(Trad.) 1122 BCE–194 BCE
Wiman Chosŏn 衛滿朝鮮	(Trad.) 194 BCE–108 BCE
Samhan 三韓	(Proto–Three Kingdoms) first century
CE—third century CE	
Mahan 馬韓	
Chinhan 辰韓	
Pyŏnhan 弁韓	
Koguryŏ 高句麗	(Trad.) 37 BCE–668 CE
Paekche 百濟	(Trad.) 18 BCE–660 CE
Silla 新羅	(Trad.) 57 BCE–668 CE
Kaya 加耶	(Trad.) 42 BCE–562 CE
Unified Silla 統一新羅	668–935
Parhae 渤海	698–926
Koryŏ 高麗	918–1392
Chosŏn 朝鮮	1392–1910
Japanese colonial period	1910–1945

SOUTH KOREAN PRESIDENTS

1948–1960	Syngman Rhee (Yi Sŭng-man) 李承晚
1960–1961	Yun Posun (Yun Po-sŏn) 尹潽善
1961–1979	Park Chung Hee (Pak Chŏng-hŭi) 朴正熙
1980–1988	Chun Doo Hwan (Chŏn Tu-hwan) 全斗煥
1988–1993	Roh Tae Woo (No T'ae-u) 盧泰愚
1993–1998	Kim Young Sam (Kim Yŏng-sam) 金泳三
1998–2003	Kim Dae Jung (Kim Tae-jung) 金大中
2003–2008	Roh Moo-hyun (No Mu-hyŏn) 盧武鉉
2008–2013	Lee Myung-bak (Yi Myŏng-bak) 李明博
2013–2017	Park Geun-hye (Pak Kŭn-hye) 朴槿惠
2017–	Moon Jae-in (Mun Chae-in) 文在寅

NORTH KOREAN RULERS

1948–1994	Kim Il Sung (Kim Il-sŏng) 金日成
1994–2011	Kim Jong Il (Kim Chŏng-il) 金正日
2011–	Kim Jong Un (Kim Chŏng-ŭn) 金正恩

HISTORICAL CHRONOLOGY OF CHINA

Shang 商	c. 1550–1045 BCE
Western Zhou 西周	1045–771 BCE
Eastern Zhou 東周	771–256 BCE
Spring and Autumn Period 春秋時代	771–c. 475 BCE
Warring States Period 戰國時代	c. 475–221 BCE
Qin 秦	221–206 BCE
Han 漢	206 BCE–220 CE
Western Han 西漢	206 BCE–9 CE
Eastern Han 東漢	25–220 CE
Six Dynasties Period 六朝	220–589
Sui 隋	581–618
Tang 唐	618–907
Five Dynasties Period 五代	907–960

Liao 遼	916–1125
Song 宋	960–1279
Yuan 元	1279–1368
Ming 明	1368–1644
Qing 清	1644–1912

INVENTED TRADITIONS IN
KOREA—CONTENTION AND
INTERNATIONALIZATION

ANDREW DAVID JACKSON

Picture the scene: you are in a restaurant, sitting with your friends on stools around a steel drum that contains a saucepan-sized container of hot coals barbecuing slivers of marinated pork ribs or beef. The walls are decorated with images of farmers clothed in traditional white: they are farming, dancing, banging drums, singing, and drinking. Your friends cut up the meat with a large pair of scissors, and you dip it in soybean paste, add a slice of garlic, some spicy green pepper, chili pepper, and marinated spring onions or maybe some kimchi. You then wrap the lot in a lettuce leaf and eat it, washing it down with beer, a shot glass of soju (a white liquor), or a bowl of local rice wine.

Anyone who has been to South Korea (the Republic of Korea, or ROK) will recognize this scene, and foreign visitors to North Korea (the Democratic People's Republic of Korea, DPRK) may be treated to a similar culinary experience. This is the stereotypical image of a traditional Korean dining experience in many parts of the world. The paintings on the walls of the restaurant, the old-fashioned furniture, everything suggests a direct link back to a distant Korean past. The owner of this establishment may even *claim* a connection between the fare in their restaurant and ancient Korean culinary traditions.[1]

Yet how traditionally Korean is any of this experience? The chili peppers that color and spice the foods? The beverages consumed? The fact that there is even a *kogi chip* (meat restaurant) at all? Although bar-becue feels like the epitome of traditional gastronomic culture in South Korea, it is actually a construct of the last three decades of the twentieth century, one only made possible by cheap food imports (Cwiertka 2010, 131). The peppers found in your kimchi and many of your side dishes are most likely the Ch'ŏngyang variety of chili pepper, commonly thought to originate in Ch'ungch'ŏng Province but in fact developed in the 1970s in a South Korean laboratory commissioned by a Japanese food manufac-turer seeking an alternative to costly Mexican imports (Chu 2015). These peppers are considerably more fiery than the version that existed on the Korean Peninsula for two hundred years. Many of your other side dishes are probably composed of cheap imports from China, and the charcoal firing the grill was probably produced in Indonesia. If expensive *hanu* (Korean cow) beef is on the menu, you can thank a 1970s feat of agricul-tural bioengineering that bred imported Angus cows with native cattle in order to produce the sought-after marbling in the meat (Müller 2016). Your meal at this typical South Korean restaurant is a case of creative culi-nary construction, an experience that suggests continuity with a distant past but is of relatively recent origin—what Eric Hobsbawm and Terence Ranger call an "invented tradition."

Hobsbawm and Ranger's 1983 book *The Invention of Tradition* was groundbreaking, both in terms of its interdisciplinary approach and its applicability to different cultural, temporal, and intellectual contexts. In his theoretical introduction, Hobsbawm noted that "'traditions' that appear or claim to be old are often quite recent in origin and sometimes invented" (1983a, 1). Traditions are usually invented in an attempt to establish continuity with a suitable historical past that fits with a par-ticular contemporary sociopolitical agenda: "However, insofar as there is such reference to a historical past, the peculiarity of 'invented' tradi-tions is that the continuity with it is largely factitious. In short, they are responses to novel situations which take the form of reference to old situ-ations" (1983a, 1). Invented traditions do not preserve the past; instead they build an idea of a past and help keep this construction intact (Linder 2012, 37). Invented traditions are premised on an "invariant" past as a means to help structure a rapidly changing social context (Hobsbawm 1983a, 2). It is this quality that is important to the separation of invented traditions from other practices such as customs, which "cannot afford to be invariant," or from traditions that Hobsbawm describes as "genuine" (Hobsbawm 1983a, 2). Curiously, Hobsbawm does not elaborate, but one potential understanding of genuine tradition is something that "has been handed down," particularly orally and anonymously transmitted practices (Edward Shils, quoted in Linder 2012, 26). According to Hobsbawm, traditions can also be invented in different ways, such as the development of new uses for old practices, or the resurrection of defunct traditions.

Hobsbawm's theory of invented traditions has been criticized on several levels. Particularly contentious was the claim that "there is probably no time and place with which historians are concerned which has not seen the 'invention' of tradition" (Hobsbawm 1983a, 4). Dipesh Chakrabarty (1998, 285) has attacked Hobsbawm's assertions of the theory's universal applicability by arguing that non-Western civilizations in the premodern period never considered their past to be invariant.[2] Guy Beiner complains that Hobsbawm's thesis is too limiting to be capable of accounting for the sheer variety of cultural practices of human society, in particular, the vernacular traditions omitted from Hobsbawm and Ranger's collection, such as the culture of indigenous groups (2001, 5). These assumptions about the universal applicability of the theory have led to criticisms about how invented traditions have gone on to be used in much academic discourse. Beiner has attacked the uncritical, "ubiquitous" application of Hobsbawm's central thesis to descriptions of cultural revival in historical studies (2001, 1).

This claim of the universalism of his theory together with Hobsbawm's assertion of the distinction between genuine or invariant custom and invented tradition led to the criticism that his ideas were "structurally naïve" (Vlastos 1998, 3–4). Cultural historians and anthropologists have observed that tradition—like all aspects of culture—are "socially constructed" and therefore subject to re-interpretation (Vlastos 1998, 3–4; Beiner 2001, 1; Linder 2012, 37). Countering Hobsbawm's thesis is what Byron King Plant (2008, 179) calls the "Constructivist" view of scholars like Handler and Linnekin (1984) and the aforementioned Beiner (2001) who argue tradition is a "contemporaneous symbolic construction undertaken by societies in the present" (Plant 2008, 179). For Constructivists, tradition is a socially constructed process that involves continual re-creation (Plant 2008, 179). In some cultural musical forms such as folk songs, Roald Maliangkay (2016, 14) has observed it is virtually impossible to isolate a single fixed, all-encompassing and authentic original form since interpretation and improvisation are an "inherent aspect" of the art. Freezing "all elements of a traditional music would deny its practitioners the ability to modify their art to relate to contemporary entertainment and interpretation" (Maliangkay 2016, 14). In other words, the notion of "invariant" traditions undermines the creativity and performativity underlying cultural practices.

Hobsbawm's claims of the theory's universal applicability are all the more striking, because the case studies he examines in his introduction and that are explored by the contributors in the rest of the volume are in actual fact very specific. They are related to the revival of *distinct* types of cultural practice during periods of *particularly* extreme social and political change—especially during the process of nation building. Hobsbawm's own understanding of tradition and its uses and abuses is linked to his life's academic project—a Marxist examination of capitalist modernity— particularly, the emergence of European nation-states in the late nineteenth and early twentieth centuries. Hobsbawm argues, "The national phenomenon cannot be adequately investigated without careful attention to the 'invention of tradition'" (1983a, 14). The most striking case studies examined in Hobsbawm and Ranger's book are cultural practices closely linked to institutional power and the demarcation of political ideologies during periods of social change. Examples of invented traditions in their book with an *outwardly* official political function are the creation of public monuments, flags, anthems, and paraphernalia of nations or the newly coined rituals of the British monarchy, all developed to maintain order, loyalty, and national identity during a period of mass politics and shifting hierarchies (Hobsbawm 1983b, 263–285; Cannadine 1983, 108). Hobsbawm also argued that newly devised traditions were used as political tools by movements opposing state rule—for example, the European socialists' creation of a new left-wing iconography (red flags, May Day) to reflect the emerging political consciousness of workers during this same period (Hobsbawm 1983b, 263–286). It is within this latter context of nation and institution formation that Hobsbawm's theory is at its most effective. Hobsbawm's notion is a powerful tool to unlock the "ideological uses of the past," especially amongst governments or other elite groups seeking the legitimization of their actions and institutions or to establish social cohesion (Chakrabarty 1998, 285; Hobsbawm 1983a,

3–9). It is worth further delineating the typology of invented traditions established by Hobsbawm and highlighting the types of invented tradition that are clearly linked to institutional power and that were devised during social and political transformation. I call these aforementioned examples—both those types instituted by states and those in opposition to them—"monumental" invented traditions to reflect (what Hobsbawm describes as) the "statuomania" or mass production of public monuments created to ensure social cohesion and identity in an era of political transformation (Hobsbawm 1983b, 263–280).

Such traditions that serve as powerful normative forces when exploited by political leaders should be contrasted with other traditions, whose origins are little traceable—like many in North American indigenous communities (see Plant 2008, 186). There are also other inventions of tradition, which may be less explicitly tied to particular political agendas of institutional power—as in the aforementioned example of the Korean barbecue restaurant. Another example is that of folk songs in modern-day South Korea, which because they are dependent upon constant improvisation and re-interpretation by performers may in their processes of revision be less tied to specific periods of state formation. In addition, since many different interest groups are involved in the preservation of such cultural artifacts—scholars, performers, as well as the government—"the agent of change" may also be less easy to identify (Maliangkay 2016, 16). There is in the transformation of certain traditions, then, a far less obvious, traceable, and outward relationship to institutional power. Of course, there are links—in the case of folk songs through policies for preserving heritage and the control of museums, and in the case of meat restaurants through government legislation, for example—but the evident political agenda that underlies many of the monumental invented traditions that fill Hobsbawm and Ranger's book is less pronounced.

The convincing quality of *The Invention of Tradition*'s accounts of the political uses of traditional culture during state formation may explain why most academic criticisms target the theory—particularly the claims of its universality—rather than the actual use of the theory to elucidate the case studies contained in the collection. This quality may also explain why, despite the criticisms that Hobsbawm's claims undermined the innate flexibility and adaptability of tradition, almost four decades after the book's publication, scholars are still applying the notion of "invented traditions" in previously unexplored contexts of social and political change, for example in the Roman World (Boschung, Busch, and Versluys 2015) but also in Korea.

Invented Traditions in North and South Korea joins this growing body of work investigating the invention of tradition during different periods of recent Korean history. Many studies deal with the restoration of individual traditional practices, for example, Korean music in Keith Howard's *Music as Intangible Cultural Heritage: Policy, Ideology, and Practice in the Preservation of East Asian Tradition* (2012a, 2012b), and the preservation of Korean remains and relics in Hyung Il Pai's *Heritage Management in Korea and Japan* (2013). Like this current volume, two other works by Kim (1991) and Kendall (2011) consider the revival of a broader range of cultural objects and practices. The essays in Laurel Kendall's collection *Consuming Korean Tradition in Early and Late Modernity* take contrasting approaches to Hobsbawm's theory, by examining the commercial consumption of revived traditions and by portraying culture less as something fixed and unchanging, and more as something constantly made and remade. Kendall's volume was the first publication to explore invented traditions in the context of both colonial-era Korea (1910–1945) and the capitalist modernity of postwar South Korea. Her collection explores the revival of tradition by Koreans for reasons of nostalgia and as a reaction to fears of the erasure of distinctiveness, and it shows how tradition is consumed, experienced, and performed by Korean people. Kim Kwang-ŏk's article investigates the ways in which the revival of tradition was used as a political weapon by groups competing for influence in dictatorship-era South Korea (1991, 22–23). As such Kim's analysis of the use of invented traditions in the South Korea of the 1960s to the 1980s most closely resembles the analysis of monumental invented traditions explored in Hobsbawm and Ranger's collection.

Invented Traditions in North and South Korea draws on notions of tradition from both Kendall's and Kim's approaches to the revival of culture. Part of this collection—particularly the chapters in section three on music and traditional Korean objects—examine the performativity, refashioning, and consumption of traditional cultural practices, which are engaged in an ongoing process of transformation within modern South Korea. However, the chapters that make up the rest of the book, and that cover North Korea, history, language, and architecture continue in the same vein as Kim's work by paying special attention to the political uses of cultural revival, in particular the use of invented traditions by elites to socialize and mobilize populations and to legitimize institutions as well as the state. Here "elites" are those powerful institutions and groups within state and society that influence and shape political discourse. This includes the central institutions of the dictatorships that formulated cultural policy on the Korean Peninsula. In the South Korean case, this also includes influential groups—such as university academics, associations of amateur historians, and religious groups that have been able to operate with far greater independence from the central authorities than has been true in North Korea (Xu 2016, 142–146).[3] One important oppositional group is the 1970s and 1980s *minjung* movement—a broad alliance of "alienated classes" led by students and intellectuals that played a decisive role in the fall of authoritarian rule in 1980s South Korea (Lee 2007, 1; De Ceuster and Maliangkay 2003, 205).

This collection considers the use of invented traditions not only in South Korea, but in North Korea as well. There are several reasons for researching cultural practices in the two Koreas together. First, there is a common perception amongst both the South Korean public and the scholarly community that North and South Korea have diverged politically, linguistically, and culturally during seventy years of division, rendering meaningful comparison difficult (Jeong and Lee 2009, 213). This introductory essay aims to demonstrate that as far as elite use of invented tradition is concerned, meaningful comparison is vital for revealing commonly held assumptions about history, and cultural and national identity despite ideological divergence. Second, there is a lack of comparative cultural analysis between the two Koreas. Many South or North Korea scholars stay within the bounds of their own specialities and shy away from making cross-border analyses, usually for methodological reasons. A good example is cinema studies, where (with the exception of Hyangjin Lee's *Contemporary Korean Cinema: Identity and Politics*) film scholars have elided the film output of the other Korea in their cinematic analysis, treating state media and capitalist popular culture as incompatible despite similarities in subject matter (Kim and Choe 2014). Finally, too many scholars make generalizations about what constitutes "Korea" and "Korean culture" while limiting their discussion to the South (Jackson and Balmain 2016, 6). The invention of tradition provides an important platform upon which to make cross-border comparisons, and analysis of Korea and Korean culture.

The aim in considering the type of monumental invented tradition featured in Hobsbawm and Ranger's collection is to examine the role of culture in the shaping of the post-division Korean Peninsula. If we look at the history of the Korean Peninsula since 1945, we see a fertile territory for the development of invented traditions according to Hobsbawm's framework. Both Koreas have experienced a "rapid transformation of society" that weakened or destroyed "the social patterns for which 'old' traditions had been designed" (Hobsbawm 1983a, 4). Both Koreas had to deal with the perceived humiliation of a late nineteenth-century opening by the west, the loss of national sovereignty, the legacy of Japanese colonialism, periods of military rule overseen by powerful foreign administrations, the creation of separate states with opposing political ideologies, war, and rapid industrialization, all of which created immense social and demographic change. South Korea experienced political democratization and from the 1970s sustained economic prosperity, while the North, despite regime continuity and an initial period of industrial expansion, collapsed economically.

CONTENTION AND INTERNATIONALIZATION

An important feature of the Korean Peninsula is its prominent position in the global imagination. This is in part because of its perceived instability and the nuclear threats represented by the DPRK. The common view—as Hazel Smith (2015, 1) has argued—is that 25 million North Koreans are ruled by an evil and irrational totalitarian regime. The focus of foreign media on Cold War conflict on the Korean Peninsula and poverty in the DPRK has occasionally been criticized by South Korean cultural commentators as fostering a negative outlook on Korea as a whole.[4] However, since the 1988 Seoul Olympics, there has been a gradual increase in international exposure to South Korean culture abroad. Most recently, the *hallyu* phenomenon—the South Korean wave of pop music, film, TV dramas, urban lifestyles, language, and food—has dramatically increased international interest in the country and its culture, both modern and traditional (Maliangkay 2016, 2).

The chapters in this volume are best understood in the context of the two Koreas' struggle to form distinct, national cultural identities for both internal and external consumption. One aspect that has been frequently pointed out by researchers of the revival of cultural practice is the use of invented traditions as sources of and tools for contention (Howard 2012a, 2012b; Pai 2013, 7). "Contention" refers not only to academic debates that have arisen over the legitimacy of the preservation of culture by state agencies and questions of authenticity (see Howard 2012b, 114), it also refers to the expropriation of cultural revival by opposing groups within state and society to contend political legitimacy. One suitable framework for explaining contention over the invention of tradition is provided by Lisa Lowe and David Lloyd in their collection *The Politics of Culture in the Shadow of Capital*. Their comprehension of the political exploitation of culture comes close to Hobsbawm's thesis, and they have a particular interest in cultural production in decolonizing states. Lowe and Lloyd are above all concerned with what they call "contradictions" that occur in the process of decolonization. These contradictions are critical discrepancies between ideological platforms of political groups and their actual policies. An example can be seen in the case of nationalist movements that upon achieving independence from colonial administration legitimize their authority by using the same ruling discourses as their former imperial oppressors (1997, 9–10). For Lowe and Lloyd, as a result of these contradictions, and particularly after formal independence from colonialism, a state becomes a "site of" and "object of" contention for different political groups (1997, 7). This is because it "defines the terms" upon which national culture is presented, while "nationalist . . . movements confront the limits of state-oriented definitions . . . that emerge in the formation of modernity" (1997, 7–8). One Korean example of this state-society cultural contention observed by Kim Kwang-ŏk (1991, 22–23) and Timothy Tangherlini (1998, 127–131) is the use of shamanistic rituals by both the South Korean government in the opening ceremonies of the 1986 Asian Games and 1988 Olympics, and the student movement during the widespread anti-dictatorship protests of 1987. In their enactments, both sides aimed to preserve ancient Korean traditions, but both sides also appealed to different forms of nationalist thought to legitimize their political positions. The government was presenting to the world a unique national culture distinct from its colonial past and from other Asian countries, while the students were opposing the authorities by presenting themselves as the true custodians of Korean folk culture. Contention is also often an unintended consequence of the heritage protection system designed to both preserve and establish the authenticity of culture. The problem as Keith Howard observes is that the knowledge of early cultural practice is often limited and this creates scope for disagreement. In the official state system for regulating the preservation of cultural practices, what is deemed authentic is decided by experts based on the evidence available at the time. Once appointed, the cultural property is regarded as "immutable" (Howard 2012b, 133). The emergence of further evidence about cultural practices can result in conflict between competing groups of experts with much to gain from being seen as protectors of national culture. One example is the ongoing struggle over the continued preservation of the ritual music and dance performed at the Royal Ancestral Shrine (Chongmyo) and Confucian Shrine (Taesŏngjŏn), which has pitted state-funded institutions like the National Gugag Center (Kungnip kugagwŏn) and powerful Confucian groups and Sungkyungwan University against one another (Howard 2012a, 17; Howard 2012b, 118–120).

Using these ideas about culture as a site for contention and Laurel Kendall's (2011) analyses of the commodification, consumption, and performativity of invented traditions allows us to move forward into a comparative international framework. International perspectives have seldom been examined in previous research on invented traditions in Korea, but both the DPRK and ROK have produced invented traditions for consumption across and beyond their national borders, and abundant questions remain about both the target audience and impact of such traditions. Research on cultural revivals in both North and South Korea suggests important features that shed light on these questions and, by doing so, help us better understand the use of cultural practice in creating state legitimation discourses. These features—1) the open adulteration of tradition in North Korea, 2) the use of mythical figures, 3) longevity, 4) reception, and 5) cultural policy drives—combine to contextualize the recent revival of culture on the Korean Peninsula. They facilitate the identification of Korea-specific circumstances and phenomena. Finally, they raise theoretical questions about the application of Hobsbawm's framework to the Korean context, especially in relation to international reception and longevity of invented traditions.

The cultural practices discussed in this essay include cinema, heritage sites, martial arts, music, literature, and food. Subjects were chosen for their importance and their relationship to both contention and internationalization. However, these are not the only cultural practices relevant to invented traditions. The goal of this introductory chapter is not to be a theoretical end point, but rather to spark a wider debate on the use of invented traditions in the two countries.

Folk Songs, Heritage, and Re-interpretation

Hobsbawm's theory of tradition works on the assumption that when a tradition is invented, the fact and process of its revival has to be glossed over as part of the process of claiming authenticity, and that the pretense must be maintained that there has been no manipulation of the original practices. While this may be true of many invented traditions, a distinctive feature of the North Korean context is that its artists, academics, and policy makers often openly acknowledge their re-invention of traditional forms.

An official DPRK publication, for example, defines folk songs as having been created "spontaneously" through the "wisdom and artistic talent of the masses, handed down and polished through the years." These songs contain "emotions and sentiments of their cultural, historical, and ethnic quality. . . . The folk song has kept the very *essence of our national spirit, so it is also important to develop these songs in a more advanced and newly adapted format*" (quoted in Kwon 2007, 107; emphasis added). This means that the music remains unaltered, but "archaic" lyrics that include Sino-Korean structures have been transformed into odes of loyalty to Kim Il Sung (1912–1994) using native Korean vocabulary (Kwon 2007, 110–111). For the North Korean authorities, such formal changes have done nothing to alter the "national spirit" contained within the songs, which has been updated to exclude foreign forms. There seems to be no contradiction in the idea that if a folk song has been rewritten or reinterpreted (*chaehyŏngsanghwa*), it still provides a direct link to the spontaneity, creativity, and wisdom of the past (Kwon 2007, 108).

Other researchers have observed the same phenomenon in the revival of classical Korean literature and traditional musical instruments in the DPRK. Investigating modern adaptations (*yunsaek*) of traditional literary texts in the 1980s and 1990s, Sonja Häussler (2011, 101) discovered widespread changes to these texts: transformed narrative trajectories, the omission of incidents and characters, and the addition of conflicts to emphasize patriotic elements absent in the original text. Meanwhile, Keith Howard (2011, 181) has observed that official state policy made calls to "improve" Korean traditional instruments by altering their physical shape, size, and tone as early as 1961.

In both cases, officials and artists justified changes that stressed the "progressive and popular" and that rendered traditional forms suitable to the "reality of contemporary times" (Häussler 2011, 101; Howard 2011, 181–187). Practices were altered to encourage audiences to interpret cultural forms in ways approved of by the DPRK leadership. Häussler argues that the transformation of traditional forms was a means of maintaining loyalty in a context of economic decline, reduced foreign support, and increasing inter-Korean dialogue (2011, 103). Faced with a need for autonomy and indigenous forms, scholars revived classical Korean literature but changed the original texts to bring them into line with contemporary party policy. Howard notes that the North Korean changes to musical instruments were practical and served the new reality of mass performance in a state-socialist society. Changes were encouraged, as long as the instruments did not end up sounding too much like Western instruments—officials insisted that instruments retain their distinctive Koreanness, to be a third way between the West and the Korea of old (Howard 2011, 183–189).

Official pronouncements about the 1960s redevelopment of the DPRK's heritage sites provide clues to another fundamental principle underlying this open alteration of tradition. A case in point is the redevelopment of the Taesŏngsan (Great Fortress Mountain) area of Pyongyang. The area is perhaps best known for its Revolutionary Martyrs' Cemetery; however, it contains ruins of one of the largest forts of the Koguryŏ kingdom, built to defend the route into the capital. The authorities in charge in the 1960s considered the ruins appropriate for redevelopment, since Koguryŏ had famously managed to fend off attacks from far more powerful Sui and Tang dynasty forces. This image aligns perfectly with

North Korea's self-perception as a nation threatened by foreign (particularly US and Japanese) imperialism. The DPRK authorities reconstructed the ruins beyond recognition. They constructed a cemetery, zoo, botanical garden, and funfair around them, turning the site into a one-stop historical, ideological, and leisure theme park.

One important justification for such widespread changes to ancient ruins came from Kim Il Sung in a speech on heritage in which he argued that it was imperative for the government "to restore all the historical remains which were ravaged by the Japanese imperialists" (quoted in Atkins 1996, 203). According to Kim Il Sung, such structures—buildings, walls, temples, and shrines—were not in disrepair because they were old, neglected, or had been looted by locals, but because of Japanese colonialism. Following this logic, the open restoration and reconstruction of heritage was not a break with the past. It was Japanese colonialism that had created a break from the past, and the present-day restoration represented a return to the spirit of resistance against foreign domination that was exemplified by Koguryŏ, the kingdom that had built the fort being restored. In addition, for DPRK authorities, the rewriting of folk songs and classical literature represented a cleansing of undesirable past elements— especially those associated with cultural borrowings from China or with what the North condemned as primitive elements of the past. In this view, form and physical structure could be altered, as they merely constituted a receptacle for something more important, simultaneously intangible and truly Korean: the Korean essence, the national spirit. With their open admission of changes, the North Koreans demonstrate a sense of ownership of the past, a claim of control over the essence of national spirit. By changing traditional musical instruments, altering literature and lyrics, and rebuilding its physical heritage, the DPRK government signalled its autonomy over cultural heritage, its resistance to foreign domination, and its opposition to what it considered outdated and repressive rule.

The Park Chung Hee dictatorship in the ROK used many of the same legitimizing discourses as Kim to justify both his rule and the restoration of traditional culture. However, the DPRK government's openly acknowledged changes of traditional culture to convey messages about national autonomy stood in some contrast to the use of heritage by Park. The Park administration also invoked the "Korean spirit" (Chosŏn *chŏngsin*) as a criterion in the selection of which cultural objects and sites should represent the identity of the nation, and like Kim in the North, the Park administration also stressed the importance of preserving culture they claimed had been systematically destroyed and plundered by the Japanese. They also saw a Korean history driven by the "spirit" of national resistance against foreign enemies (Pai 2013, 11–12). For Park the preservation of national heritage from historic sites, to music, dance, art, and literature was a cornerstone of his political and economic policy. Only by instilling a sense of national pride through the restoration of Korean culture and through the invocation of this unique "spirit" could the population be mobilized to make sacrifices to develop the country's wrecked economy, accept his authoritarian rule (Maliangkay 2016, 3–4), and overtake a North Korea that had raced ahead economically in the post-1953 period.

An example of Park's cultural restoration policies is visible in one important case that has attracted much scholarly attention. From 1966 to 1975, the ROK government worked to restore a Chosŏn-period shrine dedicated to the sixteenth-century admiral Yi Sun-sin (1545–1598). The shrine, located in Ch'ungch'ŏng Province, is known as Hyŏnch'ungsa (Shrine of the famous and loyal one). Park Chung Hee used Yi Sun-sin's heroism during the Imjin War (1592–1598) as part of a legitimizing discourse. Yi's battles with the invading Japanese forces and his struggles to overcome the opposition of civil officials resonated with the ROK's more modern history of "overcoming national difficulties" (kungnan kŭkpoksa), a South Korean discourse that presents the peace-loving Koreans as being forced to defend themselves against both foreign aggression and domestic weaklings (Sìntionean 2014, 257). For Park, Yi was a military hero who had come to the aid of his nation but had also been maligned by Chosŏn civilian officials. Park saw himself as a military general who had overthrown an ineffective civilian government in the name of "national salvation" (Park 2010, 13). In their reconstruction of Hyŏnch'ungsa and its ceremonial function as a place honoring the memory of Yi, the ROK authorities presented heritage as a direct continuation of tradition, whereas in fact, the site broke considerably from traditional practice. Descendants had previously performed private family ritual practice at Hyŏnch'ungsa, but were now excluded by Park Chung Hee, and rituals were made into national televised events (Park 2010, 8–10). Buildings were enlarged and the site made monumental with modern building materials, but at the same time, traditional-looking colors and roof features were retained to give an impression of continuity (Park 2010, 4; Sîntionean 2014, 265; see also Codruţa Sîntionean's chapter in this volume). Both Koreas expressed similar political messages about national autonomy and foreign resistance but through contrasting presentations of traditional cultural forms. In these notable examples in the DPRK, what is interesting is the act of change itself. These openly admitted and defiant changes to traditional practice remain a feature that stands in some contrast to the revival of heritage by the Park Chung Hee administration for whom the pretence of continuity was important for the formation of its state and cultural identity. Park's policy of heritage reconstruction and its pretense of continuity with a Korean past untainted by outside influence emphasized a unique and morally superior national culture that resisted foreign invasion and that was incomprehensible to non-Koreans. However, there were central contradictions in Park's administration and management of heritage (Lowe and Lloyd 1997, 9–10). Park largely recycled colonial-era cultural policy, and his economic policies aimed at "westernization" were largely dependent upon foreign and especially Japanese capital (Maliangkay 2016, 3–5; Pai 2013, 19–25).

These contrasting uses of culture also reveal some underlying assumptions common to both regimes that influenced the invention of traditions on both sides of the border. Here, culture is not seen as a blend of indigenous and external forms that have been negotiated and reformulated over the years, but instead as something that can be cleansed of its individual or politically undesirable parts. Such a view is necessary for the selective appropriation of a single representative aspect of a common Korean past—resistance to foreign political rule, for example.

Tan'gun and National Legitimacy

In Hobsbawm's analysis, political elites use the invention of tradition to legitimize their rule over national subjects. The DPRK regime actually took this one step further in its use of the Tan'gun myth to project its own legitimacy both within and outside the nation-state. Tan'gun is a mythical figure conventionally understood to be the progenitor of the Korean race and founder of its first kingdom, Old Chosŏn (Kojosŏn). In 1993, North Korean archaeologists announced the discovery of Tan'gun's tomb close to Pyongyang, claiming that the human remains found at the site proved his existence (treated in more detail in chapter 2 of this volume). The DPRK authorities alleged that the site demonstrated that the Koreans had emerged as a distinct race and that the region around the North Korean capital was the cradle of human civilization (Seth 2013). Kim Il Sung personally ordered the excavation and restoration of the Tan'gun site along with the tombs of the founding fathers of Koguryŏ and Koryŏ (Scheidhauer 2011, 148). With these excavations, Kim Il Sung connected himself and the DPRK with both important ancient states and the founder of the Korean people.

Kim Il Sung was not the first Korean political leader to make use of this particular myth. The South Korean regime of Syngman Rhee (1875–1965) had established National Foundation Day or Kaech'ŏn chŏl (Opening of heaven festival) as a public holiday on the date that Tan'gun was supposed to have created his kingdom. And in 1964, the Park Chung Hee administration had designated two sites on Kanghwa Island—allegedly constructed by Tan'gun himself—as historic treasures: Ch'amsŏngdan (Altar of the castle and moat), and Samnangsŏng (Fortress of Three Sons). Park was heavily influenced by the nationalist historiography of the colonial period, and by championing these sites he was both historicizing the progenitor of the Korean race and associating Tan'gun with the ROK regime (Sîntionean 2014).[5] This represented a considerable break with Chosŏn dynasty practice, since the Tan'gun myth was never central to premodern Korean identity (Seth 2013).

In the North Korean case, the "discovery" and promotion of Tan'gun's tomb was not the invention of a tradition: instead, it was the adoption of a tradition associated with myth and superstition, which meant that this tradition also clashed with previous official representations of history. For example, prominent North Korean historian To Yu-ho (1905–1982) considered nations to be "constructed entities" rather than the product of mythical figures, and argued the Korean nation truly began with unification by tenth-century Koryŏ (Scheidhauer 2011, 117). Historical dictionaries of the 1970s described Tan'gun as a myth from "feudalistic history books" (Sahoe kwahagwŏn ryŏksa yŏn'guso 1971, 472–473), while as late as the 1980s, the DPRK's *Chosŏn T'ongsa* (Comprehensive history of Korea) made no reference to Tan'gun (Seth 2013). By relocating the birth of Korean civilization to Pyongyang, North Korean historians were also revising earlier narratives that the earliest capital of a Korean kingdom was found farther north (Xu 2016, 153).[6] In other words, the official DPRK line was not initially in favor of Tan'gun, but shifted its position around 1993 after portraying Tan'gun as a feudal myth just a decade prior.

Many scholars assume that the DPRK authorities, faced with an economic crisis, were appealing to a domestic audience in their revival of the Tan'gun myth.[7] However, Tan'gun also seems to be part of a competitive dialogue between the two Korean states. In the 1960s and 1970s, Park Chung Hee made broadcasts on National Foundation Day that addressed both South and North Koreans, while the DPRK authorities announced their alleged discovery of Tan'gun's bones on the eve of National Foundation Day in 1993. Following the discovery, South Korean historical groups were invited to Pyongyang to confirm the findings and participate in joint North-South seminars on Tan'gun (Seth 2013). Thus, one compelling fact about the selection, popularization, and institutionalization of Tan'gun in North Korea is the myth's utilization in competing historical narratives with the South.

The post-1945 division of the Korean Peninsula led to contested national legitimacy, a struggle that was fought militarily and diplomatically—and also culturally (Gills 1996, 221). Within this cultural sphere, the struggle for domination of the historical past is fiercely contested by historians both within the state (see the first section of this collection for examples) and between states. Official DPRK literature depicts the South as betrayers of the Korean people because of their collaboration with the United States. North Korean historians trace this loss of autonomy and subservience to foreign domination to the ancient past (Xu 2016, 148–149). The DPRK has claimed that its historical independence and its uncontaminated racial and linguistic purity proves its superiority over the South (Smith 2015, 65; see Xu 2016, 148–149). Seen as a response to the association of Tan'gun with sites in the South in the 1960s, the 1993 discovery in the North set down a cultural challenge to the legitimacy of the ROK and helped shore up North Korea's claims to superiority. By linking the founding father of the Korean race to its own geographical territory, the DPRK was claiming the right to lead not just its own 25 million citizens, but the entire Korean *minjok* (ethnic nation). This represents the use of invented traditions not only in support of state formation—as was implied in Hobsbawm's formulation—but perhaps more unusually as an appeal to the loyalty of people beyond national borders.

To give the site the sense of grandeur befitting Tan'gun's status as progenitor of the race, the DPRK authorities constructed a Koguryŏ-style
pyramid-shaped monumental tomb that also featured modern architectural techniques (Portal 2005, 106–108). It was of little import to the
authorities that there was no uniformity in architectural styles, just as
it did not matter to them that the figure given historical agency at the
site had never physically existed. Geographical or physical space was an
imperfect marker of Koreanness at this point, since neither the South
nor the North could claim to speak for the entire Korean *minjok* on the
basis of the territory each side controlled. Legitimacy could come from
whichever Korea had the strongest link to an essence that transcended
physicality—in this case the mythical progenitor of the Korean race.

The North's revival of the Tan'gun myth is important for another
reason, since the internationally publicized discovery of Tan'gun's remains
gave South Koreans new insight into the North's use of invented traditions as a tool to legitimize political leadership. The South Korean media
described the North's claims that Tan'gun was an actual historical figure
as "ludicrous" and a "fabrication" (Ha 1993). Given these reactions and
the benefit of external insight into the North's actions, it is difficult to
account for the continued assertions by nationalist pressure groups in
the South that Tan'gun should be recognized as an actual figure and that
this should be reflected in school history textbooks (Seth 2013, 6–9).[8] In
other contexts, researchers have blamed naïve cultural revivals on a lack
of critical reflection, but this does not explain the perpetuation, reclama-
tion, and transformation of the Tan'gun myth.[9]

Taekwondo and Longevity

Like the resuscitation of the Tan'gun myth, the case of taekwondo offers
another pertinent example of the prolonged acceptance of invented traditions with unlikely origins. However, more than this, the taekwondo case
reveals an attempt to repackage wholly concocted traditions as authentic
indigenous culture and market them on a worldwide level. The example
of taekwondo also reveals a failure to recognize that what is of value in
cultural practice often lies less in ancient historical or indigenous origins
but in more recent technical development. Taekwondo is the nominal
national sport of South Korea, an Olympic event, and enjoyed by millions

worldwide. The principal reason for its popularity is the dynamic, fluid, and highly technical sparring of sports taekwondo, which uses body armor to enable safe and effective practice, and a scoring system to evaluate the effectiveness of strikes (Moenig 2015, 36–56). Over the course of many years, South Korean and non-Korean practitioners have developed taekwondo into a full contact sport. However, the roots of taekwondo actually lie in Japanese karate, which was introduced to the Korean Peninsula during the colonial period. Evidence for these origins can be found in well-documented links between pioneering Korean martial artists and the Japanese instructors who taught them. These origins are not widely known; in fact, they are still denied by South Korean taekwondo's ruling bodies: The World Taekwondo Federation (now World Taekwondo, hereafter WT) and the Korean Taekwondo Association (KTA). Some of the early taekwondo pioneers—General Choi Hong Hi (Ch'oe Hong-hŭi, 1918–2002), Hwang Ki (1914–2002), and Yi Sŏn-gun (1905–1983)— helped concoct indigenous origins for taekwondo dating back thousands of years. They made claims that taekwondo had developed from fighting skills developed by the *hwarang*, an obscure, elite youth group often associated with military activities from the Silla Kingdom (Moenig and Kim 2016, 6). Early practitioners also associated taekwondo with folk games like *t'aekkyŏn*, and even claimed that these fighting arts had subsequently spread from the Korean Peninsula to Okinawa and then into Japan (Capener 2016).[10] Early Korean martial artists believed this would help popularize taekwondo domestically by inventing a tradition for the sport as well as disassociating it from its colonial roots.

From the early 1960s onward, taekwondo became a particularly important vehicle for the Park Chung Hee administration to further its agenda abroad. Taekwondo was not only a means of soft power, it may also have been a front for spying, money laundering, and the intimidation or elimination of Park's political opponents (Gillis 2011). Despite these borderline nefarious activities, taekwondo spread widely overseas. Its narrative of ancient origins imbued taekwondo with an "authoritative Korean pedigree" to make it more marketable to an overseas audience (Capener 2016, 70). Park's administration established WT to centralize control of the various styles of the martial art still practiced in South Korea. WT rivaled General Choi Hong Hi's International Taekwondo Federation (ITF), and this led to bitter antagonism between the two organizations.

Feeling persecuted by the Park regime, Choi moved his ITF to Canada in the early 1970s and then in 1980, following promises of financial support, openly affiliated his organization with the DPRK (Moenig and Kim 2016, 3). The North's sudden recognition of tackwondo was somewhat of a *volte face*, since traditionally the country, like others in the communist bloc, had frowned upon martial arts, regarding them as reactionary activities (Moenig and Kim 2016, 3). However, the DPRK authorities recognized that ITF taekwondo had potential as a front organization for its own international activities. The North Korean ITF adopted wholesale the falsified narrative of taekwondo's origins that had been developed in the South. With its North Korean connections, Choi's ITF went into terminal decline. Taekwondo practitioners in the South, however, succeeded in revolutionizing sparring practice, taking it further away from its Japanese origins. WT engineered the exponential growth of its brand of taekwondo and its admission as an Olympic sport. Despite the fact that WT-style taekwondo has been firmly established as an Olympic sport since 2000, the practice has been left with the legacy of a founding myth that was in fact invented by martial artists and then nurtured by political elites. To this day, the history of taekwondo remains controversial in debates over authenticity and origin.

Stephen Vlastos raises the important question of just how it is that the authority of certain traditions is not impaired even if they have both "startlingly recent origins" and their histories are frequently tailored and embellished (1998, 7). For example, bushido, a Japanese code of samurai warrior ethics, has retained its domestic and international authority despite having relatively recent origins. Writing on bushido and tradition, Oleg Benesch argues that the more complex the answers are to "how, by whom, and to what social and political effect" traditions are formulated, the "greater the resilience of the invented tradition in question" (2014, 10). However, this hypothesis does not work when applied to the founding mythology of taekwondo in South Korea. The Japanese origins of taekwondo are well documented, but the myth of indigenous and ancient roots lives on in official WT doctrine and publications.

It is unclear whether taekwondo's popularity would be impacted if the Japanese colonial origins of taekwondo were to become more widely known, given that it is competitive at the international level. What is certain is that there is more at stake than taekwondo's membership. For

taekwondo governing bodies and the South Korean taekwondo community as a whole, rewriting their history and admitting to a previous falsifi-
cation of facts—created during a different political context—could result
in a loss of both institutional and national prestige. This origin myth plays
an important role in the creation and maintenance of the identities of its
practitioners whose personal level of investment in taekwondo is high.
The result is that due to the sustained challenge by those who have uncov-
ered evidence of the Japanese roots of taekwondo, other narratives have
emerged to offer a face-saving historical explanation for the discipline's
origins. So-called neo-traditionalist historians admit that the sport has
partial influences from Japan, but still insist on maintaining the pretense
of taekwondo's ancient origins (Capener 2016, 71).

The taekwondo case is also interesting because it suggests a deeply
ambivalent sense of cultural self-worth. It is not enough that WT or ITF
taekwondo each developed their own distinct cultural identity from other
martial arts. The sport's value is also premised upon a unique, distinct, and
native heritage, not just on technical achievements. Taekwondo shares
characteristics with other Korean cultural practices—in particular, the
desire of its practitioners for external recognition of the uniqueness and
difference that help demarcate Korea from both East Asia and the west
(see Don Baker on new religious movements, Keith Howard on music,
and Codruța Sîntionean on architecture in this volume, for example).

Sopyonje *and International Reception*

In addition to the use of taekwondo as a vehicle for South Korean governments to promote their interests overseas and to garner popular recognition for Korean culture, film is now another important cultural export.
The 1993 release of the film *Sopyonje* (dir: Im Kwŏn-taek) marked an
important point in the internationalization of culture from South Korea.
The timing of the film's appearance is also key to understanding its impact.
At the time of the film's domestic release, local cinematic production
was thought to be on the verge of collapse, and there was great concern
about the destruction of traditional cultural forms by Western intrusion.[11] Domestic audiences and critics saw clear parallels between the
subject matter of the film and these cultural concerns. The decline of local
film production was largely blamed on the opening of the South Korean

cinematic industry to direct distribution from US majors. *Sopyonje* is particularly famous for helping to popularize the Korean musical story-telling tradition of *p'ansori*, performed by a vocalist and drummer, which had been, prior to the film's release, largely ignored by the South Korean public. The film is also important for what it tells us about the consumption of invented traditions and how drastically responses vary according to different perceptions of authenticity.

The narrative of *Sopyonje* is constructed around a family of *p'ansori* performers in which the father brutalizes the son until he flees and then blinds his own daughter so she can perfect her technique by developing *han*—the Korean term for a feeling of anger generated by unfulfilled wishes and injustices perpetrated by past governments, foreign aggression, or the fickle hands of fate (De Ceuster and Maliangkay 2003, 201–202). The narrative focuses on the son's wanderings through the South Korean landscape in search of his blind sister so they can be reunited in song for one final time. The film caused a sensation amongst the media and public alike, sparking a debate about the place of traditional culture in South Korea. *Sopyonje* stirred complex and often contradictory responses in domestic audiences. The film symbolized a simultaneous desire for global recognition and a belief that only Koreans could understand, perform, or truly represent Korean tradition. It also revealed a concomitant sense of cultural superiority and inferiority versus Western culture (Cho 2002, 136–146). Cho Hae-joang suggests that *Sopyonje* was the moment South Koreans truly entered the "modern age" by gaining a sense of what tradition meant (2002, 148).

Sopyonje broke domestic box office records in 1993 and domestic audiences saw in the film a celebration of what they perceived to be authentic Korean culture, here represented by the film's shots of a pristine natural environment, excerpts of *p'ansori* performances, and the father's struggle to induce *han* into his daughter. It was also widely predicted to be the film that revived South Korean cinema's fortunes by bringing it international acclaim. However, *Sopyonje* flopped abroad (Cho 2002, 136; Stringer 2002, 157). Julian Stringer provides one account for its overseas failure, describing a screening of *Sopyonje* at which non-Koreans expressed their disappointment in the film (2002, 161). Stringer argues one problem was non-Korean audiences perceived a highly manipulated, consumable, and watered-down version of a traditional art within a film that appealed to emotional and nationalistic responses. This reception was caused by the complexity of presentation of the art of *p'ansori*: while via the plot it is clear that the director is mourning the loss of Korean culture, the film itself reinvents traditional practice within its own construction. The music and singing style presented in the film was not the Sŏp'yŏnje or Western School that prevailed in Chŏlla Province in southwest Korea, but from another school.[12] *P'ansori* can last several hours, so the film only features excerpts. In addition, the sound design mixed the voices of three female singers to represent the main performer (Stringer 2002, 174, 178). While foreign audiences may not have known the different forms of *p'ansori*, at the screening attended by Stringer, overseas spectators were particularly frustrated by the central scene, which united the two siblings of the family of *p'ansori* performers for one final performance. At the climax, as they begin their song, the real *p'ansori* fades out to be replaced by non-diegetic music or music originating outside the frame of the movie, here performed on flute and synthesizer (Stringer 2002, 164). For Stringer, a fuss had been made "about the authenticity and beauty" of *p'ansori*, but at the "crucial juncture" the audience was denied "its full expression" (2002, 164). Also, the film's reliance on notions of *han*—a phenomenon with which non-Koreans are supposedly unfamiliar—felt to the non-Korean audience like a nationalistic attempt to manipulate traditional practice in order to claim a distinctive culture (Stringer 2002, 167). *Han* is itself an invented tradition—a term popularized by the *minjung* movement opposing military dictatorship from the 1970s onward. *Han* was a useful metaphor that helped mobilize a generation into actively opposing the military government—and it faded with the advent of directly elected governments and the growing obsolescence of the *minjung* movement (De Ceuster and Maliangkay 2003, 209).

The differing receptions reveal a dichotomy. Domestic audiences saw the film's representation of culture as internally authentic, while international audiences were disappointed by the perceived contradiction between assertions of pure tradition in promotional literature and an inauthentic cultural exterior that used obvious manipulation of traditional forms. This raises theoretical questions about cultural reception, something largely ignored by Hobsbawm, whose theories of invented tradition appear to assume both domestic and more passive consumption. Hobsbawm never explicitly analyzed how invented traditions looked to the consumer outside the specific cultural and political context of its creation. One wonders: in Hobsbawm's contexts of nation building and institution building (in which elites devised invented traditions to mobilize, institutionalize, and socialize), are invented traditions jarring to outsiders looking in? It could not therefore be assumed that traditional forms or their representations would be consumed in the same way outside the Korean Peninsula. The overseas reception of *Sopyonje*'s representations of revived traditional forms were particularly important, as they came at a time when the foreign consumption of South Korean culture was increasing.

Kimchi, Policing International Consumption, and Cultural Policy

Sopyonje was released just before President Kim Young Sam's (1993–1998) *segyehwa* or globalization drive, which, amongst other goals, aimed to improve South Korea's national image by showing that it could produce not only cars and electronics for foreign consumption, but also culture. *Segyehwa* marked the start of a long-term shift in government cultural strategy. Previous administrations had argued that Korea's "national cultural identity" had been lost to colonialism and westernization, and thus required reconstruction and protection from external influences (Yim 2002, 37–41). However, *segyehwa* was premised upon the overseas marketability of Korean culture. Korean culture could be globalized and bring the ROK not just recognition but also economic benefits (Yim 2002, 37–41). *Segyehwa* meant direct state intervention into both domestic cultural industries and overseas activities. This included the introduction of Korean Cultural Centers overseas to promote both popular and traditional culture.

Greater cultural engagement with the outside world also brought occasional attempts by ROK governmental agencies to intervene more aggressively in the overseas consumption of Korean culture. These state interventions demonstrated sensitivity to overseas responses and an official belief that foreign consumption of Korean culture could be influenced by South Korean governmental policies. An example is the so-called kimchi wars that took place during the administration of Kim Young Sam and that reoccurred in 2020.[13] Kimchi is the fermented dish made from cabbage, garlic, chili peppers, and fish sauce that is an essential component of traditional Korean culinary culture. Sales of kimchi in Japan began after the success of the 1986 Asian Games and 1988 Olympics that attracted foreign visitors to Seoul. As the Japanese market grew, local Japanese producers successfully competed with Korean manufacturers by producing a cheaper product they called *kimuchi* (to reflect local pronunciation) that left out the traditional fermentation process and the pungent fish additives (Han 2011, 157). The South Korean media ridiculed the Japanese *kimuchi* as an inferior tasting and inauthentic product. But Japanese manufacturers were increasingly expanding into lucrative world markets (Han 2011, 60), and even went so far as to propose *kimuchi* as an official food of the 1996 Atlanta Olympic Games. The South Korean media and public were outraged, fearing that *kimuchi*'s commercial exposure would gain international recognition for Japan's variety of kimchi rather than Korea's (Han 2011, 60).

As a result of the controversy, ROK governmental agencies appealed to the World Health Organization and Food and Agriculture Organization's Codex Alimentarius Commission (CAC) to establish an international standard to control the quality of kimchi based on ingredients and production processes. This was an attempt to designate the Japanese variety as "inauthentic" and "inferior" and block its exposure on international markets. The problem was, as Kyung-Koo Han (2011) argues, the South Korean governmental claims of authenticity were themselves premised upon heavily modified traditional practice created to meet the need for cheaper mass food production. Traditionally, there had been great regional variety in kimchi ingredients and taste, but South Korean manufacturers selected the Seoul-Kyŏnggi Province (the area around the capital) variety as the standard for international markets; this variety was itself the product of culinary engineering. Manufacturers had adopted it— out of hundreds of regional varieties—as the Korean national standard, not because of superior taste or greater historical authenticity but simply because producers considered it less likely to offend different consumers' palates. In addition, the Seoul-Kyŏnggi Province variety of manufactured kimchi had become popular because fewer South Korean women were making or consuming kimchi in the traditional way (*kimjang*),[14] preferring instead to eat cheaper varieties produced in South Korean factories in mainland China where manufacturing costs were lower. In the end, the government's attempts were unsuccessful and the CAC recognized both *kimuchi* and kimchi as different variations of the same type of food (Han 2011, 153–159).

The ROK government used arguments about authenticity to achieve international market dominance with a domestically produced invented tradition. But the controversy also shows the conflict inherent in the desire to expand Korean culture to foreign audiences and the fear of losing control over the process of internationalization. Exporting Korean culture to the outside world not only brought attention and national benefits, but also unintended consequences, such as the Japanese reinvention and successful commercial production of Korean kimchi.[15]

Kim Young Sam was not the first Korean leader to intervene in the foreign consumption of Korean culture in an attempt to improve the national image. Between the 1960s and 1980s, the DPRK used traditional culture to influence relationships with other countries despite the fact that heritage and traditional cultural artifacts occupied an ambiguous place in the former communist bloc. The contradiction for the North Korean government, along with other communist states, was this: on the one hand, traditional culture should be rejected in the name of progress, but on the other hand, in the historical, materialist sense, it was vital, objective evidence of the development of human society to a more advanced stage. Given this ambiguity, state policies on the destruction or preservation of heritage could be reversed according to ideological shifts and whims of the political elite. In the DPRK, policy could also shift according to the state's international relations priorities.

Balázs Szalontai (2009) argues that the DPRK used cultural diplomacy to gain favors from allies in the fraternal socialist bloc over the years as well as from South Korean audiences during moments of detente. The DPRK would temporarily revive Korean traditions at strategic points in order to demonstrate its openness and flexibility. Then, after it had achieved (or failed to achieve) its goals, cultural policy would revert to anti-traditionalist stances (Szalontai 2009, 155). An example is the revival of cultural nationalism in 1972, which took place during a brief improvement in ROK-DPRK relations when the two regimes released a joint declaration stressing their common cultural identity (Szalontai 2009, 156). During this period, the DPRK government in Pyongyang began to celebrate folk music more actively and established a new Museum of Ethnography to house items from recently excavated royal tombs and Buddhist sites. The sudden celebration of Buddhist and historical artifacts took place in a country where such objects had been previously rejected as primitive tools of a repressive ruling class. However, after a subsequent decline in relations between the two regimes, the North Korean government moved to antagonistic attitudes toward tradition. Suddenly, Korean folk music became the "music of slaves, serfs, landlords, and drunkards" and heritage was again regarded as "obsolete" and associated with "bourgeois lifestyles" (Szalontai 2009, 154–156). This apparent reversal in attitude toward traditional culture was most likely an attempt to show proximity to domestic policy within the People's Republic of China, thereby facilitating the improvement of relations with China during the last three years of Mao's Cultural Revolution (Szalontai 2009, 154–156). Szalontai argues that the DPRK's attempts at cultural diplomacy using traditional music and objects were largely unsuccessful in this period, as both fraternal socialist nations and the South Koreans saw the sudden revivals of traditions as temporary and disingenuous. Cultural diplomacy is important because it is part of a package of measures the DPRK uses to attempt to influence overseas perceptions of the country, and such sudden reversals in official attitudes to traditional culture reoccur periodically to this day (despite their apparent lack of success).[16]

The discussion thus far has concerned itself with a variety of cultural artifacts and practices; what links them is that in all cases examined above, deliberate choices were taken about the selection of which version should be adopted to represent the "authentic" form for domestic and international consumption. In some cases, the cultural forms or objects themselves—like *p'ansori* or kimchi—were diverse and with many hundreds of years of development on the Korean Peninsula. Taekwondo on the other hand only had a few decades of history. Yet the decisions about how and why to revive the cultural forms and how to present this revival were often made not by practitioners themselves as part of a cycle of cultural development but by bureaucrats or politicians for other motives than the enjoyment of the art.

The ROK and DPRK revived tradition to show entirely opposing impressions of their respective societies. The ROK's attempts to police the overseas distribution and consumption of its traditions had the objective of displaying a Korean uniqueness or distinctiveness that differentiated the country and culture from its East Asian neighbors, despite their cultural and geographic proximity. Meanwhile, in moments when it was politically prescient, the DPRK attempted to show to the outside a more humane face of a dictatorship. The revival of tradition showed the DPRK to be normal in the sense that—like other countries—it respected traditional arts and culture and did not simply fund and promote art dedicated to the Kim regime. The actions of ROK and DPRK state organs are similar in that they were defensive and ultimately unsuccessful moves to manipulate foreign perceptions of culture and nation.

INVENTED TRADITIONS IN KOREA

With their ideologically antagonistic regimes, opposing economic trajectories, and a widespread perception of completely divergent cultural practices, there are both significant commonalities and contrasts in the two Koreas' use of invented traditions. This use of invented traditions tells us a great deal about how the North and South Koreans remember the past, conceptualize their modernity, and project their culture to the outside world.

In her essay "The Invention of Edo," about how a modern Tokyo was created in opposition to a "traditional" Edo, Carol Gluck (1998, 262) argues: "Modernity, by definition, foresaw the future by setting itself off from the past. Newness was all, but it could only be grasped by juxtaposition to what was old."[17] The Japanese formulated the cultural identity of modern Tokyo in relation to an imaginative recreation of its Edo past. The imaginative recreation of both a modern North and South Korean cultural identity was complicated by several problems, and the invention of tradition has been a way of overcoming these.

First, the invention of tradition has been a way to re-establish cultural agency by political leaders in two nations that lost their historical agency due to foreign intervention and colonial rule. One example is the DPRK authorities' open admission of changes to folk songs, instruments, and archaeological sites as an expression of authority over the historical past. Second, for many Koreans, foreign involvement in Korea—especially the latter part of Japanese colonial rule—felt like a full-scale foreign assault upon Korean cultural identity. Korean political leaders saw the re-estab-lishment of a "lost" national cultural identity—often with non-native forms excluded—as a duty. The invention of tradition was a tool that could help achieve this. Such a task was based on an understanding of culture and identity not as something negotiated, fluctuating, and polysemic, but as something fixed, uniform, and subject to loss (Burgi-Golub 2000, 213). Culture and identity could be attacked and destroyed, but they could also be reconstructed. Finally, the remembering of the Korean past—especially of the period between the late nineteenth-century opening of Korea and its colonization—was complicated by inter-Korean competition. Both Koreas drew on a shared cultural legacy and selected elements that fell within their own geographical jurisdiction—such as Yi Sun-sin in the South and Koguryŏ in the North—to establish a cultural identity both different and superior to their opposite number.

Invented traditions are often evidence of contention between moder-nity and what it displaces in a moment of social change. Andrew Gordon (1998, 19–36) argues that the attempt to cloak the supposedly harmo-nious relationships or *wa* between management and labor in Japanese industry in a discourse of ancient social traditions reveals the ambiva-lence on the part of many Japanese toward modernity. Early Japanese reformers embraced the modern, but also identified it with social decay and cultural loss, and the result was a tendency to invent tradition to fill gaps left by change. The same could be said of the invention of tradition in most countries, including South Korea. In the Korean case, we find a special intensity in the nation's ambivalence to modernity. This modernity was developed under colonialism, in particular by a Japanese power that partly justified its rule by pointing to the "backwardness" of the country and its supposed reliance on Chinese culture. Invented traditions in both North and South Korea work to diminish the appearance of foreign influ-ences and to display a cultural identity distinct from not only Japan and the west but from the *other* Korea. Modernity on the Korean Peninsula, in both its socialist and capitalist forms, has been experienced in the context of division. As a result, Koreans have dug deep into a well of past cultural practice in order to project a more stable and unified tradition on to an imperfect modernity that is dominated by a fractured national agency. This includes myths of a static, solid, and native past, as found in taekwondo, and of unifying figures representing Korean commonality like Tan'gun.

Korean ruling elites in particular have used invented traditions as ways to legitimize their rule during periods of political transition. Many historians have observed that rather than clear-cut breaks between dynasties, historical periods, shifts in the political system (for example from military to civilian and from authoritarian to democratic rule), we often see considerable overlap with persistent ideas and influences. John Duncan (2000), for example, has argued that the transformation from the Koryŏ to the Chosŏn dynasties was not characterized by the seismic cultural and political shifts that had previously been claimed but by significant continuity. Perhaps the most contentious overlap in Korean history concerns the transition from Japanese colonial to native Korean rule, as evidenced by the ongoing arguments over allegations of Japanese collaboration amongst post-Liberation South Korean elites. Chungmoo Choi (1997, 461) and Roald Maliangkay (2016, 5) have argued we can see significant continuity between colonial ideas, institutions, and modes of rule in post-1945 Korean administrations. In order to mask this contentious "contradiction" and cover up the continuity between their rule and that of the Japanese colonizers, postwar Korean political elites have invented traditions—they have reframed the colonial as native, the foreign as national, and the hybrid as unique. Nowhere is this better exemplified than in the case of taekwondo—a practice lifted directly from Japanese colonizers and adopted by both the South and North Koreans at convenient historical moments as a diplomatic and political tool and that has been represented as a cultural practice emblematic of ancient Korean tradition.

Reimagining and re-creating a suitable past have moved beyond domestic consumption, as both Koreas have sought an international audience for their cultural output, although for different purposes. To show that it has found its place on the world stage both economically and culturally, South Korea has made greater efforts to export its traditions to an international audience. Another commonality between the Koreas is a desire to define cultural identity through intangible, internal qualities. This intangible, internal quality could be "spirit," "inner meaning," myth, or *han*. It is Korean culture unencumbered by physicality, and as such, the external aspect can change as long as the essence is preserved. However, this notion of an essential Korean culture and quality can have a purist and isolationist effect, which keeps out the outside world, thereby negatively impacting the desired external recognition by foreign audiences. This is one of several problems associated with using the revival of tradition to reach out to the world. Another problem with discourses of invented traditions is that they obscure the perspective that something of cultural value may not have ancient or indigenous origins, but may instead have been formed through hybridization and technical development, as is the case with taekwondo. Invented traditions figure highly in how the two Koreas remember the past, shape their divergent modernities, and present themselves to the world.

The four sections in this book explore the invention of traditions in the two Koreas and show how a "suitable" past has been reimagined, rewritten, consumed, performed, and embodied. Three of the sections deal specifically with those monumental invented traditions closely and explicitly linked to institutional power. As such, these chapters take the reader on a journey through Korea's epic twentieth century, examining the revival of culture in the context of colonialism, decolonization, national division, dictatorship, and modernization. The two chapters on the DPRK, where the locus of political power is centered around a Pyongyang dynasty, introduce specific examples of invented traditions created to lend legitimacy to the leadership. In the case of the chapters on the ROK, we see the manipulation of culture by political leaders intending to shape a specific national identity. We also see culture as a site of contention between influential institutions and groups in the South Korean state and society, all of which were attempting to support their own national vision.

The book's first section investigates how the Korean nation is remembered and represented in historical and spiritual terms. This remembrance sometimes results in the creation, rather than the recall, of a suitable religious or historical past—a creation often based on small quantities of evidence and huge doses of speculation. These manipulations are complex features of "popular" histories and new religions in South Korea and for the practitioners deadly serious since their accounts of an ancient Korean past were developed to overcome historical humiliation and national fragmentation in the present. The second section continues in the same vein as the first by examining intellectual debates that arose from the nineteenth century onward over the character of the Korean language and those attempts by linguists to distinguish Korean culture from Sinitic civilization and establish historical uniqueness.

With the exception of the final chapter examining the invention of a food tradition in the DPRK, the cultural revival explored in section three is less obviously related to those monumental invented traditions closely linked to political power. The chapters consider the interactions between academics, practitioners, and state administrators in the development of musical forms and traditional artifacts, but their main emphasis is on the role of human agency and performativity in cultural transformation. These chapters investigate the type of invented traditions neglected by Hobsbawm and Ranger's collection, but one that holds a vitally important place in the cultural landscape of the Korean Peninsula. The chapters focus on the cycles of transformation that have led to the creation of cultural icons that represent Korean heritage today.

The final section examines the ways in which the two Korean states have imagined, projected, and recreated legitimizing and competing visions of modernity physically, with a focus on space. This section returns the reader to a formative moment in South Korean history and examines the huge impact the Park Chung Hee dictatorship had on the popular acceptance of traditional architecture. The section also interrogates the more recent efforts of a DPRK leadership whose legitimacy has been severely dented by economic collapse and famine to shore up its political rule through the invention of pilgrimages to a landscape representing former glories.

By examining those traditions whose construction is closely tied to institutional power during formative periods in both North and South Korean history, as well as other cases of invented traditions, we hope to provide a more comprehensive picture of how cultural practices have shaped the two Koreas.

GLOSSARY

Ch'amsŏngdan 塹星壇
Chaehyŏngsanghwa 재형상화
Chongmyo 宗廟
Chosŏn chŏngsin 朝鮮 精神
Chosŏn T'ongsa 조선통사
han 恨

Hanu 韓牛
hwarang 花郎
Kaech'ŏn chŏl 開天節
kimjang 김장
Kogi chip 고기집
Koguryŏ 高句麗

Kojosŏn 古朝鮮
Koryŏ 高麗
Kungnip kugagwŏn 國立國樂院
minjok 民族
p'ansori 판소리
Samnangsŏng 三郎城

t'aekkyŏn 태껸
Taesŏngjŏn 大成殿
Taesŏngsan 大成山
Tan'gun 檀君
To Yu-ho 도유호
Yodong 遼東

NOTES

This work was supported by the Core University Program for Korean Studies through the Ministry of Education of the Republic of Korea and Korean Studies Promotion Service of the Academy of Korean Studies (AKS-2017-OLU-2250002). Thanks to Christopher Bae, Suzanne Wertheim, Gregory S. Kailian, Roald Maliangkay, Udo Moenig, Anders Riel Müller, Perry Iles, the eight anonymous peer reviewers for their input into this introductory essay, and my fellow editors Remco Breuker, CedarBough T. Saeji, and especially Codruţa Sîntionean. Thanks also to Lucien Brown, Ahn Heekyung, and my colleagues at Monash University for giving me research time to finish this project.

1. Kim Jin-young, the proprietor of the Chosŏnok Restaurant in Seoul, claims this type of dining experience dates back to the Chosŏn dynasty (McKechnie 2020).
2. He provides the example of aboriginal peoples of Australia.
3. In the case of the autonomy of groups operating in the DPRK historically, Xu (2016, 140) asserts that between the 1950s and the 1960s there was an "unprecedented" amount of open discussion amongst historians working on topics like ancient history. On the autonomy and influence of intellectual groups operating outside the state authorities, see Smith 2015, 172; Hassig and Oh 2015, 189–191.
4. For example, in the controversy over the James Bond film *Die Another Day* (dir: Lee Tamahori, UK, 2002).
5. Ch'oe Nam-sŏn (1890–1957) challenged Japanese colonial historians who downplayed the myth of Tan'gun because of the duration of civilization that it would have given Korea (Scheidhauer 2011, 102–103).
6. Stella Xu observes that until the discovery of Tan'gun's tomb, the official stance had been that the first Korean kingdom, Old Chosŏn, had been located north of Pyongyang at Yodong (2016, 146).
7. Xu argues there was a shift in the North's historical studies from a class-based analysis stressing the DPRK's social development to a nation-focused

analysis emphasizing its national uniqueness. The latter line was emphasized by historians aligned to Kim Il Sung's ruling group and became ortho-
doxy by 1993 (Xu 2016, 148–156).

8. Like the Federation of the Civic Movement of the National Spirit (Seth 2013).

9. Jong Hyun Lim (2008), for example, complains that the recent boom in the "conjectural reconstructions" of historic houses has led to widespread uncritical and "unreflective public acceptance" of structures as accurate representations of those that existed in the past.

10. It was not until the 1970s, that a more unified narrative of taekwondo's origins was created, cleansed of all foreign influences. This occurred with the declaration of taekwondo as South Korea's national sport (Moenig and Kim 2016, 27).

11. In 1993, only 16 percent of films screened in South Korea were made domestically, the lowest recorded figure.

12. The Eastern School, or Tongp'yŏnje. The subject of *p'ansori* is revisited in chapters 7 and 8 in this volume.

13. In 2020, a dispute occurred between the People's Republic of China and South Korea over the international recognition of the historical origins of kimchi; see Sharma (2020).

14. The "kimchi network" of kinswomen communally prepared a winter's supply of the food and exchanged information about improving their art (Han 2011, 151). More than a condiment, kimchi production was an edu-cation, a rite of passage, and a socialization process for newlywed moth-ers (Han 2011, 151).

15. Another example of such unintended consequences is provided by Katar-zyna Cwiertka who demonstrates why Korea's failed bid to have Royal Cui-sine of the Chosŏn dynasty recognized is ironically partly responsible for another newly crafted Japanese tradition called Washoku; see Cwiertka (2018).

16. A more recent example is the Manwŏldae palace excavations in Kaesŏng.

17. Edo was the former name for Tokyo.

REFERENCES

Atkins, Peter. 1996. "A Séance with the Living: The Intelligibility of the North Korean Landscape." In *North Korea in the New World Order*, edited by Kevin Magill, 196–211. London: Palgrave MacMillan.

Beiner, Guy. 2001. "The Invention of Tradition?" *The History Review* 12:1–10.

Benesch, Oleg. 2014. *Inventing the Way of the Samurai: Nationalism, Internationalism, and Bushidō in Modern Japan.* Oxford: Oxford University Press.

Boschung, Dietrich, Alexandra W. Busch, and Miguel John Versluys, eds. 2015. *"Reinventing the Invention of Tradition"? Indigenous Pasts and the Roman Present.* Munich: Wilhelm Fink.

Burgi-Golub, Noelle. 2000. "Cultural Identity and Political Responsibility." *International Journal of Cultural Policy* 7 (2): 211–223.

Capener, Steven D. 2016. "The Making of a Modern Myth: Inventing a Tradition for Taekwondo." *Korea Journal* 56 (1) (Spring): 61–92.

Cannadine, David. 1983. "The Context, Performance and Meaning of Ritual: The British Monarch and the 'Invention of Tradition,' c. 1820–1977." In *The Invention of Tradition,* edited by Eric Hobsbawm and Terence Ranger, 101–164. Cambridge: Cambridge University Press.

Chakrabarty, Dipesh. 1998. "Afterword: Revising the Tradition/Modernity Binary." In *Mirror of Modernity: Invented Traditions of Modern Japan,* edited by Stephen Vlastos, 285–296. Berkeley: University of California Press.

Cho, Hae-joang. 2002. "*Sopyonje*: Its Cultural and Historical Meaning." In *Im Kwon-Taek: The Making of a Korean National Cinema,* edited by David E. James and Kyung Hyun Kim, 134–156. Detroit: Wayne State University Press.

Choi, Chungmoo. 1997. "The Discourse of Decolonization and Popular Memory: South Korea." In *The Politics of Culture in the Shadow of Capital,* edited by Lisa Lowe and David Lloyd, 461–484. Durham, NC: Duke University Press.

Chu Yŏng-ha. 2015. "Sikt'aki ont'ong 'hat, hat'" [The table is completely hot, hot]. Pressian.com, August 28.

Cwiertka, Katarzyna J. 2010. *Cuisine, Colonialism and Cold War: Food in Twentieth-Century Korea.* London: Reaktion Books.

———. 2018. "Serving the Nation: The Myth of Washoku." In *Consuming Life in Post-Bubble Japan: A Transdisciplinary Perspective,* edited by Katarzyna J. Cwiertka and Ewa Machotka, 89–106. Amsterdam: Amsterdam University Press.

De Ceuster, Koen, and Roald Maliangkay. 2003. "The Fashionability of Han." In *Sentiments doux-amers dans les musiques du monde,* edited by Michel Demeuldre, 201–212. Paris: l'Harmattan.

Duncan, John. 2000. *The Origins of the Chosŏn Dynasty.* Seattle: University of Washington Press.

Gillis, Alex. 2011. *A Killing Art: The Untold Story of Taekwondo.* Toronto: ECW Press.

Gills, Barry. 1996. *Korea Versus Korea: A Case of Contested Legitimacy.* New York: Routledge.

Gluck, Carol. 1998. "The Invention of Edo." In *Mirror of Modernity: Invented Traditions of Modern Japan*, edited by Stephen Vlastos, 262–284. Berkeley: University of California Press.

Gordon, Andrew. 1998. "The Invention of Japanese-Style Labor Management." In *Mirror of Modernity: Invented Traditions of Modern Japan*, edited by Stephen Vlastos, 19–36. Berkeley: University of California Press.

Ha Tong-gŭn. 1993. "Pukhan Tan'gun yugol ch'ult'o chujang hŏguil kŏsŭro ch'ujŏng" [The claims that Tan'gun's remains have been excavated in North Korea is thought to be a fabrication]. Sisapress.com, October 21.

Han, Kyung-Koo. 2011. "The 'Kimchi Wars' in Globalizing East Asia: Consuming Class, Gender, Health, and National Identity." In *Consuming Korean Tradition in Early and Late Modernity: Commodification, Tourism, And Performance*, edited by Laurel Kendall, 149–166. Honolulu: University of Hawai'i Press.

Handler, Richard, and Jocelyn Linnekin. 1984. "Tradition, Genuine or Spurious." *Journal of American Folklore* 97 (385): 273–290.

Hassig, Ralph, and Kongdan Oh. 2015. *The Hidden People of North Korea: Everyday Life in the Hermit Kingdom*. Lanham, MD: Rowman and Littlefield.

Häussler, Sonja. 2011. "Revived Interest in Literary Heritage: Changes in DPRK Cultural Policy." In *Exploring North Korean Arts*, edited by Rüdiger Frank, 88–112. Nürnberg: Verlag für moderne Kunst.

Hobsbawm, Eric. 1983a. "Introduction: Inventing Traditions." In *The Invention of Tradition*, edited by Eric Hobsbawm and Terence Ranger, 1–15. Cambridge: Cambridge University Press.

———. 1983b. "Mass-Producing Traditions: Europe, 1870–1914." In *The Invention of Tradition*, edited by Eric Hobsbawm and Terence Ranger, 263–308. Cambridge: Cambridge University Press.

Hobsbawm, Eric, and Terence Ranger, eds. 1983. *The Invention of Tradition*. Cambridge: Cambridge University Press.

Howard, Keith. 2011. "Redefining Koreanness: North Korea, Musicology, Ideology, and 'Improved' Korean Instruments." In *Exploring North Korean Arts*, edited by Rüdiger Frank, 181–191. Nürnberg: Verlag für moderne Kunst.

———. 2012a. "Introduction: East Asian Music and Intangible Cultural Heritage." In *Music as Intangible Cultural Heritage: Policy, Ideology, and Practice in the Preservation of East Asian Tradition*, edited by Keith Howard, 1–22. London: Routledge.

———. 2012b. "Authenticity and Authority: Conflicting Agendas in the Preservation of Music and Dance at Korea's State Sacrificial Rituals." In *Music as Intangible Cultural Heritage: Policy, Ideology, and Practice in the Preserva-*

tion of East Asian Tradition, edited by Keith Howard, 113–140. London: Routledge.

Jackson, Andrew David, and Colette Balmain. 2016. "Introduction." In *Korean Screen Cultures: Interrogating Cinema, TV, Music and Online Games*, edited by Andrew David Jackson and Colette Balmain, 1–11. Oxford: Peter Lang.

Jeong, Cheol Hyun, and Sang Hoon Lee. 2009. "Cultural Policy in the Democratic People's Republic of Korea." *East Asia* 26:213–225.

Kendall, Laurel. 2011. "Introduction: Material Modernity, Consumable Tradition." In *Consuming Korean Tradition in Early and Late Modernity: Commodification, Tourism, and Performance*, edited by Laurel Kendall, 1–17. Honolulu: University of Hawai'i Press.

Kim, Kwang-ŏk. 1991. "Socio-Cultural Implications of the Recent Invention of Tradition in Korea: An Overview." *BAKS* (British Association of Korean Studies) *Papers* 1:7–28.

Kim, Kyung Hyun, and Youngmin Choe. 2014. *The Korean Popular Culture Reader*. Durham, NC: Duke University Press.

Kwon, Ohsong. 2007. "The Re-formation of Traditional Folksongs in North Korea." *The World of Music* 49 (3): 107–118.

Lee, Hyangjin. 2001. *Contemporary Korean Cinema: Identity and Politics*. Manchester: Manchester University Press.

Lee, Namhee. 2007. *Making of Minjung: Democracy and the Politics of Representation in South Korea*. Ithaca: Cornell University Press.

Lim, Jong Hyun. 2008. "Giving Reconstruction a History: Architectural Renaissance of Invented Tradition in Modern Korea." In *Traditional Dwellings and Settlements Review* 20:1.

Linder, Gunnar Jinmei. 2012. "Deconstructing Tradition in Japanese Music: A Study of Shakuhachi, Historical Authenticity and Transmission of Tradition." PhD diss., Stockholm University, Sweden.

Lowe, Lisa, and David Lloyd. 1997. "Introduction." In *The Politics of Culture in the Shadow of Capital*, edited by Lisa Lowe and David Lloyd, 1–32. Durham, NC: Duke University Press.

Maliangkay, Roald. 2016. *Broken Voices: Postcolonial Entanglements and the Preservation of Korea's Central Folksong Traditions*. Honolulu: University of Hawai'i Press.

McKechnie, Ben. 2020. "Is this the Most Authentic Korean Barbecue?" *BBC News*, January 28. Accessed January 28, 2020. http://www.bbc.com/travel/story/20200127-is-this-the-most-authentic-korean-barbecue

Moenig, Udo. 2015. *Taekwondo: From a Martial Art to a Martial Sport*. London: Routledge.

Moenig, Udo, and Minho Kim. 2016. "The Invention of Taekwondo Tradition, 1945/1972: When Mythology Becomes 'History.'" *Acta Koreana* 19 (2) (December): 1–34.

Müller, Anders Riel. 2016. "Beef, Barbecue and Nationalism." Paper presented at the University of Copenhagen Seminar Series, September 29.

Pai, Hyung Il. 2013. *Heritage Management in Korea and Japan: The Politics of Antiquity and Identity.* Seattle: University of Washington Press.

Park, Saeyoung. 2010. "National Heroes and Monuments in South Korea: Patriotism, Modernization and Park Chung Hee's Remaking of Yi Sunsin's Shrine." *The Asia-Pacific Journal* 8 (24/3) (June): 1–27.

Plant, Byron King. 2008. "Secret, Powerful, and the Stuff of Legends: Revisiting Theories of Invented Tradition." *The Canadian Journal of Native Studies* 28 (1): 175–184.

Portal, Jane. 2005. *Art Under Control in North Korea.* London: Reaktion Books.

Sahoe kwahagwŏn ryŏksa yŏn'guso. 1971. *Ryŏksa Sajŏn* [Historical dictionary]. Pyongyang: Sahoe kwakhak ch'ulp'ansa.

Scheidhauer, Ruth. 2011. "A Historiography of Cultural Heritage Interpretation and Policy in Kaesŏng, DPR Korea and their Possible Impact on Inter-Korean Rapprochement." PhD diss., University College London.

Seth, Michael J. 2013. "Myth, Memory and Reinterpretation in Korea: The Case of Tan'gun" (in Chinese). The Center for Korean Studies Peking University, *Collected Papers of the Study of Korea* 22:113–123.

Sharma, Shweta. 2020. "Cabbage Wars: South Korean Anger after China Claims Kimchi as its Own." *The Independent*, December 1. Accessed February 20, 2021. https://www.independent.co.uk/news/world/asia/south-korea-china -standard-kimchi-world-domination-b1764405.html

Sîntionean, Codruţa. 2014. "Heritage Practices During the Park Chung Hee Era." In *Key Papers on Korea: Essays Celebrating 25 Years of the Centre of Korean Studies, SOAS, University of London,* edited by Andrew David Jackson, 253–274. Leiden: Brill.

Smith, Hazel. 2015. *North Korea: Markets and Military Rule.* Cambridge: Cambridge University Press.

Stringer, Julian. 2002. "*Sopyonje* and the Inner Domain of National Culture." In *Im Kwon-Taek: The Making of a Korean National Cinema,* edited by David E. James and Kyung Hyun Kim, 157–181. Detroit: Wayne State University Press.

Szalontai, Balázs. 2009. "Expulsion for a Mistranslated Poem: The Diplomatic Aspects of North Korean Cultural Politics." In *Dynamics of the Cold War in Asia: Ideology, Identity, and Culture,* edited by Tuong Vu and Wasana Wongsurawat, 145–164. New York: Palgrave Macmillan.

Tangherlini, Timothy R. 1998. "Shamans, Students and the State: Politics and the Enactment of Culture in South Korea, 1987–1988." In *Nationalism and the Construction of Korean Identity*, edited by Hyung Il Pai and Timothy R. Tangherlini, 126–147. Berkeley: Center for Korean Studies, Institute of East Asian Studies, University of California.

Xu, Stella. 2016. *Reconstructing Ancient Korean History*. Lanham, MD: Lexington Books.

Yim, Haksoon. 2002. "Cultural Identity and Cultural Policy in South Korea." *International Journal of Cultural Policy* 8 (1): 37–48.

Vlastos, Stephen. 1998. "Tradition: Past/Present Culture and Modern Japanese History." In *Mirror of Modernity: Invented Traditions of Modern Japan*, edited by Stephen Vlastos, 1–16. Berkeley: University of California Press.

PART I

Reimagining Tradition

History and Religion

Introduction

REMCO BREUKER

> False tales are, first of all, tales, and tales, like myths, are always
> persuasive.
>
> —*Umberto Eco*, "The Force of Falsity" (1999, 25)

The (re-)invented traditions, historical forgeries, and other fake objects, practices, and notions this section discusses have been proven to be always persuasive, as Umberto Eco argued, because they tell tales that find popularity with an audience. The reason these tales enjoy such popularity is because they stem from familiar historical contexts, often idealized, but all the more desirable on account of these contexts. Alfred Hiatt posited the notion that a historical forgery manifests the idea of the way history *should* look (2005, 3). Eco remarked that for forgeries, the problem lies not so much in determining what is fake, but what is genuine: "The truly genuine problem does not consist of proving something false but in proving that the authentic object is authentic" (1999, 26). Bringing these two notions together leads us to the products of the forgers that in a most probably unintended nod to Jean Baudrillard's notion of the hyperreal ultimately results in the creation of discourses in which what is considered "real" is "a real without origin or reality" (Hiatt 2005, 4).

It is therefore not always useful (although sometimes possible) to distinguish between the authentic and the fake or forged. We need to talk about these terms in some more detail. The English language (the same goes for the Korean language and I imagine many other languages as well) has the unfortunate tendency to only have available words with a definitively negative connotation to designate what otherwise may perhaps be termed as the products of creative prevarication or ingenious circumvention instead of fake or forgery. The verbosity of the previous sentence underlines the poverty of our languages to accurately and completely describe forgeries and so on. Yes, deception is a *sine qua non* for any forgery or invented tradition, but we should not mistake the means for the goal. Forgeries are not only meant to replace the genuine, but also, as this volume shows, to correct it, add to it, make it whole again, understandable, relevant. In this sense, forgeries and fakes try to move *beyond* the genuine. Due to the loftiness, urgency, the importance of the Platonian idea (of a group's history for example) they manifest, they may very well be considered by the forger and believers alike as more important than the genuine artifact. Even as more authentic.

The professional historian will disagree of course. As one should because the criteria used by the professional historian are not those of the forger who only desires the approval of those criteria but not their true application. At the same time, the professional historian should realize that a forgery is both something that intends to deceive and something that has been forged, that has been created anew. A forgery in its instrumental mode is deceptive; in its teleological mode however it is authentic. Forgeries are rarely completely derivative. All forgeries carry within them the context of their creation, and not of their supposed provenance. It is a matter of context, in other words:

> The practice of decontextualization forms the basis, I will argue, for an alliance between forgery and antiquarianism, an alliance that depends at the same time upon historiography to provide a complementary practice of recontextualization. That is, the antiquarian project of retrieval is predicated upon the survival of decontextualised fragments, relics of the past, around which (recontextualising) histories can be written. The project of the forger of historical documents is to produce precisely such an artefact, a text which seems to narrate, more or less fully, its own context, which seems to invoke the story of its genesis. However, because of its status as artefact, this text appears to be removed from its original surroundings, transported out of its initial context, and it is therefore susceptible to further contextualisation, often undertaken by the forger or forgers themselves. (Hiatt 2005, 4)

Rather than to understand forgeries as the polar popular opposite of the products of the professional historian (also because many a forger turned out to be a professional historian), the notion of decontextualization is helpful in understanding what forgeries are, what pseudohistory is, what invented traditions are. They are complex features of counternarratives put forth by marginalized groups. This marginalization is also contextual: a group that may be marginal internationally, may be dominant in its own country. It is undeniably the feeling of being marginalized that provides a major impetus to forge something that had been lost, that should have still been there but no longer is. I hesitate to equate this with popular amateurism versus elitist professionalism, if only because the case of South Korea has shown clearly that often it is the pseudo-historians who have political support, economic means, and easy media access, where the professional historian only has institutional sheltering. The slew of lawsuits and political accusations against professional historians by the pseudo-historians demonstrates that the dichotomy between popular and elitist is ambiguous at the very least and of little practical use here.

Yet another point to be taken under consideration is this: without the particular skill set of the professional historian, the prestige associated with it, and the professional discourse, the forgeries of the forger would fall flat. Historical forgeries need the academic discourse of the professional historians; for their encroachment upon the margins of formal discourse, a veneer of professional respectability becomes available.

In connection to the last point, the term "pseudo-historian" which Andrew Logie uses for the revisionist and ultranationalist amateur historians whose work he analyses, merits some more explication. Like the term "forgery" this term also carries a heavily negative connotation: "pseudo" here is shorthand for "would-be" or "pretend." Unlike "forgery" however, there is no layering of meanings to "pseudo" that can set off this negative connotation. Still, I think Logie is right in using this term. The amateur historians he describes pride themselves on their superiority as proper historians—they call themselves historians, yet lack the professional skills that make a historian. Their vision on what history is supposed to be is extremely strong, their command of the methodology of the trade correspondingly weak. "Pseudo-historian," then, fits this positioning well. This epithon should be taken literally to mean "pretended historian."

This section houses the chapters that deal with history and religion as the themes around which inventors draped the often-existential concerns they wanted to see addressed. In this sense, religion and history turn out to be close cousins, borrowing freely from one another, religion using history's ancient sources or if these turn out not to be suitable, making do with the aura of authority that ancient historical sources dispense. Invented traditions that center around history on the other hand often do the same, relying on intangible attraction of religious meaning to imbue its narratives with something that other narratives do not possess.

Despite the fact that the forgeries at the heart of historical and religious invented traditions have been easily spotted by historians and other academics, these forgeries have nonetheless, as Andrew Logie argues in his contribution to this volume and Don Baker shows in his chapter, made possible invented traditions that have been around long enough to have obtained the functional characteristics of authentic traditions due to their "developmental depth" (Logie's term), garnering the (semi-)professional and popular support to speak of and be accepted as a tradition.

The pseudo-historians Logie discusses in his chapter are an example of an invented tradition based on clearly identified historical forgeries and other methodologically unsound practices, resulting in fantastic historical narratives that have gained a momentum of their own. Such invented traditions seek to replace dominant historical narratives by challenging their authenticity on the grounds that the newer, fantastic narratives not only satisfy the needs of the nation, but also that they uphold real academic rigor in a way professional narratives have not been able to. These discourses are increasingly removed from those of the professional historians, calling to mind Baudrillard's hyperreal "without origin or reality," although their respective margins by necessity touch.

The same phenomenon also emerges from the chapters in this section. Don Baker's contribution to this volume delves into one of the more intriguing phenomena of modern Korea: the emergence of new religions with very strong views on history. These religions *grosso modo* adhere to the characteristics of neo-nativism discussed earlier (Breuker 2013), attaching crucial importance to a considerable time-distance between its invented origins and the time that the religion actually arises (Sŏndo, "an ancient religious tradition that predates Buddhism by centuries" vs. the present in which this ancient tradition is active). Baker also shows how Sŏndo rejects the civilizing influences of Sinitic culture, rejecting the scholarly *communis opinio* in favor of revisionist and nativist theories.

In the face of modernization (that has been more brutal on the Korean Peninsula than in many other places), Baker argues:

> [I]t is not surprising that some people will seize upon elements from their culture's past as markers of a distinctive identity that can resist absorption by that homogenized world. It is also not surprising that they often inadvertently create something new out of those old elements, since, after all, they are creating cultural markers that they hope will survive in the modern world and therefore must produce something that is a modernized version of tradition.

The postcolonial context in divided Korea in which Sŏndo arose made it inevitable that it would position itself as an underdog, emphasizing ethnic unity and rejecting universalist tendencies associated with colonialism. The emphasis on Tan'gun fits well with this inclination. Baker reconstructs the three separate elements that came to make up Sŏndo: the belief that Tan'gun indeed lived for almost a millennium and a half and became a sinsŏn (godlike immortal), the belief that other mortals can attain that same goal, and the techniques of Chinese internal alchemy practiced during the Chosŏn dynasty in Korea. Combined with a plethora of historical forgeries purported to have been written in ancient times, Baker draws a convincing picture of a "living" invented tradition serving a readily identifiable purpose.

Remco Breuker's chapter delves into the methodology and motives of the forgers of historical texts. He notes the structural affinity between historians ardently wishing for a more useful history and the forgers who cherished the same desires. Both the historians and the forgers acted upon their existential desires: a historian like Kim T'aeg-yŏng ended up recompiling and partly reimagining medieval sources to prepare the ground for a new, more vital, and less vulnerable reading of Korean history. Forgers contemporary to Kim tried to obtain the same goal by relying on much of the same methodology, but going just a bit further, they crossed the blurry line between historiography and historical fantasy. Where Kim T'aeg-yŏng created a thoroughly researched reorganization of historical sources in the *Sin Koryŏsa* (which has its own serious problems as a historiographical work, but is not a forgery, in that it clearly declares what it is), the forgers (whose identities are often obscure) forged historical texts such as the *Tan'gi kosa* (Ancient history of Tan'gun and Kija), which masqueraded as something that they were not: written contemporary testimonies to events shrouded in the mists of myth and history. Breuker argues that texts like this were forged not to simply deceive, but out of a desire to fill in the gaps in the historical record that would then undoubtedly show the true nature of the history of the Korean people (and thus their destiny) at the moment when the very identity of the Korean people was under threat of annihilation with the advent of Japanese colonialism. The power of these texts can be seen in the fact that almost a century after their creation, they still generate works by amateur historians that attract a massive popular readership today and that generate significant political influence as well. The fabrications were justified by the forgers because the fabricated histories preserve a national essence that was lost as a result of Sinitic influence over the course of the Koryŏ dynasty and Chosŏn dynasty. The dividing lines between forgers, historians "filling in the gaps," and more rigorous forgers turn out to be blurrier than would seem methodologically safe.

Andrew Logie's chapter is an extremely urgent study of a peculiar historiographical phenomenon that has come to exercise significant political influence in present-day South Korea. The increasingly fantastic (in the original sense of the word) re-interpretation of the ancient history of the Korean nation expanded both the age of the Korean nation by several millennia and its territorial reach (in some accounts all the way to Europe). Logie traces the historiographical and intellectual traditions in which the pseudo-historians (his term) work and notices that historically groundless as their theories may be, their activities have amassed sufficient developmental depth as to constitute a complex of invented histories on their own. Importantly, Logie uses his meticulous tracing of the arguments and sources invoked not only to draw a picture of the network over time in which the pseudo-historians have been active, but also to show, in conjunction with the aggressive politics of a number of these pseudo-historians, what happens when academic rigor is sacrificed for its mere appearance. The ensuing political, social, and academic mess (and damage done to individual academics) has been well documented and is, truth be told, a sorry sight to behold. This also falls within the realm of the monumental invented tradition (outlined in the introduction to this volume): it may or may not support the hegemonic narrative, it may or may not negatively affect those who oppose it, or as in this case, are opposed by it. It may not always be easy to discern the same mechanisms behind the activities of the pseudo-historians (because of the overtly political angle and the offensive aggression aimed at individual scholars), but structurally and in terms of the process, Logie's observations coincide with those of Baker.

POST SCRIPTUM

Considering to what extent invented traditions in the fields of history and religion are or are not built on authentic source materials is not the purpose of this exercise. Deconstructing an invented tradition is a tool rather than a goal. Besides, a serious argument can be made that most if not all traditions were at some point invented, that is, they all went through the same stage of coming together before they obtained the "developmental depth" needed to generate sufficient weight to stand by themselves. As the chapters in this book show, invented traditions are always under discussion, both the discursive field itself and its—provisional—product. Historical and religious invented traditions have functioned as key elements of the construction of neo-nativist identities in late nineteenth- and early twentieth-century Korea. In general, historiographical narrative strategies that are employed in nativist invented traditions typically reveal a number of characteristics that seem to be compatible with what can be observed in the context of Korea. Nativistic discourse typically contains a considerable time-distance between its projected or invented origins and the time that the nativist discourse actually arises (at least 3,500 years here and perhaps as much as 7,000 years). The chapters in this section satisfy this criterion rather generously. Nativist discourse is also explicitly revisionist: Logie's pseudo-historians are explicitly revisionist in their rejection of traditional historiography and rely on values considered nativist, while Baker's understanding of Sŏndo reinforces this point. Further characteristics include expressly donning the garb of the eternal underdog; and consciously developing anti-syncretistic tendencies (the emphasis on authenticity in an ethnic and cultural context does precisely this). As made clear by the traditions scrutinized by Baker and Logie, in a postcolonial context these traditions also express a clash between the universalistic values of colonialism (or at least its pretenses as such) and localized strategies to deal with these pretenses. It may be useful to consider the emergence of these invented traditions as one possible local response trying to create a momentum of autonomous self-conscious identity. Mostly, these invented traditions have been understood as isolated cases, but I wonder whether they should not be looked at as a systematic "tradition of invention" specifically driven by underlying cultural and historical dynamics.

Let me conclude with a poem by Yu Ŭng-du from Yi Kwan-gu's *Ŏnhaengnok* (Record of words and deeds), which succinctly captures the urgently felt need for the discovery of lost traditions, knowledge, and historical texts that "fill in the gaps" (and that ironically and fittingly may be a forgery itself). The poem is about a strange script he discovered, the remains of an ancient past unknown to him and his countrymen (and, it should be added, as an authentic ancient script, it is still unknown to academics today):

九月山 石碑	The stele at Kuwŏl-san Mountain
村名稱馬韓	Mahan is the name of the village
別有殊常石	Where they have a very strange stone
址荒躑躅紅	Its stand dilapidated, red azalea traces
字沒莓苔碧	The moss grows green, but the characters are worn away
生於剖判初	Having been created when heaven and earth were separated
立了興亡夕	It was erected in the dusk of the rise and fall [of a nation]
文獻俱無跡	Documents contain no traces at all [of those times]
徜非箕氏跡	Can't these be the traces of Ki-ssi?

When Yi Kwan-gu reached P'ungch'ŏn Saga-ri he pulled free a small stele from under a large zelkova tree. When he studied it closely, there turned out to be traces of characters on the surface of the stone. These characters were not Chinese (Hanmunja) nor were they Korean (Chosŏnmunja), but they were similar to the traces of characters on a stele in Mahan-ch'on at Kuwŏl-san. The people said that this was the original script (kungmun) from the period of Tan'gun Chosŏn.

GLOSSARY

Chosŏn 朝鮮
Chosŏnmunja 朝鮮文字
Hanmunja 漢文字
Kim T'aeg-yŏng 金澤榮
Koryŏ 高麗
kungmun 國文
Kuwŏl-san 九月山

Mahan-ch'on 馬韓 村
Ŏnhaengnok 言行錄
P'ungch'ŏn Saga-ri 豐川 四佳里
Sŏndo 仙道
Tan'gun 檀君
Yi Kwan-gu 李觀求
Yu Ŭng-du 柳應斗

REFERENCES

Breuker, Remco. 2013. "O fleeting Joyes of Paradise or: How Nativism Enjoyed its 15 Minutes of F(r)ame in Medieval Korea." In *Challenging Paradigms: Buddhism and Nativism: Framing Identity Discourse in Buddhist Environments*, edited by Henk Blezer and Mark Teeuwen, 229–257. Leiden: Brill.

Eco, Umberto. 1999. "The Force of Falsity." In *Serendipity: Languages and Lunacy*, 1–28. London: Phoenix.

Hiatt, Alfred. 2005. *The Making of Medieval Forgeries: False Documents in Fifteenth-Century England*. Toronto: University of Toronto Press.

CHAPTER 1

Authenticating the Past

Filling in Gaps with the Tan'gi kosa

REMCO BREUKER

In a lament characteristic for his profession when confronted with an obvious historical forgery, renowned historian of the ancient history of the Korean Peninsula Cho In-sŏng, sighed that even though academics had sufficiently proven allegedly ancient historical works such as the *Tan'gi kosa* (supposedly an eighth-century text), *Hwandan kogi* (purportedly a 1911 collection of four texts from antiquity), and *Kyuwŏn sahwa* (a 1675 text purporting to transmit the last of the 47 Tan'gun rulers over the Korean Peninsula) to be modern forgeries, so-called *cheya sasŏ* or amateur histories based on these works continued to appear in bookstores and libraries. The interest of lay readers in these works did not seem to diminish either (Cho 2003, 33–49). His solution to this irritating conundrum unfolds in the remainder of his article: his aim is "to compare the contents of the *Tan'gun segi* contained in the *Hwandan kogi* with the *Tan'gi kosa* and *Kyuwŏn sahwa*," in order to "show even more clearly that the *Tan'gun segi* and the book that contains this text, the *Hwandan kogi*, are historical forgeries" (Cho 2003, 34). But alas, despite Cho's good intentions, the *Hwandan kogi* and related texts continue to inspire new *cheya* histories of Korea and continue to exhibit more romantic, political, nationalist, and commercial appeal than the works of professionally trained historians. After the government-backed claims by Chinese scholars in 2005 that the history of the ancient kingdoms of Koguryŏ and Parhae belonged to Chinese ancient history rather than to Korean ancient history, which is the scholarly *communis opinio*, the writings of the pseudo-historians in South Korea (as well as their public and political support), angrily defending the nation, reached new, sometimes absurd heights (Rawski 2015; Ahn 2019). In this chapter, I analyze the story of the fabrication of texts like the *Tan'gi kosa* and discuss their continued importance in understanding popular understandings of Korean history. At the same time, I would like to draw attention to the structural relationship forged historical texts possess with authentic(-ated) historical texts, as well as the discursive context in which they function alongside authentic historical texts. I would like to draw attention to the serendipitous layering of meanings that the word "forged" possesses in this context: it is perhaps tempting to just focus on "forged" in its negative sense of "made in fraudulent imitation of something genuine; counterfeit, false, spurious." That, however would be a denial of the constructive (if also creative) use of history forged historical texts tend to make (Breuker 2009). In order to fully appreciate a forged historical text, the notion of "forged" in the sense of "fashioned at the forge" should be given equal significance, signifying both the illuminating and obfuscating properties of a forged historical text.

INVENTING ANCIENT TEXTS

The forging of historical texts is one example in a much wider field of what may in a broader sense be called invented traditions: ready-made traditions as "responses to novel situations which take the form of reference to old situations," as Hobsbawm and Ranger (1983) put it in their classic *The Invention of Tradition*. To be sure, much of what in historical and religious terms has been invented, (re-)imagined, (re-)conceptualized on the Korean Peninsula can be said to more or less fit this definition. The example given above certainly does. At the same time, it has proven to be too restrictive, too reductive, and perhaps even too Eurocentric to limit the function of the invented tradition to the category of reaction to novel situations.[1] This not only smacks of by now rather outdated models that explicitly or implicitly presuppose some kind of unified decisive action to have taken place (for example, the intervention by a colonial power) for invented traditions to emerge, but is also not borne out by empirical investigation. Examples from the Korean Peninsula, even if only limited, as this section is, to the categories of history and religion, show that invented traditions are as conformity inducing as they are subversive, depending on the context and place whence the tradition is made to emerge. Invented traditions not only react; especially from a subaltern position, they also act or instigate. Indeed, invented traditions institutionalize, mobilize, and socialize as much as they have been remade, constructed, and forged. It is this essential duality of the invented tradition that has often been overlooked in previous studies. There is practical use to be found in the invented tradition as a tool to effect change that is either desired or deemed necessary. The inventors of traditions on the Korean Peninsula found out, in particular in the late nineteenth and early twentieth centuries, that rather than by a sharp break, the authentic and the newly made are separated by degrees of difference, positioned on a sliding scale. This enabled creative minds to fill in the gaps, where necessary, of a past that was no longer entirely accessible. This is a point that I also argue in the section introduction, which in different forms and contexts returns in the chapters that follow.

Let us first return to the example that started this introduction. Cho's reaction to the widespread credibility attached to works that have been repeatedly and consistently exposed as twentieth-century forgeries instead of the ancient historical works they claim to be, may be considered both typical and proper for a professional historian. Forgeries that nonetheless, as Andrew Logie argues in his contribution to this volume and Don Baker demonstrates in his chapter, have made possible invented traditions that have been around long enough to have obtained the functional characteristics of authentic traditions due to their developmental depth, garnering the (semi-)professional and popular support to speak of it as a tradition.[2] These inventions are still invented traditions; they were based on forgeries, and as such prima facie antithetical to the pursuit of the serious historian, substituting fancy for fact, imagination for inference. Or are they? It is undeniably so that invented traditions resting on the assumed authority of historical forgeries may sabotage some of the key components of the modern (religious) historian's profession: the integrity, historicity, and authenticity of source materials. It has been suggested that forgeries, in particular in art, are a reaction against modernity and its key emphases on individuality, novel solutions to artistic problems, and historicity (Radnoti 1999). This, however, would seem to fly in the face of the fact that forgeries, whether in historiography, art, or other fields of endeavor, have been around almost as long as writing. There is a subversive side to forgeries—and to invented traditions: this is a point that needs to be driven home again and again. As art historian Ian Haywood eloquently argued, art forgeries are "subversive artifacts" that challenge "the cult of the original." (1987, 2, 10). Haywood belongs to a category of art historians that do not lament forgeries per se, but take into account the background of their coming-into-being, relishing, as it were, the way art forgeries expose and problematize the notion of the authentic and the cult of the original, while drawing attention, slightly paradoxically perhaps but also understandably, to the economic underpinnings of the contemporary art world and its study. Essentially an optimist, Haywood (1987, 18) appreciates the potential in forgeries for radical revaluation of prevailing values. In this vein, forgeries are understood as products of the underdogs of society and forgers as artistically inclined Robin Hoods, deftly relieving the rich of their money by taking advantage of their lack of artistic refinement to see the difference between a forgery and an original.[3] Such an approach, however, does not really mount a challenge to the cult of the original, but merely confirms its pervasiveness and significance by imitating it. The pseudo-historians Logie discusses in his chapter are an example of this, pseudo-historians who do not rely on empirical data of historical records, believing these records to show a distorted historical view that diminishes Korea's national essence. Instead they attempt to fill in the lacunae left in the records and rely on forged histories created by twentieth-century nationalist scholars. Their invented traditions seek to replace dominant historical narratives by challenging the authenticity of the narratives put forward by professional historians only on the grounds that the professional narratives were never held to the rigorous academic standards demanded from anyone else. While for the professional historian methodology and handling of sources come first and the analysis is the necessary outcome of the application of methodology to the sources, for the pseudo-historian the teleologically determined outcome of his/her historical analysis takes precedence, necessitating a fundamentally different approach to methodology and sources. Only if these yield the desired outcome, are they valid and worthy of recognition.

It could also be argued, perhaps, that forgeries are antidotes to (or ironically the epitome of) what Charles Lindholm (2008) describes as a modern affliction: the pervasive desire for authenticity is in his estimation a consequence of a modern loss of faith and meaning, offering its seekers a sense of belonging, connection, and solidity. Interestingly and alarmingly, Lindholm shows that the notion of authenticity is not only imagined in the realms of art, music, and food, but also plays a part in the way belonging to the nation is constructed, described, and even proscribed. While Lindholm is rather negative in appreciating the consequences of allowing the notion of authenticity as the arbiter of who belongs and who does not to a certain community, this notion of authenticity may also work to include rather than to exclude, when put to use in a subaltern position. Again, the Korean Peninsula, in particular with regard to its colonial period, provides us with examples of how this might work. The appropriation of objective historiographical methodology to retell Korean history is a case in point: here, the instrumentarium of the colonial elite was repurposed to turn the concept of "truth" around and use it to prepare for Korean independence (Breuker 2006).

For the sake of argument, let us focus on the invention of historical and historically undergirded religious traditions here, in particular on the acquisition and uses of the historical facts and artifacts (often texts) that are indispensable in the creation of different historical narratives.

FORGING OR FILLING IN?

Using the notion of authenticity, the line between the invented (or forged) and the authentic is not easily drawn, despite the protestations of professional academics that it is. And even if historians were to put, for example, any suspected text along a truth-falsehood or forged-authentic axis, we may reasonably question how useful the results would be, except in purely technical historical or even antiquarian terms. There are obviously instances in which knowing if a text (or a practice) is what it purports to be is decisive in order to achieve historical understanding. More often, such inquiry only leads to the obfuscation of what is perhaps any invented tradition's most important characteristic: that it is the product of a process, that it is a process itself, and that as such it functions in a discursive field that is both professional and non-professional. This is in fact tantamount to considering the process by which an invented tradition is conceived, created, made public, and authenticated (or denounced) as a complex of sources in their own right (this is the "developmental depth" Logie refers to in chapter 2). Where does this get us? Let's take a look at two concrete examples.

Reconsidering forgeries in a positive manner, rather than lamenting their very existence, and situating these explicitly in a context immediately identifiable with that of the (ex-)colony, Derek Pearsall had the following to say:

> They work with the material they have, which may not have been insubstantial, and in a plain and circumstantial style simply fill out the narrative with the details of battles fought, soldiers killed and truces signed that have unfortunately been lost in the passage of time. Like Geoffrey [Geoffrey of Monmouth—c. 1100–c. 1155], they supply the gaps in the historical record, and in the absence of information, provide it. (2003, 10)

Interestingly, this is precisely what we find when looking at Korean historical forgeries and the invented traditions associated with or built upon them. A medieval text like the *Ten Injunctions* (*Hunyo Sipcho*), for instance, was forged to complement the historical records that had been lost during the sacking of Kaesŏng in 1011 by the Liao army (Breuker 2009), but more recent forgeries on the Korean Peninsula show the very same ambition, as these words—purportedly by Sin Ch'ae-ho (1880–1936) reveal:

> Oh oh! I also think that we absolutely must have a real 5000-year old history starting with Tan'gun, the only reason why we cannot see it yet, is because we have not been able to preserve our history due to our experiencing several political upheavals. How can I not lament this? But the bright heaven has not let this fact ruin [this prospect] and has made Mr Yu Ŭng-du appear with his manuscript. Who cannot rejoice when reading it, who cannot speak of it and pass it on, since it was not coincidental that Mr Yu came to possess it, for he obtained it from the passion he had cherished for so long. (Tae 1986)

It should be noted that Sin Ch'ae-ho, perhaps colonial Korea's most famous and influential intellectual (particularly in the realm of historiography), who here seems to knowingly endorse a forgery (if indeed Sin's text isn't a forgery as well, in which case an impersonator is speaking), was not easily satisfied with anything that would merely complement the incomplete historical records of the Korean nation.[4] He severely criticized other historical forgeries that he thought were just bad, low-quality forgeries and not pertinent reimaginations of the past. It should not pass unnoted that the historical forgery discussed here is meaningless if not placed in the context of the larger—invented—tradition of a particular type of perennial Korean independence. Sin (or his impersonator), however, does not dwell on what the criterion for reimagining rather than forging the past would be. This is unfortunate, because this criterion is exactly what gives historical forgeries their raison d'être. We can try to deduce the contents of this criterion, however, and come to a reasonable approximation.

In order to do this, we must cast our net wider than the obvious forgeries related to the reconstruction of Tan'gun Chosŏn, which is traditionally placed in the third millennium BCE. But interestingly, not much wider. A closer look at one of the twentieth century's more famous forgeries that gave rise to the continuing importance of perhaps the most significant invented tradition on the Korean Peninsula, that of Tan'gun, will open up avenues for further investigation. The *Tan'gi kosa* (Ancient history of Tan'gun and Kija), an account of the mythical proto-Korean states of Tan'gun Chosŏn and its rulers and Kija Chosŏn, is prefaced by three separate texts, one of which—purportedly—was by Sin Ch'ae-ho. The first preface is by Yi Kyŏng-jik (b. 1852), the director of the government educational publishing department (Hakpu pyŏnjipkuk).[5] Yi writes how Yi Yun-gyu had been entrusted with the original *Tan'gi kosa* manuscript in Literary Sinitic by his teacher Yu Ŭng-du.[6] Yu had chanced upon it in a secondhand bookstore in China. Amazingly, Yi Kyŏng-jik also writes about how a Chinese scholar had earlier given him a similar old and battered book (this description is a staple ingredient of the provenance narratives of Korean historical forgeries). This of course turned out to be another copy of the *Tan'gi kosa*, made by Yi Yun-gyu in order to safeguard against a renewed loss of this valuable manuscript (apparently, many copies were made at the same time; none seem to have survived though).[7] Yi's preface laments the many missing sources in Korean history. Those ancient sources that did survive, such as the *Samguk sagi* (Histories of the Three Kingdoms, 1146) by Kim Pu-sik (1075–1151) or the *Samguk yusa* (Memorabilia of the Three Kingdoms, 1285) by Ir'yŏn (1206–1286) are perceived as inherently worthless due to their ideological constraints (Tae 1986, 8–9). This is noteworthy, because this kind of historical revisionism ties these textual forgeries to a discourse that may be characterized as religious neo-nativism, creating some of the most vibrant Korean invented traditions (see Breuker 2013). Upon reading the book he had received from Yi Yun-gyu, Yi Kyŏng-jik found that it was a historian's and patriot's dream come true. It had been originally written by Parhae prince and scholar Tae Ya-bal (fl. early eighth century BCE), translated into Literary Sinitic by one Hwang Cho-bok (dates unknown) three hundred years later, and still later had been annotated by the equally unknown Chang Sang-gŏl. The style of the Literary Sinitic was similar to the *Book of Documents*, while the institutions devised by Tan'gun and Kija described in it were similar to what Song dynasty Chinese historian Sima Qian had written about in his extremely influential *Zizhi Tongjian* (Comprehensive mirror to aid in government, 1065). Most importantly, the manuscript celebrated Chosŏn culture in a way Confucian culture never could have and indeed never had.

The *Tan'gi kosa*, the story continued in the preface, had been hidden for a thousand years on account of those who tried to destroy Korean culture (it is not specified who these persons might have been). Although the edition that was transmitted to Yi Yun-gyu was in Literary Sinitic, the original had been written in the no longer extant language of Parhae in 727 by Tae Ya-bal. This edition, which Yi Kwan-gu had received from his father, was, conveniently perhaps, destroyed when Yi's father's house in Sŏngbuk-tong in Seoul was destroyed during the Korean War (1950–1953), not before having made a translation into Korean in 1949 by Kim Tu-hwa and Yi Kwan-gu, though, which is the version still extant.

The link through Yi Kyŏng-jik with the educational publishing department is significant, because Yi Kyŏng-jik is said to have tried to publish the text in a Literary Sinitic edition in 1907. Although details are not given, pro-Japanese forces successfully opposed this, fearing that the publication of such a book might stir nationalist sentiments amongst the Korean population. Five years later, it is further stated in the book's preface, Yi Kyŏng-jik and Sin Ch'ae-ho tried to have the book published in Manchuria, but again this plan is said to have failed, this time apparently because of a lack of funds. Finally, in 1949, the hangul vernacular version was published in South Korea with financial and intellectual support from influential persons,[8] but it was completely ignored by historians, whose craft

Yi Kwan-gu—whose credentials as an independence fighter are impeccable—characterizes as "toadyist historiography" (*sadaesahak*). This kind of historiography by professional historians allegedly ignored the native history of Korea and only focused on Chinese influences, again showing the revisionism inherent in this text. This is a direct predecessor to the pseudo-historians' characterization of professional historians as "pro-Japanese" traitors described in Logie's chapter.

The 1959 preface by the impersonator of Sin Ch'ae-ho agrees on many points with the original 1949 preface by Yi Kyŏng-jik. The "authentic" Sin's argument is familiar: one can only call oneself a patriot if one knows one's national history. Without history, he states, there is quite literally nothing. The style of the preface is lyrical and, as always, contains a diatribe against Kim Pu-sik,[9] who not only represents sinocentric toadyism for Sin, but was also almost held to be singlehandedly responsible for Korea's ancient sources disappearing from the historical record by not including them in his *Samguk sagi*. As noted above, Sin's preface, whilst outspoken and very lyrical, is also rather subtle in that it seems to endorse the *Tan'gi kosa* without confirming its factual veracity. Rather, Sin maintains that serendipitously the *Tan'gi kosa* could serve to complement the lacunae of the Korean historical record. If rephrased in a more contemporary manner, this would be the reimagining of the gaps and breaks in Korean history.[10] Given the subtle wording of this preface to the *Tan'gi kosa*, it seems as if Sin hints at knowing that the *Tan'gi kosa* was not authentic in the sense that there was no way to prove it was a faithful copy of the original. Still, he imagined it to be what it could not be proven to be, but what historical and national necessity had determined it should be.

The final preface is supposedly the original preface by the author of the version in the Parhae language, Tae Ya-bal. Here, the provenance of the text is established; the tradition of Tan'gun is being invented in front of the eyes of the reader. Again, the theme of lost historical records is prevalent and according to Tae the main reason for the compilation of the *Tan'gi kosa*. When the Tang armies had destroyed first the ancient kingdom of Paekche in 660 and then Koguryŏ in 668, they also destroyed the historical archives of the two states. It turns out that the *Tan'gi kosa*, written on the command of the ruler of Parhae, the state into which the survivors of Koguryŏ's destruction had coalesced, was not a new work. Rather, it was an attempt at restoring as much of the damaged historical record as possible. It was meant to represent the history of the nation (which included both the ancient state of Koguryŏ, the medieval state of Parhae, and the long line of—historically unattested—states that preceded them) until the moment of compilation. It does so by providing a detailed history of the states and rulers on the peninsula since Tan'gun and explaining the origin of divine rule. To emphasize the status of the *Tan'gi kosa* as a historical text, in effect the only truly national history in existence, created by adhering to the professional criteria of the historian, Tae writes that he composed the text using documents and inscriptions (presumably rubbings mostly) stored in a secret stone chamber, and that he visited the region of Tolgwŏlguk (glossed in the text on page 112 as the region of the Altai Mountains) twice in order to retrieve old documents.[11] The *Tan'gi kosa* was considered to be so valuable, once it was completed, that it was carved onto woodblocks that were then stored in the national library of Parhae.[12]

There is a significant sequel to the (putative) translation history of this text. The prefaces maintain that the text was written in Parhaean and then translated into Literary Sinic, from which it was translated into modern Korean in 1949. Ten years later, in 1959, it was translated (or partially reconstructed) as a text using mixed script (known as *kukhanmun*), perhaps to add to its perceived authenticity by the liberal use of Chinese characters (Tae 1959). At the same time, the text was equipped with appendices, tables, chronologies, and maps, giving it the same attributes a history produced by professional historians would have had. This version, annotated by professional historian Ko Tong-yŏng in 1986, is the one that is still commercially available (and that to the lament of Cho In-sŏng still sells well). Andreas Schirmer's chapter (in the next section) on the—inadvertent—creation of an invented tradition when works in Literary Sinic are translated wholesale into contemporary Korean clearly brings out the nuances involved in creating and positioning authentic texts and their translations, showing how in South Korea the attempt at preserving an empirically acknowledged tradition (producing texts in Literary Sinic) gave rise to a new tradition when these texts were transposed to another language. The negotiations involved are clearly recognizable also in what happened with the *Tan'gi kosa*, although the main difference there of course is the absence of the authentic tradition in the first place. Interestingly, however, Schirmer's conclusions seem to hold even when the authentic tradition from which the translations are made, is in fact invented.

THE FORGER VERSUS THE HISTORIAN

Before delving deeper into the *Tan'gi kosa* and related forgeries, I would like to contrast the *Tan'gi kosa*, which is almost unanimously seen by scholars as a twentieth-century forgery, with a historical record compiled by a contemporary of Sin Ch'ae-ho, also a historian and intellectual who had to flee colonial Korea and died in exile in China and a person who saw the proper understanding of history as the way to save the nation from its increasingly dark colonial predicament. Here the similarities end, for where Sin is—deservedly—remembered as the epitome of modern things (anarchist, nationalist, activist, publicist), as one of the founding fathers of modern Korean historiography, and as an intellectual and nationalist giant, the intellectually much more conservative Kim T'aeg-yŏng (1850–1927) is all but forgotten as a historian and intellectual. If he is remembered at all, it is on account of his beautiful prose in Literary Sinitic. I think, however, that the example of Kim T'aeg-yŏng may help in understanding the importance of invented historical and historically contextualized religious traditions in Korean history and particularly last century, because what Kim did was in effect not much different from what the person(s) behind well-known forgeries such as the *Tan'gi kosa*, the *Ch'ŏnbugyŏng*, the *Hwarang segi*, the *Hwandan kogi*, and so forth did.[13] He also complemented the gaps in the historical record and did this out of a strong sense of dissatisfaction with the usability of the Korean historical records with regard to the predicament Korea was facing in the early twentieth century. But he did so as a professional historian. As a result, his handiwork was accepted (although subsequently forgotten) as proper history. He in fact invented a new historical tradition, which unfortunately turned out to lack any longevity or permanence; the ties that bound him to authentic texts were too strong for his creations to be found useful as either subversions or as establishment-confirming challenges.

Kim T'aeg-yŏng was a historian who, like Sin Ch'ae-ho, had received a classical education and who had attained the licentiate degree not long before the state examinations were abolished (see Ch'oe 1996, 17–19).

Unlike Sin Ch'ae-ho (and Pak Ŭn-sik) he looked for solutions in a cleansed and reinvented version of the Classical Learning (*sŏngnihak*) he had grown up with,[14] even though he was no stranger to new ideas.[15] He was acquainted with many of Korea's leading intellectuals in the late nineteenth and early twentieth century and was in contact with Chinese progressive intellectuals such as Liang Qichao (1873–1929).[16] It should be no surprise, then, that Kim shared Sin Ch'ae-ho's views on the importance of firmly grasping one's own history in order to remain a nation. Before he decided in 1908 that "it is better to grow old and die in China than to become a slave of Japan," he was a prolifically published historian in Korea (see Ch'oe 1996, 29).[17] During his time as one of the highest official historiographers of Chosŏn, he published several histories of the Chosŏn state.[18] Meanwhile, he also continued to publish histories on his native Kaesŏng.[19] In exile, he continued both strands of writing, that of the state and the local.[20]

Perhaps the most important reason why Kim T'aeg-yŏng is a neglected historian is the fact that unlike his colleagues Pak Ŭn-sik and Sin Ch'ae-ho, he did not attach any credence to Tan'gun as the progenitor of the Korean nation.[21] The chapters by Logie and Baker show the unrivaled importance the invented tradition of Tan'gun has had in late nineteenth- and twentieth-century Korea, religiously, historically, culturally, politically. Kim, however, sensibly dated the ethnogenesis of the Korean people to after the unification of the peninsula by Silla. He also did not consider Parhae as properly belonging to the genealogy of Korean states (see *Tongguk yŏktae saryak* 1977, 2:1). Again, his historical judgment is sensible: available historical evidence suggests that Parhae belongs in the category of Manchurian empires rather than Korean proto-states, even if the border dividing the two is thin.

Kim T'ae-gyŏng's classically inspired historiography was epitomized by his last project, an ambitious re-editing, recompilation, and de facto reinvention of the entire *Koryŏsa*—the official dynastic history of Koryŏ. In 1927 the *Sin Koryŏsa* (*New history of Koryŏ*) was already anachronous before it had even been published. It was the culmination of centuries of sincere and extremely skillful classical historiography. But it was something else as well. In reinventing a past that never had been, the historical vision in the *Sin Koryŏsa* was stronger than its historical technical aspects (I wonder whether this may not be a useful working definition of a historical forgery). Different from forgeries such as the *Tan'gi kosa*, the *Sin Koryŏsa* is a huge work as it consists of fifty-four volumes (*kwŏn*).[22] In trying to address the deliberate distortions of Koryŏ history by later historians, Kim not only inserted historical comments (traditionally one of the most powerful methods for a historian to advocate his views),[23] but added information to the *Sin Koryŏsa* that had been missing in the *Koryŏsa*, such as the inclusion of a Buddhism section (*sŏkchi*).[24] In an attempt to reclaim the imperial aspirations Koryŏ had had, he even adapted the section names to reflect an imperial status.[25] And interestingly, Kim turned away from a purely political history, devoting as much space as possible to apolitical (or even anti-political) categories such as "arts," "recluses," and "remaining officials" (those who refused to serve under the new dynasty). As far, at least, as he could stretch his meager sources for these traditionally underestimated categories. The result was a reinvention of the Koryŏ period at the level of the primary source.

There are a number of similarities and convergences that make the *Tan'gi kosa* and the *Sin Koryŏsa* (and the respective historiographical traditions they may be said to represent) appear much closer than one would expect at first sight. First, there is the often underestimated element of training and background. Both Kim Tae'gyŏng and Yi Kwan-gu came from similar intellectual backgrounds (scholarly *yangban* families) and received a classical education as the last persons of their generation. This meant that in terms of actively commanding Literary Sinitic, they were unrivaled (as Kim T'ae-gyŏng's reputation bears out); they belonged to the last generation that could feasibly forge a manuscript in proper Literary Sinitic. This similarity inevitably stretched into the domain of professional positions: Kim T'aeg-yŏng was responsible for the publication of historical textbooks for Chosŏn until 1905. Yi Kyŏng-jik, who clearly was well acquainted with Yi Kwan-gu, was a close colleague of Kim T'ae-gyŏng.[26]

Second, the purpose of the *Tan'gi kosa* and the *Sin Koryŏsa* was identical: correcting distorted historical views, but more importantly, filling in the gaps in the historical record that would undoubtedly reveal the true nature of the history of the Korean people (and thus their destiny). In essence, both works attempted to create a new foundation for proper historical traditions to emerge. Kim T'aeg-yŏng did so on a far more modest scale (and far more professionally), but he also acknowledged the unrecognized greatness of Korean history, for example when he emphasized that the Koryŏ state had been an empire ruled by an emperor, rather than a vassal's kingdom. And Kim T'aegyŏng admitted that Tan'gun was not a figment of the imagination, merely that there was no evidence of his historical existence left (Ch'oe 1996, 77). For our purposes here, this is an exceedingly important point, for it points straight at an important similarity between Kim T'aeg-yŏng and the forger(s) of the *Tan'gi kosa* (and some would argue any historian): the importance of the existential preferences of the historian in the reconstruction, reimagining, and reinvention of the past. This point leads us straight to the third similarity: methodology.

Methodologically, works such as the *Tan'gi kosa* share similarities with the *Sin Koryŏsa*. They were heavily reliant on traditional textual criticism and the fruits of the linguistic philology of Japanese and Korean historians such as Shiratori Kurakichi (1865–1942) and Ch'oe Nam-sŏn (1890–1957). Kim T'aeg-yŏng was trained as a classical historian and while working for the Chosŏn state, he was heavily influenced by Japanese historians such as Hayashi Taisuke (1854–1922), who were using the rhetoric of the latest European historical methodologies, even when Kim wrote in Literary Sinitic. Kim T'ae-gyŏng's historical methodology has been examined several times and despite his tendency to borrow from politically suspect historians, little criticism has been voiced with regard to his command of the métier of the historian (see Ch'oe 1996; also see Breuker 2004). The *Tan'gi kosa*'s authors, on the other hand, are not distinguished by their meticulous application of the same historiographical methodology, but they apply it nonetheless. There is a distinct lack of historical sophistication that seems to have been replaced by a badly articulated sense of urgency. This, again, should remind one of today's pseudo-historians who have also replaced strict methodological rigor with political urgency, dubious and methodologically outdated linguistic arguments, and with the positioning of individual works in an established historiographical tradition (of pseudohistory). Nonetheless, the published versions of the text (the only ones that were possibly scrutinized by people who were not connected to the emergence of the manuscript) adhere to academic practice with regard to annotation.[27] At a glance, the *Tan'gi kosa* certainly passes muster as an academically annotated and published text and this is of course exactly what was intended by its authors, translators, editors, and annotators. But behind the parade of hard-to-believe factoids

(Tan'gun Chosŏn invented democracy, the first coins, held the first ever census, used paper money for the first time ever, and so forth and so on) (Tae 1986, 63, 87–88, 105–106), there is a notion that these nonsensical claims come very close to the kind of historiography that Kim T'aeg-yŏng (and many others) wrote. There is the reliance on ancient texts with the implicit assumption that antiquity adds to the intrinsic value of the text; there is intertextuality in the footnotes that continually refers to other (suspected) forgeries such as the *Tan'gun segi*, the *Tan'gun'gi*, and the *Kyuwŏn sahwa*, to no longer extant texts such as the *Koch'ilbu sosa*, but also to historical texts that are accepted as genuine in academic circles (Tae 1986, 51). Referring to lost texts is not something that is the prerogative of the amateur historian. Hundreds of pages have been written by professional historians about Koryŏ works that are no longer extant and that might not have existed in the first place.[28] The debate about (and analysis of!) the no longer extant *Ku Samguksa* (The old history of the Three Kingdoms) is but one example.

The *Tan'gi kosa* also employs historical intertextuality by inserting itself in established historical narratives by claiming kinship with earlier traditions allegedly involving Tan'gun.[29] It clearly shows its age by using the kind of pseudo-historical linguistic reasoning that was perfected by Japanese colonialist historians such as Shiratori Kurakichi: the text gives the geonym *shibiro*, which in the footnotes is etymologically connected to *sŏbaengnia* or the rather modern transcription of Siberia in Chinese (Tae 1986, 39).

There is a fourth important similarity between histories such as written by Kim T'aeg-yŏng and Sin Ch'ae-ho, and historical forgeries such as the *Tan'gi kosa* or the *Hwandan kogi*. They emerged against the same colonial background and kept on being developed (mainly by secondary scholarship) during the postcolonial period. The historical writings by Sin Ch'ae-ho and Kim T'aeg-yŏng were shaped by the colonial experience, but a careful reading of the *Tan'gi kosa* and like works reveals similar preoccupations with rebutting colonialist logic. The *Tan'gi kosa* is emphatic in its reconstruction (in the footnotes added in 1959) of a national religion that would evolve into Taejonggyo, but that started out as something that was exactly like Japanese shintō, almost to the character (Sin'gyo). Acknowledging the inevitable appeal of the colonizer's techniques, the historiographical methodology associated with Japanese historians (objective textual criticism) was applied (or at least, efforts were made to apply it) in these texts.[30] In this sense, the authors of the *Tan'gi kosa* did not differ fundamentally (but decidedly in terms of skills) from their famous contemporaries such as Ch'oe Nam-sŏn (Breuker 2006, 1–38). Another factor in this is the fact that all persons involved with the *Tan'gi kosa* (and later also the persons allegedly involved with the *Hwandan kogi*) were active in the independence movement. Yi Kwan-gu, for instance, is a famous independence fighter. There can be little doubt that texts such as the *Tan'gi kosa* should be seen as (post-)colonial expressions to take hold of the "inner domain" as Partha Chatterjee has argued (while Yi Kwan-gu's other activities as an active resistance fighter were aimed at taking back the "outer domain") (see Chatterjee 1986).

It is necessary to view a text such as the *Tan'gi kosa*, whether it is a forgery or not, as belonging to the same discursive field, to the same invented tradition, as a publicly acknowledged history such as the *Sin Koryŏsa*. I have little doubt that the *Tan'gi kosa* is a forgery in the sense that it is not what it says it is. Exposing the text as a forgery and leaving it at that, however, is not very conducive to thorough analysis and certainly does not help us any further along toward understanding what these texts mean, what kind of role they play in society, and why they retain their popularity with the public, despite the warnings of professional historians. The *Tan'gi kosa* substitutes fancy for fact and imagination for inference. Its historical vision is strong, while its historical methodology is fatally weak. It undeniably sabotages the integrity, historicity, and authenticity of source materials. But it does more than that. In doing so, it gives a voice to otherwise marginalized groups, in this case a specific group of (recently de-)colonized Koreans. It is active in a wider discursive field, which for all purposes is a tradition in the process of being invented. As such there is a subversive side to these forgeries, to these invented traditions, and they do resemble the "subversive artifacts" Haywood (1987) discusses. At the same time, in sabotaging the integrity, historicity, and authenticity of what historians as a community have labeled authentic source materials (see Trouillot 1995 and Novick 1988), these texts also "challenge the cult of the original," problematizing legitimate historiographical undertakings to the extent of sabotaging academic inquiry not in line with their own political views. It would seem, though, that it is not sufficient to understand the *Tan'gi kosa* as the work of a subaltern party aiming at the establishment, whether political and economic (the colonizer) or technical (the professional historian). This text does something more. In a rather paradoxical way since it is not an authentic text itself, it establishes a criterion for authenticity (the historical authenticity of the people of Tan'gun). The notion of authenticity may also work as an including rather than excluding force, when put to use in a subaltern position. A historical forgery such as the *Tan'gi kosa* is almost defined by its subalternity; the flipside of this argument is that when the social group that is associated with such a forgery leaves its subaltern position, the potential for hegemony is large, as has been shown by the abuse of power by pseudo-historians through South Korean Members of Parliament to castigate any professional historian not deemed sufficiently patriotic or nationalist.

More in-depth research should bear this out, but the publication history of works like the *Tan'gi kosa* shows the process of (alleged and real) translation, annotation, publication, and authentication that culminated in the 1959 version of the *Tan'gi kosa* (which is the one available commercially now). If anything, this process is a social process that cuts across the boundaries of the discursive fields of professional and non-professional historiography. It is an invented tradition in itself, having gathered sufficient developmental depth to stand on its own. The juxtaposition with Kim T'ae-gyŏng's *Sin Koryŏsa* served the goal of illustrating the similarity in terms of people, institutions, methodological notions, and goals involved in the compilation and dissemination of both types of works. The process by which a forgery is conceived, created, made public, and authenticated (or denounced) is altogether not very different from the process through which a historical work written by a professional historian goes. As a result, invented traditions are a gray area where the authentic and the inauthentic meet, and where hybridity in different degrees is the norm. At the risk of simplification, it is a matter of degree rather than substance. This, I would suggest, shows most clearly in the contents of invented traditions relating to history and religion, where genuine and forged artifacts and texts are purportedly measured with the same yardstick and used with the same opportunistic gusto.

GLOSSARY

Chang Sang-gŏl 張上傑
Ch'oe Nam-sŏn 崔南善
Ch'ŏnbugyŏng 天符經
Chŏng Hae-bak 정해박
Chǔngbo munhŏn pi'go 增補文獻
　備考
Hakpu pyŏnjipkuk 學部編輯局
Han'gukhak munhŏn yŏn'guso 韓
　國學文書硏究所
Hayashi Taisuke 林泰辅
Hunyo sipcho 訓要十條
Hwandan kogi 桓檀古記
Hwang Cho-bok 皇祚福
Hwarang segi 花郎世紀
Iryŏn 一蓮
Kim Pu-sik 金富軾
Kim T'aeg-yŏng 金澤榮
Kim T'aeg-yŏng chŏnjip 金澤榮
　全集
Ko Tong-yŏng 高東永
Koch'ilbu sosa 居漆夫小史
Kojong sillok 高宗實錄
kukhanmun 國漢文
p'yŏnnyŏnch'e 編年體
sadaesahak 事大史學

Samguk sagi 三國史記
Samguk yusa 三國遺事
shibiro 西非路
shintō 神道
Shiratori Kurakichi 白鳥倉吉
Sima Qian 司馬光
Sin Koryŏsa 新高麗史
Sin'gyo 神敎
sŏbaengnia 西伯利亞
Sŏkchi 釋志
sŏngnihak 性理學
Sungyang kigujŏn 崧陽耆舊傳
Tae Ya-bal 大野勃
Taehan yŏktae saryak 大韓歷代
　史略
Tan'gi kosa 檀奇古史
Tolgwŏlguk 突厥國
Tongguk yŏktae saryak 東國歷代
　史略
Tongsa chimnyak 東史輯略
Yi Kyŏng-jik 李庚稷
Yi Yun-gyu 李允珪
Yŏksa chimnyak 歷史輯略
Yu Ŭng-du 柳應斗
Zizhi Tongjian 資治通鑑

NOTES

The research that resulted in this publication was funded by the European Research Council under the Starting Grant Scheme (War of Words—Proposal 338229).

1. To my knowledge, there is no general study of Korean forgeries set in their respective historical contexts, which releases these artifacts from their status as mere counterfeit products. Partial studies in Korean have

appeared from time to time, but none in English. Although Korean discourses also tend to gravitate along a true-false axis, the application of categories extrapolated overwhelmingly from European examples does not help in bringing a more objective balance to the field. In that sense, Hobsbawm and Ranger's work needs conceptual and empirical rejigging.

2. This statement of course immediately problematizes the notion of tradition on a rather existential level.

3. See for example the diary of Eric Hebborn (1997) for a self-congratulatory description of the modern forger. On the mythology surrounding Dutch master forger Han van Meegeren, see van den Brandhof (1979) and Werness (1983). It is telling that the Robin Hood comparison was made by the forgers themselves.

4. Most often, of course, Kim Pu-sik is blamed for this.

5. See the references in the *Kojong sillok* and the *Chŭngbo munhŏn pigo*.

6. I should mention explicitly here that further research should establish whether the persons mentioned in the text such as Yi Kyŏng-jik were at all involved with this text. The authenticity of the text, or rather the concrete details of the persons behind its (re-)creation are not very important in the context of this book, however. The ascription of that process to certain historical persons, is.

7. Which may be because it was copied from the *Tan'gi kosa* preface into that of, for example, the *Hwandan kogi*.

8. People like Han Chae-yŏng (who provided the money) and vice president Yi Si-yŏng who proofread the text, for example.

9. The style of the preface is lyrical and, as always, contains a diatribe against Kim Pu-sik who not only represents sinocentric toadyism for Sin, but was also almost singlehandedly responsible for the disappearance of Korea's ancient sources from the historical record by not including them in his *Samguk sagi*. Kim Pu-sik was a twelfth-century statesman whom Sin's writings led to his becoming the most popular scapegoat for Korea's loss of independence. Had Kim Pu-sik, argued Sin, not surpressed the—in Sin's reading—nativist revolt of Myoch'ŏng in 1136, Korea's fate would have been fundamentally different. Instead of a country bowing to China and then to Japan, it would have been powerful, proud, and independent.

10. And this is a legitimate way of thinking about history for most historians.

11. It is interesting that Tae mentions Tolgwŏlguk here instead of the more obvious choice of the Tang.

12. There is an intriguing but politically unpopular argument to be made here that understands the inclusion of Koguryŏ and Parhae as proto–Korean states as an invented tradition in its own right.

13. The Ch'ŏnbugyŏng is considered a sacred text in the Korean religion of Taejonggyo. It was allegedly discovered carved on a stone wall near Mount Myohyang by the mysterious (and perhaps completely fictitious) figure of Kye Yŏn-su (d. 1920) in 1916 and transmitted to Tan'gun-gyo (the religion of Tan'gun, later Taejonggyo) the following year. The *Hwarang segi* (Chronological annals of the Hwarang) is a set of allegedly Silla-period chronicles of elite figures from the early sixth to the late seventh century (162 pages in a hand-copied version), written in the language of Silla by Silla scholar Kim Tae-mun (fl. early eighth century). The text was discovered in the Imperial Archives of the Japanese Imperial Household by Pak Ch'ang-hwa (1889–1962), who worked in the archives in the 1930s and 1940s. The text was only published in 1989 by his pupils. Pak was an amateur historian who composed poems in *hyang'chal*, the written language of Silla, and taught this skill to selected students. The veracity of the *Hwarang segi* is still under debate, although most historians have come down on the side of it being a forgery by Pak—although Pak may not have meant it to be passed off as an authentic historical text. Interestingly, contemporary Silla sources attest to the fact that a text called *Hwarang segi* by the hand of Kim Tae-mun had indeed existed.
14. The fact that Kim T'aeg-yŏng never abandoned his classical ideas is the main factor for his relative neglect by later historians of Korean historiography. His official publications and his private writings have been influential, but to contemporary historians his inability to "overcome" his outdated ideas compares him unfavorably with Sin Ch'ae-ho, for example.
15. Kim's open-minded attitude toward Japan and the West can also be surmised from his acceptance of Japanese historical theories and his acceptance of Homer Hulbert's historiography. Having read Hulbert's history of Korea in China, Kim later wrote that he received the inspiration to write his own comprehensive history of Korea from the fact that a foreigner had taken the trouble to write a history of Korea. See Ch'oe (1996, 130).
16. Kim Yun-sik (1835–1922), Yi Kŏn-ch'ang (1852–1898), Hwang Hyŏn (1855–1910), Pak Ŭn-sik (1859–1926), and Chang Chi-yŏn (1864–1921). See Ch'oe (1996, 29).
17. Paradoxically, Kim was simultaneously open to Japanese historical scholarship, a fact for which he is still condemned by historians. The biggest Japanese influence on Kim was Hayashi Taisuke's *Chōsenshi* that had been translated into Korean by Hyŏn Ch'ae. Hayashi's book is full of colonialist and nationalist arguments, some better disguised than others, but it claimed legitimacy with an appeal to its methodology, which was purported to be objective. The weapon of historical objectivity was a powerful one and

Kim T'aeg-yŏng was by no means the only intellectual to fall for it. He later reconsidered his views on, for instance, the existence of a Japanese colony during the Three Kingdoms period or the invasion of Silla by Empress Jingū, but the damage had already been done. He never envisioned any other role for himself than that of the scholar, who "protected the country by writing." When that was about to become impossible in Korea, he went into exile to continue his research and writing. See Yu (1993, 93–97).

18. As the official state historiographer, he compiled and published the *Tongguk yŏktae saryak*, the *Taehan yŏktae saryak* (1899), the *Tongsa chimnyak* (1902), and the extended version of the last work, the *Yŏksa chimnyak* (1905).

19. Such as a new edition of the *Sungyang kigujŏn* (1903) that can be imagined to have served as a counterweight to Kim's official publications, because of its strong criticism of the corruption in Chosŏn society, its emphasis on the role of Kaesŏng literati, scholars, and bureaucrats, and its consistent if unassuming advocacy of neo-Confucianism. See Breuker (2004, 65–102).

20. In exile, he wrote the following historical works: the *Hansagye*, the *Han'guk yŏktae sosa*, the *Chungp'yŏn Handae Sungyang kigujŏn*, the *Kyojŏng Samguk sagi*, the *Kim-ssi sabo*, the *Koryŏ kyese ilsajŏn*, and the *Sin Koryŏsa*.

21. See *Tongguk yŏktae saryak* 1977, 1:1; *Tongsa chimnyak pŏmnye* 1, in Kim (1902). Kim further stuck to the use of the *p'yŏnnyŏnch'e*, accepted the classical idea of an organic and responsive cosmos, and wrote histories of Korea that were basically political histories.

22. Kim did not intend to write a comprehensive history of Koryŏ. He intended to compile a reference history that would replace the *Koryŏsa*. In 1916, he had undertaken a similar work, when he revised the *Samguk sagi* to rid it of its obvious mistakes. As the title of his version of the *Samguk sagi* suggests, *Kyojŏng Samguk sagi* (Revised histories of the Three Kingdoms), his revision of the *Samguk sagi* was similar in nature to his re-editing of the *Koryŏsa*, but far less drastic. The table of contents of the *Sin Koryŏsa* consists of Basic Annals (1–11), Special Sections (12–28), Tables (29), and Biographies (30–53). The *Sin Koryŏsa* was published in China at *Namdao hanmolin shuju* publishers. The foreword was written by Kim Kŭn-yong, the afterword by Pak Chae-sŏn. The contents were corrected by Kim T'ae-gyŏng's disciples Chang Pong-sang, Kim Kŭn-yong, Kong Sŏng-hak, Kim Chong-gi, and Pak Chae-sŏn.

23. The *locus classicus* for this kind of historical comment is the *Shiji* by Sima Qian. Kim Pu-sik also successfully used it in the *Samguk sagi*. In fact, Kim Pu-sik's historical vision is to be found in its most articulated manner in the historical comments.

24. This did not mean that Kim renounced his Neo-Confucian convictions; it was rather the opposite. Nonetheless, in Kim's estimation Buddhism had been very important during the Koryŏ dynasty, which is why, while not a Buddhist believer himself, he included a "Section on Buddhism," following the example of the *Bei Weisi* (History of the Northern Wei). Kim's attitude toward Buddhism may be summarized as an aversion to the decadence of Buddhism during the Koryŏ. He regretted the decay of Silla Buddhism, but his criticism not so much concerned Buddhism *an sich*, as the decadent splendor and corruption that came to be associated with it during the Koryŏ period. See Ch'oe (1996, 151).

25. This attitude tied in with the attitude apparent from the *Tongguk yŏktae saryak* for which Kim wrote in the explanatory notes. In it he states that in the contemporary world order there is no more place for the exclusive reverence of great countries, such as the Middle Kingdom. Instead, especially the cultures and histories of the smaller countries, of which there were hundreds, should be respected and protected. This respect was tantamount to adhering to mankind's necessary moral rules and examples of righteousness. For an account of the editing and censoring of the original Koryŏ sources into the *Koryŏsa*, see Pyŏn (1983).

26. Yi compiled the *Man'guk yaksa* in 1896 and a translation into Literary Sinitic of Parsons Williams's law books, which would be hugely influential in the 1899 reforms.

27. The annotation of the translation of the original(-ly translated) text looks all right (when one refrains from actually reading it).

28. I myself have been guilty of this. See Breuker (2010).

29. Such as the no longer extant works of Myoch'ŏng (if these ever did exist). These works have enjoyed a long afterlife in all kinds of nativist writings from the Chosŏn period until now.

30. The footnotes on almost every page bear this out.

REFERENCES

Ahn, Yonson, 2019. "The Contested Heritage of Koguryŏ/Gaogouli and China-Korea Conflict." *The Asia-Pacific Journal: Japan Focus*. https://apjjf.org /-Yonson-Ahn/2631/article.html

Breuker, Remco E. 2004. "History With a Capital H: Kaesŏng's Forgotten Claim to Capital History." *Acta Koreana* 7 (2): 65–102.

———. 2006. "Contested Objectivities: Ikeuchi Hiroshi, Kim Sanggi and the

Tradition of Oriental History (*Tōyōshigaku*) in Japan and Korea." *East Asian History* 29:69–105.

——. 2009. *Forging the Truth: Creative Deception and National Identity in Medieval Korea.* Special issue of *East Asian History* 39. Canberra: Australian National University.

——. 2010. *Establishing a Pluralist Society in Medieval Korea, 918–1170: History, Ideology, and Identity in the Koryŏ Dynasty.* Leiden: Brill.

——. 2013. "O Fleeting Joyes of Paradise, or: How Nativism Enjoyed its 15 Minutes of F(r)ame in Medieval Korea." In *Framing Discourse in Buddhist Environments: The Special Case of 'Nativist' Strategies,* edited by Mark Teeuwen and Henk Blezer. Brill Paradigm Series, vol. I.2. Boston/Leiden: Brill.

Chatterjee, Partha 1986. *Nationalist Thought and the Colonial World: A Derivative Discourse.* London: Zed Books.

Cho In-sŏng. 2003. *"Hwandan kogi-ŭi Tan'gun segi-wa Tan'gi kosa, Kyuwŏn sahwa"* [The *Tan'gun segi* as part of the *Hwandan kogi* and its relation with the *Tan'gi kosa* and the *Kyuwŏn sahwa*]. *Tan'gunhak* 2:33–49.

Ch'oe Hye-ju. 1996. *Ch'anggang Kim T'aeg-yŏng ŭi Han'guksaron* [Ch'anggang Kim T'aegyŏn's discourses on Korean history]. Seoul: Hanul Ak'ademi.

Han'gukhak munhŏn yŏn'guso, ed. 1977. *Han'guk kaehwagi kyogwasŏ ch'ongsŏ: kuksa p'yŏn* [Collection of Korean textbooks from the Enlightenment Period—Korean history]. 10 vols. Seoul: Asea munhwasa.

Haywood, Ian. 1987. *Faking It: Art and the Politics of Forgery.* Brighton, UK: Harvester.

Hebborn, Eric. 1997. *The Art Forger's Handbook.* New York: Overlook.

Hobsbawm, Eric, and Terence Ranger, eds. 1983. *The Invention of Tradition.* Cambridge: Cambridge University Press.

Kim T'aeg-yŏng. (1899) 1977. *Taehan yŏktae saryak* [Comprehensive history of the Great Han Empire]. In *Han'guk kaehwagi kyogwasŏ ch'ongsŏ* 13.

——. (1899) 1977. *Tongguk yŏktae saryak* [Concise historical chronicles of the Eastern Country]. In *Han'guk kaehwagi kyogwasŏ ch'ongsŏ.* Vols. 12–13.

——. (1902) 1977. *Tongsa chimnyak* [Concise eastern history]. *Han'guk kaehwagi kyogwasŏ ch'ongsŏ* 15.

——. (1903) 1978. *Sungyang kigujŏn* [Biographies of Kaesŏng worthies]. In *Kim T'aeg-yŏng chŏnjip* 1.

——. (1905) 1977. *Yŏksa chimnyak* [Concise history]. *Han'guk kaehwagi kyogwasŏ ch'ongsŏ* 12.

——. 1924. *Sin Koryŏsa* [New standard history of Koryŏ]. Shanghai: Nandao hanmolin shuju. 54 vols.

———. 1978. *Kim T'aeg-yŏng chŏnjip* [Complete writings of Kim T'aeg-yŏng].
6 vols. Compiled by Sin Yongha, Sin Ilch'ŏl, and Yi Kwangnin. Seoul: Asea
Munhwasa.

Lindholm, Charles. 2008. *Culture and Authenticity*. Oxford: Blackwell.

Novick, Peter. 1988. *That Noble Dream: The "Objectivity Question" and the
American Historical Profession*. Cambridge: Cambridge University Press.

Pearsall, Derek. 2003. "Forging Truth in Medieval England." In *Cultures of Forgery:
Making Nations, Making Selves*, edited by Judith Ryan and Alfred Thomas,
3–24. New York: Routledge.

Pyŏn T'ae-sŏp. 1983. *Koryŏsa ŭi yŏn'gu* [A study of the *Koryŏsa*]. Seoul:
Samyŏngsa.

Radnoti, Sandor. 1999. *The Fake: Forgery and Its Place in Art*. Lanham, MD:
Rowman and Littlefield.

Rawski, Evelyn Sakakida. 2015. *Early Modern China and Northeast Asia: Cross-
Border Perspectives*. Asian Connections. New York: Cambridge University
Press.

Tae Ya-bal. 1959. *Tan'gi kosa* [Ancient history of Tan'gun and Kija]. Translated
by Chŏng Hae-bak. Ch'ŏngju: Ch'ungbuk sinbosa.

———. 1986. *Tan'gi kosa*. Translated by Ko Tong-yŏng. Seoul: Hanppuri.

Tongguk yŏktae saryak. 1977. In *Han'guk kaehwagi kyogwasŏ ch'ongsŏ: kuksa p'yŏn
2* [Collection of Korean textbooks from the Enlightenment Period—Korean
history]. Seoul: Asea munhwasa.

Trouillot, Michel-Rolph. 1995. *Silencing the Past: Power and the Production of
History*. Boston: Beacon Press.

van den Brandhof, Marijke. 1979. *Een vroege Vermeer uit 1937: Achtergronden
van leven en werken van de schilder/vervalser Han van Meegeren*. Utrecht:
Spectrum.

Werness, Hope B. 1983. "Han van Meegeren fecit." In *The Forger's Art: Forgery
and the Philosophy of Art*, edited by Denis Dutton. Berkeley: University of
California Press.

Yu Pong-hak. 1993. "Chosŏn hugi Kaesŏng chisigin-ŭi tonghyang-gwa Pukhak
sasang suyong: Ch'oe Han'gi-wa Kim T'ae-gyŏng-ŭl chungsim-ŭro" [Trends
among late-Chosŏn Kaesŏng intellectuals and their acceptance of Northern
Learning thought]. In *Kyujanggak* 16:85–98.

CHAPTER 2

Enticement of Ancient Empire

Historicized Mythology and (Post)colonial Conspiracies in the Construction of Korean Pseudohistory

ANDREW LOGIE

> If bestsellers on Korean and ancient history stopped at making people feel good [about the past] there would be no problem. However, it is a problem if those reading such books believe them to be actual history and become prisoners to an empty delusion. As for those who create such content, to say it coldly, regardless of their own intentions, they are actively deceiving society.
>
> —Shim 2016, 272

Take a moment to peruse the history section of any of South Korea's commercial bookstores, and you will encounter a seemingly diverse range of paperbacks on topics relating to Korea's ancient history. Similar to popular histories of other countries, their covers are evocatively designed and advertise enticing claims therein of either new, or better argued, truths about Korea's early past.

Reading through such works, most can be classified according to two variant topical foci, which will here be descriptively labeled as "empire" and "pan-Altaic." The empire type argues the ancient Korean people to have possessed an expansive continental territory centered on southern Manchuria—present-day Liaoning and Jilin provinces of China—and spreading in all directions. Pan-Altaic variants concern themselves with long-range migratory schemes and a deeper search for origins that looks to Central Asia.[1] These schemes need not be mutually exclusive as the empire conceptualization may still be premised on initial migrations.

A third categorization is works explicitly promoting a historiographical scheme associated with the new religion of Taejonggyo. Established around 1909, Taejonggyo doctrine is based on Korea's traditional foundation story of Hwan'in, Hwan'ung, and Tan'gun first attested in written sources from the 1280s but pertaining to the "first Korean" state of Old Chosŏn. While sharing aspects in common with the other two variant imaginings of Korea's ancient past, current-day Taejonggyo-type histories make explicit reference to several apocryphal texts, chief of these being *Hwandan kogi* (Old records of the Hwan and Tan [empires]), a work only finalized in 1979 but typically placed in or near to bookstores' early history sections.[2] Since the 2010s, *Hwandan kogi* has been mostly actively promoted by Sangsaeng, a media group affiliated to the millenarian religion of Chŭngsando (est. 1974), headed by second-generation hereditary patriarch, An Kyŏng-jŏn. The most prominent edition of *Hwandan kogi* in bookstores today is An's own annotated translation (An 2012).

These three categorizations collectively rely on a set of claims supported by a shared canon of false arguments—textual, linguistic, and archaeological—that was established during the middle decades of the twentieth century. Nevertheless, new books with new covers claiming fresh arguments are regularly published. A sample from 2017, for example, included: *Yi Tŏk-il's Grand Korean History*, the latest from prominent empire advocate Yi Tŏk-il (b. 1961) containing arguments of continental dominance; *The Paekche We Have Learnt of Is False: The Ancient History of Korea and Japan Read through the History of Puyŏ*, a reiteration by pan-Altaicist Kim Un-hoe (b. 1961) of a hypothesis in which early Japanese states are established as the termini in a chain of transeurasian migrations; and *Actual Proof for the History of the Paedal State*, a new Taejonggyo-inspired history by Chŏn Mun-gyu (b. 1965), Paedal being an invented term of Taejonggyo discussed below (Yi 2017; Kim Un-hoe 2017; Chŏn 2017). Another work, meanwhile, promotes a hypothesis that indigenous Amerindians were descendants of early Koreans: *Our Ethnic Nation's Great Migration: American Indians Are Our People* (Son 2017). This last example represents a less often addressed extension of long-range migration theories, and is also in the mold of classic hyperdiffusion schemes of Grafton Elliot Smith (1871–1937) and William James Perry (1887–1949) in which a single archaic civilization is argued to have been spread across the globe by specific peoples, in this case as an offshoot of ethnic Korean civilization. While hyperdiffusion schemes are still promoted in the West by pseudo-archaeologists such as Graham Hancock (b. 1950), they are most actively promoted in Korea within the extensive introduction of An Kyŏng-jŏn's *Hwandan kogi*.

If 2017 was an unusual year for popular history publications, it is because alongside such titles, there also began to be published a number of paperbacks either problematizing or explicitly critiquing these popular writings as pseudohistory.[3] The timing of this critical response represented a reaction to a recent point of climax in an ongoing government-level dispute, wherein populist advocates of empire, and Taejonggyo schemes in particular, have come to wield political influence and have ultimately obstructed the work of professional historians.

To elaborate briefly, in Seoul during 2014–2015, a series of special committee hearings was held at the National Assembly targeting their own government-funded Northeast Asian History Foundation. The foundation had initially been established in 2006 to counter a perceived threat of mainland Chinese historiography that itself continues to make claims to early polities long regarded as a part of Korean history but whose historical territories at least partly lie within China's present-day borders. Two of these committee sessions, in particular, triggered the shutdown of two flagship projects: the Early Korea Project (2006–2017) based at Harvard University, and a digital Northeast Asian historical atlas project (2008–2015) on which South Korean scholars had been working for some seven years.[4] The line of questioning during these hearings utilized a reductionist and well-established polemic, promoted most recently by vocal empire advocate Yi Tŏk-il and his associates, that paints the domestic academic establishment as a "pro-Japanese, treasonous cartel" (Yi 2014, 2015). This polemic is a conspiracy theory that has evolved to explain the lack of evidence and scholarly support for the notion of an ancient Korean empire. It should be critically distinguished from more legitimate critiques of right-wing South Korean historical revisionism pertaining to modern and contemporary history that are widely rejected by professional historians.[5]

Stepping back, we can observe that although any history of the early past written within a modern national frame may be treated from an invented traditions angle, on the Korean Peninsula the concept is reified most in what today must be designated as unequivocal *pseudohistory*. Characterized by a lack of critical objectivity, reductionist polemics, and wanton manipulation of sources, the development of this phenomenon has spanned the past century and traversed both the modern North and South Korean states.[6] Together with a summary genealogy of its evolution, we will continue now by surveying some of the key topics and fallacies, particularly of the empire and Taejonggyo-ist schemes that have proven most politically influential and damaging to professional scholarship.

GENEALOGY OF EMPIRE TYPE AND TAEJONGGYO-IST SCHEMES

Both empire and Taejonggyo-ist schemes trace back to colonial-era popularist scholarship, beginning with Sin Ch'ae-ho (1880–1936) and Kim Kyo-hŏn (1868–1923), respectively.[7] The empire narrative was further developed by Sin's contemporary, journalist Chŏng In-bo (1893–1950), and later systematized under the name of North Korean scholar, Ri Chi-rin (fl. 1950–1970s). Suspected to be a product of anonymous group authorship, Ri's 1963 work contains the first positive utilization of archaeology, and is so comprehensive that most arguments contained in present-day South Korean iterations of the secular empire variant can be sourced from this single work alone.[8]

During the period of Park Chung Hee's military rule in South Korea, the three main strands of popularist pseudohistory—empire, pan-Altaic, and Taejonggyo—coalesced among a coterie of nationalist amateur historians. Alongside the likely author of *Hwandan kogi*, Yi Yu-rip (1907–1986), this group included South Korea's first minister for education (1948–1950) and lifelong Taejonggyo believer, An Ho-sang (1902–1999).[9] An authored Taejonggyo doctrinal philosophy and notably was the first to reference Ri (1963) (An 1979, 30). It was variously through Yi Yu-rip's and An's works that the secular empire narrative came to be more closely fused to Taejonggyo periodization and religio-philosophical elements.

The empire scheme was subsequently promoted by academic historian Yun Nae-hyŏn (b. 1939), who gained tenure at Dankook University, leading to a blurring in distinction between amateur and professional pseudohistory (Yun [1986] 2017). From Yun the torch has been figuratively passed to Yi Tŏk-il (b. 1961), who holds a doctorate in history but works under the affiliation of his own research institute, currently housed within the Suun building of the Ch'ŏndogyo church, another twentieth-century new religion claiming its lineage from the nineteenth-century religious movement of Tonghak (Eastern Learning).[10] Today, the all-inclusive synthesis of the Park-era amateurs is principally maintained by An Kyŏng-jŏn, while more generic popular histories have re-diverged along the three interpretative tendencies, albeit with the empire variants indelibly inflected by Taejonggyo. Thus in the cases of Yun and Yi, their textual and archaeological proof for empire is the same as Ri's (1963) while both have been reluctant to disavow apocrypha such as *Hwandan kogi*.

Although the content of the empire scheme has remained largely unchanged since its first full exposition by Sin Ch'ae-ho, the context and motivation for its writing have adjusted according to period. The first generation, including Sin, Kim Kyo-hŏn, and Chŏng In-bo, were all responding to the immediate reality of the Japanese annexation of Korea and imposition of colonial rule. All three were anti-Japanese activists and Sin and Chŏng were major figures of the cultural strengthening movement of the 1920s onward. By contrast, the amateur historians of the later Park Chung Hee era, styled themselves as Korean nationalists, but like Park himself, their backgrounds and outlook were themselves a product of Japanese empire. Reflecting contemporary political circumstance, their brand of nationalism was right-leaning and ostensibly anti-communist.

In the subsequent era of South Korean democracy and collapse of communist ideology, however, Yun and Yi have positioned themselves on the left of the political spectrum. This left is best defined as anti–Park Chung Hee and anti-US while being sympathetic to the North, and espousing an explicitly pan-Korean chauvinism that popularly defines itself against the memory of Japanese colonialism. From late 2003, these empire advocates consequently found themselves well equipped to lead the populist response to mainland Chinese government historiography and its assertions of historical jurisdiction over the north of the Korean Peninsula.

HISTORY DISPUTE WITH CHINA: THE HAN COMMANDERIES AND EARLY NORTHERN EAST ASIAN POLITIES

This historiography dispute with China initially came to public awareness through South Korean media coverage of the Chinese Academy of Social Science's Northeast Project (Dongbei Gongcheng, 2002–2007) (Byington 2004). The two topics that provoke ire are first, the assertion that Chinese states, beginning with the Han dynasty, directly ruled over the north of the Korean Peninsula for around four centuries, and second that the early kingdom of Koguryŏ, whose territory straddled both modern-day China and North Korea but that has long been regarded as a part of Korean history, should be treated as a part of China's retroactive "multiethnic history." Here we should note that memory of Chinese commandery rule, principally that of Lelang Commandery (108 BCE—c. 313 CE) located at modern Pyongyang (P'yŏngyang), had been a long-held tradition of pre-twentieth-century Korean historiography. The historicity of Lelang was confirmed in the twentieth century, first by Japanese excavations of the colonial era and subsequently through the published results of North Korean archaeologists.

Today, the colonial-era Japanese concern in highlighting the Han commanderies is regarded to have been a part of their legitimization strategy for the contemporary annexation of the Peninsula. According to this postcolonial discourse, for the Japanese, confirming the fact of the commanderies demonstrated first that Korea had initially developed as a state under an earlier period of imperial rule, and second that Korea was only "liberated" from long-term Chinese hegemony tracing back to Lelang, by modern Japan. Negating the historical existence of the commanderies has consequently been a core revisionist concern of the empire narrative. Paradoxically the view that Korea's sociocultural development was restricted by long-term subservience to China is maintained by empire advocates who from Sin Ch'ae-ho onward have traced this perceived national decline not quite as far back as to Lelang—the peninsular location of which they reject—but to the 668 overthrow of Koguryŏ and accompanying loss of continental territory.

By contrast, Beijing's claim to Koguryŏ as a part of Chinese history is itself a recent phenomenon and can be principally read as a strategy to consolidate Chinese jurisdiction over its three northeastern provinces, collectively known today as Dongbei, formerly Manchuria. Aside from the recent memory of the Manchukuo state (1932–1945) established under the Japanese, and deeper associations of the region with an ethnically distinct Jurchen-Manchu identity, a motivating factor for Beijing is to counter revisionist Korean claims of empire, which are known to have come to Chinese attention when Ri Chi-rin studied in Beijing from 1958 to 1961.[11] From a geographical perspective, Koguryŏ history may objectively be understood as a part of the history of the present-day territories of both China and North Korea. However, history in the modern East Asian states has tended to be defined by notions of ethnicity as much as geography. Thus, although, only the peninsular, southern half of Koguryŏ's territory was absorbed by subsequent Korean states, the incorporation of Koguryŏ into Korea's orthodox historiography and founding traditions has resulted in its entirety being regarded by Koreans as of exclusive ethnic Korean heritage.

If treated in isolation, there would perhaps only be limited motivation for Beijing to assert historiographical jurisdiction over Koguryŏ, but this historical state has a key position as the chronological intermediary between two polities that were more fully centered in China's present-day northeast: the early state of Puyŏ (c. second century BCE—346 CE), and the medieval state of Parhae. Although peripheral to Korean peninsular identity, both Puyŏ and Parhae constituted a distant northern aspect of Korea's orthodox historiography while, similar to Koguryŏ, they remained outside the purview of Chinese self-identity. Puyŏ was a historical state centered on the Songhua River basin in present-day Jilin Province, China. In Koguryŏ and subsequent Korean historiography Puyŏ functioned as the homeland to Koguryŏ's mythological founder, Chumong, and indeed, this Koguryŏ foundation legend was itself an adaption of the earlier attested Puyŏ foundation legend of King Tongmyŏng. The Puyŏ heritage was further laid claim to by the Korean Three Kingdoms–era state of Paekche, located south of Koguryŏ across the central west of the Korean Peninsula (Byington 2016, 277). Puyŏ consequently features prominently in Korean schemes of continental empire.

More significant to China's modern concerns, however, is Parhae, which during its zenith achieved an expansive domain across much of Manchuria. In contrast to Koguryŏ, which had its early political center just north of the modern Sino-Korea border at Ji'an and subsequently at Pyongyang, Parhae was more of a continental entity centered on the east of Manchuria, a locus that would later become the point of origin for the Manchu Qing. Through the traditional "Puyŏ → Koguryŏ → Parhae" genealogy, Korean empire advocates today project back an invented territorial claim, arguing each period to represent ethnic continuation and cyclic restorations of their supposed ancient, Manchuria-centered Korean empire. China's claim to Koguryŏ, thus functions in no small part to forestall Korean irredentism, though in projecting back present-day ethnopolitical configurations it is just as problematic.

THE ORTHODOX NARRATIVE OF OLD CHOSŎN

The ancient Korean empire imagined by Sin Ch'ae-ho and subsequent advocates corresponds in name to the early polity of Chosŏn, referred to in Korean tradition as Old Chosŏn. From the thirteenth century onward, Chosŏn has functioned as the imagined charter state of Korean history and was divided into three periods of Tan'gun Chosŏn, Kija Chosŏn, and Wiman Chosŏn.[12] The historical Chosŏn state is first attested in early Chinese sources, including *Shiji* (87 BCE) and *Sanguozhi* (280 CE), from which three main facts can be known: 1) during the Warring States period Chosŏn was a rival polity to the east of Yan (centered at modern Beijing) and contracted as Yan expanded into Liaodong (modern Liaoning, c. 280 BCE); 2) around 194 BCE Chosŏn's rulership was usurped by Yan native (Wi) Man causing the deposed Chosŏn king to relocate southward to Mahan, the largest of the three Samhan polities that occupied the south of the Korean Peninsula; and 3) under the third generation of the usurper dynasty's rule, Chosŏn was conquered by the 109–108 BCE Han invasion leading to the establishment of the Chinese commanderies. In at least its final period, the capital of Chosŏn, Wanghŏm (in Korean sources Wanggŏm) was located at Pyongyang and replaced by the Chinese commandery of Lelang.

In orthodox tradition the usurpers are given the family name of Wi—a Han-period invention—and their rule corresponds to the period of Wiman Chosŏn. Of the preceding line of rulers, only the last two kings are named and treated as the fortieth and forty-first generation of rulers descended from the legendary Chinese figure of Kija (Ch. Jizi). This notion of Kija Chosŏn is based on the legend of Kija, a royal sage of the Shang dynasty, who upon Shang's demise to Zhou, departs east for Chosŏn; upon arrival he introduces core articles of classical Chinese civilization including rites, ethics, agriculture, and weaving. Although Kija—Viscount of Ki—may have been a historical Shang personage and hereditary title, the legend of his traveling to Chosŏn and bringing knowledge of Chinese civilization with him was clearly an invented tradition, likely introduced by Han China post-108 BCE to legitimize the commandery presence (Shim 2002). Whether from this time, or only with the later reintroduction of Confucianism, the legend was ultimately embraced by peninsular Koreans as it provided a route by which to claim themselves as inheritors of classical Chinese civilization, distinguishing themselves from other supposed "barbarians."

The earliest period of Tan'gun Chosŏn, meanwhile, was derived from a more local tradition that only fully emerged in the late thirteenth century, within a milieu then under the influence of esoteric Buddhism. The first attestation occurs in two contemporaneous sources of the 1280s, *Samguk yusa* and *Chewang un'gi* (Rhyming record of [Chinese] emperors and [Korean] kings). According to the myth, the deity Hwan'in sends his son Hwan'ung from heaven to rule on earth; following a union between Hwan'ung and a girl transformed from a bear, Tan'gun is born and consequently establishes the state of Chosŏn at a date corresponding to 2333 BCE; after a thousand years Tan'gun removes himself to a mountain; Kija then arrives 164 years later. From its initial coalescence the story underwent a gradual process of rationalization that has continued until the present day. Official recitations soon eliminated the bear story, while Tan'gun was increasingly interpreted as a human ruler and founding ancestor of a dynasty that could fill the thousand-year period ascribed to Tan'gun Chosŏn.

By the mid-fifteenth century an episode was further innovated in which Tan'gun has a son, Hae Puru, who participates in the Xia king Yu's gathering of vassals at Mount Tu, a celebrated event of orthodox Chinese tradition found in the *Shujing* (Book of documents). Puru is a name earlier attested from the Koguryŏ foundation story as the king of Puyŏ who is displaced by Chumong's arrival. This episode thus functioned both to incorporate the Puyŏ-Koguryŏ legendarium under the newly invented Tan'gun paradigm, as well as to push back Korea's association with ancient China to a near mythical period preceding even that of the Kija legend. The Tan'gun-Kija symbiosis was maintained as state historiography throughout the Chosŏn dynasty. Therein the capitals of all three ancient Chosŏn periods, as well as the seat of Lelang Commandery and the Koguryŏ capital, were all regarded as having been located at Pyongyang. To the extent that they were treated, the continental aspects of Puyŏ and early Koguryŏ were also collapsed to within a peninsular conceptualization. In the case of Koguryŏ, for example, Pyongyang was considered to have been the location for early heritage sites associated with the Koguryŏ foundation story despite records stating the capital to have been relocated southward more than once, and to Pyongyang only centuries after.

For modern-day empire advocates, their charter civilization corresponds in name and time depth to Tan'gun Chosŏn but they seek to match this to a continental conceptualization closer to that of historical Puyŏ, Koguryŏ, and Parhae, which they consequently portray as restorations of Chosŏn. A further task is to neutralize the Chinese aspects of Kija, Wi Man,[13] and the Han commanderies. Much of this was achieved in Sin's revisionist narrative, which has provided an archetypal blueprint for all subsequent iterations and to which we can now turn.

SIN CH'AE-HO'S NARRATIVE OF ANCIENT EMPIRE

Sin's historiography includes at least four integrated aspects: a narrative of the political and cultural "rise and fall" of ancient Korean civilization; a corresponding historical geography that lays claim to continental Manchuria; the elaboration of diachronic traditions linking this invented past to attested historical memory; and finally, a conspiracy-type narrative pertaining to official historiography required to explain the empire's lack of attestation.[14] The most compelling strengths of Sin's writing are found in both his overarching narrative as well as the specific mechanics by which he establishes a picture of the continental empire, albeit largely through misappropriation of later sources and linguistic speculation. The two aspects of his work that have proven most foundational to current lineages of pseudohistory, however, are his historical geography and conspiracy narrative of historiography.

Sin delineated the boundaries of the ancient Chosŏn empire as extending north to the Amur River, east to the present-day coast of Russian Primorye, southward to incorporate the entire Korean Peninsula, and westward to include at least the region of modern-day Liaoning Province, China, with further "colonies" extending down much of the east China seaboard. These borders are the same as those depicted on maps drawn by present-day empire advocates such as Yun Nae-hyŏn and Yi Tŏk-il. Although a small number of Chosŏn dynasty scholars had recognized that until the Yan expansion, Old Chosŏn's territory must have extended significantly westward, the northern and eastern boundaries were not conceptualized in such an expansive manner until the works of Sin and Kim Kyo-hŏn, Kim sketching a similar territory to Sin.[15]

Under the first generation of empire advocates, including Sin, Kim, and Chŏng In-bo, the construct of these borders can be understood in two overlapping ways. The first is as a straightforward appropriation of Qing Manchuria, wherein the northern border had come to be defined through early encounters with Russia and the introduction of modern cartography (Kim Seon-min 2017, 50). The second is from a historiographically Korean perspective, wherein the central and northern limits correspond to the territory of Puyŏ, the political heartland of which during the early twentieth century was believed to have been in the vicinity of modern Harbin. The eastern maritime region corresponds both to a Koguryŏ-centric notion of "East Puyŏ"—a designation found only in Koguryŏ and later derived sources—and subsequently to Parhae. The western extent, meanwhile, is established through combining toponymic associations of Chosŏn and the Han commanderies seemingly attested in the region of Liaoning, together with Koguryŏ's actually attested conquest territory of the same Liaodong Peninsula region. This toponymic tradition is a key "proof" utilized by empire advocates today. Discussed further below, it is, however, the product of historical circumstances postdating the historical commanderies.

The interpretation constructed from historiographically Korean elements becomes transparent in Sin's conceptualization of ancient Chosŏn. In a bold revisionist stroke, he performed both a temporal and spatial flattening of the orthodox notion of the Three Chosŏn, re-interpreting them as three internal domains of a single charter territory—the original empire—each ruled by a *tan'gun* priest-lord (Sin 1995, 91). Therein, he located the primary capital at modern Harbin with two secondary capitals, one at Yingchengzi, located ten kilometers southeast of Haicheng in Liaoning and known for the site of a later Koguryŏ fortress, and the other at Pyongyang on the Korean Peninsula. The Harbin location corresponds to the Puyŏ homeland and functions to make Chosŏn a continental entity. Yingchengzi provides an alternative "Chosŏn" subdomain to which Sin could then provincialize the Chinese encroachments of Kija, Wiman, and the commanderies, serving to keep both the Korean Peninsula and Manchurian heartland undefiled. Pyongyang, meanwhile, represents Korean Peninsula identity and ensures continuity between the ancient Chosŏn of the continent and the historical Korean states of the Peninsula. Following his "decline and fall" narrative, the initial empire first breaks into its three domains, which, in turn, are gradually forced to retreat into the Korean Peninsula. Puyŏ and Koguryŏ are then portrayed as later ethnic revivals of former continental Chosŏn. In this way, the borders of Sin's "charter empire" and characterizations of Puyŏ and Koguryŏ as territorial restorations constitute core irredentist elements maintained in present-day Korean pseudohistory.

Beginning from Sin and maintained by pseudo-historians today, the invasive Chinese elements of Kija, Wi Man, and the commanderies are diminished by narrating them to have played out only in the westernmost part of the imagined continental empire, in the region of modern Liaoning and eastern Hebei provinces of China. Sin and all empire advocates since contend that the 108 BCE invasion attested in Chinese sources, was in reality a failure thwarted by an emergent Koguryŏ, and that the commanderies were established to the west but named after their failed campaign objectives to hide the supposed reality of defeat (Sin 1995, 114, 139). They thus assert Lelang Commandery to have been the namesake for a purely indigenous *state* of Nangnang—the Korean pronunciation for Lelang—centered on the orthodox position of the commandery at Pyongyang.

The textual evidence cited by pseudo-historians that would appear to place Lelang in eastern Hebei comes from sources postdating the historical commandery's demise of c. 313. They indeed describe circumstances of relocated namesakes but crucially of a later date than Lelang's historical existence at Pyongyang. The notion of a peninsular Lelang/

Nangnang state, meanwhile, is first encountered in the late thirteenth-century Korean source, *Samguk yusa*, anticipated by mention of a Lelang/Nangnang "king" in the earlier *Samguk sagi* (1145). We may best explain these later Korean-authored intimations of a Nangnang state as being the product of an internalized though already distant memory of the historical Lelang Commandery that had existed on the Korean Penin-sula for some four centuries, outlasting the Han dynasty itself, and that at times had lapsed to periods of near autonomous rule with its name consequently diffusing to usage in titles of local rulers across the Peninsula. Sin's provincialization of perceived Chinese elements and the notion of an indigenous Nangnang state both remain core features of the empire narrative.

In present-day North Korea, scholars officially maintain the hypothesis of an indigenous Nangnang state at Pyongyang with the commanderies located outside of the Peninsula. However, subsequent to colonial-period Japanese excavations, a large number of mortuary sites have been discovered by North Korean archaeologists themselves, the construction and associated artifacts of which, as assessed from available reports, are clearly identifiable to international scholars as commandery related. In particular, around 1992 there occurred the discovery of census tablets for Lelang that provide population figures for the year 45 BCE and thus constitute primary source evidence for the commandery's location at Pyongyang.[16] Such tombs and their contents are necessarily explained *ad hoc* by both North Korean scholars and South Korean empire advocates as having belonged to Chinese defectors granted refuge by Nangnang (Son 2006, 118).

DONGYI CONFLATIONISM AND THE URAL-ALTAIC LANGUAGE HYPOTHESIS

An accompanying means through which empire advocates seek to substantiate the territorial aggrandizement of ancient Korea is through the attribution of a common ethnic identity among all northern East Asian peoples but expressly excluding and in opposition to the Han Chinese nation. From Sin onward, this strategy has married two conceptual premises, both of which are false. One is a long-standing feature of Korea's pre-twentieth-century identity discourse, which we can label here as "Dongyi conflationism." The other is the Ural-Altaic language hypothesis, a newly introduced paradigm contemporary to Sin.

Dongyi (eastern barbarian), and similar terms occur in Chinese sources to refer to surrounding non-Chinese peoples. With the adoption of Confucianism and through the Kija tradition, peninsular Koreans came to positively self-identify as "civilized Dongyi." This exceptionalist construct was based on a conflation of China's ancient Dongyi who, as attested from pre-Qin period sources and unearthed epigraphy, were located east of the Central Plain in the region of the Shandong Peninsula, and the subsequent reuse of the same label in Chinese sources for peoples newly encountered when the Qin and Han empires expanded northeastward into Manchuria.[17] The pre-Qin Dongyi are an integral part of China's own early historiography and include various culture heroes such as Emperor Shun of Yu (Yu Shun), Xia king Yu, and Jizi (K. Kija). Sin, and pseudo-historians today, again reverse the hierarchy of the traditional conflation, re-casting the original Dongyi of Shandong as a secondary branching from a Manchuria-centered ethnic homeland.

Through the conflation of Koreans with the culture heroes of the ancient Chinese Dongyi, inclusive of the entire Shang dynasty, Sin and some scholars today assert fundamental aspects of Chinese culture such as the Five Elements (*wuxing*), and even the notion of a celestial emperor, to have in fact been imported from ancient Chosŏn (Sin 1995, 82, 406).[18] In narrative terms, this undercuts the received tradition of civilization having been introduced to Chosŏn by Kija, with Sin narrating instead that it had initially been transmitted to the ancient Dongyi *from* Chosŏn during the earlier episode of Hae Puru participating in Xia king Yu's gathering of vassals, an episode that as we saw was only created in the fifteenth century CE. Radically revisionist though it was, Sin's approach was ultimately rooted in his own classical training and a deeper familiarity with Chinese sources than is possessed by his self-appointed successors. Secular empire advocates today maintain the ethnic aspect of Dongyi conflationism but tend to eschew broader claims to Chinese cultural elements. Such claims have rather been asserted by Taejonggyo advocate An Ho-sang and are again maintained today by An Kyŏng-jŏn.

The ethno-nationalist aspect that pervades Korean pseudohistory today is, however, drawn from another aspect of Sin's historiography, which advocates the rediscovery of an indigenous, non-Chinese heritage, premised on language as a marker of ethnicity. Then as now, advocates assume the language of the ancient empire to be ancestral to modern Korean, and beginning with Sin, this has been situated within the paradigm of the Ural-Altaic language hypothesis, which in its maximal form premises a shared ethno-linguistic commonality among the peoples of the transeurasian steppe.

From west to east, the core Altaic language groups are Turkic, Mongolic, and Tungusic.[19] During the formative stage of the hypothesis in the nineteenth century, the Uralic languages, which include Finnish and Hungarian and are located principally to the west, were also considered to be a part of the same language family, leading linguists to place the linguistic homeland centrally in the region of the Altai Mountains. A relationship between Korean and Japanese had separately been conjectured by a small number of Japanese scholars, and from the late nineteenth century, beginning from the work of Shiratori Kurakichi (1865–1942), these languages were tentatively added to the Ural-Altaic belt. This is the stage at which the hypothesis was introduced to Korea and at which point it has since fossilized. However, by the 1930s, the Uralic phylum was already regarded as genetically unrelated to the remaining eastern language groups. The linguist who during this same period worked most systematically to incorporate Korean and Japanese into the Altaic hypothesis, G. J. Ramstedt (1873–1950), himself abandoned the notion of a homeland situated in Central Asia. Instead he argued Manchuria to have been the homeland of a language family that, owing only to convention, retained the now misleading yet enigmatic moniker of "Altaic" (Ramstedt 1928).

Although the notion of a Manchurian homeland would seem advantageous to Korean chauvinism—in particular to more recent advocates of an indigenous northeast Asian empire—popular and pseudo-historiography in Korea has generally been reluctant to shift from the idea of long-range Central Asian origins.[20] For pan-Altaicists the "search for origins" and associated migration theories are their primary concern for which the fossilized form of the Ural-Altaic hypothesis is their core premise. *Hwandan kogi* also maintains the starting premise of eastward migrations. For empire advocates, however, the distant migration constitutes only a vaguer starting point of prehistory.

Regardless of focus between Altaic origins and the Manchurian empire, in both cases advocates assert for there to have been a secondary point of early convergence and expansion farther east. Initially this was Lake Baikal, but a seemingly more tangible candidate emerged with the 1979 discovery of a ritual enclosure at Niuheliang, Liaoning, associated with the Neolithic Hongshan archaeological culture (4500–3000 BCE), the geographical area of which straddles western Liaoning and Inner Mongolia.[21] Whether the focus is placed on Central Asia, Lake Baikal, or Hongshan, advocates maintain the premise of a shared ethno-linguistic identity among non-Chinese peoples. Consequently the underlying Ural-Altaic language hypothesis implicitly functions as scientific support for Dongyi conflationism; the hypothesis further enables the incorporation of other historically attested peoples to the north of early China such as the Xiongnu and Xianbei who in orthodox historiography had been classified separately to the Dongyi.

MATERIALITY OF EMPIRE: ARCHAEOLOGY AND HONGSHAN

Discussion of archaeology in popular history writing began with Chŏng In-bo. In order to maintain Sin's hypothesis of the Han commanderies having been located outside of the Peninsula against the counterevidence being produced by Japanese-led excavations, Chŏng argued that diagnostic artifacts, including clay seals and roof tiles with imprinted characters naming Lelang and a number of subordinate districts, were all fabricated.[22] This conspiracy theory of fabrication is maintained by empire advocates still today.[23]

Beginning from Ri Chi-rin, empire advocates have also sought to substantiate their expansive Chosŏn domain through the distribution of supposed diagnostic material artifacts and remains. These include polished stone implements, various earthenware types, dolmen graves, bronze daggers, and fine-lined bronze mirrors. For each case, Ri (1963) argues that their distribution matches Chosŏn territory, stretching from the Korean Peninsula to southeastern Inner Mongolia, that the typology is entirely distinct from those of China, and that they were products of local innovation originating in the Liaodong region rather than from any outside influence. Today, advocates continue to emphasize bronze daggers and dolmen in particular to define the territory and to represent a physical testimony of an otherwise elusive civilization. Additionally, they claim a type of bladed coin, known as *ming* (K. *myŏng*) knife coins, as the currency of Old Chosŏn. The distribution of *ming* coins, however, is limited to Liaoning and farther west in historical Yan territory, and are therefore to be associated with Yan rather than Chosŏn (Byington 2016, 58n88).

By starting with the distribution of stone implements across Inner Mongolia and northeastern China, Ri projected Chosŏn's origins back to the Neolithic. His emphasis on indigenous innovation marked a shift away from presumptions of Central Asian origins and is reflected today in the derivative works of Yun Nae-hyŏn and Yi Tŏk-il. While the premise of linguistic affinity remains, in Yun and Yi the sense of transeurasian solidarity invoked by pan-Altaicists is replaced by a narrower, northern East Asian nativism, which may be characterized as "Dongyi chauvinism." Ri's projection to the Neolithic also anticipated the subsequent interest in the Hongshan culture. Predating the Yellow River Yangshao culture, that had long been associated with Central Plain civilization, from the mid-1980s certain Chinese archaeologists including Su Bingqi (1909–1997) have asserted Hongshan to be an early source of northern Chinese civilization inclusive of the Dongyi (Su [1987] 1997). With Hongshan seeming to offer material evidence for their ancient civilization, South Korean advocates have at once adopted Su's characterization of Hongshan as an early state while contesting the Chinese claim over "proto-Dongyi" culture.

Through both the physical culture and name itself, Hongshan (red mountain) has lent itself well to pseudo-historical interpretations. Artifacts include bracelet-sized carved jade rings with zoomorphic features, which Chinese scholars have variously interpreted as boars, bears, and dragons. Among these, Koreans emphasize the bear as preeminent and interpret it as a totemic symbol evocative of the Hwan'ung-Tan'gun foundation myth. They further interpret female stone idol remains found at Niuheliang as evidence that ancient Chosŏn was a more egalitarian and even matriarchal society, to be contrasted to the patriarchal Confucianism of China. Hongshan features prominently in An Kyŏng-jŏn's *Hwandan kogi* as the cradle of Northeast Asian civilization.

CH'OE NAM-SŎN AND THE ROOTS
OF PURHAM MOUNTAIN

Just as evocative for pseudo-historians, however, is the coincidence of the name "red mountain." First, mountains are a recurrent feature of Korean origin explanations, occurring in the case of the Tan'gun story, as well as the Altaic hypothesis. Today they remain important to both Korean states, including locally to vernacular religious practices as well as at the level of state mythology. Second, the qualifier "red," pronounced in vernacular Korean as *ppalk-* or *pulk-*, fits into a well-established popular assertion that the ancient Korean people worshipped the sun and brightness. From the mid-fifteenth century, scholars suggested "light of the morning sun" as a semantic interpretation for the characters used to write Chosŏn, which in reality, however, are almost certainly phonetic renderings of a non-Sinic term. Adopting the semantographic interpretation, Sin Ch'ae-ho posited a common vernacular name of various toponyms and polities—including both Puyŏ and Harbin—as *pul*, the modern Korean word for "fire," which according to Sin, was indicative of slash-and-burn practices of early settlers arriving from the Pamir Mountains of Central Asia.

The popular associations of brightness and mountains, however, received their most definitive treatment by Ch'oe Nam-sŏn (1890–1957), whose works on long-range culture zones have been a foundational influence particularly on pan-Altaic schemes starting from the Park Chung Hee–era hyperdiffusionists. One of several iterations, the scheme that proved most enduring has been his *Purham Culture Thesis* in which he sought to define an expansive civilization primarily evinced through the distribution of oronyms (mountain names) whose etymologies, according to Ch'oe, could supposedly all be derived from the proto-terms *părk(an)* or *taigăr*, to which he attributed meanings in Korean of "bright/white" and "sky/heaven," respectively.[24]

The eponymous Purham is the Sino-Korean pronunciation for the name of a mountain associated with the early Sushen people. In pre-Qin sources, the Sushen were originally recorded as residing to the north of Zhou China, in the vicinity of a Purham mountain. Through a process analogous to Dongyi conflationism, later Chinese tradition identified these ancient Sushen of northern China as direct ancestors to the Yilou people of southeastern Manchuria. In turn this tradition misidentified Mount Paektu, that straddles the modern China-Korea border, as the original Purham mountain of the Sushen (Byington 2016, 35). In perhaps the first study of Korean toponyms working within the Ural-Altaic paradigm, Shiratori (1896) consequently suggested the etymology of *Purham*—in reference to Mount Paektu—to be Mongolic *burkhan*, with the meaning "god/heaven." In subsequent writings he further suggested *burkhan* to be one of two Mongolic words meaning "god," the other being *tä(n)gri* (Shiratori, cited in Laufer 1916, 394; Shiratori 1907). Thus it becomes apparent that Ch'oe simply appropriated these terms from Shiratori.

Through suggesting Korean *park* as the etymology of Purham and adopting Shiratori's etymologies, however, Ch'oe was able to create an enduring linkage between Chosŏn's preexisting associations of "light," both to mountains and, critically, to the wider transeurasian Altaic hypothesis. Thus, if not for Ch'oe's Purham thesis the coincidental enigmaticism inherent in the name of Hongshan would carry less significance for advocates today.

RATIONALIZATION OF HWAN'UNG AND TAN'GUN

Ch'oe Nam-sŏn's seminal analysis of the Old Chosŏn foundation story, meanwhile, remains the single strongest influence on mainstream interpretations. As noted, Tan'gun has undergone a continued process of rationalization from the thirteenth century until the present. While Sin rejected the content of the myth as a later invention and interpreted *tan'gun* as a title, Ch'oe applied a folkloristic approach that sought to rationalize the fullest version of the Hwan'ung-Tan'gun account, including the bear and tiger episode as recorded in *Samguk yusa* but that was omitted from other extant renditions.[25] Ch'oe's motivation was to counter contemporary Japanese arguments that variously dismissed the myth either as primitive folklore, or as an esoteric Buddhist–flavored invention of the Koryŏ period created in response to the Mongol invasions.[26] Ch'oe's counterstrategy was to demonstrate underlying "shamanistic" roots supposedly predating what he then characterized as Buddhist embellishments from the period the account was first written down. The final product of this Hwan'ung-Tan'gun apologism saw a new structural analysis dividing the account into three parts: the *heavenly descension myth* of Hwan'ung; *totemic origin myths* of the bear, tiger, and sun; and finally, a *proto-historical account* of Tan'gun's rule.

Ch'oe then sought to argue that these aspects were evidence for an expansive "archaic civilization" of which Koreans were the chief inheritors. In his first attempt to explicate this civilization, he explicitly situated it within the hyperdiffusionary scheme of William Perry's *The Children of the Sun* (1923) that premised all civilizations of the world to have originated from Egypt. The second version was the *Purham Culture Thesis*. Today Ch'oe's inductive explanation of shamanic origins and totemism remains a standard popular interpretation, while the proto-historical characterization of the Tan'gun section has been expanded on by Yun Nae-hyŏn. Ch'oe's culture-zone schemes were utilized by the Park Chung Hee–era amateur historians. Their innovations are today reflected in An Kyŏng-jŏn's *Hwandan kogi*, wherein the Sumerian and Egyptian civilizations are presented as a westward branch from a "father civilization" located in Central Asia, named Hwan'guk, with attributed dates of 7197–3897 BCE.

Distinct from both Sin and Ch'oe, Kim Kyo-hŏn early on established a wholly more inventive periodization scheme that is, nevertheless, loosely derived from the Hwan'ung-Tan'gun account and that continues to provide a framework for Taejonggyo-ist historiography found in the *Hwandan kogi*. Kim divided the ancient era into three periods of Sinsi, Paedal, and Puyŏ (Kim 1923, 45–52). According to this scheme, the Sinsi period corresponds to Hwan'ung's descent and initial period of governance, although to remove Buddhist overtones, Kim substituted Hwan'ung's name with "celestial god." Paedal commences with the inauguration of the same divine figure as "great lord" and the newly established state being named "Tan" (the *tan* of Tan'gun), which according to Kim, was pronounced in vernacular Korean as Paedal. During the ensuing 1,026-year Paedal era, the state expands to the same territory as defined by Sin; this expansion and associated migrations lead to cyclic regeneration of the Manchurian heartland, ushering in Kim's next designated period of Puyŏ. While Sinsi is a term found in the *Samguk yusa* account and Puyŏ is self-evident, Paedal appears to be an invented term exclusive to Taejonggyo. An Ho-sang later claimed Paedal to be attested in the twelfth-century Chinese-Korean glossary, *Jilin leishi*, supposedly given there as the vernacular Korean pronunciation for the *tan* character of Tan'gun, but no such entry exists (An 1964, 35, 206).[27] In *Hwandan kogi*, Sinsi is renamed Hwan'guk.

More recently, Yun Nae-hyŏn has sought to blend Ch'oe's folkloristic analysis with Kim's three-part periodization, further matching this to standard neoevolutionary archaeological periodizations. According to Yun: the heavenly descent of Hwan'ung corresponds to the migration of a Paleolithic "Hwan'ung tribe" that worshipped a sky god named Hanŭ-nim, rendered in Chinese as Hwan'in; Hwan'ung's initial rule corresponds to the early Neolithic period, which sees the introduction of agriculture; and the establishment of Old Chosŏn under Tan'gun then corresponds to the Bronze Age, with the traditional foundation date of 2333 BCE "roughly matching" the introduction of bronze, that Yun dates to c. 2550 BCE (2003, 48).

Here, two points are of note. First, while Yun's sky god originates with Ch'oe's emphasis of Northeast Asian shamanism, the Hanŭ-nim term itself derives from a vernacular Korean term for the Christian god coined by Protestant missionaries during the late nineteenth century. Usage of Hanŭ-nim and similar variants represents an invented tradition of Korean monotheism that is present as a feature of new religions, including both Taejonggyo and Chŭngsando (Baker 2002). Second is a concern among empire advocates to substantiate the orthodox date for Tan'gun's assumption of power that reflects the continuing process of Tan'gun historicization. Stated in the *Samguk yusa* account, Tan'gun's coming to rule corresponds to the 25th year of China's legendary Emperor Yao, 2333 BCE. The specific date of Emperor Yao's ascension was fixed in China only in the third century CE and not transmitted to Korea until significantly later. Treatment of this date in pseudo- and popular historiography assumes two aspects. One is a chauvinistic inclination to push it still further back in order to predate its Chinese or Japanese analogues. The other is an apologetic approach to the myth where advocates seek to suggest that, even when the notion of Tan'gun is not to be understood as a deity or historical personage, a significant "civilization event," such as the introduction of rice or bronze, must nevertheless have occurred around the third century BCE, the distant memory of which was then codified in orally transmitted mythology. Indeed, even in cases including *Hwandan kogi*, where supernatural elements of the Hwan'ung-Tan'gun tradition are rationalized to a point of negation, there remains an indelible imprint, which, even as it replaces the story, circularly legitimizes the tradition. Present-day views of empire advocates in the South continue to be shaped by North Korean historiography. Reasons for this include: the foundational influence of Ri Chi-rin and other revisionist North Korean scholars, the continued inaccessibility—and therefore mystification— of the territory, and finally, the political inclinations of South Korean pseudo-historians themselves. In particular, through jurisdiction of historical Pyongyang, the DPRK has inherited a monopoly over the region's archaeological sites, previously examined only by Japanese scholars who focused on identifying Lelang Commandery. In the South, anti-communist state-led nationalism of the Park Chung Hee–era ROK gave way to a pro-North, people's nationalism born of the 1980s democracy and workers' movement that continues to inform ostensibly left-leaning idealism today. However, mainstream nationalism has been partially tempered through globalization aspirations and, paradoxically, the continued presence of the US military. By contrast, in the wake of the Soviet Union's collapse, the ensuing domestic food crisis, and the first hereditary leadership transition, North Korea turned inward, shifting to an emphasis of ethnic chauvinism centered on its own peninsular territory.

In 1993 the North Korean regime consequently announced the "restoration" of Tan'gun's grave site in northeastern Pyongyang, constructing a large stepped mausoleum over what is known to have been a Koguryŏ-era tomb. This location was not wholly arbitrary as a tradition of Tan'gun's tomb had been attested there from the early fifteenth century, and activists had erected a modest stele during the colonial era. Claiming to have analyzed the skeletal remains of Tan'gun and his wife, North Korea has hereafter placed the foundation of a historical Tan'gun Chosŏn state as having occurred at around 3000 BCE. Concomitantly, they proclaimed the Taedong River basin as the center of a fifth civilization of the ancient world supposedly rivaling, and even surpassing, those of the Nile, Euphrates, Indus, and Yellow Rivers (Ryŏksa P'yŏnjipsil 1994). According to this Pyongyang-centric scheme, Tan'gun Chosŏn is modeled as only secondarily expanding into Manchuria from the northwest of the Korean Peninsula, thus erasing Ri Chi-rin's arguments for Liaodong origins (Son 2005). The responses of Yun Nae-hyŏn and Yi Tŏk-il have differed. Yun embraced the mausoleum and led a civil delegation to Pyongyang in 2002 (Yun 2003,

14). Yi, however, has maintained Ri Chi-rin's work to be correct, going so far as to republish it in 2018 (Yi 2014, 147).

INCORPORATION OF CHIYOU

The North Korean regime's decision to utilize Tan'gun is indicative of both an inherent strength and weakness of the tradition. With a long-established prestige position in pre-twentieth-century Korean historiography and continued associations with Pyongyang and the northwest of the Peninsula, Tan'gun remains a unifying Korean figure from which the North can derive a certain legitimacy compelling even to compatriots in the South. However, this same peninsular nativism, together with the lack of attestation in either pre-thirteenth-century Korean, or any Chinese sources at all, as well as the lack of narrative detail in the *Samguk yusa* account, all render Tan'gun less productive for claims to the continent or wider Dongyi conflationism. We may speculate that for this reason, among empire advocates an alternative mythical ancestor, Ch'iu (Ch. Chiyou) has also come to be emphasized, largely independent of Tan'gun.

Chiyou is a figure of early Chinese myth, principally known for having been defeated by the equally legendary Yellow Emperor (Huangdi), who has long been elevated as the founding ancestor of central Chinese civilization.[28] As a consequence Chiyou became a symbol of non-Chinese otherness and the evolution of the Chiyou tradition has occurred in more than one place and across time periods. During the twentieth century separate earlier traditions variously associating Chiyou with the ancient Dongyi of Shandong, and with the present-day Miao minority of southern China, were both reemphasized. From the 1940s certain Chinese scholars beginning with Xu Xusheng (1888–1976) sought to match legends found in early records to archaeological cultures; in this reductionist process Chiyou was proposed as the chieftain of the Dongyi and matched to the Longshan culture of Shandong in order to function as an antithesis to the Yellow Emperor of the Xia, who was matched with the Yangshao Yellow River culture (Kim In-hŭi 2017, 168).

During the early 1990s, China moved to fully historicize two mythical figures, the Yellow Emperor and Emperor Yan (Flame Emperor), asserting them as the dual ancestors to the modern-day Chinese nation. Chiyou was to remain as the non-Chinese other whose role is to be vanquished by the two emperors; however, vocal elements within the Miao successfully lobbied for the incorporation of Chiyou as a third ancestor.

In Korea, meanwhile, Ch'iu came to prominence only in the Park Chung Hee era. First mention is in a colossal one-thousand-page work by Ch'oe Tong (1896–1973), *History of the Ancient Korean People* (1966), that presaged the work of the other Park-era amateurs (Yi 2018, 92). Ch'iu was subsequently given an important position in *Hwandan kogi*, wherein his defeat is recast as a victory. In 1999, graphic designer Chang Puda (b. 1969) created an image of Ch'iu as the emblem for the supporters' association of the national football team. This design fused the Chinese image of Chiyou as a horned god with the preexisting "red devil" moniker of the supporters' association. From the outset the emblem has been referred to with a title previously only attributed to Ch'iu in *Hwandan kogi*: *Ch'iu ch'ŏnwang*, "Celestial King Ch'iu." As excitement swept Korea during the 2002 FIFA World Cup, the Ch'iu emblem became a familiar national symbol. Building on this very recent popular appropriation, *Hwandan kogi*–influenced empire advocates have consequently emphasized Ch'iu as their own Dongyi ancestor and, in a manner analogous to their claims over the Hongshan material culture, they have created a straw man argument, charging that China's rehabilitation of Chiyou is another strategy to lay claim to non-Chinese Dongyi heritage that should otherwise belong to Koreans (Yi and Kim 2006, 234).

MIMANA AND THE COLONIAL VIEW OF HISTORY

Led by Yi Tŏk-il, present-day empire advocates regularly characterize the academic establishment as a "pro-Japanese cartel" promoting a "colonial view of history." Advocates' definition of this colonial view is composed of two core aspects. First, they assert that two entities of early peninsular history, both associated with the imposition of foreign rule, were created solely in order that Japanese scholars could argue early Korea to have begun as a divided colony under the control of imperial powers. These entities are the aforementioned Chinese commanderies occupying the north of the Peninsula, and a Japanese outpost termed the Mimana

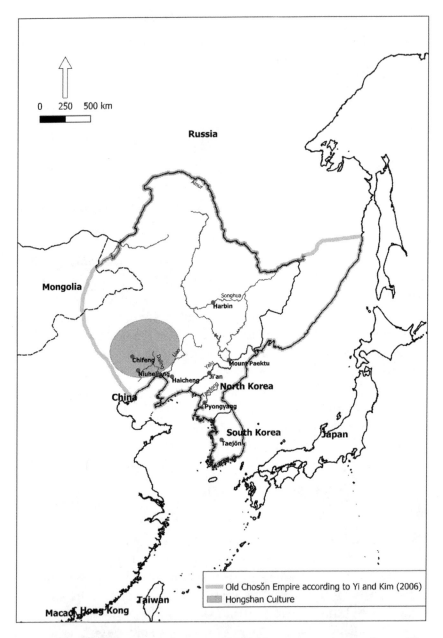

FIGURE 2.1. Map showing location of Old Chosŏn empire according to Yi and Kim (2006); map created by Elspeth McVey. Courtesy of Elspeth McVey and Adrian Tear.

Nihonfu (K. Imna ilbonbu, "Mimana Japan government") occupying the south. Second, they allege that colonial Japanese scholars rejected the historicity of early entries found in the *Samguk sagi* covering the first century BCE through to the third century CE, and replaced them with the notion of the pre-state-level Samhan polities. The supposed motivation was to reduce the orthodox dates for the establishment of Three Kingdoms–era polities, in particular those of the southern Peninsula, in order that Japanese scholars could assert Korean state formation to have occurred later than Japan.

As a term, Mimana Nihonfu only occurs in the eighth-century Japanese source, *Nihon shoki*, but Mimana (K. Imna) alone, as well as Imna Kara (Kara being a variant of Kaya), are attested in various earlier sources including the Kwanggaet'o stele (414 CE) and Chinese histories, as well as the later *Samguk sagi*. Similar to the commanderies, Japanese historians conducted research on the Mimana Nihonfu. Taking the *Nihon shoki* references at face value they described it as an organ of colonial control governing the south of the Peninsula. Unlike the commanderies, however, archaeologists failed to find any material evidence. The colonial historiography polemic is thus another straw man argument because neither Japanese nor South Korean scholars maintain this colonial-era interpretation. Korean scholars have long rejected the Mimana Nihonfu, but do acknowledge the historicity of Mimana/Imna, variously hypothesizing connections to Paekche or emphasizing its own agency as a Kaya entity, while recent archaeology is providing a more complex picture of the early south and multidirectional interactions with the Japan islands (Sin 2016).[29]

Advocates' second accusation, concerning the *Samguk sagi* dating, meanwhile, would seem to reflect a purely chauvinistic desire to both maintain the earliest possible dates while promoting Korean-authored sources over Chinese, regardless of chronological precedence. The traditional first-century BCE dates for the foundation of the Korean Three Kingdoms–era polities, as given in the *Samguk sagi*, and for Kaya in *Samguk yusa*, represent a retrospective construct of history, for the fact is that contemporary Chinese sources do not attest the southern polities of Paekche, Kaya, or Silla until around the late third century CE, but do attest the preceding Samhan in the same region during the early third century CE (Best 2006, 31).

Advocates' insistence on the existence of a "colonial view of history" is a conspiracy theory that can be understood as a continuation of a similar narrative constructed by Sin Ch'ae-ho, in his case pertaining to pre-twentieth-century sources that functioned to explain the lack of attestation for his imagined continental empire. Sin charged that in the process of the Chosŏn civilization's *longue durée* decline the elite became both politically and culturally subordinate to a Sinocentric Confucian mentality, and that from the Unified Silla period onward, having lost aspirations to recover continental territory, they destroyed evidence of Korea's early territorial greatness both in deference to China and because this greatness had been longest sustained by Silla's defeated rival, Koguryŏ (Sin 1995, 36–37). Ironically, Sin characterized *Samguk sagi* as the epitome of Sinocentric historiography for its failure to include more of Korea's continental history. The premise that both Chinese and orthodox Korean sources actively distort early history, consequently provided the justification for Sin's revisionist interpretations as he could accuse the sources of a cover-up, such as in the case of his claiming the 108 BCE Han invasion recorded in Chinese sources to have in fact been a failure.

Today Sin's reductionist portrayal of pre-twentieth-century Sinocentrism continues to be promoted by pseudo-historians in order to explain both the orthodox Korean tradition of locating Lelang at Pyongyang, which otherwise undermines their charge of this being a colonial-era conspiracy, and also the lack of attestation for Tan'gun in *Samguk sagi*. If Sin's writings sought to explain Korea's loss of continental greatness, the pro-Japanese cartel hypothesis promoted by Yi Tŏk-il *cum suis* now functions as a sequel to explain why the invented tradition of ancient empire has not been more actively embraced by the academic establishment.

AN INTERNALIZED EMPIRE AND THE VALUE OF MYTHOLOGY

As noted at the start of this chapter, the empire tradition has come to constitute a staple of popular history writing and to wield political influence. Against the context of geopolitical rivalries between the nation-states of East Asia these two aspects continue to have a mutually reinforcing effect. Korean pseudohistory concomitantly thrives at the intersection of popular nationalism and religious practice. It is distinguished from academic history by its wanton subordination of the scientific method to its own ethnocentric subjectivity such that critical objectivity concerning sources and archaeological evidence is severely compromised. This circumstance is exemplified by the continued presence of mythological elements, and through the motivation of its advocates to frame their exaggerated conceptualization of Korea's early past as a second front on which to bolster national identity and fight present-day wars of words with regional rivals.

The Taejonggyo-inflected empire narrative is a more complex phenomenon built on an accumulation of invented traditions spanning from early sources to the present day. Owing both to its developmental depth across the twentieth century, and the level to which it has been internalized within society, it constitutes a tangible modern tradition.

Of course, neither the presence of medieval mythology within popular treatments of early history, nor chauvinist assertions of ancient exceptionalism are unique to South Korea. We need only evoke the long-standing obsession with King Arthur in British mass media. However, the aspect of political interference concomitantly exhibited is more often associated with states of a totalitarian disposition than those with intellectually freer societies as South Korea otherwise is.

We may finish by speculating that that which is more particular and influential to the circumstances of both Koreas is that these two aspects found in the present-day phenomenon of Korean pseudohistory have long been present in its pre-twentieth-century historiography, namely the state sponsorship of history writing and the embedment of prestige foundation mythology within. Concerning state sponsorship, few countries even within the East Asian Sinosphere could boast such a developed and sustained system of government historiography than that maintained throughout Chosŏn dynasty Korea. During the colonial era this practice was co-opted by the Japanese, a historical circumstance providing the seed for conspiracy arguments endemic today. In South Korea it has come to be exemplified both positively, for example, in the level of government support for the digitalization of sources—including the same Chosŏn dynasty government records themselves—but also in the political expectations placed on scholarship: political expectations shaped by the popular internalization of pseudohistory.

Mythology, meanwhile, is typically regarded as ahistorical but, pertaining to discourses of antiquity and national identity mythology, nevertheless maintains a parallel claim to authenticity. In certain instances of modern nation-state formation, "rediscovered" mythologies fueled National-Romantic movements that were principally pursued as literary art rather than academic history, though archaeology has from its inception intimated a tantalizing promise to bring history and myth together. In the case of Korea, however, until the twentieth century the primary and even sole function of the Hwan'ung-Tan'gun foundation story had been to signify the beginning of Korean history, and critically it does not possess enough of an independent narrative text or story universe to exist outside of history.

In contrast to pure fiction, the perceived authenticity of mythology further imbues it with a certain legitimizing function: hence its utility to both state historiography and religion. In Korea, these circumstances have ensured that, even as the Old Chosŏn foundation story was adopted by colonial-era intellectuals for purposes of cultural resistance and revitalization, it remained closely intertwined with popular perceptions of and expectations toward early history, even as the academic field of history underwent exposure to new levels of empirical rigor, and fused with archaeology. Previously a function shared with the figure of Kija, from the twentieth century onward it has been the Tan'gun myth alone that legitimizes ancient Chosŏn as the charter state of Korean history, and even while pseudo-historians who promote ancient empire have embraced the more dynamic figure of Ch'iu, their own popular legitimacy derives solely from Tan'gun.

GLOSSARY

An Chŏng-bok 安鼎福
An Ho-sang 安浩相
Chewang un'gi 帝王韻紀
Ch'iu (Ch. Chiyou) 蚩尤
Ch'iu ch'ŏnwang 蚩尤天王
Ch'oe Nam-sŏn 崔南善
Ch'oe Tong 崔棟

Chŏlmŭn yŏksa hakcha moim 젊은역사학자모임
Chŏng In-bo 鄭寅普
Chŏng Yak-yong 丁若鏞
Chōsen oyobi chōsen minzoku 朝鮮及朝鮮民族
Chosŏn Ilbo 朝鮮日報

Chosŏn sanggo munhwasa 朝鮮
上古文化史
Chosŏn sanggosa 朝鮮上古史
Chumong 朱蒙
Chŭngsando 甑山道
Dongbei 東北
Dongbei Gongcheng 東北工程
(abbreviation of 東北邊疆歷
史與現狀系列研究工程)
Dongyi 東夷
Hae Puru 解夫婁
Han 漢
Hongshan 紅山
Huangdi 黃帝
Hwandan kogi 桓檀古記
Hwan'guk 桓國
Hwan'in 桓因
Hwan'ung 桓雄
Im Sŭng-guk 林承國
Imna 任那
Imna Kara 任那加羅
Inha (University) 仁荷大學校
Ji'an 集安
Jilin (Province) 吉林
Jilin leishi 鷄林類事
Jizi 箕子
Jurchen-Manchu 女眞·滿洲
Kaya 加耶
Kija 箕子
Kija Chosŏn 箕子朝鮮
Kim Jong Il 金正日
Kim Kyo-hŏn 金敎獻
Kim Pu-sik 金富軾
Koguryŏ 高句麗
Kojosŏn 古朝鮮
Kojosŏn Yŏn'guso 고조선 연구소
Kwanggaet'o (stele) 廣開土王碑

Kwŏn O-jung 權五重
Kyŏnghŭi (University) 慶熙大學
校
Lelang ([Nangnang] Command-
ery) 樂浪郡
Liaodong 遼東
Liaoning 辽宁
Longshan 龍山
Lunyu 論語
Mahan 馬韓
Manchukuo 滿洲國
Miao 苗
Mimana 任那
Mimana Nihonfu 任那日本府
ming 明
Nihon shoki 日本書紀
Niuheliang 牛河梁
Ŏ Yun-jŏk 魚允迪
Och'ŏnnyŏngan Chosŏn ŭi ŏl 五
千年間 朝鮮의 얼
Paedal 倍達
Paekche 百濟
Paektu (Mount) 白頭山
Parhae 渤海
Park Chung Hee 朴正熙
Purham 不咸
Puyŏ 夫餘 (in Korean sources 扶
餘)
Pyŏlgŏngon 別乾坤
Pyongyang 平壤
Qing 清
Ri Chi-rin 李址麟
Ryŏksa P'yŏnjipsil 력사 편집실
Samguk sagi 三國史記
Samguk yusa 三國遺事
Samhan 三韓
Sangsaeng 相生

Sasanggye 思想界
Shandong 山東
Shang 商
Shiji 史記
Shiratori Kurakichi 白鳥庫吉
Shujing 尚書
Silla 新羅
Sin Ch'ae-ho 申采浩
Sinsi 神市
Songhua 松花
Sŏul Sinmun 서울신문
Su Bingqi 苏秉琦
Taejonggyo 大倧敎
Tan'guk taehakkyo 단국대학교
   (檀國大學校)
Tan'gun 檀君 (in *Samguk yusa* 壇
   君)
Tan'gun Chosŏn 檀君朝鮮
Tan'gun kogi chŏnsŏk 檀君古記
   箋釋
Tan'gun kŭpki yŏn'gu 壇君及其
   研究
Tan'gunnon 壇君論
Tong'a Ilbo 東亞日報

Tongbug'a yŏksa chaedan 東北亞
   歷史財團
Tonghak 東學
Tongmyŏng (King) 東明王
Tongsa yŏnp'yo (1915) 東史年表
Tu (Mount) 塗山
Wanghŏm 王險城 (in Korean
   sources Wanggŏm 王儉城)
Wi Man 衛滿
Wiman Chosŏn 衛滿朝鮮
wuxing, K. *ohaeng* 五行
Xia Yu 夏禹 Xia king Yu
Xianbei 鮮卑
Xiongnu 匈奴
Xu Xusheng 徐旭生
Yamato 大和
Yan (Emperor) 炎帝
Yan 燕
Yangshao 仰韶
Yi Ik 李瀷
Yi Yu-rip 李裕岦
Yu Shun 虞舜
Yun Nae-hyŏn 尹乃鉉
Yun Yong-gu 尹龍九
Zhou 周

NOTES

Research for this chapter has been completed with support from the ERC *A War of Words* project at Leiden University. In addition to the editors, special thanks are extended, in order of surnames, to Ahn Kanghun, Mark Byington, Javier Cha, Chris Green, Jean Hyun, Juha Janhunen, Fresco Sam-sin, Barbara Wall, and Sixiang Wang.

1. Pan-Altaic interpretations share much in common with early twentieth-century pan-Turanism, which was promoted by Japan during the war years.

2. Initially written in literary Chinese, one of the more influential Korean translations renders the title as *Handan kogi* (Im 1986).
3. The first was Shim (2016). This continued with Song Ho-jŏng in Han (2017), Chŏlmŭn yŏksa hakcha moim (2017, 2018), Kim Hyŏn-gyu (2017), Kim In-ŭi (2017), and Yi (2018). *Hankyoreh 21* magazine, affiliated with the politically left-leaning *Hankyoreh* (*Han'gyŏre*) newspaper, also carried a six-part series of articles under the title "Real Ancient History" authored by the Chŏlmŭn yŏksa hakcha moim, an organized group of younger academic historians (*Hankyoreh 21* 2017).
4. For a retrospective of the Early Korea Project see Byington (2017).
5. This New Right historiography actively apologizes for both Japanese imperialism and South Korean autocracy of the postwar and developmentalist decades. See Tikhonov (2019).
6. Ki Kyoung-ryang observes that the practice of Korean pseudohistory matches the definitions given by Fritze (2009, 12–16). These include: approaching a topic with preconceptions and hidden agendas; cherry-picking evidence to support a theory while ignoring evidence to the contrary; making use of earlier scholarship that has since been disproven; interpreting myths and legends as historical fact; failing to distinguish between remote possibility and actual likelihood of a given scenario occurring; and finally, taking issue with basic facts such as whether a historical event occurred or not, or whether a certain place or personage really existed. See Ki in Chŏlmŭn yŏksa hakcha moim (2017, 32). For a more detailed discussion and debunking of Korean pseudohistory, see Logie (2019).
7. Sin Ch'ae-ho is often claimed by Taejonggyo as part of their tradition, but while he may have had some interactions, his work was essentially secular and shows only limited adoption of Taejonggyo notions or terminology. For details of Taejonggyo and Kim Kyo-hŏn, see N. Kim (2017, 158–244).
8. On Ri Chi-rin and the likelihood of group authorship, see Kang (2015).
9. For extensive discussion of the Park-era coterie see Yi (2018, 99–134).
10. Empire-type interpretations have more recently gained institutional representation through Inha University's Kojosŏn Yŏn'guso (Old Chosŏn Research Institute), which has been active since 2015. By contrast, in the same year Kyung Hee (Kyŏnghŭi) University established the Institute of Korean Archaeology and Ancient History (IKAA) with an explicit mission to counter pseudohistory.
11. See Kang (2015, 34), and in English, Lugar (2012, 31) and Xu (2016, 145).
12. My usage of the term "charter state" to describe Chosŏn's position in Korean historiography is adapted from Lieberman (2003, 23) who uses it to denote

early polities of mainland Southeast Asia that "in varying degrees, provided a religious, political, and administrative charter for subsequent empires."

13. Founder of Wiman Chosŏn.

14. Discussion of Sin is principally based on his *opus magnum, Chosŏn sanggosa* written (c. 1924) together with an earlier work, *Chosŏn sanggo munhwasa* (estimated c. 1914). These broadly complementary works were both serialized in the *Chosŏn Ilbo* newspaper 1931–1932.

15. Characterization of Kim Kyo-hŏn's historiography is based on Kim (1923), the exact date of which is uncertain. Prominent Chosŏn dynasty scholars recognizing Old Chosŏn's continental western territory prior to the Yan expansion include Yi Ik (1681–1763) and Chŏng Yak-yong (1762–1836). Their writings are often invoked by empire advocates; however, in all cases these scholars regarded both the Wiman capital of Wanghŏm and Lelang Commandery to have been located on the Peninsula at Pyongyang.

16. Bamboo strips of *Lunyu [The Analects]* were also found in the same tomb and made known sooner, but the existence of the census tablets was revealed only in 2006, with photographs released on the back cover of the journal *Chosŏn kogohak yŏn'gu* in 2008. See Yun (2010, 19, 153) and An (2016, 267).

17. On pre-Qin Dongyi see Li (2006, 313), and on the Dongyi conflation see Byington (2016, 34) and Pak (2018, 50–63).

18. A notable omission is Chinese script. Sin asserts Chosŏn to have had its own script that was lost. *Hwandan kogi* makes a similar claim, and includes a set of characters broadly resembling the Korean hangul script (Im [1986, 67] and An [2012, 222]). However, hangul is documented to have been created only in the mid-fifteenth century CE, prior to which it is wholly unattested.

19. On the flaws of the Altaic hypothesis, see Janhunen (1996, 237).

20. During the Park Chung Hee era, Ch'oe Tong (1966) postulated Koreans to have been a tribe descended from the "Turanian civilization" of Babylon, while Mun Chŏng-ch'ang (1979) later also argued that Koreans were one of the lost tribes of Israel, but in both cases the proposed migration routes still went from west to east, via Central Asia.

21. For an overview of Hongshan archaeology, see Li (2008, 73–132).

22. Chŏng's representative work on ancient history was serialized in the *Tonga Ilbo* newspaper from 1931 to 1935 under the title "Five thousand years of the Chosŏn spirit" (Och'ŏnnyŏngan Chosŏn ŭi ŏl). It was subsequently edited into two volumes by *Sŏul Sinmun* in 1946. For a recent Korean edition of the first volume, see Chŏng (2012).

23. Aside from the continued results of North Korean archaeology, a further counterargument is why the Japanese did not also fabricate artifacts for the Mimana Nihonfu, which colonial-era scholars asserted as having been a base of early Japanese control south of Lelang.
24. This thesis was originally written in Japanese, being included in the 1927 publication *Chōsen oyobi chōsen minzoku*. It was apparently first published in Korean in his posthumous collected works in 1974. For a modern Korean edition see Ch'oe (2013b).
25. Ch'oe's three main theses on Hwan'ung-Tan'gun comprise *Tan'gunnon*, serialized in the *Tong'a Ilbo* newspaper in 1926, *Tan'gun kŭpki yŏn'gu* published in the magazine *Pyŏlgŏngon* in 1928, and *Tan'gun kogi chŏnsŏk* published in *Sasanggye* in 1954. For modern editions see Ch'oe (2013a).
26. The charge of Buddhist invention had previously been made by scholars An Chŏng-bok (1712–1791) and Chŏng Yak-yong (1762–1836). An believed Tan'gun to have been a historical personage but otherwise rejected the content of the extant myth.
27. According to Yi Mun-yŏng (2007), this claim originates in *Tongsa yŏnp'yo* (1915) by Ŏ Yun-jŏk (1868–1935).
28. The earliest attestations of Chiyou occur in the *Book of Documents*, predating those of the Yellow Emperor that first occur in *Shiji*.
29. On recent archaeology, see Byington, Sasaki, and Bale (2018).

REFERENCES

An Chŏng-jun. 2016. "Onŭl nal ŭi Nangnanggun yŏn'gu" [Present-day research on the Lelang Commandery]. *Yŏksa-bip'yŏng* 114 (Spring).

An Ho-sang. 1964. *Paedal ŭi chonggyo wa ch'ŏrhak kwa yŏksa* [Religion, philosophy and history of Paedal]. Seoul: Ŏmungak.

———.1979. *Paedal tong'i nŭn tong'i kyŏre wa tong'a munhwa ŭi palsangji* [Paedal and Dongyi were the place of origin of the Dongyi people]. Seoul: Paeg'ak munhwasa.

An Kyŏng-jŏn (annotator). 2012. *Hwandan kogi (pogŭp p'an)* [Old records of the Hwan and Tan empires (popular distribution edition)]. Daejeon-si: Sangsaeng.

Baker, Donald. 2002. "Hananim, Hanŭnim, Hanullim, and Hanŏllim: The Construction of Terminology for Korean Monotheism." *Review of Korean Studies* 5 (1).

Best, Jonathan W. 2006. *A History of the Early Korean Kingdom of Paekche: Together with an Annotated Translation of the Paekche Annals of the Samguk Sagi*. Cambridge, MA: Harvard University Press.

Byington, Mark E. 2004. "A Matter of Territorial Security: China's Historiographical Treatment of Koguryŏ in the Twentieth Century." *Nationalism and History Textbooks in Asia and Europe—Diverse Views on Conflicts Surrounding History*. Seoul: The Center for Information on Korean Culture, Academy of Korean Studies.

———. 2016. *The Ancient State of Puyŏ in Northeast Asia: Archaeology and Historical Memory*. Cambridge, MA: Harvard University Asia Center.

———. 2017. "A Retrospective Account of the Early Korea Project at Harvard." Institute of Korean Archaeology and Ancient History (IKAA) website, Kyung Hee University. Accessed February 27, 2020. http://www.ikaa.or.kr/home.php

Byington, Mark, Ken'ichi Sasaki, and Martin T. Bale, eds. 2018. *Early Korea-Japan Interactions*. Early Korea Project. Cambridge, MA: Korea Institute, Harvard University.

Ch'oe Nam-sŏn. 2013a. *Ch'oe Nam-sŏn Han'gukhak chongsŏ 7: Tan'gunnon* [Ch'oe Nam-sŏn collected writings 7: Thesis on Tan'gun]. Seoul: Kyŏng'in munhwasa.

———. 2013b. *Ch'oe Nam-sŏn Han'gukhak chongsŏ 8: pulham munhwaron·salman'gyoch'agi* [Ch'oe Nam-sŏn collected writings 8: *Purham Culture Thesis* and notes on shamanism]. Seoul: Kyŏng'in munhwasa.

Ch'oe Tong. 1966. *Chosŏn sanggo minjok-sa* [History of the ancient Korean people]. Seoul: Tongguk munhwasa.

Chŏlmŭn yŏksa hakcha moim [Young historians' collective]. 2017. *Han'guk kodaesa wa saibiyŏksahak* [Early Korean history and pseudo-historiography]. Goyang: Yŏksa pip'yŏngsa.

———. 2018. *Yongmang nŏmŏ han'guk kodaesa* [Early Korean history beyond (chauvinist) greed]. Paju: Sŏhaemunjip.

Chŏn Mun-gyu. 2017. *Siljŭng paedalguksa 1* [Actual proof for the history of the Paedal state]. Seoul: Bungnaep.

Chŏng In-bo. 2012. *Chosŏnsa yŏn'gu (sang)* [Research on Korean history]. Seoul: Uriyŏksa yŏn'gu chaedan.

Fritze, Ronald H. 2009. *Invented Knowledge: False History, Fake Science and Pseudo-Religions*. London: Reaktion Books.

Han Myŏng-gi, ed. 2017. *Chaengjŏm Han'guksa: chŏn'gŭndaepyŏn* [Disputed points of Korean history: Premodern period]. Goyang: Ch'angbi.

Hankyoreh 21. 2017. "Chintcha kodaesa" [Real ancient history], vols.

1172–1178. *Han'gyŏre*. Accessed February 27, 2020. http://h21.hani.co.kr/arti /SERIES/260/

Im Süng-guk. 1986. *Handan kogi*. Seoul: Chŏngsin segyesa.

Janhunen, Juha. 1996. *Manchuria: An Ethnic History*. Helsinki: Finno-Ugrian Society.

Kang In-uk. 2015. "Rijirin ŭi 'kojosŏn yŏngu' wa chojung kogo palguldae" [Ri Chirin's research on Old Chosŏn and the joint DPRK-China excavations]. *Sŏnsa wa kodae* 45:29–58.

Kim Hyŏn-gu. 2017. *Singminsahak ŭi k'arŭt'el* [Colonial historiography cartel]. Seoul: Isang midiŏ.

Kim In-hŭi. 2017. *Ch'iu, orae toen yŏksabyŏng* [Chiyou, an old disease of history]. Seoul: P'urŭn yŏksa.

Kim Kyo-hŏn. 1923. *Sindanminsa* [History of the divine Tan people]. Handwritten mimeograph, accessed from Harvard Library Hollis database (HOLLIS Number 005066685).

Kim, Nuri. 2017. "Making Myth, History, and an Ancient Religion in Korea." PhD diss., Harvard University. Accessed February 27, 2020. http://nrs.harvard .edu/urn-3:HUL.InstRepos:41140212

Kim, Seon-min. 2017. *Ginseng and Borderland: Territorial boundaries and political relations between Qing China and Chosŏn Korea 1636–1912*. Oakland: University of California Press.

Kim Un-hoe. 2017. *Uri ka paeun Paekche nŭn katcha ta: Puyŏsa ro ingnŭn Hanil kodaesa* [The Paekche we have learnt of is false: The ancient history of Korea and Japan read through the history of Puyŏ]. Goyang: Wisdom House.

Laufer, Berthold. 1916. "Burkhan." *Journal of the American Oriental Society* 36:390–395.

Li, Feng. 2006. *Landscape and Power in Early China: The Crisis and Fall of the Western Zhou 1045–771 BC*. Cambridge: Cambridge University Press.

Li, Xinwei. 2008. *Development of Social Complexity in the Liaoxi Area, Northeast China*. Oxford: BAR Publishing.

Lieberman, Victor. 2003. *Strange Parallels*. Vol. 1, *Integration of the Mainland Southeast Asia in Global Context, c. 800–1830*. Cambridge: Cambridge University Press.

Logie, Andrew. 2019. "Diagnosing and Debunking Korean Pseudohistory." *European Journal of Korean Studies* 18 (2): 37–80.

Lugar, Richard G. 2012. "Senate Committee Print, 112th Congress: China's Impact on Korean Peninsula Unification and Questions for the Senate: A minority staff report prepared for the use of the Committee on Foreign Relations United States Senate." Washington, DC: U.S. Government Printing Office.

Mun Chŏng-ch'ang. 1979. *Han'guk syumerŭ isŭra'el ŭi yŏksa* [Korea and Sumer—Israel history]. Seoul: Paengmundang.

Pak Chaebok. 2018. "Chŏllae munhŏn kwa ch'ult'o charyo ro pon tong'i ŭi yŏnwŏn" [On the origin of the Dongyi as seen through transmitted texts and excavated sources]. In Tongbug'a yŏksa chaedan hanjung kwan'gye yŏn'guso. *Chungguk sandong chiyŏk ŭi tong'i* [The Dongyi of the Shandong region of China], 47–80. Seoul: Yŏksa konggan.

Perry, W. 1923. *The Children of the Sun: A Study in the Early History of Civilization*. London: Methuen.

Ramstedt, G. J. 1928. "Remarks on the Korean Language." *Journal de la Société Finno-Ougrienne* 58. Helsinki: Suomalais-Ugrilainen Seura.

Ri Chi-rin. 1963. *Kojosŏn yŏn'gu* [Research on ancient Chosŏn]. Pyongyang: Kwahak'wŏn ch'ulp'ansa.

———. (1963) 2018. *Ri chirin ŭi kojosŏn yŏn'gu: taeryuk kojosŏn ŭl ch'ajasŏ* [Ri Chirin's *Research on ancient Chosŏn: In search of continental Old Chosŏn*]. Seoul: P'ip'ŭllain.

Ryŏksa P'yŏnjipsil [History compilation room]. 1994. *Tan'gun kwa kojosŏn e kwanhan yŏngu nonmunjip* [Collected research papers relating to Tan'gun and ancient Chosŏn]. Pyongyang: Sahoe kwahak ch'ulp'ansa.

Shim, Jae-hoon. 2002. "A New Understanding of Kija Chosŏn as a Historical Anachronism." *Harvard Journal of Asiatic Studies* 62 (2): 271–305.

———. 2016. *Kodae Chungguk e ppajyŏ Han'guksa rŭl paraboda* [Immersed in early China, examining Korean history]. Seoul: Purŭn yŏksa.

Shiratori Kurakichi. (1896) 1970. "Chōsen kodai chimeikō" [Study on early Korean toponyms]. In Shiratori Kurakichi, *Shiratori Kurakichi Zenshū dai 3 ken* [Shiratori Kurakichi collected works, vol. 3], 37–68. Tokyo: Iwanami shoten.

———. (1907) 1970. "Mōko minzoku no kigen" [On the origins of the Mongol peoples]. In Shiratori Kurakichi, *Shiratori Kurakichi Zenshū dai 4 ken* [Shiratori Kurakichi collected works, vol. 4], 23–62. Tokyo: Iwanami shoten.

Sin Ch'ae-ho, Tanjae. (1972) 1995. *Tanjae sin-chaeho chŏnjip (sanggwŏn)* [Collected works of Tanjae Sin Ch'ae-ho, part 1]. Seoul: Tanjae Sin-chaeho sŏnsaeng kinyŏm saŏphoe.

Sin, Ka-yŏng. 2016. "Research on the 'Mimana Nihonfu' and the Colonialist Historical Perspective." *Yŏksa-bip'yŏng* 114 (Spring).

Son Sŏng-tae. 2017. *Uriminjok ŭi taeidong: Amerik'a indiŏn ŭn uriminjok ida—Meksik'op'yŏn* [Our ethnic nation's great migration: American Indians are our people—Mexico volume]. Seoul: K'ori.

Son Yŏng-jong. 2005. "Tan'gun Chosŏn ŭi sŏngnip" [The establishment of Tan'gun

Chosŏn]. In *Nambuk hakcha-dŭr-i hamkke ssŭn Tan'gun-gwa Kojosŏn yŏn'gu,* edited by Tan'gun hakhoe, 249–283. Seoul: Chishik sanŏpsa.

———.2006. *Chosŏn tandaesa (Koguryŏsa 1)* [Chosŏn history by period (Koguryŏ 1)]. Pyongyang: Kwahak paekkwa sajŏn ch'ulpansa.

Su, Bingqi. (1987) 1997. "Hua people—Descendants of the dragon—Chinese: An archaeological seeking after roots." *Antiquity* 71:37–39.

Tikhonov, Vladimir. 2019. "The Rise and Fall of the New Right Movement and the Historical Wars in 2000s South Korea." *European Journal of Korean Studies* 18 (2).

Xu, Stella. 2016. *Reconstructing Ancient Korean History: The Formation of Korean-ness in the Shadow of History.* Lanham, MD: Lexington Books.

Yi Mun-yŏng. 2007. "Paedal ŭi yurae" [The origin of *paedal*]. *Ch'orokpul ŭi chaphaktasik,* March 10 (personal blog). Accessed February 27, 2020. http://orumi .egloos.com/3043922

———.2018. *Yusayŏksahak pip'an: hwandan kogi wa ilgŭrŏjin kodaesa* [Critique of pseudohistory: *Hwandan kogi* and distorted early history]. Goyang: Yŏksa pip'yŏngsa.

Yi Tŏk-il. 2014. *Uri an ŭi singminsagwan: haebang toeji mothan yŏksa, kŭdŭr ŭn ŏttŏk'e uri rŭl chibae haenŭnga* [The colonial view of history within us: Unliberated history, how have they controlled us?]. Seoul: Man'gwŏndang.

———.2015. *Maeguk ŭi yŏksahak, ŏdi kkaji wanna* [Treasonous historiography, how far has it come?]. Seoul: Man'gwŏndang.

———.2017. *Yi Tŏk-il ŭi tangdanghan'guksa* [Yi Tŏk-il's grand Korean history]. Seoul: Arami.

Yi Tŏk-il and Kim Pyŏng-gi. 2006. *Uri yŏksa parojapki 1: Kojosŏn ŭn taeryuk ŭi chibaeja yŏtta* [Correcting our history 1: Old Chosŏn were rulers of the continent]. Koyang: Wisdom House.

Yun Nae-hyŏn. 1986. *Han'guk kodaesa sillon* [A new history of early Korea]. Seoul: Ilchisa.

———.2003 (2014, 5th repr.). *Uri kodaesa: sangsang esŏ hyŏnsil ro* [Our early history: From imagination to reality]. Paju: Chisik san'ŏpsa.

———.(1986) 2017. *Han'guk kodaesa sillon* [A new history of early Korea]. Seoul: Man'gwŏndang.

Yun Yong-gu. 2010. "Nangnangguk ch'ogi ŭi kunhyŏn chibae wa hogu paak" [Understanding the system of commandery-prefecture rule and the census during the early period of the Lelang Commandery]. In *Nangnang-gun hogubu yŏngu* [Research on the Lelang census tablets], edited by Kwŏn O-jung, 152–206. Seoul: Northeast Asian History Foundation.

CHAPTER 3

Imagining Ancient Korean Religion

Sŏndo, Tan'gun, and the Earth Goddess

DON BAKER

In what may be the most widely used university-level Korean history textbook in the Republic of Korea (hereafter, ROK), Han Young Woo (Han Yŏng-u), one of the most respected historians of Korea in the last quarter of the twentieth century, says that the religious beliefs of people who lived on the Korean Peninsula 3,000 or so years ago are best described as "Seongyo" ([Sŏn'gyo], religion of immortality) or "Sin'gyo" (religion of God) (Han 2010, 74–75; 2001, 60). A few pages later he writes that the ancient myth of Tan'gun tells us that the guiding principle of the first kingdom of Korea, established by Tan'gun over 3,000 years ago, was *hongik in'gan* (broadly benefit humanity). Moreover, he cites the Tan'gun myth's claim that, after ruling Korea for around 1,500 years, Tan'gun retreated to the mountains, where he became a mountain-hermit immortal.[1]

Han Young Woo is too good a historian to take the Tan'gun myth literally. However, his nationalistic inclinations have caused him to drop his guard a bit and assert that nevertheless we can learn much about ancient Korea from that myth, such as its religious beliefs. This causes him to make some assertions for which there is no archaeological or contemporaneous evidence. The oldest extant version we have of the Tan'gun story is less than 800 years old, making it difficult to use it, as Han unfortunately does, to give us information about Korean beliefs and practices 3,000 years ago. A careful study of the Tan'gun myth itself gives us even more reason to doubt the usefulness of relying on that tale for information on any distinctive religious beliefs and practices of the inhabitants of the Korean Peninsula several millennia ago. For one thing, it is replete with esoteric Buddhist references, which suggests it was composed after Buddhism entered the Korean Peninsula around 1,700 years ago and reflects the religious beliefs of that later time (Jorgensen 1998). Moreover, there is not much uniquely Korean about that myth, other than place-names. The entire text in which that revered prescription to "broadly benefit humanity" is introduced is written in classical Chinese. Even the grammar of *hongik in'gan* is classical Chinese grammar (adverb-verb-object) rather than Korean (which would be object-adverb-verb), casting doubt on any claim to ancient Korean roots. (Though hangul had not yet been invented when that text was written, Koreans had already begun using Chinese characters for their phonetic value to reproduce Korean vocabulary and grammar when they felt it useful to do so. If that myth were really as ancient as has been claimed, it would have been passed down orally over the centuries. If that were the case, surely there would have been at least nods to that vernacular version in the classical Chinese rendition.)

Despite these caveats about the reliability of the Tan'gun myth for information on ancient Korean religious beliefs and practices, a growing number of South Koreans today agree with Han Young Woo that the ancient ancestors of the Korean people today had their own indigenous religion, different from what could be seen in China or Japan at that time (Kim 1988, 49–60; Lee, Park, and Yoon 2005, 79–81). Moreover, many of them believe that religion involved the pursuit of immortality and the worship of God (Ch'oe 1994, 93–94). The most popular name for that imagined ancient Korean religion today is Sŏn'gyo, the religion of immortality, or Sŏndo, the way of the immortals.

CONSTRUCTING A TRADITION

The lack of any specific evidence for the existence of anything resembling an organized religion of Sŏn'gyo or an organized practice of Sŏndo on the Korean Peninsula thousands of years ago, or at any time before the late twentieth century, indicates that this is a constructed tradition. New traditions claiming ancient roots are rarely, if ever, concocted out of thin air. Usually such traditions emerge when bits and pieces extracted from the past are woven together to create a new fabric designed to appear traditional. That is precisely what happened with the assertion heard in recent decades that Sŏn'gyo/Sŏndo is an indigenous longevity-enhancing spiritual tradition that is thousands of years old.

Said to have been first promoted by Tan'gun himself, Sŏndo is often defined as a combination of physical exercises and breathing practices that enhance physical and mental health, allowing practitioners to live longer and healthier lives than non-practitioners normally do.[2] Sometimes practitioners are even promised that they can become *sinsŏn*, the legendary godlike "immortals" who were believed to live for centuries in the mountains of the Peninsula, subsisting on little more than air and whatever edible vegetation they could find up there (Kukhak yŏn'guwŏn 2010, 305). Moreover, due to the influence of the early twentieth-century creators of the new religion of Taejonggyo [the religion of the great progenitor], a sizeable minority of those who insist that Sŏndo is an ancient tradition link it with a purported ancient belief in God, often described as a trinitarian God like the God of Christianity, though in this case consisting of Tan'gun, his father Hwan'ung, and his grandfather Hwan'in. Such addition of a theological framework for Sŏndo is, of course, strongest among the followers of Taejonggyo, a religion focused on worship of Tan'gun. However, it also appears among those who, often without realizing it, have been influenced by Taejonggyo teachings (Kim 1971, 130; Yi 2015, 170–195).

Korea has a long tradition of belief in *sinsŏn*, in the benefits of internal alchemy (the belief that certain breathing practices and physical exercises can transform human physiology so that the bodily decay normally associated with aging is halted or even reversed), and in Tan'gun. But only in the second half of the twentieth century did those three beliefs coalesce. The constructed tradition of Sŏn'gyo, now more often called Sŏndo by those practicing internal alchemy techniques, has its roots in a belief emerging into prominence during the colonial period that Tan'gun had created, or, at least, practiced and promoted, a distinctly Korean religion. Since Tan'gun was said to have lived for centuries, he was also identified as a *sinsŏn*. Later, in the second half of the twentieth century, internal alchemy was added to this story to provide concrete content for the purported ancient teachings of Tan'gun.

Claims that Korean Sŏndo has ancient roots gained growing acceptance over the last few decades for at least three reasons. First of all, many of those who promote this claim point to statements in texts presented as thousands of years old, even though textual evidence suggests most of them were written in the twentieth century (Cho 2001, 210–239; Sŏ 1994, 47–81). A second reason so many people have come to believe in the claim of an ancient Korean tradition of Sŏndo is that they have conflated some key terms. For example, they assume that any reference to someone of unusual longevity, such as Tan'gun, especially if that person is referred to as a *sŏn* or *sinsŏn*, means they must have practiced the breathing practices and physical exercises associated with internal alchemy, which provides enhanced longevity. And, since they believe Tan'gun is the first *sinsŏn* to appear as such in Korea's histories, they believe those practices must have originated with Tan'gun.

A third reason for the growing acceptance of the claim that Sŏndo is a unique Korean religious tradition with ancient roots is that Koreans, after coming out from under the thumb of Japanese colonial rule from 1910 to 1945, which denigrated the value and distinctive character of Korean culture, have wanted to shine a spotlight on anything that demonstrates that for thousands of years they have had their own civilization, one that was and still is quite different from what is seen in China and Japan because it emerged before either China or Japan had any cultural impact on the Peninsula (Chŏng 2009, 93). Koreans are justified in claiming cultural originality, of course. Koreans have been a distinctive people with a distinctive culture for millennia. However, not every claim of some unique cultural product appearing in Korea's long history is justified by reliable historical evidence or sound reasoning.

Modern attempts to claim ancient roots for Sŏndo are one example of such unsubstantiated assertions. Statements that, long before they were influenced by their neighbors, the Korean people had their own unique religion are based on a misreading of truly ancient documents and a misplaced trust in recently manufactured documents. For example, a close reading of the Tan'gun myth in its earliest version, in the *Samguk yusa* (Memorabilia of the Three Kingdoms), a late thirteenth-century text, reveals that that text says nothing about Tan'gun engaging in any sort of religious practices. Moreover, nothing is said about Tan'gun engaging in any type of breathing practices or physical exercises. Nor is anything said about his teaching such techniques to anyone else. All that is said, at the end of the Tan'gun story, is that he left the mundane world and moved into the mountains, where he became a mountain spirit (Kim 1992, 17).

The only way this story can be read as a story of the origins of a distinctive Korean Sŏndo is if the reader, first of all, assumes that since Tan'gun is described as becoming a mountain spirit after living among human beings for well over a thousand years, he must have engaged in the sort of breathing practices and physical exercises that are believed to promote such longevity. In other words, he must have been a practitioner of Sŏndo, since such exercises are identifying characteristics of Sŏndo. In addition, the reader must assume that Tan'gun was a good person who believed in broadly benefiting humanity and therefore Tan'gun surely would have shared those techniques with human beings. And those human beings must have passed those techniques down to the next generation, and then on to the next generations without a break over more than 3,000 years so that the Sŏndo tradition today is directly inherited from Tan'gun. And, since Tan'gun, according to that story, lived long before we see any signs of Daoism in China, Korea's Sŏndo tradition must have arisen not only independently of China's Daoism but predate it as well and therefore is Korea's indigenous religious tradition.

Clearly, the only way the Tan'gun story can be read as supporting the belief that Tan'gun pioneered the same Sŏndo practices many modern Koreans engage in today is if a reader sees more in that story than actually appears on the written page, adding to that story things it does not say, based upon the assumption that, since Tan'gun was the founder of Sŏndo, that must be what that story is telling us between the lines. The argument that the Tan'gun myth proves that Tan'gun founded Sŏndo can only persuade someone who already believes that Sŏndo is an indigenous Korean tradition founded by Tan'gun.

MISREADING AUTHENTIC EARLY TEXTS

The construction of a tradition often requires the creative reading of a much earlier text, as shown above. However, it also sometimes requires ignoring texts that cannot be so easily misconstrued. Such is the case with the claim that Sŏndo has not only ancient roots in Korea but also a continuous history.

There are Chinese accounts, apparently based on personal observations, describing the customs, including religious practices, of the ancient inhabitants of the Korean Peninsula. Those accounts were written in the third and fifth centuries, yet nothing is said about Tan'gun, Hwan'ung, or Hwan'in being worshipped, revered, or even remembered. Moreover, nothing is said about any activities that involve the pursuit of immortality through anything that resembles internal alchemy. Worship of Heaven is mentioned, but that is not linked in any way to the Tan'gun story. Moreover, the Chinese accounts suggest that there were a variety of cultures in and around the Korean Peninsula back then, and different cultures showed ritual respect for Heaven in different ways, undermining any claim that there was one Korean religion that far back in time (Lee 1993, 13–24; Byington 2009, 132–152).

A somewhat more recent text, one that is Korean-authored and is often cited as proof that Sŏndo is an ancient and uniquely Korean tradition, is a ninth-century (or early tenth-century) inscription on a Silla stele (Min 2016; Mason 2016, XI:1). That inscription is said to have been carved by Ch'oe Ch'i-wŏn (858–910). Ch'oe is famous for moving to Tang China when he was a young boy, passing the civil service examination and gaining a post in the Tang bureaucracy, but then returning home to live out the rest of his life in the Silla countryside. The oft-quoted part of that stele (which is no longer extant; that inscription survives in the *Samguk sagi* [The history of the Three Kingdoms], a twelfth-century work) reads, "Our country has a mysterious Way which we call p'ungnyu. The origin of this teaching can be found in detail in the history of the *sŏn*" (Kim Pu-sik 2012, 131).

There are three common misreadings of this brief passage. First of all, "p'ungnyu" is misread as a noun, as the name for a distinctive Korean tradition. However, as Peter Lee points out, that Sino-Korean term is normally used in Chinese sources as an adjective to mean elegant, sophisticated, or refined (Kakhun 1969, 67–68). A reading more faithful to the normal use of that term would have that first sentence say that Korea has an elegant way of doing things.[3] That this is the more accurate reading is clear from the sentences that follow, in which we are told that elegant way consists of a combination of Confucianism, Buddhism, and Daoism.

The second misreading is to add "unique" to that first sentence, making Ch'oe say that Korea has its own unique "p'ungnyu" Way. There is no character in that line saying that this Way is unique to Korea. Moreover, the fact that Ch'oe goes on to say that Way is a combination of three traditions from China makes clear that he is not claiming that Korea has a religious tradition of its own. There is nothing in those few lines quoted from that stele that justifies a recent scholarly claim that "p'ungnyudo, originating from the ancient times, was based on a belief in the heavens and native beliefs" (Ch'oe 2016, 215).

The third mistake is to read the second line, that the origin of this teaching can be found in detail in the history of the *sŏn*, as a reference to a history of Sŏndo. That the text gives the name of the history referred to as *Sŏnsa*, literally "the history of immortals," does not mean it is a history of Sŏndo. *Sŏn* was a term used loosely in Silla times to refer to some members of the *hwarang* (young men from elite families training to be future leaders of Silla), not in the sense of immortals but in the sense simply of extraordinary young men. Since this stele is cited in a section of the *Samguk sagi* that discusses the origins of the *hwarang*, it is more faithful to the text to read it as a reference to a no-longer-extant history of the *hwarang* that tells the story of how the three teachings from China were combined into one elegant Way (Kim 1976, 80).

It is important to note that there is no mention of Tan'gun on that stele, nor is there any reference to internal alchemy practices as part of the "mysterious way" it refers to. Even a forced reading of this inscription to make it appear to say that Korea in the ninth century had a unique indigenous religious tradition called p'ungnyu does not link that purported indigenous tradition to Tan'gun or internal alchemy.

Another argument for an ancient indigenous Korean religious tradition of pursuing immortality through breathing practices and physical exercises draws on references in Korea's oldest histories to people called *sŏn* among the *hwarang* of the Silla Kingdom. As already noted, *sŏn* was a term used loosely to refer to anyone seen as having extraordinary abilities. That could include the ability to live a very long time but not necessarily. An oft-quoted reference to four particularly famous *sŏn* among the *hwarang*, found in *Lives of Eminent Korean Monks*, written in the early thirteenth century, is translated by Peter Lee as "knights" rather than immortals (Kakhun 1969, 68). He has solid grounds for translating that term that way. Nothing is said in that text about those four "*sŏn*" being immortals. Rather they are portrayed as outstanding warriors. Moreover, other uses of the term *sŏn* in Silla texts, such as references to a *kuksŏn*, "a *sŏn* of the court," also appear to refer more to leaders of the band of young warriors known as *hwarang* than to mountain-dwelling immortals (McBride 2008, 39, 75).

The four *sŏn*, and the *hwarang* in general, are given more traditional traits of mountain-dwelling immortals in a text called *Hwarang segi* (Chronicle of the Hwarang) (Kim et al., 2001, 32–42). However, the version of the *Hwarang segi* used today is a twentieth-century text that uses the name of an earlier text now lost (McBride 2005). It cannot be relied on for accurate information about what Koreans believed centuries ago. The original text by that name is no longer extant and we have no way of knowing what it says. A more accurate depiction of what the *hwarang* were, drawing on other, more reliable, documents, is provided by Richard Rutt (1961).

Even if these references to *sŏn* found in authentic early Korean texts referred to those who have acquired the ability to live much longer than an average human being, they still do not support the story that Korea has a unique religious tradition of Sŏndo going back thousands of years. First of all, those references from Silla times to people labeled *sŏn* say nothing about any connection to Tan'gun. The same is true of poetry in the Koryŏ era about *sinsŏn*. Neither in Silla nor Koryŏ do we find assertions that the breathing practices and physical exercises associated with Sŏndo today were created by Tan'gun. In fact, we find no evidence at all that such longevity-enhancing techniques were practiced at all that far back in Korean history (Yi 1989, 46). And, of course, there is no use of the term Sŏndo or any claim that the *sŏn* represents a uniquely Korean organized religious tradition. Moreover, it is hard to distinguish what those old Korean sources say about *sŏn* from what equally old Chinese sources say about *xian*. *Xian* is the Chinese pronunciation of the same character Koreans pronounce *sŏn*, and refers to the same sort of extraordinary human beings. Han Young Woo (2014, 56–57) insists the term *sŏn/xian* originated in Korea rather than in China. However, he presents no textual evidence for that claim other than citing its first appearance in a Han dynasty dictionary, which makes no mention of Korea.

Not only is the term for immortals the same in China and Korea, so, too, are the other terms used in Korea's purported indigenous tradition of pursuing immortality through internal alchemy. The absence of any distinctive Korean terminology for what is claimed to be an indigenous Korean tradition suggests that, instead of being homegrown, Korea's Sŏndo is an offshoot of a tradition that originated in China. Nevertheless, many contemporary Korean scholars who have examined the possibility that Sŏndo is Chinese in origin have rejected that possibility (Im 2011). Some other Korean scholars, however, share my skepticism (Chŏng 2004).

RELYING ON UNRELIABLE SOURCES

The same reliance on Chinese characters, both for the core terminology of what is proclaimed to be the Korean indigenous tradition of Sŏndo and for the actual body of texts that, though written in Sino-Korean in standard Chinese grammar, are presented as ancient Korean texts, can be found in some recently "discovered" texts that play a central role in supporting the claim that Sŏndo has ancient Korean roots. (Tamul Minjok yŏn'guso 1993) One of the most frequently cited of those texts, alleged to date back to the Tan'gun era, is the *Chŏnbugyŏng* (Celestial amulet sutra). This is a short text, only 81 Chinese characters long. Not only is the *Chŏnbugyŏng* of doubtful authenticity, since no versions predating its twentieth-century "rediscovery" have been found, even if it were authentic it could not be used to prove that Tan'gun invented Sŏndo, since there is nothing in that text that explicitly refers to Sŏndo or any longevity-enhancing breathing practices or physical exercises (Baker 2001; Kim 2006).

On the other hand, there are a few pre-twentieth-century works that draw a specific connection between Tan'gun and the pursuit of a much longer life span. The *Chŏnghak chip* (Collected anecdotes of Master Blue Crane) of Cho Yŏ-jŏk (dates unknown), a late sixteenth-century collection of stories about the Korean search for longevity, lists Tan'gun, along with Tan'gun's equally mythical father and grandfather, as the founders of the Korean *sŏn* tradition. However, the grandfather, Hwan'in, is said to have learned about *sŏn* techniques from the Chinese immortal Guangchengzi. Guangchengzi, who is introduced in chapter 11 of the *Zhuangzi*, is also said to have taught the secrets of immortality to Huangdi, the legendary first emperor of China, blurring the distinction between Chinese *xian* and Korean *sŏn* (Cho and Ham 1992, 218). A similar work, the *Haedong ijŏk* (Traces of extraordinary people in Korea), written by Hong Man-jong (1643–1725) in 1666, gives Tan'gun a more important role, crediting him with being the actual founder of Sŏndo, with no mention of a Chinese connection (Kim 2005, 84). Though these two works are not twentieth-century forgeries, nonetheless neither can be trusted as reliable accounts of what happened almost 3,000 years before they were written, since they provide no corroborating documentation. On the issue of when Sŏndo as the pursuit of longevity through breathing practices and physical exercises emerged in Korea, they are no more trustworthy than such works as *Hwandan kogi* (Old records of the Hwan and Tan [empires]), *Kyuwŏn sahwa* (Tales of history from the garden of discernment), and *Pudoji* (Chronicle of the heavenly seal capital), which are twentieth-century creations masquerading as ancient texts (Cho 2001).

INTERNAL ALCHEMY IN CHOSŎN KOREA

We are on firmer ground when we discuss actual internal alchemy practices, since we have several accounts of such practices from Chosŏn dynasty authors, starting as early as the fifteenth century. We can find the sorts of breathing exercises and physical exercises associated with internal alchemy recommended in some of the most important medical works of the entire Chosŏn dynasty period. For example, a 1445 court-commissioned compilation of medical advice, the *Ŭibang yuch'wi* (Classified collection of medical prescriptions), included a section on "promoting longevity." That section drew on several Chinese works with the character for *sŏn/xian* in their titles. It borrowed from them to provide a detailed description, with illustrations, of the sorts of physical exercises Chinese internal alchemists used to transform their physiology so that they could live much longer. We do not see any reference in this text to Tan'gun, to any purported ancient Korean religion of Sŏndo, or even to indigenous Korean antecedents for these exercises (Chŏng, Han, and Kim 2014; Kim 1981, 221–226; Yi 1999, 52–57).

The Chosŏn dynasty's most famous medical encyclopedia, *Tongŭi pogam* (A treasury of eastern medicine), compiled in 1613 by Korea's most respected premodern physician, Hŏ Chun (1539–1614), has similar advice drawn from Chinese sources on how to enhance longevity. Hŏ shared with his readers the Daoist assumption that they could use certain breathing practices and physical exercises to expel decaying or weak *ki* [animating matter-energy] from their bodies and replace it with fresh, healthy *ki*, and could then use their "cinnabar fields" (sites for processing *ki* that are believed to be located in the abdomen, the chest, and the forehead) to refine that *ki* further so that it could support both a healthier body and a more enlightened mind (Hŏ Chun 1998, 72–78; *Dongui bogam* 2013 Part I: 21–40). He suggests one particular practice which sounds very Daoist. He advised rising early in the morning to sit facing east while exhaling three times to get rid of all your old *ki*. Then he suggested holding your breath for a while before breathing in clean *ki* through your nose. While doing that, he suggested further, let saliva collect in your mouth, swirl it around in your mouth for a while, then swallow it. This, he argued, will send *ki* to its rightful abode, your lower cinnabar field, where processing can begin (Hŏ 1998, 75–76; *Dongui bogam* 2013, 29–32).

Though some non-Daoists, including some Buddhists and even some Neo-Confucians, used some of the techniques Hŏ Chun recommends (after all *ki* was an important component of the overall East Asia view of both the human body and universe in general and nourishing one's *ki* was generally considered essential for maintaining a healthy body and mind), these techniques find their most elaborate justification and elaboration in Daoist texts and therefore are normally associated with Daoism (Engel-hardt 1989). They are never, before the twentieth century, associated with any indigenous Korean tradition of longevity-enhancing practices. Moreover, as is the case with the *Ŭibang yuch'wi*, nothing is said in Ho Chun's work about Tan'gun or Sŏndo. Instead, all of his references are to Chinese sources.

Since Confucian filial piety required sons to maintain their health as long as possible so they could take care of their parents, we also find dis-cussions in writings by non-physician Confucian scholars of techniques they believed could enhance their health and longevity. The oldest such discussion extant today is found in the writings of the fifteenth-century eccentric Kim Si-sŭp (1425–1493). He wrote that by breathing in a certain way, men can slowly expel harmful *ki* from their bodies while accumulating good, life-prolonging *ki*. One specific technique he suggested is to rise early and sit facing the east, welcoming the *ki* that you breathe in through your nose (you are supposed to breathe in through your nose only and breathe out only through your mouth). He wrote that then you should slowly close your mouth so that less and less *ki* escapes, allowing you to accumulate more and more life-enhancing *ki* with each breath (Yi 1977, 214–225; Kim 1973, 294 [17:191–120a]).

Kim Si-sŭp promised that if we couple such bodily practices with virtuous conduct and also cultivate a composed mind, we can become *sinsŏn*, godlike immortals, though he makes no reference to Tan'gun as a pioneer *sinsŏn*. A century later, Chŏng Nyŏm (1506–1549) made a similar promise. Elaborating on the techniques Kim Si-sŭp had introduced, Chŏng wrote that the way to cultivate our own internal elixir of longevity was quite simple. We should begin by retaining the *ki* we breathe in, refraining from excessive exhalation that would allow *ki* to escape, and then store that accumulated *ki* in the part of our body in which it can be most effectively utilized. We do this by lowering our eyes to focus on our nose while we point our nose toward our navel. This ensures that we focus on the lower cinnabar field, where we want our *ki* to go, since that is the only place that can process it properly. Chŏng makes no reference to this technique originating with Tan'gun (Cho and Han 1992, 275–278; Yi 1977, 229–239; Yi 2003).

Evidence of how widespread, and mainstream, interest in the internal alchemy techniques introduced in books from China became during the Chosŏn era can be seen in the life of T'oegye Yi Hwang (1501–1570), one of the greatest Neo-Confucian philosophers in all Korean history. T'oegye dedicated most of his scholarly time to explicating the moral psychology of *li* [the network of patterns governing appropriate interaction throughout the universe, embracing both human society and the natural world] and *ki*, arguing for the need to clearly distinguish between moral emotions generated by *li* and selfish emotions generated by *ki*. However, T'oegye also took the time to copy by hand a Ming dynasty text called in Korean *Hwarin simbang*, compiled by Zhu Quan (1378–1448). This work includes both specific directions for physical exercises as well as directions for cinnabar-field meditation, with the usual injunctions to rise early in the morning, face east, and breathe out more than you breathe in to get rid of your bad *ki* (Yi Ch'ŏl-hwan 1993; Yi 1992). T'oegye also wrote to one of his disciples that the best way to nurture your innate moral nature is to combine regulating breathing with conscientiously fulfilling the obligations of your everyday life. He noted, "practicing breath control over a long period of time will not only keep you healthy, it will also help you preserve the moral nature you were endowed with at birth" (Yi 1999, 316).

The belief that Daoist-style breathing exercises and physical exercises could significantly enhance longevity was widespread enough that even Chŏng Yak-yong (1762–1836), known for his skeptical approach to fengshui and even to some aspects of Neo-Confucian metaphysics, gave it some credence. Chŏng reported that there was a bookseller people called "Cho the Immortal." He got that appellation because, Tasan wrote, he appeared to never grow older.

> In 1776, I happened to run into him in Seoul. He looked like he was only 45 years old or so. When I ran into him again 24 years later, in 1800, he hadn't changed a bit. He looked like he was still only 45 or so. I haven't seen him personally since then, but some people I know who ran across him after that say that he still looked the same in 1821. And someone who saw him way back in 1756 reported he looked like he was around 45 then as well! If he was 45 then and is still alive today, he must be over 100 years old. How can he still have a full beard without a touch a grey in it? (Chŏng 1970, I, 17, 32b–33a)

Neither T'oegye, nor most of his fellow Chosŏn Koreans who practiced internal alchemy, or even non-practitioners like Chŏng Yak-yong who nevertheless suspected such practices might be effective, connected those breathing practices and physical exercises with Tan'gun or an ancient tradition of Sŏndo. Instead, they recognized their Chinese origins. It was not until after the Chosŏn dynasty fell in 1910 and after Koreans had suffered under Japanese colonial rule for thirty-five years that the nationalism Japanese rule stimulated gave birth to the claim that Korea had an ancient religious tradition of Sŏndo dating back to at least the time of Tan'gun, and that Sŏndo included those breathing practices and physical exercises previously identified as Chinese in origin.

THE CLAIM OF AN ANCIENT
TRADITION OF SŎNDO EMERGES

As noted above, already in the Chosŏn dynasty there were a few writers who connected Tan'gun with a Korean tradition of *sinsŏn*, mountain immortals. However, none of them linked him to any of the specific physical exercises and breathing practices that were being practiced by a few Chosŏn scholars and physicians. Early in the twentieth century, the notion of religion as a distinct component of human culture was introduced to Korea (Baker 2006). That inspired a few nationalistic writers, such as Ch'oe Nam-sŏn (1890–1957) and Yi Nŭng-hwa (1865–1945), to claim that Tan'gun had founded a religion in Korea long before the foreign religions of Buddhism and Daoism, and the philosophy of Confucianism had become part of Korean culture (Yun 2012). However, they failed to point out any specific practices associated with that religion, other than claiming that Tan'gun taught Koreans to worship heaven (or, in the case of Taejonggyo, worship Tan'gun along with his father and grandfather as a trinitarian God). It was not until the last quarter of the twentieth century that we begin to see the emergence of the invented tradition that linked the notions that Tan'gun not only had an extremely long life and that Korea had its own tradition of enhancing longevity with the specific physical exercises and breathing practices that had previously been associated with China but were now credited to Tan'gun (Chŏng 2009, 97).

The best-known examples of this constructed tradition can be found in the writings of Yi Sŭng-hŏn, better known as Ilchi Lee. Yi is the promoter of something he calls Dahn Hak, which he teaches through a chain of exercise studios under the brand name Dahn World or Dahn Yoga (Dahn refers to the cinnabar fields in the human body). One of his earliest English-language introductions to his teachings claims:

> The origin of Dahn Hak goes back approximately 10,000 years. . . . The inspired teachings of Shin Shon Do [Sinsŏndo] were handed down through the three ancient Korean scriptures, Ch'on Bu Kyong [Ch'ŏnbugyŏng], Sam Il Shin Go, and Ch'am Jon Kye Kyong [Ch'amjŏn kyegyŏng]. . . . After the Great Korean Master Il Tchi, Lee Seung Heun had been enlightened through a long and agonizing self-training, he realized his disciplines of exercise were the same as those of Shin Shon Do. (Lee 1997, 19)

Yi Sŭng-hŏn was not the first person to make that claim, however. In 1967 a man named Ko Kyŏng-min began teaching what he called Kuksŏndo (the way of our country's immortals) (Im 1986). He claimed he had learned those techniques, which were almost 10,000 years old, from some immortals he had met when he became lost in Korea's mountains (Na 2014). At first he did not attract much interest, but in the 1980s, after a best-selling novel entitled *Tan* (cinnabar) reintroduced Koreans to the notion of immortals and the supernatural powers they said they possessed, more and more Koreans began to read his books and learn his techniques (Kukhak yŏn'guwŏn 2010, 737).

Ko was soon joined by others who claimed that they were reviving the ancient longevity-enhancing techniques taught by Tan'gun. One such claimant was Kwŏn T'ae-hun, who provided the material Kim Chŏng-bin drew on to write the best-selling novel *Tan* (Cinnabar) (Kim 1984), and was also the head of Taejonggyo (the religion based on worship of Tan'gun) from 1982 until 1992. In 1986, building on the popularity of that novel, Kwŏn founded the Korean Society for the Study of Cinnabar Meditation (Han'guk Tanhakhoe) in order to promote Kwŏn's teachings about what he called Korea's unique spiritual tradition and its associated practices (1997, 339). However, he was not alone. In the early 1980s an explicitly religious movement, known both as Ch'ŏnjonhoe (The Society of Celestial Majesty) and as Ch'ŏndo Sŏnbŏp (The Celestial Way of the Immortals), also started teaching what it claims are internal alchemy-like health-enhancing techniques invented in Korea over 6,000 years ago (Ch'ŏndo sŏnbŏp 2017). In addition, Gicheon (Kich'ŏn, the *ki* of Heaven), a group that says it is not religious at all and is only interested in promoting health and longevity, appeared about the same time Kuksŏndo appeared in the 1970s and grew in prominence over the decades that followed (Ten 2017). Gicheon, too, maintains that its teachings and practices have been passed down secretly by Korean mountain immortals for thousands of years.

However, the most visible proponent of the claim that Tan'gun taught longevity-enhancing techniques that have been rediscovered in the late twentieth century is Yi Sŭng-hŏn and his Dahn Hak/Dahn World/Dahn Yoga movement (Yi Sŭng-hŏn 1993a, 7–12). Yi reports that, in 1980, he climbed up to what he describes as a Buddhist temple on the slopes of Mount Moak outside of the city of Chŏnju in southwestern Korea to go without food or sleep for twenty-one days in a row in order to concentrate on experiencing the power of *ki* in the cosmos as well as within his own body. It is there, he writes, that he was enlightened to the fact that his true self was nothing other than the cosmic energy (*ki*) that fills the universe. Only later, he writes, did he realize that he had become enlightened to the teachings and practices of the ancient Sŏndo practitioners (Yi Sŭng-hŏn 1993b, 207–216; Lee 2011, 31–40).

A few years after he descended from Mount Moak, he began renting rooms under the name Tanhak sŏnwŏn (Centers for becoming *sinsŏn* through cinnabar field respiration) to provide more formal instruction of what he had learned during his spiritual quest. Those first few Tanhak sŏnwŏn halls were soon joined by many more, at first in Korea and then, starting in the 1990s, in the United States and Japan as well, eventually growing into a multinational organization under the umbrella title of Dahn World. In the 1990s, Yi also began publishing books, first in Korean and then later in English, explaining the breathing practices and physical exercises he recommended as well as the philosophy behind them. For his books, he adopted the pen name Ilchi, "he who points to the Way."

Ilchi has established a Sŏndo empire that spans the globe. In the process, he has modified his message in order to reach a larger audience. He insists that his teachings and practice are a "religion which is not a religion" (Yi Sŭng-hŏn 1993b, 6), and now downplays the emphasis on the three sacred scriptures of Taejonggyo (including the *Ch'ŏnbugyŏng*) that was a conspicuous feature of his teachings in the 1990s, though he has continued to emphasize respect for Tan'gun. However, his organization has spun off an explicitly religious organization (though it denies any connection) that was once called Sŏnbulgyo (the teachings of the Sinsŏn and the Enlightened One), but recently changed its name to simply Sŏn'gyo to express the belief that it is a revival of the ancient indigenous religion of Korea (Yun 2016; Han Sang-jin 2010).

Within his own organization, one of his most dramatic changes has been to rename his breathing exercises. Since the early part of this century, he has downplayed the traditional Daoist term "cinnabar field respiration" and began using the term "brain respiration" (*noe hohŭp*) instead, though the basic techniques he teaches have not changed. In another dramatic change, he has gone beyond Tan'gun and now promotes belief in Mago, whom he claims is the goddess of the earth who was once worshipped by humanity and should be so honored again (Lee 2002).

Mago is a name that has been used in Korea in the past for female mountain gods as well as for anthropomorphized creative forces of nature, but Mago was never given the position of supreme deity that Ilchi and his organization try to give her now (Kang 1992). She was a god but not God. Ilchi bases his claim to the contrary on a book called *Pudoji* (The chronicle of the heavenly seal capital), which was published for the first time in 1986 but is presented as an ancient text. (As is usual with such texts, we are told that the original text is no longer available but fortunately a man who escaped from North Korea to the South in the late 1940s, leaving the original manuscript behind, had memorized it and was able to reproduce it [Pak 2002, 5–9].) That book claims that Mago created the human race 10,000 years ago and presided over a paradise (called Mago's castle—Mago sŏng) in which the first humans lived until they were expelled for eating fruit Mago had forbidden them to eat.

There is no mention of any specific techniques for enhancing longevity in the *Pudoji*. Nevertheless, followers of Ilchi claim that Mago is the actual origin of Sŏndo, which provides the basis for Ilchi's assertion that Sŏndo is 10,000 years old. Ilchi now claims the point of his breathing exercises is to "feel the energy of Mago," so you can be in touch with the soul of the earth. He has written that chanting Mago's name while engaged in breathing meditation will be particularly helpful (Lee 2002, 77–84). Mago is important enough to Ilchi and his followers that in 2009 a twelve-meter-tall statue of Mago was erected near a highway, near Ilchi's Mago's Garden retreat center, in Sedona, Arizona (Chŏng 2015, 177). However, opposition from Sedona residents led to that statue being torn down the next year (Lemons 2010). A statue of Tan'gun, however, remains in Ilchi's Sedona retreat center.

Another Tan'gun statue, recently joined by a statue of Mago, has been erected near the University of Brain Education built by Ilchi in Ch'ŏnan in South Korea. That is a small university but nonetheless supports a research institute for Dahn Hak as well as a research institute for Kukhak (literally, "national studies," but defined as actually the study of Sŏndo) (Kukhak yŏn'guwŏn 2010, 760). Since 2006 the University of Brain Education has also been publishing a scholarly journal called *Sŏndo munhwa* (*Journal of Korean Sŏndo Culture*). With his university and its associated research centers, along with his practice halls around the world and his retreat center in Arizona, as well as his publications and even that

scholarly journal, Ilchi Yi Sǔng-hǒn has done more than any other Korean
to promote the assertion that Korea once had an ancient spiritual tradition of Sǒndo, which has been revived in the modern world.

As this volume shows, Sǒndo is not Korea's only invented tradition.
Nor is Korea the only country on earth to paint new traditions with the
patina of age. At a time when modern means of transportation and communication are stimulating globalization that threatens to erase cultural
differences, it is not surprising that some people will seize upon elements
from their culture's past as markers of a distinctive identity to help them
resist absorption by that homogenized world. It is also not surprising
that they often inadvertently create something new out of those old elements, since, after all, they are creating cultural markers that they hope
will survive in the modern world and therefore must produce something
that is a modernized version of tradition. That is precisely what some
Koreans have done with the invented tradition of Sǒndo.

Sǒndo has been constructed from ancient Korean tales of a legendary
first ruler who became a mountain god, from an equally ancient tradition
of belief that some human beings are able to overcome normal physical frailty and live for hundreds of years, and from the actual practice of
Chinese internal alchemy techniques during the Chosǒn dynasty. They
have added to that mix the imported concept of religion and created the
argument that, long before Korea was exposed to Chinese culture and
Chinese religions, Korea had its own ancient religion, or at least its own
spiritual tradition, which involves breathing practices and physical exercises that enhance longevity. The absence of any reliable documentary evidence for such an ancient belief system is irrelevant. Equally irrelevant is
the fact that all the terminology for those practices is Sino-Korean. There
are no indigenous Korean terms for either the theoretical underpinnings
of those practices or for the actual practices themselves. Even the term
Sǒndo itself is a Sino-Korean term. Nevertheless, the pressure to resist
cultural homogenization and assert an ancient distinctive Korean cultural
identity that survives into the modern world and distinguishes Korean
culture from other cultures has led many Koreans to believe that, just as
the Chinese can claim Daoism and Confucianism as distinctive cultural
markers and the Japanese can do the same with Shinto, Koreans can point
to Sǒndo as proof that Koreans in the distant past were just as original
and just as creative as their neighbors.

GLOSSARY

Cho Yŏ-jŏk 趙汝籍
Ch'oe Ch'i-wŏn 崔致遠
Ch'oe Nam-sŏn 崔南善
Ch'ŏnan 天安
Ch'ŏnbugyŏng 天符經
Ch'ŏndo Sŏnbŏp 天道仙法
Chŏng Nyŏm 鄭磏
Chŏng Yak-yong 丁若鏞
Ch'ŏnghak chip 青鶴集
Ch'ŏnjonhoe 天尊會
Chŏnju 全州
Dahn Hak 丹學
Gicheon (Kich'ŏn) 氣天
Guangchengzi 廣成子
Haedong ijŏk 海東異蹟
Han'guk Tanhakhoe 韓國丹學會
Hŏ Chun 許浚
Hong Man-jong 洪萬宗
hongik in'gan 弘益人間
Hwandan kogi 桓檀古記
Hwan'in 桓因
Hwan'ung 桓雄
hwarang 花郎
Hwarang segi 花郎世紀
Hwarin simbang 活人心方
Ilchi 一指
ki 氣
Kim Si-sŭp 金時習
Ko Kyŏng-min 高庚民
Kukhak 國學

kuksŏn 國仙
Kuksŏndo 國仙道
Kwŏn T'ae-hun 權泰勳
Kyuwŏn sahwa 揆園史話
Mago 麻姑
Mago sŏng 麻姑城
Moaksan 母岳山
noe hohŭp 腦呼吸
Pudoji 符都誌
p'ungnyu 風流
Samguk sagi 三國史記
Samguk yusa 三國遺事
Sin'gyo 神教
sinsŏn 神仙
sŏn 仙
Sŏnbulgyo 仙佛教
Sŏndo 仙道
Sŏn'gyo 仙教
Sŏnsa 仙史
Taejonggyo 大倧教
Tan 丹
Tan'gun 檀君
Tanhak sŏnwŏn 丹學仙院
T'oegye Yi Hwang 退溪 李滉
Tongŭi pogam 東醫寶鑑
Ŭibang yuch'wi 醫方類聚
Yi Nŭng-hwa 李能和
Yi Sŭng-hŏn 李承憲
Zhu Quan 朱權
Zhuangzi 莊子

NOTES

1. Han Yŏng-u (2010, 89–90) says he became an immortal; Han (2001, 67–68)
   says he became merely a mountain spirit, which is what the original text
   of the myth says.

2. One scholar at least pushes the origins of Sŏndo much further back than Tan'gun, claiming it originated over 10,000 years ago with Tan'gun's grand-father Hwan'in (Chŏng 2009, 100).
3. Evidence that p'ungnyu refers to an elegant lifestyle can be found in Ch'oe (2016, 211).

REFERENCES

Baker, Don. 2001. "The Heavenly Amulet Sutra." In *Korea Between Tradition and Modernity: Selected Papers from the 4th Pacific and Asian Conference on Korean Studies*, edited by Yunshik Chang et al., 236–249. Vancouver: Institute of Asian Research, the University of British Columbia.

———.2006. "The Religious Revolution in Modern Korean History: From Ethics to Theology and from Ritual Hegemony to Religious Freedom." *Review of Korean Studies* 9 (3): 249–275.

Byington, Mark E., ed. 2009. *Early Korea: The Samhan Period in Korean History*. Cambridge, MA: Korea Institute, Harvard University.

Cho In-sŏng. 2001. "Chaeyasasŏ wisŏron: *Tan'gi kosa, Hwandan kogi, Kyuwŏn saghwa*rŭl chungsimŭro" [A discussion of the authenticity of the histories favored by amateur historians: Focusing on *Tan'gi kosa, Hwandan kogi*, and *Kyuwŏn Sahwa*]. In *Tan'gun kwa Kojosŏnsa* [Tan'gun and the history of Old Chosŏn], edited by No T'ae-don, 210–239. Seoul: Sagyejŏl ch'ulp'ansa.

Cho Yŏ-jŏk and Han Mu-oe. 1992. *Haedong chŏndorok. Ch'ŏnghak chip* [A record of the transmission of the Way to Korea and collected anecdotes of Master Blue Crane]. Original texts with translation by Yi Chong-ŭn. Seoul: Posŏng munhwasa.

Ch'oe Chun-sik. 1994. "Yi Nŭng-hwa ŭi Chosŏn Togyosa" [The history of Daoism in Korea according to Yi Nŭng-hwa]. In *Uri Munhwa ŭi ppurirŭl ch'annŭn Yi Nŭng-hwa yŏn'gu: Han'guk chonggyo sahagŭl chungsimŭro* [Studies of Yi Nŭng-hwa who sought the roots of our culture: Focusing on his study of the history of religion in Korea], Yi Chong-ŭn et al., 87–108. Seoul: Chimmundang.

Ch'oe Kwangsik. 2016. "Ch'oe Ch'iwŏn's P'ungnyudo and Present-day Hallyu." *International Journal of Korean History* 21 (1): 193–220.

Ch'ŏndosŏnbŏp. 2017. "Ch'ŏndosŏnbŏp." Accessed July 17, 2017. http://www.chundo .org/pages.php?p=1

Chŏng Chi-hun, Han Pong-je, and Kim Tong-nyul. 2014. "Ŭibang yuch'wi ŭi doindo-e kwanhan yŏn'gu" [A study of the charts for Daoist physical exercises in the Ŭibang yuch'wi]. *Journal of Korean Medical History* 27 (1): 41–50.

Chŏng Kyŏng-hŭi. 2009. "Han'guk sŏndo wa Tan'gun." [Korean sŏndo and Tan'gun]. *Togyo munhwa yŏn'gu* 30:91–135.

———. 2015. "Hyŏndae 'Tan'gun undong' ŭi saeroun chŏn'gae wa tanhak" [The contemporary Tan'gun movement and new developments of cinnabar field studies]. *Sŏndo munhwa* 19:143–194.

Chŏng Se-gŭn. 2004. "Han'guk sinsŏn sasang ŭi chŏn'gae wa punp'a" [The development and fragmentation of the notion of mountain immortals in Korea]. In *Han'guk Koyu sasang munhwaron* [The debate over Korea's indigenous thought and culture], Hŏ Ch'ang-mu et al., 266–299. Sŏngnam: Academy of Korean Studies.

Chŏng Yak-yong. 1970. *Yŏyudang chŏnsŏ* [The complete writings of Yŏyudang Chŏng Yak-yong]. Seoul: Kyŏngin munhwasa.

Dongui bogam: Treasured Mirror of Eastern Medicine. 2013. Translated by An Sang-wu, Kwŏn Oh-min, and Lee Jŏng-hwa (Yi Chŏng-hwa). Seoul: Ministry of Health and Welfare.

Engelhardt, Ute. 1989. "Qi for Life: Longevity in the Tang." In *Taoist Meditation and Longevity Techniques*, edited by Livia Kohn, 263–296. Ann Arbor: Center for Chinese Studies, University of Michigan.

Han Sang-jin. 2010. "Tan wŏltŭ." *Sindonga*, January. Accessed July 17, 2017. http://shindonga.donga.com/3/all/13/109037/3

Han Yŏng-u. 2001. *Tasi Ch'annŭn Uri Yŏksa* [Recovering the history of our nation]. Seoul: Kyŏngsewŏn.

———. 2010. *Han'gu Sŏnbi Chisŏngsa: Han'gugin ŭi munhwajŏk DNA.* P'aju: Chisik sanŏpsa.

Han, Young Woo (Han Yŏng-u). 2010. *A Review of Korean History.* Vol. 1, *Ancient/ Goryeo Era.* Translated by Hahm Chaibong. Paju: Kyongsaewon.

———. 2014. *An Intellectual History of Seonbi in Korea.* Translated by Cho Yoon-jung. Paju: Jisik-sanup Publishing (translation of Han Yŏng-u [2010]).

Hŏ Chun. 1998. *Tongŭi pogam: Wŏnbon* [The original edition of the *Tongŭi pogam*]. Seoul: Namsandang. (An English translation is available: *Dongui bogam: Treasured Mirror of Eastern Medicine* [2013]).

Im Ch'ae-u. 2011. "Han'guk Sŏndo ŭi kiwŏn kwa Kŭn'gŏ munje" [The origin of Korean Sŏndo and the problems with the material used to address that question]. *Togyo munhwa yŏn'gu* 34:39–65.

Im Kyŏng-t'aek. 1986. "Kuksŏndo." *Korea Journal* 26 (8): 26–34.

Jorgensen, John. 1998. "Who Was the Author of the Tan'gun Myth?" In *Perspectives on Korea*, edited by Sang-oak Lee and Duk-soo Park, 222–255. Sydney: Wild Peony Press.

Kakhun. 1969. *Lives of Eminent Korean Monks: The Haedong Kosŭng Chŏn.* Translated by Peter H. Lee. Cambridge, MA: Harvard University Press.

Kang Chin-ok. 1992. "Mago halmi sŏlhwa-e nat'anan yŏsŏngsin kwannyŏn" [The goddess seen in the folktales about Grandmother Mago]. *Han'guk minsokhak* 25:3–47.

Kim Chŏng-bin. 1984. *Tan* [Cinnabar]. Seoul: Chŏngsin segyesa.

Kim Duk-Whang. 1988. *A History of Religions in Korea*. Seoul: Daeji Moonhwasa.

Kim Kyŏng-il. 2006. "A Study on the Research History of the Cheonbugyeong." *Research Journal of Korean Studies* 9 (3): 229–247.

Kim Kyŏng-t'ak 1971. "Han'guk wŏnsi chonggyosa, II: hanŭnim kwannyŏm paldalsa" [The original religion of Korea, II: The development of the concept of the God of Heaven]. In *Han'guk munhwasa tagye* [A survey of the cultural history of Korea], edited by *Koryŏ Taehakkyo minjok munhwa yŏn'guso* vi, 115–176. Seoul: Koryŏ Taehakkyo minjok munhwa yŏn'guso.

Kim Nak-p'il. 2005. *Chosŏn sidae ŭi naedan sasang: Kwŏn Kŭk-chung ŭi Togyo ch'ŏrhakchŏk sayu wa kŭ chŏn'gae* [Internal alchemy thought in the Chosŏn dynasty: The Daoist philosophical speculations of Kwŏn Kŭkchung and how his thinking developed]. Seoul: Taewŏn ch'ulp'an.

Kim Na-p'il, Pak Yŏng-ho, Yang Ŭn-yong, and Yi Chin-su. 2001. "Han'guk sŏndo sasang ŭi chŏn'gae" [The unfolding of Korean belief in immortals]. *Togyo munhwa yŏn'gu* [Research on Daoist culture] 15:9–180.

Kim Pu-sik. 1976. *Wanyŏk Samguk sagi pu wŏnmun* [A complete translation of the Samguk Sagi, with the original text attached]. Translated by Kim Chonggwŏn. Seoul: Kwangjo ch'ulp'ansa.

———. 2012. *The Silla Annals of the Samguk Sagi*. Translated by Edward J. Shultz and Hugh H. W. Kang with Daniel C. Kane. Sŏngnam: Academy of Korean Studies.

Kim Si-sŭp. 1973. *Maewŏldang chŏnjip* [The complete works of Kim Si-sŭp]. Seoul: Taedong munhwa yŏn'guso.

Kim Tu-jong. 1981. *Han'guk ŭihaksa* [The history of medicine in Korea]. Seoul: T'amgudang.

Kim Yong-ok. 1992. *Samguk yusa indŭk* [Index to the Memorabilia of the Three Kingdoms]. Seoul: T'ongnamu.

Kukhak yŏn'guwŏn [Institute for the study of our nation's history], ed. 2010. *Han'guk sŏndo ŭi yŏksa wa munhwa* [The history and culture of Korea's Sŏndo]. Ch'ŏnan: University of Brain Education Press.

Kwŏn T'ae-hun. 1997. *Minjok pilchŏn chŏngsin suryŏnbŏp* [The secret teachings of our people and the way to train the mind]. Seoul: Chŏngsin segyesa.

Lee, Hyun-hee, Park Sung-soo, and Yoon Nae-hyun. 2005. *New History of Korea*. Paju, Gyeonggi-do: Jimoondang.

Lee, Ilchi (Yi Sŭng-hŏn). 2002. *Unchain your Soul through Mago's Dream: Communing with the Earth's Soul*. Las Vegas: Healing Society.

————.2011. *The Call of Sedona: Journey of the Heart.* Sedona: Best Life Media.

Lee, Peter H. ed., 1993. *Sourcebook of Korean Civilization.* Vol. 1, *From Early Times to the Sixteenth Century.* New York: Columbia University Press.

Lee, Seung Heun (Yi Sŭng-hŏn). 1997. *Dahn Meditation: A Spiritual Exercise for Perfect Health and Happiness.* Seoul: Dahn Publishing.

Lemons, Stephen. 2010. "Mago Statue Dismantled, *Rolling Stone* Article Blasts Dahn Yogo as a Cult." *Phoenix New Times,* February 23. Accessed July 13, 2017. http://www.phoenixnewtimes.com/blogs/mago-sculpture-dismantled -rolling-stone-article-blasts-dahn-yoga-as-cult-6501433

Mason, David A. 2016. *Solitary Sage: The Profound Life, Wisdom, and Legacy of Korea's "Go-un" Choi Chiwon.* Seoul: Sanshinseon Publishing (ibooks edition).

McBride, Richard D., II. 2005. "The Hwarang Segi Manuscripts: An In-Progress Colonial Period Fiction." *Korea Journal* 45 (3): 230–260.

————.2008. *Domesticating the Dharma: Buddhist Cults and the Hwaŏn Synthesis in Silla Korea.* Honolulu: University of Hawai'i Press.

Min Yŏng-hyŏn. 2016 "Koyu sangŭrosŏ-ŭi p'ungnyudo wa Han'guk sŏndo-ŭi sangho yŏn'gwan mit kŭ silch'e-e kwanhan yŏn'gu [A study of the actual connections between p'ungnyudo and Sŏndo as Korea's unique way of thinking]. *Sŏndo Munhwa* [Sŏndo Culture] 20:45–81.

Na U-gwŏn. 2014. "Ch'ŏngsan sŏnsa Ko Kyŏng-min saengae wa sasang: Ch'ŏnin habil-e irŭnŭn yangsaengbŏp" [The life and thought of Ch'ŏngsan Master of Immortality Ko Kyŏng-min: His longevity-enhancing techniques that unite heaven and humanity]. *Togyo munhwa yŏn'gu* 41:67–93.

Pak Che-sang. 2002. *Pudoji* [The chronicle of the heavenly seal capital]. Translated by Kim Ŭn-su. Seoul: Han munhwa wŏn.

Rutt, Richard. 1961. "The Flower Boys of Silla (Hwarang): Notes on the Sources." *Transactions of the Royal Asiatic Society, Korea Branch* 38:1–66.

Sŏ Yŏng-dae. 1994. "Tan'gun kwan'gye munhŏn charyo yŏn'gu" [A study of the documentary material related to Tan'gun]. In *Tan'gun: kŭ ihae wa charyo* [Tan'gun: Documents and interpretations], edited by Yun I-hŭm et al., 47–81. Seoul: Seoul National University Press.

Tamul Minjok yŏn'guso, ed. 1993. *Yohae Han minjok ŭi pisŏ: Ch'ŏnbugyŏng esŏ Chŏnggamnok Kkaji* [Summary and exegesis of the hidden classics of the Korean people: From the *Ch'ŏnbugyŏng* to the *Chŏnggamnok*]. Seoul: Tamul.

Ten, Victoria. 2017. "Body and Ki in Gicheon: Practices of Self-Cultivation in Contemporary Korea." PhD diss., Leiden University.

Yi Chin-su. 1992. "T'oegye chŏ'lhak ŭi yangsaeng sasang-e kwanhan yŏn'gu" [Studies on ideas of longevity in T'oegye's philosophy]. In *Han'guk Togyo ŭi hyŏndaejŏk chomyŏng* [Korean Daoism in the light of the present day], 81–142. Seoul: Asea munhwasa.

——. 1999. *Han'guk yangsaeng sasang yŏn'gu* [A study of Korean thinking on prolonging life]. Seoul: Hanyang University Press.

——. 2003. "Yonghogyŏl-e Kwanhayŏ" [On dragon-tiger breathing]. *Togyo munhwa yŏn'gu* 19:97–142.

Yi Ch'ŏl-hwan. 1993. *Swipke ponŭn Hwarin simbang* [An easy introduction to the *Hwarin simbang*]. Seoul: Iljungsa.

Yi Kyu-gyŏng. 1959. *Oju yŏnmun changjŏn san'go* [Random expatiations of Yi Kyu-gyŏng]. Seoul: Tongguk munhwasa.

Yi Nŭng-hwa. 1977. *Chosŏn Togyosa* [The history of Daoism in Korea]. Translated by Yi Chong-ŭn. Seoul: Posŏng munhwasa.

Yi Sŭng-ho. 2015. *Han'guk Sŏndo wa Hyŏndae Tanhak* [Korea's Sŏndo and contemporary internal alchemy]. Seoul: Kukhak Charyowŏn.

Yi Sŭng-hŏn. 1993a. *Ch'ŏnjiin: Sae hanŭl kwa sae ttangŭl yonŭn saram* [Humans, heaven, and earth: People who open the door to a new heaven and a new earth]. Seoul: Hanmunhwa.

——. 1993b. *Tanhak: kŭ iron'gwa suryŏnbŏp* [Tanhak: The theory behind it and its methods of cultivation]. Seoul: Hanmunhwa.

Yi Yŏn-jae. 1989. *Koryŏsi wa sinsŏn sasang ŭi ihae* [Understanding the poetry of Koryŏ and thoughts about immortals]. Seoul: Asea munhwasa.

Yun Han-ju. 2016. "Sŏn'gyo ŭi ch'anggyo paegyŏng kwa sin'gwan yŏn'gu" [A study of the background to the founding of modern Sŏn'gyo and its concept of god]. *Sŏndo munhwa* 21:73–103.

Yun Yŏng-sil. 2012. "Tan'gun kwa Sindo: 1930nyŏndae chungban Ch'oe Nam-sŏn ŭi Tan'gun sinang buhŭngnon kwa simjŏn kaebal" [Tan'gun and Sindo: Ch'oe Nam-sŏn's attempt to revive worship of Tan'gun in the mid-1930s and the Mind Development Movement]. *Han'guk hyŏndae munhak yŏn'gu* 36:347–387.

PART II

Rewriting Tradition

Language

Introduction

ANDREW DAVID JACKSON
AND REMCO BREUKER

Prys Morgan (1983, 43–44) writes of the eighteenth-century revival of Welsh tradition and imagining of a Welsh identity distinct from that of England: "In this period Welsh scholars and patriots rediscovered the past, historical, linguistic and literary traditions, and where traditions were inadequate, they created a past which had never existed. Romantic mythologizing went to quite extraordinary lengths in Wales, leaving a permanent mark on its later history." One area of particular revival for the scholars and patriots was the Welsh language—for them it was the native tongue that provided a "pure and undefiled direct link" to early history (Morgan 1983, 71). Welsh intellectuals conflated linguistic origins with ethnic identity. For these intellectuals, Welsh was the backbone of a cultural identity that was truly distinct from that of the English who had politically dominated Wales for centuries and who had attempted to suppress the language from 1536 onward. As a result, the number of Welsh speakers had fallen, the quality of Welsh spoken had declined, and the uniqueness of Welsh and its beauty, creativity, and difference (in comparison to English) was no longer appreciated by its population. Morgan continues that within the arguments of these Welsh scholars, notions of "[d]ecay and revival are curiously intermixed, because very often those who bewailed the decay were the very ones who brought about the revival" (1983, 43).

The discussions of these eighteenth-century Welsh intellectuals provide many interesting parallels with nineteenth- and twentieth-century Korean movements to revive interest in the Korean language. From the late nineteenth century onward, Korean linguistic intellectual movements have sought to not only investigate their linguistic history, but to revive, restore, and preserve Korean. For these Korean intellectuals questions about the origins, development, and preservation of the Korean language and links between language and notions of ethnic identity and national identity became *particularly* important in the years between 1895 and 1910. This period saw the 1894–1895 Sino-Japanese War that reversed the traditional power balance of East Asia and the eventual loss of Korean sovereignty to Japanese colonialism. The seismic shifts that saw the demotion of China from a dominant position to the sick man of East Asia, the decoupling of Korea from Sinitic civilization, the growth of early Korean nationalism, and the eventual incorporation of Korea into a Japanese imperial Empire (Schmid 2002, 56). During the 1890s, intellectuals began to re-evaluate hangul in a more positive light and linked national language to modernity and efficiency by means of comparison with Western societies that used alphabetic scripts. Meanwhile, many nationalists saw the use of Chinese characters, along with Confucian thought and systems of governance, as part of Sinitic civilisation that was preventing the progression of both Korea (and Qing China) into a modern nation. This intellectual reassessment of hangul intensified because of the colonial experience (Lee and Ramsey 2011, 13; Schmid 2002, 257).[1] After the 1910 annexation of the Korean Peninsula by Japan, the Japanese colonial authorities imposed their own tongue as the national language and increasingly Korean people were pressured into using Japanese in order to get by in daily life (Ramsey 2006a, 58; Robinson 2007, 95). Following the imperial Army's invasion of Manchuria in 1937, Japanese colonial authorities intensified the attempt to assimilate the Korean population into a greater Japan and the promulgation of Japanese was a cornerstone of this effort. The colonial administration gradually closed all Korean publications, enforced Japanese language use in schools, arrested Korean linguists, and made colonial citizens adopt Japanese family names (Robinson 2007, 95; Schmid 2002, 258). Although researchers like Michael Robinson have argued that this language policy was often inconsistently and incompetently enforced and achieved mixed results (2007, 95), these colonial period efforts are popularly perceived by many in both the South and North to have been a full-blown attempt at cultural genocide (Ramsey 2006a, 58; Kim Jin-p'yŏng 1988, 97–98).

Given this understanding of the colonial period and the precolonial intellectual reassessment of the influence of Sinitic civilization on

Korean culture, it is perhaps unsurprising that before, during, and after the colonial period, Koreans have made concerted efforts to remove foreign influences from the language. The North and South Korean governments have succeeded in removing from popular use, vocabulary that had been adapted from Japanese during the colonial period such as *pyŏntto* (lunch box), *waribasi* (wooden chopsticks), and so on (Ramsey 2006a, 59). Both governments have sought to reduce the use of Chinese characters in everyday use and promote the exclusive use of the Korean alphabet, hangul (Sohn 2006, 55). North Korea has promoted a hangul-only policy for seventy years, and replaced Sino-Korean vocabulary with new formulations coined from native words (Sohn 2006, 55; Lee Hee-jae 2013). In the meantime, nationalistic movements in the South are still attempting to replace Sino-Korean words with Korean native words and remove Chinese character combinations of Japanese origin associated with politics or technology (Kim Hyŏng-gyu 1988, 125–127). Language has been stressed by Korean intellectuals not only because it helped establish a distinct national identity in relation to other East Asian neighbors. For intellectuals in both Koreas, preserving and reviving the Korean language and even purifying it of foreign influences represented something akin to the protection of a national cultural identity that had been under threat of annihilation under colonialism. This process of nativizing is still an unfinished and ongoing project.

One major obstacle for those governmental and non-governmental agencies attempting to cleanse the Korean language of its non-native influence, is the massive historical influence of foreign culture especially that of imperial China and Japan on Korean language, culture, and society. The Korean lexicon, for example, is made up of Sino-Korean, Sino-Japanese, and other foreign loanwords that account for between 50 and 70 percent of the total lexis and is therefore, in the words of Ho-min Sohn, "integral and indispensable" to communication (2006, 44; Kim Hyŏng-gyu 1988, 125). Language like culture is not, as Andre Schmid (2002, 64) has observed, "as objective as shards of pottery . . . [that can be] sought, retrieved and restored—in short, returned to an untainted, original state." With this obstacle in mind, the effort to renew, revive, and preserve Korean, and trace the historical development of the language has provided fertile ground for the invention of traditions about language.

One area that has been the source of great controversy has been about the origins, use, and spread of the native Korean alphabet. Hangul is a remarkable creation because as Gary Ledyard (1997, 35) observes, in most cases alphabets evolve over many years and are the products of many individuals, not a single man or a small group of intellectuals.[2] In comparison to Chinese characters, hangul is relatively straightforward to learn, and rules of spelling and pronunciation consistent. Yet many questions remain about the precise function of the alphabet, why it never spread until long after its creation and how it was eventually popularized. Conventional wisdom has it that King Sejong (1397–1450; r. 1418–1450) commissioned the script as an educational gift to his people (Lee 1988, 74; Kim 2005, 13; Ramsey 2006b, 26). That the alphabet was painstakingly created and then immediately shelved was due solely to the opposition of a conservative bureaucracy opposed to any reform that might take Chosŏn rule away from Sinitic civilization (Kim 2005, 13; Ledyard 1997, 73).

The explanation of its original function is backed by empirical evidence in the *Hunmin chŏng'ŭm haerye* (Explanations and examples of the correct sounds for the instruction of the people), which states that the alphabet was created for the benefit of the population as an attempt to increase general literacy (Kim-Renaud 1997, 2–3; Kim 2005, 13). This narrative in which an enlightened Korean king acts for the benefit of his people against foreign cultural influence also sits well with nationalistic interpretations of the development of Korean (Wang 2014, 59–60). Yet this version also raises questions that have never been answered within this narrative: Especially, why go to the bother of creating an alphabet to empower the people but never enforce it? How was it that a Korean king was encouraging universal literacy many centuries before enlightened rulers were doing the same in other geographical contexts? Why was hangul used only by some of the least empowered in society?[3]

Over the years this popular narrative has been challenged from many directions. For example, the Korean alphabet was not developed in a vacuum but in the context of the creation of alphabets in other parts of East and Central Asia (Lee 1988, 71; Ledyard 1997). The prime function of the alphabet may not have been just to promote literacy amongst the population but to help train Korean interpreters in the pronunciation of the Ming-style Chinese vernacular for their vital interactions with their counterparts at the Ming court (Wang 2014). The reason the Korean script was never enforced is because the Chosŏn court wished to keep the invention of the new tool secret from the Ming court that would have seen the creation of hangul as a direct challenge to its cultural sovereignty (Wang 2014).

Of course not all of these revised historical discourses have been generally accepted, but this may account for the difference between a historical discourse and an invented tradition. The difference is the depth to which the narrative is embedded within the collective consciousness. The universal literacy and empowerment thesis runs deep.

The two chapters in this section evaluate two other invented traditions related to the history of the Korean language. As with the aforementioned case of Welsh, the chapter authors interrogate the intellectual movements that bemoaned the decay of the national language in an attempt to simultaneously revive Korean. In her chapter, Eunseon Kim discusses the construction of the notion that Korea has historically always been "a nation of propriety" or *Tongbang yeŭi chi kuk*. She reaches the conclusion that politeness or propriety (*yeŭi*) now functions "as a marker of an ethno-national character," but her research shows that historically, the concept of *yeŭi* has not been unified or consistently understood. *Yeŭi* in a Neo-Confucian context carries a very different bandwidth of possible meanings than *yeŭi* in its present-day incarnation of common politeness. The historical examples mobilized to promote *yeŭi* as a defining national characteristic employ both authentic source materials (but possibly interpreted out of a proper context) and forged materials presented as more authentic than anything else. Ancient descriptions of cultures on the Korean Peninsula, vague ascriptions of the characteristic of "propriety" to possible ancestors of later peoples on the Korean Peninsula, even Tan'gun, is roped in to support the historical politeness of Korean civilization. Interestingly, Kim also shows how this invented tradition of always having been proper or polite could be interpreted to mean completely different things, depending on who did the interpreting.

Andreas Schirmer's contribution to the analysis of invented traditions comes from the perspective of translation studies. Schirmer charts in considerable detail how a country that for centuries produced most of its literary and other written texts in Literary Sinitic, made the transition to writing in hangul almost exclusively. Interestingly, rather than focusing on the invention of a new tradition, Schirmer concentrates on what happens when a society cuts itself off from the major traditions that have shaped it for a millennium if not longer. He does so by invoking notions prevalent in heritage studies and devotes considerable attention to state-sponsored cultural policies to protect the "authentic" traditions of writing in Literary Sinitic. Noting the existential difficulties that inevitably accompany radical transitions such as this, he reaches the conclusion that in dealing with the fact that South Koreans now are effectively cut off from their historical heritage, the government has invested heavily in countenancing this by translating as many works in Literary Sinitic into contemporary Korean as is feasible. This gives rise to yet another invented tradition because the texts, and their crucial intertextuality and original context, are lost in translation, replaced by a hangul-based understanding of the world of Literary Sinitic—a new tradition, freshly invented, with the added bonus of being entirely Korean (where works in Literary Sinitic always were multivalent in this aspect), especially important in the age of globalization.

GLOSSARY

Hunmin chŏng'ŭm haerye 訓民正音解例

NOTES

1. Thanks to Lucien Brown for his help with this section introduction. As Lee and Ramsey observe: Koreans are often told that their language is related to Mongolian and Manchu, producing romantic visions of ancestors arriving on the Peninsula as "horse-riding warriors" (2011, 13).
2. There is disagreement over whether King Sejong was the sole inventor of hangul or whether he invented it together with a group of other scholars; see Yeon (2010).
3. It is commonly claimed that women and monks mainly used hangul; however, many members of these groups also used *hanmun* throughout the Chosŏn period.

REFERENCES

Kim, Hyŏng-gyu. 1988. "Chinese Characters and the Korean Language." In *The Korean Language*, edited by The Korean National Commission for UNESCO, 121–127. Seoul: Si-sa-yong-o-sa Publishers.

Kim, Jin-p'yŏng. 1988. "The Letterforms of Han'gŭl: Its Origin and Process of Transformation." In *The Korean Language*, edited by The Korean National Commission for UNESCO, 80–102. Seoul: Si-sa-yong-o-sa Publishers.

Kim-Renaud, Young-Key. 1997. "Introduction." In *The Korean Alphabet: Its History and Structure*, edited by Young-Key Kim-Renaud, 1–9. Honolulu: University of Hawai'i Press.

Kim, Zong-su. 2005. *The History and Future of Hangeul: Korea's Indigenous Script*. Translated by Ross King. Folkestone, UK: Global Oriental.

Ledyard, Gary. 1997. "The International Linguistic Background of the Correct Sounds for the Instruction of the People." In *The Korean Alphabet: Its History and Structure*, edited by Young-Key Kim-Renaud, 31–87. Honolulu: University of Hawai'i Press.

Lee, Hee-Jae. 2013. "How North Korea Made Its English Korean Dictionary." In *Key Papers on Korea: Essays Celebrating 25 Years of the Centre of Korean Studies, SOAS, University of London*, edited by Andrew David Jackson, 135–150. Leiden: Brill.

Lee, Ki-moon (Yi Ki-mun). 1988. "Foundations of Hunmin Chŏngŭm." In *The Korean Language*, edited by The Korean National Commission for UNESCO, 71–79. Seoul: Si-sa-yong-o-sa Publishers.

Lee, Ki-moon (Yi Ki-mun), and S. Robert Ramsey. 2011. *A History of the Korean Language*. Cambridge: Cambridge University Press.

Morgan, Prys. 1983. "From Death to a View: The Hunt for the Welsh Past in the Romantic Period." In *The Invention of Tradition*, edited by Eric Hobsbawm and Terence Ranger, 43–101. Cambridge: Cambridge University Press.

Ramsey, Robert S. 2006a. "Korean in Contact with Japanese." In *Korean Language in Culture and Society*, edited by Sohn Ho-min, 57–62. Honolulu: University of Hawai'i Press.

———. 2006b. "The Invention and Use of the Korean Alphabet." In *Korean Language in Culture and Society*, edited by Sohn Ho-min, 22–30. Honolulu: University of Hawai'i Press.

Robinson, Michael. 2007. *Korea's Twentieth-Century Odyssey: A Short History*. Honolulu: University of Hawai'i Press.

Schmid, Andre. 2002. *Korea Between Empires, 1895–1919*. New York: Columbia University Press.

Sohn, Ho-min. 2006. "Korean in Contact with Chinese." In *Korean Language in Culture and Society*, edited by Sohn Ho-min, 44–56. Honolulu: University of Hawai'i Press.

Wang, Sixiang. 2014. "The Sounds of Our Country: Interpreters, Linguistic Knowledge, and the Politics of Language in Early Chosŏn Korea." In *Rethinking East Asian Languages, Vernaculars, and Literacies, 1000–1919*, edited by Benjamin A. Elman, 58–95. Leiden: Brill.

Yeon, Jaehoon. 2010. "Was the Korean Alphabet a Sole Invention of King Sejong?" *Journal of Korean Culture* 14:183–216.

CHAPTER 4

The Language of the "Nation of Propriety in the East" (東方禮儀之國)?

The Ideological History of the Korean Culture of Politeness

EUNSEON KIM

Politeness has been treasured as a pillar of national culture in modern East Asian societies (Kádár and Mills 2011). *Yeŭi*, variously defined as "politeness; etiquette; good manners; observance of proper ritual; or propriety" in contemporary Korean societies, has come to mean more than a code of conduct or ethics; it can be further circulated as a marker of an ethno-national character—as a distinctive and often superior quality to distinguish self from others. The collective identity of Koreans has often been characterized by the epithet *Tongbang yeŭi chi kuk*, "Nation of Propriety in the East" (*Tongbang ryeŭi ji kuk* in the DPRK; henceforth NPE). According to the *P'yojun kugŏ taesajŏn* (Standard Korean dictionary),[1] there are two definitions of *yeŭi*: With the sinograph *yì* (K. *ŭi*) "proper, right or correct conduct," *yeŭi* refers to "etiquette and obligations that a person is supposed to observe." *Yeŭi* with the sinograph *yí* "ceremony, rites" (K. *ŭi*) offers a narrower meaning: "proper ways of speaking or demeanor that indicate one's respect." Among the many customary practices of *yeŭi* at present, the complicated linguistic system used to index politeness (*nop'im-mal* or *chondaet-mal*; henceforth honorifics) in Korean is a recurrent example of NPE. The Korean honorifics system is usually understood as the aggregate of grammaticalized and lexicalized

149

forms of "respect," primarily for one's superior by age or social status (see Hwang 1990).

YEŬI, COLLECTIVE IDENTITY, AND NATIONAL LANGUAGE

Popular discussions of Korean linguistic practice often consider the salient linguistic phenomenon of politeness as a sign that represents certain features of the linguistic community—something that Harkness (2015, 492) refers to as a "linguistic emblem." For example, an introductory booklet for general speakers of Korean compiled by the National Institute of Korean Language (henceforth, NIKL) presents a chapter titled "Polite Korean" as follows: "Koreans have valued etiquette so highly that Korea has been referred to as NPE. This life attitude is evident in language-use, which led to the development of honorifics" (Pak 2010, 81). Similarly, Korean language textbooks for foreigners teach a variety of Korean kinship terms as a manifestation of the shared characteristic of traditional Korean culture, specifically social hierarchism and collectivism (see Cho, Lee, and Schultz 2000, 51).

This chapter is intended as an attempt to critically approach the symbolic value of Korean linguistic politeness and honorifics as a hallmark of Korean ethno-national culture. Both lay speakers and linguists of Korean tend to presuppose as a premise that politeness culture has been a remarkable trait of Korea and Koreans. The hallmark of deferential culture in Korean is often attributed to Confucian tradition (see Yum 1988; Hong 2006). According to the NIKL's survey of national citizens' awareness of the Korean language in 2010, 78.1 percent of the total respondents agreed that the Korean cultural identity as NPE needs to be maintained through the use of honorifics. By contrast, some language professionals and social activists have criticized Korean honorifics as a "badge of social rank" and have called for linguistic reforms in an effort to build a more egalitarian and civil society (see Yi et al. 2018). This chapter considers a question raised at the start: how did the grammaticalized dimension of linguistic politeness come to carry such weight as a salient marker of Korean group identity?

Language has certainly lived with the speakers in a community throughout history, but the social meanings of language should not be simply seen as a natural outcome of society. People can employ language as an instrument to mobilize "imagined communities" (Anderson 1991), and the modern invention of tradition demanded a standardization of national language (Hobsbawm 1983). The vernacular language on the Korean Peninsula was no exception. The rise of linguistic nationalism from the late nineteenth century in Korea depended on the notion of language as "a vessel for the Korean spirit" in contemporary Korea (Kim 1994). The making of a national language called for the standardization of grammar, orthography, and regional variations, and the inculcation of nationalism in the language community (see King 2007).

A few studies have discussed the ideological aspects of Korean honorifics in the ROK (see Brown 2011), while most studies have focused on the DPRK's standard model of linguistic politeness as a cultural tool to propagate communist or socialist ideologies (see Yi 1996; Kim 1997; King 2014). This chapter turns attention away from language to the ideological history of NPE itself. Has the epithet always been part of a distinctive identity discourse that distinguishes Korea from others? How did the group of relevant epithets about politeness evolve as a recognizable cultural trope which epitomized the nation-bound notion of ethno-national tradition? What drove the search for a particular feature of "Korean" culture? The central goal of this chapter is to contextualize the creation of politeness as an ethno-national culture and its changes. My discussion focuses on the ideological construction of nationalist elites who appropriated the preexisting epithet to position their nation in the changing world order, primarily between the first decades of the twentieth century and 1945. Primary sources are drawn from a discourse analysis of NPE as illustrated in historical records and print media.

This chapter proceeds as follows. The first part calls into question the popular conception concerning the history of NPE and discusses why a particular forged text has been circulated widely but uncritically in popular discourses. The following section considers the cultural-political awareness of the notion of the "state of propriety" by examining how similar epithets were perceived in ancient Chinese and premodern Korean records. The latter part of this chapter deals with the initial transition whereby the conventional epithet came to prominence as an icon of group identity and underwent interpretive mutations. Central to this discussion is the transition from a cultural identity bound to Chinese civility to the ethno-national character of NPE used to distinguish one group from Others. Finally, I point out that the nature of the ethno-national group or traditional society produced by colonial intellectuals' ethno-national rhetoric was summoned again as an ideological mechanism in order to foster national identities and create national citizens in postwar Korea and later.

THE FORGED SOURCE OF
TONGBANG YEŬI CHI KUK

There are a few ancient Chinese historical texts frequently mobilized in South Korean popular media as putatively objective pieces of evidence in support of claims of historical depth for the epithet *Tongbang yeŭi chi kuk*. For example:

Book Nine, "Haiwai dong jing" (Classic of the Overseas East), in *Shanhai jing* (Classic of mountains and seas [c. fourth–first centuries BCE]). The sinographs qiang 羌 (tribe name) under Radical *yang* 羊 (sheep) and *yi* 夷 (barbarian) under Radical *da* 大 (big) in the *Shuowen jiezi* (Explaining the unit characters and analyzing the compound characters [c. second century CE] compiled by Xu Shen [c. 58–c. 148]). "Dongyi zhuan," article 75, in the *Hou Han shu* (The history of the Later Han dynasty [Fan Ye, 445, vol. 115]).

Although there are no specific mentions of the exact phrase *Tongbang yeŭi chi kuk* in them, these Chinese records are the earliest accounts to use the terms "land of gentlemen" (Ch. *junzi guo*; K. *kunja kuk*) or "land where gentlemen never die." In these records, the Yi tribe in the East or the Eastern Yi tribe (henceforth, Dongyi) is described as a people who are morally virtuous and culturally advanced, or else their territory is depicted as the ideal land where even Confucius wanted to live.[2] Attempts to trace the connections between the Dongyi and ancient Korean territory located in what is now Northeast China are rather commonplace in South Korean popular and even some scholarly discourses (see O 2015). However, as

I will discuss later, historians have come to understand "Dongyi" as a generic term used by the Han Chinese to refer to peripheral non-Chinese groups to the East of China in general, rather than as a term limited to the early states on the ancient Korean Peninsula.

There remains an additional supposedly ancient Chinese source that personal blogs, web pages of public groups, and popular books related to the historical origins of politeness in South Korea cite frequently. "Tongi yŏlchŏn" (Arrayed traditions of the Dongyi by Zi Shun, c. 266 BCE) became known to the public as an appendix to the *Tan'gi kosa* (Ancient history of Tan'gun and Kija) (Tae 1950, 164–165) translated by Kim Tuhwa and Yi Hwasa. Among the several modern published editions of *Tan'gi kosa*, it is only this 1950 edition that includes "Tongi yŏlchŏn."[3] The putative author of the text, one Kong Bin, is alleged to be an eighth-generation descendant of Confucius (c. 551–479 BCE). According to the "Tongi yŏlchŏn," Zi Shun (dates unknown), who is mostly known as Kong Bin or Kong Qian, wrote the text in the tenth year (c. 266 BCE) of King Anxi (276–243 BCE) of the State of Wei (403–225 BCE). Although the title in sinographs is similar to that found in the *Hou Han shu*, these two texts are completely different. To the best of the author's knowledge, the existence of this ancient text has never been mentioned in other historical texts or recognized as legitimate by contemporary historians. Nonetheless, the entire passage in Literary Sinitic has been widely circulated in on- and off-line publications targeted at a general audience. Where is the original source from? This question has been often neglected by those who cite this as putatively the most ancient piece of evidence.

It is less known to the public that "Tongi yŏlchŏn" is highly questionable in its authenticity, despite the widespread presence of this text in popular media. The *Tan'gi kosa* is well known now as a modern forgery, created as part of the construction of a nationalist history (Jorgensen 2004). In 1950, the Cooperative Association for Police Education reprinted it, intending to facilitate the "awareness of ethnic independence" (*minjokchŏgin chajuŭisik*) in Korea during the Cold War (Kyŏngch'al chŏnmun hakkyo 1956, 68). The Police College (Kyŏngch'al chŏnmun hakkyo) published *Tan'gi kosa* and distributed 15,000 copies to police officers as well as to those who worked for the good of local communities. "Tongi yŏlchŏn" is known to be a preface to another text about the history of Tan'gun titled *Hongsa* (The prosperous history). Judging from the text

translated and annotated by Song Hosu (2005, 361–363) into modern
Korean, the general narrative of the preface is similar to that of "Tongi
yŏlchŏn." Some details have been modified, including the title of the
source material as "Tongguk yŏlchŏn" (Arrayed traditions of the Eastern
State) instead of "Tongi yŏlchŏn." Another text titled *Hongsa han'ŭn*
(The prosperous history of Tan'gun), the putative historical records of
the homeland of Tan'gun and his parents, also includes a text that looks
similar to "Tongi yŏlchŏn."[4]

Neither *Hongsa* nor *Hongsa hanŭn* are verified historical texts. They
are considered forgeries by mainstream historians; the historical existence of "Tongi yŏlchŏn" and other similar versions remains unconfirm-
able. Why do these highly dubious texts appeal to laypeople and get cited
broadly but uncritically? To ordinary people who are interested in Korean
history and manners, "Tongi yŏlchŏn" offers by far the earliest and most
similar epithet to NPE in comparison with other ancient Chinese sources.
Besides, Kong Bin's account of the Dongyi is centered on the history of
Tan'gun, the mythical founding progenitor of the Korean nation. "Tongi
yŏlchŏn" relates that Tan'gun from the Dongyi was selected as king by the
nine tribes. It goes on to say that Dongyi was a cultivated country whose
people and culture was on a par with or even surpassed China, illustrating the alleged impact of Dongyi's descendants on ancient China. "Tongi
yŏlchŏn" endorses the moral and cultural standards of the Dongyi as represented by Tan'gun, and Kong Bin proclaims the land of the Dongyi as "a
country which might well be called the 'Land of Gentlemen and Propriety
in the East'" (Tae 1950, 164).

However, the accounts of Tan'gun and Dongyi in "Tongi yŏlchŏn" and
the two divergent copies of "Tongi yŏlchŏn" in *Hongsa* and *Hongsa hanŭn*
present several problems that cast doubt on the authenticity of this text.
According to Breuker (2010, 102–105), the myth of Tan'gun was created
during the Koryŏ period. If the myth of Tan'gun did not exist before the
late thirteenth century, it is safe to assume that the year when Kong Bin
allegedly wrote "Tongi yŏlchŏn" in 266 BCE is spurious. Moreover, it is
crucial to note that Dongyi used to be a general term whose territorial
boundaries were malleable up until the fifth century. It was in the *Hou Han
shu* that the identification of Dongyi shifted from disparate tribal states
in the north of the Shandong Peninsula to the new regions of present-day

Northeast China, and included also the three proto-Kingdoms of Korea as well as the Japanese (Chŏn 1979, cited in Yi 2010, 103–104). The afore-mentioned Chinese source has a note in volume 1 (*Guangwu diji* [The record of Emperor Guangwu]) by Li Xian (654–684) from Tang China who refers to the Dongyi people in "the state of Han" (Ch. Hanguoren) as the three proto–Three Kingdoms comprised of Chinhan, Pyŏnhan, and Mahan. The association between the ancient Korean people and the *yi* tribes in the Eastern "land where gentlemen do not die" is not entirely groundless, which might be why "Tongi yŏlchŏn" has a title so similar to the "Dongyi zhuan" of the *Hou Han shu*. By the same token, the (later, spurious) subtitle, "Tongguk yŏlchŏn," looks like a tactical choice to allow these forged texts to capitalize on the *Hou Han shu* as the grounds for incorporating Dongyi into the history of the ancient states of Korea.

The point to be made, however, is that "Tongi yŏlchŏn" fixes the mal-leable term Dongyi as a synonym for a particular ethnic group, namely the people on the Korean Peninsula. Furthermore, "Tongi yŏlchŏn" evinces a strong sentiment of cultural sovereignty and national polity. The romanticized character of Korea as a group of people with a civi-lized culture and decent morals could be mobilized to bolster cultural pride. As Yi Mun-yŏng (2010, 101) contends, the nationalist concept of *minjok* (ethnic nation) applied to ancient Korea invokes the notion of an imagined community created by modern Western nation-states. The public's strong attachment to "Tongi yŏlchŏn" seems to be related to the aspiration to speak with authority and authenticity about an ideal past. Take, for example, one of the South Korean civic organizations called the Nationwide Courtesy Movement Association (Pŏm-gungmin yeŭi saeng-hwal silch'ŏn undong ponbu).[5] As part of a historical overview of *yeŭi*, its website introduces Kong Bin's text as one of the extant Chinese accounts. The text is treated as an authoritative ancient reference along with clas-sical Chinese Confucian texts such as *Confucius* and *Mencius*. If "Tongi yŏlchŏn" was allegedly written by the descendants of Confucius, there would be no other more authoritative ancient evidence for the primordial origins of NPE than this. If the ancient history of Tan'gun's Dongyi as an ethnic group is taken to be as authentic as the "Tongi yŏlchŏn" claims, the epithet would not be self-generated but historically owing to and certified by the Chinese, the center of civilization in premodern East Asia. Popular discourse is engaged in the uncritical citing of the "Tongi yŏlchŏn" as an effective means to endorse the ancient and original ethno-national tradition of Korea as "the state of propriety."

Accounts of NPE in Premodern History

In Korean sources, historical records show that both Koryŏ and Chosŏn referred to themselves or were referred to by several terms related to propriety, such as the "region of propriety" (*yeŭi chi pang*), and the "country of propriety" (*yeŭi chi kuk*).[6] Such claims to propriety in premodern Korea seem to be closely related to aspiring to, meeting, and sharing Chinese standards of value and culture. This conceptualization of propriety began with the history of worshipping Jizi (K. Kija) as the originator of culture ever since the early Koryŏ period (Breuker 2010, 100). The emphasis on Kija as the origin of propriety became even more commonplace in the Chosŏn dynasty. As discussed in Koh (2002), the concept of *li* (K. *ye*) "propriety, rites or rituals" was of great importance as the East Asian counterpart to Western concepts of "civilité" and "civilization." Chosŏn valued the Confucian concepts and code of *ye* in society and politics as a means of cultivating oneself and governing the nation (Koh 2002). In particular, study and discussions of ritual studies (*yehak*) bloomed throughout mid- and late Chosŏn. The reference to Chosŏn as the successor of Kija legitimized the authentic origins and status of the Chosŏn court. Ch'oe Pu (1454–1504), a Chosŏn literatus, noted in "Tongguk T'onggam-non" (A theory of the comprehensive mirror of the Eastern Country) that the title of *kunja yeŭi chi kuk* (state of gentlemen and propriety) for the Chosŏn dynasty derives from Kija's edification. Peninsular references to premodern Korea as the state of propriety were mutually acknowledged in diplomatic interactions with successive Chinese dynasties. The Chosŏn dynasty took pride in itself as a "state of propriety" complying with Confucian norms, while Ming China recognized and praised the standards of ethics and rituals in Chosŏn as deserving of special diplomatic prestige (Ku 2015).

As sketched above, China and Chosŏn referred to Chosŏn as a state of propriety in terms of moral and cultural eminence, and China was the ultimate standard of propriety. By worshipping Kija and claiming itself as his authentic successor, the Koryŏ and Chosŏn courts and literati looked to Chinese morals and rites as the standards of authenticity and authority with regard to propriety, and Chosŏn's claims to the "country of propriety" in diplomatic relationships with China attested to its loyalty to imperial China. In return for performing its duties well, Chosŏn was accredited as a morally upright country versed in Confucian norms. But such an attempt to locate the legitimacy of Korean culture in Chinese standards is absent in "Tongi yŏlchŏn." Instead, by creating a decent past out of Dongyi, the customary metaphor of "propriety" serves as an original source of cultural pride and national identification, bypassing China. The alleged impact of the Dongyi on ancient China nonetheless implicitly gives less credence to China as the legitimate source of civilization, which is in fact at odds with what was generally perceived in attested historical accounts, as seen above. The discrepancy between the conception of NPE in "Tongi yŏlchŏn" and how Koryŏ and Chosŏn societies actually coped with the trope suggests that Korea's cultural dependence on China was effaced in order for NPE to serve as a national icon of traditional culture as known in modern days.

THE NATIONALIZATION OF THE NPE

The cultural identity of Chosŏn as linked to China began to be redefined at the turn of the last century. After the Chosŏn dynasty was forced to establish relations with outside powers in the latter half of the nineteenth century, the repositioning of Korea's national identity away from the Middle Kingdom (China) soon thereafter was inevitable. Close ties with Qing China diminished as the Empire of Japan gained power over the Korean Peninsula following the First Sino-Japanese War (1894–1895). At the same time, narratives of "civilization and enlightenment" (K. *munmyŏng kaehwa*) in late nineteenth-century East Asia pressured Korea to reform itself to keep up with the fast-paced global ideologies of capitalist modernity (Schmid 2002). Accordingly, the conventional meanings of NPE encountered a transitional moment. The cultural identity gained through long-lasting interactions with China began to stand for the nature of the ethno-national group, a distinct Korean identity that the

Chosŏn court and literati could use to distinguish themselves from the foreign invaders. Political elites took the Confucian norms of propriety as a point of reference for their own identity rooted in the past.

This collective identity was repackaged as an index of the superior nature of the ethnic group through nationalist efforts to encourage the public's support for various purposes. A letter from a Chosŏn military camp written to denounce the military incursion of a French warship in 1886 proudly referred to its country as a *yeŭi chi kuk* where kindness and generosity to other countries had been observed for generations.[7] While some believed the glory of NPE to be perpetual, others considered that Korean society had failed to maintain it. The luster of a previous glorious history seemed to have evaporated when the Korean Empire was demoted to the status of a protectorate of Japan in 1905. The epithet NPE was synonymous with the ideal past of Korea inhabited by "the most excellent racial group in the world" (*injong chŭk myŏngsi segye udŭng*) (Konghaksa Sangho 1906). This contrast between the glorious NPE of bygone times and the current disgraceful situation as lamented in major newspapers stirred up a moral panic or sense of crisis and provided a rationale for invoking public concern over the national fate as Korea teetered on the verge of losing its sovereignty.

Nonetheless, various nationalist groups discovered the trope of NPE as a driving force to overcome a national crisis. The old claims to the state of propriety grounded in (Neo-)Confucian tenets became nationalized as a shared moral and cultural pride and worked as a catchphrase to secure national sovereignty. For example, an article on June 26, 1907, in the *Taehan Maeil Sinbo* newspaper appealed to the gentlemen of the nation of propriety (*yeŭi chi kuk*) for the National Debt Repayment Movement. A young adult Korean-Christian group in Japan asserts in an article on September 22, 1907, that the title of *yeŭi chi kuk* has been a perpetual characteristic of Korean nature and culture since the ancient times of Tan'gun and Kija. This nationalist group adapted the old Confucian legacy of propriety to a cultural trait that was supposedly widespread even among ignorant people in rural Korea and was so outstanding as to draw the admiration of Europeans. An article on December 8, 1907, expresses faith in this potential, stating that the outstanding nature of Korean morals and culture could propel Korea to stand out as the number-one country in the world. As annexation by Japan loomed, the popular pride in NPE mobilized spiritual unity among the masses for national revival in opposition to savage Japan. A written appeal for anti-Japanism in 1908 pronounces "our nation" (*uri nara*) as the "small region of Propriety in the East" (*Tongbang yeŭi chi pang*), whereas Japan is described as a country of those who only pursue utility and self-interest (T'onggambu munsŏ 1908). With this popular and proud identity, various nationalist groups discovered a driving force to mobilize spiritual unity among the masses for national revival. A political cartoon from the newspaper *Sinhan Minbo* (see fig. 4.1) in San Francisco specifically names the core strength needed

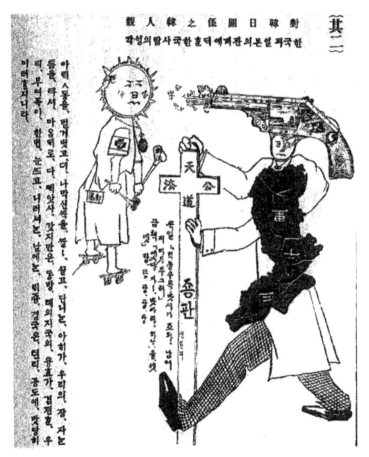

FIGURE 4.1.   "Koreans' perspective on the Korea-Japan relationship" (Sinhan Minbo, September 15, 1909). Courtesy of National Library of Korea.

to resist the soon-to-be colonial authorities in 1909: "The Nation of Propriety in the East should show loyalty and filial piety and stand up as the
tribe of ancient Korea, even though Japan has taken everything away
from Korea."[8]

CONTENTION IN THE
INTERPRETATIONS OF THE NPE

As discussed above, the old title of "state of propriety" began to serve as
an identity marker that distinguished Korea from others, invoking cultural pride and unity to cope with a national crisis in a rapidly changing
world. The legacy of NPE was replaced with skepticism and used as a reference for self-criticism after Korea fell under Japanese colonial rule in
1910. Many Korean political elites began to question the legacy of NPE.
To reform-minded nationalists, the collective identity seemed to be a
culprit for the political and economic struggles of colonized Korea. For
instance, an editorial on June 20, 1909, in the *Hwangsŏng Sinmun* newspaper states that Koreans tended to bow down to Japanese demands with
honeyed words since they like to be humble to others as people of *yeŭi
chi kuk*. The editorial goes on to say that foreigners who see through the
Koreans' nature will simply keep asking for things. Similarly, in an article
on September 15, 1920, in the *Tonga Ilbo*, the lagging economic status of
the Korean Peninsula is ascribed to the obsolescent ideology of NPE that
makes Korean society believe in national success without working, while
despising other countries as barbaric.

The old legacy rooted in Confucianism was losing its authority and
validity. Modern values and customs such as civility or public etiquette
from abroad were emerging as the new model for social and cultural
advancement. Western codes of ethics and behavior were introduced
as an alternative model for civil society instead of the old model of NPE.
Voices espousing the Western model of civility were heard from the
informed group of people who had lived abroad. A man under the pen
name Kŭmsŏng (1923) laments in his essay titled "Chaos upon returning to my home country after four years" that Chosŏn's pride in NPE is a
cause for extreme embarrassment. For a civilized life in his native land,
he proposes modernized manners or etiquette such as punctuality, a

dress code, and respect for women and one's personality. Pride in NPE turned into shame as colonial Korea struggled with the demands of daily life. A column on July 7, 1936, in the *Tonga Ilbo* invokes shame in NPE because a public code of ethics and behavior was needed for mundane functions such as using public bathrooms properly, rather than a Confucian model of propriety that belongs only to noble sages. The perceived lack of practical applications for it justified revamping the cultural value of NPE. Sŏ Sang-guk in his column on December 24, 1928, in the *Tonga Ilbo* assumed that literati who proclaim their country as NPE would see modern sports as an insane thing to do after taking a meal because they obstinately disdain martial matters. Similarly, a column on world legal systems for divorce on November 15, 1933, in the *Tonga Ilbo*, sees proclamations of NPE saturated with Confucian ideology among Koreans as accounting for their disposition to deal with divorce as a matter of ethics rather than as a legal issue.

Social Darwinism and socialism were also seeping into Korea from Western Europe via Japan. An article on December 29, 1925, in the *Tonga Ilbo* denounces the epithet NPE as originating from class discrimination between the proletariat and property-owning classes and advocates the social need for egalitarianism. Similarly, in a series of columns in the *Tonga Ilbo* under the title "The Culture and Tradition of Chosŏn" on November 2, 1937, Yi Chŏng-wŏn expressed second thoughts about NPE because Confucian morals in social relations fundamentally denied the opinions and autonomy of individuals.

The national identity of NPE was critically reassessed in the emergence of modern notions of civility and ethics. Reform-minded elites readopted the title of NPE in order to confront political and economic struggles and to pursue new visions of sociocultural reform. To progressive elites, the national character was no longer a proud legacy for Koreans to preserve. The past of a valued tradition was reimagined as a target of cultural reforms—the root of social problems particularly associated with (Neo-)Confucianism. The cultural identity of NPE was personified as a conservative member of the learned class who clung to obsolete ideals and empty formalities. The unviable and impractical morals and practices lingering in Korean society in the name of NPE were blamed for the fall of Korean society and painted as an obstacle to national power and prosperity. The perceived social evils of Confucian morals and customs represented a stark contrast with the new cultural model for *yeŭi* necessary for the future.

Criticism of Blind Imitation of China

The trope of NPE offered Korean nationalists another reform agenda item in addition to premodernity or backwardness: Sinocentrism. While standing as a notable cultural characteristic of Koreans, the historical origins of NPE recalled the shadow of China over Korean culture. In his review of the "true colors" (*ponsaek*) of Korean people on December 27, 1930, in the *Tonga Ilbo*, Kim Tu-hŏn notes that renowned Korean intellectuals understood politeness (*yeŭi* or *ye*) as one of the fundamental attributes of Koreans. Kim mentions ancient Chinese historical accounts such as the *Hou Han shu* as evidence for NPE. However, his assessment of the attributes of Korean culture goes on to say that the deeply rooted contacts with China from early on had diluted national awareness and led to a blind imitation of China. At the end of his article, his interpretation of the Korean cultural character as inclined to worshipping China expands into a concern with the phenomenon of post-pro-Chinese sentiments like pro-Japanism, pro-Americanism, and pro-Russianism.

The Chinese origins of Korea's alleged superior cultural identity provoked many colonial Koreans to advocate political self-reliance or independence. In some quarters, cynicism regarding cultural pride led to a backlash against cultural nationalism. In an editorial on economic competence on December 7, 1933, in the *Tonga Ilbo*, Ch'ang Paek-cha (a pen name) lambasts the sense of moral superiority underpinning NPE as an example of the current discourse of "self-respect" imposed by socially authoritative figures. The author's scathing critique of the discourse of NPE targets Koreans who cite the "certificate of proper demeanor accredited by China." This author summarizes such attempts to scavenge "Korean boasts" as a form of ultranationalism and antiquarianism, driven by the faulty expectation of upgrading the lives of the ethnic group. From the author's perspective, the cultural model from which nationalists sought to instill national pride symbolizes the disgraceful tradition of Sinitic and Confucian elite culture in the Korean past. Political elites mentioned the epithet of NPE to condemn the obsolescent and subservient attributes of Korean culture as a rationale for cultural nationalism and sociocultural reforms, two key agenda items for Korean elites.

The Birth of the Language of the NPE

Although treated by many as useless and troublesome, the NPE epithet was not going to fade away. As sketched above, Korean nationalists treated the cultural tropes of NPE in identity politics as either an item for their reform agenda or as an element of indigenous tradition. Paradoxically, while NPE was typified as an obsolescent ideology of the Confucian tradition, the deference-oriented notion of politeness became positively valorized as the core virtue of ethnic Koreans. As noted in Yi Kwang-su's (1892–1950) well-known essay titled "A Theory of National Reconstruction" (1922), respect for *ye*, the Confucian notion of propriety, was entrenched in Korean society as one of the fundamental characteristics of the Korean ethnic group. According to him, the target of reform was not the nature itself inherent in the group but concomitant flaws such as empty formalities. In fact, cultural nationalists advocated that distinctive national tradition held significance in the global order. As Ko Yŏng-hwan stated in his column on August 26, 1931, in the *Tonga Ilbo*, it was important for Koreans with their 5,000-year history to possess unique customs such as their wedding ceremony, in order not to humiliate their country, which after all enjoyed the title of NPE. The discourse of NPE seemed to hold out promise as an effective vehicle for nationalist writers as a positive identity marker that celebrated Korean tradition.

The Korean language also gained attention as a resource for cultural nationalism. In particular, Korean honorifics came to serve as the linguistic embodiment of the NPE. For instance, An Hwak (1886–1946), nationalist scholar and linguist and one of the most influential Korean intellectuals, mentioned "politeness/etiquette" (*yejŏl*) as one of the seven national characteristics of the Korean people in his book titled *Chosŏn munhaksa* (History of literature in Korea):

> Korea has been referred to as the Nation of Propriety in the East because etiquette and manners (*yeŭi chakpŏp*) have been highly developed. [. . .] Greetings and manners among the Westerners are extremely simple.

[. . .] Korean people have thought much of social intercourse and strove to distinguish the virtue of kindly feelings (*injŏng ŭi michŏm*), thus politeness is highly developed. [. . .] In terms of meanings expressed through language, [Korean] has plenty of honorific expressions (*kyŏngŏ*) and humble expressions (*kyŏmŏ*). [. . .] One might say that they originated from social hierarchy (*kyegŭp-che*), but they came to exist as the expressions of endearment (*ch'inae*) and graceful affection (*umi ŭi chŏong*). (An Hwak [1922] 1994, 146–152)

In his attempt to search for cultural resources to reveal Korean civilization, An Hwak presented honorific and humble language as the manifestation of Koreans' endearment and affection through linguistic distinctions in social relations, rather than social hierarchy. In comparison with the simple expressions of Westerners, the Korean language reflects the indigenous and virtuous tradition of Confucianism.

The deference-oriented notion of politeness associated with Korean honorifics and NPE also appealed to Japanese intellectuals as an excellent and indigenous tradition. In his article on the history of honorifics in Japan and Korea, Mikajiri (1934) romanticized etiquette in vertical relations (for example, king vs. subject, father vs. son, or elder vs. younger) from Confucianism in the Chosŏn dynasty as the nature of Korean society along with the epithet of NPE.[9] Both the Korean Empire and the Japanese colonial government promoted a form of Confucian morality centralized on loyalty, respect for elders, and filial piety in moral and citizenship education at public schools in order to inculcate docile subjects for the authorities (Hwang 2015, 182–188).

However, interpretations of Korean honorifics as an emblem of Korean characteristics were subject to the sociocultural projects envisioned by different groups of people. To reform-minded nationalists, Korean honorifics were a remnant of Confucian hierarchy and thus a prime target for cultural reforms, as the case for the trope of NPE. The non-use of honorifics with people in a lower status such as children led progressive cultural revisionists to see the linguistic structure of Korean politeness as an evil practice owing to the Confucian legacy of *changyu yusŏ* (elders take precedence; see Kim 1920). Similarly, the Enlightenment Club (Kyemyŏng Kurakpu) began a linguistic campaign to promote using honorific language with and among children in 1921 to reform society and promote cultural advancement (see *Chosŏn Ilbo*, September 25, 1921). In doing so, Korean honorific expressions were used to promote a civil and egalitarian society where fellow humans are respected regardless of social status.

POLITENESS—AN INVENTED TRADITION OF KOREAN NATIONAL CULTURE

"[T]he history which became part of the fund of knowledge or the ideology of nation, state, or movement is not what has actually been preserved in popular memory, but what has been selected, written, pictured, popularized and institutionalized by those whose function it is to do so" (Hobsbawm 1983, 13). National tradition is not a coherently defined concept inherited from the past. Not all customs from the past gain cultural significance as national tradition simply because the habitual behaviors or thoughts existed in so-called traditional society. How can we trace situations in which tradition is deliberately created? Hobsbawm (1983, 4–5) notes that the invention of tradition occurs frequently when the existing customary practices dwindle or collapse during a period of rapid change in society, requiring old traditions to be reframed under new conditions and for new purposes. He pays attention to the use of customary actions or values linked to the past as an effective resource for nation building and nationalism. Social acts underwent the evaluative process of identity politics. Newspapers and magazines provided a discursive space and a popular platform for intellectuals and ideologues to have their voices heard by general audiences.

The national identity of NPE has been an emergent process along with the experience of globalization and colonialization between the last years of the Chosŏn dynasty and Chosŏn under colonial rule. Political elites positioned the traditional epithet of NPE as a "symbolically charged sign of club membership" (Hobsbawm 1983, 11). Old wine was poured into new bottles when Confucian scholars at the turn of the last century took over ownership of the Chinese legacy. The narratives of NPE across different periods capture the ideological process whereby a conventional epithet undergoes (re-)construction as a national icon. The pride in propriety in premodern Korea was deeply grounded in China, and not the other way around. Nationalist elites pronounced their reassessments of the old epithet of the nation of propriety. Conservative elites deployed the idea of a superior moral sensibility as a potential means for saving a country. Progressive nationalists raised doubts about supposed Korean excellence in propriety as modernization shattered the old Sino-centric epistemology. Reform-minded nationalists blamed NPE as a white elephant to be discarded—as impractical traditions of the old Confucian society that no longer helped solve current issues and reform society. NPE as a metaphor for the residue of bygone ways and a target for reforms became an efficient rationale to accelerate social or economic changes for the modern Korean nation.

National tradition evolves as the artifact of a politically saturated project. Two strands of the national movement played the main role in fashioning nationalist projects in times of change and challenges. Nationalist intellectuals repeatedly called on the rhetoric of NPE for the cultivation of collective identities conceived by each political group. This cultural trope facilitated support from Koreans as a source of either self-pride or self-criticism. The reference to Chinese civilization once legitimized Korea's high standard of morals and civilization, but pride in NPE came under fire as the grounds for criticizing premodern ways and faulty (ultra-)nationalism leaning on Sino-centrism. Thus, the symbolic meanings of NPE as national tradition became imbued with national knowledge in the work of nationalism and nation building.

In postcolonial Korea after liberation from Japan, good manners were in demand again in order to rebuild the nation-state. The code of politeness became a policy issue in order to facilitate cultured elegance and social morality. For example, the initial volume of *Sae Sallim* (New life), a woman's magazine published by the US army military government in Korea, featured *yeŭi* as a national citizen's obligation in maintaining harmony in society (see Ko 1947a, 1947b). Likewise, the social meanings of NPE were tailored to the needs of the time. Critiques of NPE were replaced by the positive attributes of the ethno-national group (*minjok-sŏng*) in Korean tradition. A state-sponsored textbook, *Kugŏ* 5–2 "National Language" (Mun'gyobu 1952) notes that Koreans' value of morals has been "respected" as the NPE from ancient times. Nevertheless, the values of NPE in identity politics were a precarious basis upon which to pronounce self-reliance or an independent tradition. A special column in *Chayu Sinmun* on November 3, 1948 (National Foundational Day—also known as the Anniversary of the Tan'gun's Accession) criticizes those who proudly proclaimed themselves people of NPE as embarrassing. This article, titled "The Origins and Etymology of the Nation of Propriety in the East" sees the epithet as too oriented to China as the center. Thus, the author asserts that "we" take "our country"—there is no reason to be timidly referred to as "the East" (*Tongbang*).

The distribution of the "Tongi yŏlchŏn" in 1950 needs to be understood within an ideological context where the urge to validate the authenticity of this particularly admirable quality of the ethno-nation required the downplaying of former dependency on China in the history of NPE. "Tongi yŏlchŏn" evokes an effective historic continuity for the "land of gentlemen" dating back to the era of Tan'gun and does so by narrowing the referent of the term Dongyi to the name of a specific ancient nation in the East under the kingship of Tan'gun. On the one hand, the claim that ancient China recognized Koreans as the people of NPE lends international recognition to the epithet. On the other hand, detailed and boastful accounts of Tan'gun's Dongyi characterized as a culturally advanced ancient Korea also minimizes Korea's dependency on China as the original locus of and standards for civilization. Thus, "Tongi yŏlchŏn" presents a glimpse into how the Chinese shadow over Korean tradition could be transformed into a resource for endorsing a sense of cultural pride in Korean tradition.

The social act of shaping ethno-cultural identities has been an ongoing project in the two Koreas since the Korean War (1950–1953). The post-Liberation Koreas have created different ethno-cultural identities using the NPE trope as part of their rhetorical tool kit for rebuilding nation-states in the two different regimes. In the ROK, the notions of "moral nation" (*toŭi kukka*) and "morality for national citizens" (*kungmin toŭi*) were central to the nation-building project and creating "national citizens" (*kungmin*) under the regime of the first president, Syngman Rhee (1875–1965) (see Kang 2008). Rhee underlined the Three Bonds and the Five Relationships (K. Samgang oryun) and democracy as the objectives of national morality (Pang 1952). Accordingly, the Committee for

National Morality (Kungmin toŭihoe) published the *Silch'ŏn kungmin yepŏp* (Practical decorum for national citizens) (Kungmin toŭihoe 1954) in order to prescribe individuals' daily life in family and society along with decorum for the state, ranging from dress to polite speech. Cultivation of national morality was in full swing after Park Chung Hee (1917–1979) came into power in 1961. More printed guidelines on citizens' duties for moral culture, like *Kungmin toŭi* (Morality for national citizens) (Toŭi han'guk-chi p'yŏnch'an wiwŏnhoe 1962) and *Silch'ŏn yepŏp* (Practical decorum) (Kungmin toŭi kyoyuk hakhoe 1964) were published. In addition to morals and politeness education at schools, the Ministry of Education published *Saenghwal yejŏl* (Life etiquette) (Mun'gyobu 1972), which determined the moral and behavioral models of politeness such as speech manners as part of the cultural standards for a nation that champions democratic ideologies (equality) and cosmopolitanism. Behavioral and moral disciplines including respect, etiquette, and decorum came to take root as an important value for the state and its national citizens through public education.

The same ideological drive has engendered language as a key constituent representing the tradition of a moral/polite race (King 2014). Language planning in the DPRK began in earnest with the "instructions" (*kyosi*) of Kim Il Sung based on his conversations with a group of linguists in 1964 and 1966 in order to develop the North Korean language as a tool and weapon of the revolution. Kim Il Sung addressed the prospects of the Korean language for fostering communist morality in his first set of instruction as follows: "Because our language can express propriety and etiquette clearly, it is extremely good for people's upbringing in communist morality" (cited from Chŏng 2003, 19). One of the first morals and etiquette references in the DPRK, *Kongsanjuŭi ryeŭi todŏk kyoyang* (Communist etiquette, morals, and culturedness), was edited and published in 1964 in Japan for the education of pro-DPRK Korean residents in Japan. The preface calls for the strengthening of communist moral culture in order to break down the vestiges of capitalist and feudalistic (in other words, bourgeois and American) ideas and life patterns (1964, 4). This book also notes that ancient Chinese texts such as the *Shanhai jing* admired Korea as NPE (1964, 8). The cultural knowledge of NPE is thus evoked as a common virtue to be preserved and developed by observing proper public behavior and interactions as a good communist/ socialist citizen.

Both North and South Korea also undertook the inculcation of morality through linguistic standardization. The standardized model of polite speech in the DPRK was published as *Chosŏnmal ryejŏlpŏp* (Linguistic etiquette in the Korean language) (Kim 1983) to establish cultural and moral norms of life befitting a socialist and communist society. As discussed in King (2014), celebrating the deferential and asymmetrical practice of Korean honorifics as indigenous and excellent Korean culture served as useful rhetoric for justifying social hierarchies and gender inequalities in the DPRK. The standard models of polite speech in the ROK were promulgated in *P'yojun hwapŏp* (Explanations for standard speech) (NIKL 1992), published as the collaborative work with *Chosŏn Ilbo*, one of the major newspaper companies, under the slogan, "for correct and beautiful *Uri-mal*" (Korean speech, literally, our speech). The professed purpose of work was a public project to ease citizens' linguistic "confusion" and "difficulties" in daily life. However, such a tradition of codifying and stipulating "appropriate" social interaction in communication can hardly be apolitical. Language planning and morals education in postwar North and South Korea demonstrate that language prescription has played a significant role in behavioral and moral indoctrination as a crucial measure to mold behavioral and moral ideals and cultural identities in the two different political regimes.

The cultural politics surrounding national tradition are an ongoing process for social stability and global competence in the context of the so-called era of globalization. The Global Etiquette Campaign was one of the major strategic tasks initiated by President Lee Myung-bak in 2010, geared in particular toward the G20 Summit held in Seoul. With the slogan, "your consideration [for others] makes the world smile," this public campaign encouraged national citizens to participate in the making of a "globally polite nation" (*kŭllobŏl yeŭi chi kuk*) as ambassadors of the ROK. The vision of enhancing the positive national image like a valuable commodity (i.e., national branding) was circulated through school education and public policies by educating "charming Koreans" and "global citizens" who could be competitive and respectable on the global stage.

GLOSSARY

Anxi 安釐
changyu yusŏ 長幼有序
Chinhan 辰韓
Chosŏn 朝鮮
Chosŏn munhaksa 朝鮮文學史
da 大
Dongyi 東夷
Dongyi zhuan 夷傳
Guangwu diji 光武帝紀
Haiwai dong jing 海外東經
Hanguoren (K. Han'gugin) 韓國人
Hongsa 鴻史
Hongsa Han'ŭn 鴻史桓殷
Hou Han shu 後漢書
Hwangsŏng Sinmun 皇城新聞
Jizi (K. Kija) 箕子
junzi guo 君子國 (K. *kunja kuk*)
Kong Bin 孔斌
Kong Qian 孔谦
Korai reigi no kuni 古來禮儀の國
Koryŏ 高麗
Kui 九夷
Kunja yeŭi chi kuk 君子禮義之國
li (K. *ye*) 禮
Li Xian 李賢 (Zhanghuai Taizi 章太子)
Mahan 馬韓
Munmyŏng kaehwa 文明開化
Pyŏnhan 弁韓

qiang 羌
Shanhai jing 山海經
Shuowen jiezi 說文解字
Sinhan Minbo 新韓民報
Taehan Maeil Sinbo 大韓每日申報
Tan'gi kosa 檀奇古史
Tan'gun 檀君
tōhō kunshi no kuni 東方君子の國
Tonga Ilbo 東亞日報
Tongbang yeŭi (North Korean: *ryeŭi*) *chi kuk* 東方禮儀之國 (東方禮義之國)
Tongbang yeŭi chi pang 東方禮義之邦
Tongguk yŏlchŏn 東國烈傳 (in the *Hongsa* version) 東國列傳 (in the *Hongsa Han'ŭn* version)
Tongi yŏlchŏn 東夷列傳
Wei 魏
Xu Shen 許
yang 羊
yehak 禮學
yejŏl 禮節
yeŭi (North Korean: Ryeŭi) 禮儀 or 禮義
yi 夷 barbarian
Yi Kwang-su 李光洙
Zi Shun 子順

NOTES

1. The *P'yojun kugŏ taesajŏn* is a dictionary of the Korean language published by the National Institute of Korean Language. The definitions of *yeŭi* are cited from the online edition: https://stdict.korean.go.kr/search/searchResult.do, accessed June 3, 2021.

2. Dongyi are also referred to as the *yi* tribe or the *kui* (nine tribes).
3. This edition is available only through a few privately owned copies. I am grateful to Cho Chun-hŭi for generously sharing with me her copy of "Tongi yŏlchŏn" from the 1950 edition of *Tan'gi kosa*.
4. In an interview with the *K'orian Sŭp'irit* on January 29, 2013, Pan Chae-wŏn, the annotator of *Hongsa Hanŭn* and director of the Hunminjŏngŭm Research Institute, claims that the text was donated by one Pak Chong-ho in 2003. Based on the photoprint (Hunminjŏngŭm yŏn'guso 2012, 380), the overall structure remains the same. This particular text written in mixed-script orthography notes that *Hongsa han'ŭn* was excerpted in the year of Sinyu (60 BCE, 1 CE).
5. See Pŏm-gungmin yeŭi saenghwal silch'ŏn undong ponbu (n.d., section 1).
6. Historical records of premodern Korea associated with propriety include *History of Koryŏ*, *Annals of the Chosŏn Dynasty*, historical and literary works of individuals written during the Chosŏn dynasty. With regard to the term for *yeŭi*, "propriety," it is interesting to note that most of the terms appear with the sinograph 義 *yì*, "proper, right or correct conduct" (K. *ŭi*) with only a few cases using 儀 *yí*, "ceremony, rites" (K. *ŭi*), whereas it seems the other way around after the twentieth century in Korea.
7. See *Kojong Sillok* (n.d.) entry for September 11, 1866.
8. This copyrighted image was used from an editorial titled "[No. 2] Koreans' perspective on the Korea-Japan relationship" (n.d.) prepared by *Sinhan Minbo* in 1909 and was released under KOGL License Category 1. This work can be downloaded from the National Library of Korea, www.nl.go.kr, without cost.
9. Similarly, Unit Thirteen of *Chūtō kyōiku shūshinsho 2* (Chōsen Sōtokufu 1936) notes that Chōsen (Korea), as a "time-honored nation of politeness" (*korai reigi no kuni*), boasted good manners based upon the (hierarchical) order between old and young (*chōyō no jo*) and between husband and wife, and that the custom of worshipping ancestors was popular. While praising such a culture as a perfectly respectable culture of the "Nation of Gentlemen in the East" (*tōhō kunshi no kuni*), this unit goes on to say that this same politeness culture brought about many evils because Korean people have stuck so much to form that they squander their fortunes on a funeral.

REFERENCES

An Hwak (An Cha-san). 1922. *Chosŏn munhaksa* [History of Korean literature]. Kyŏngsŏng: Hanil sŏjŏm ch'ulp'an. 1994 reprint of Kwŏn O-sŏng, Yi T'ae-jin, and Ch'oe Wŏn-sik, eds., *Chasan An Hwak kukhak nonjŏjip* [Collected works of An Hwak]. Seoul: Yŏgang Ch'ulp'ansa.

Anderson, Benedict. 1991. *Imagined Communities: Reflections on the Origin and Spread of Nationalism.* London: Verso.

Breuker, Remco E. 2010. *Establishing a Pluralist Society in Medieval Korea, 918–1170: History, Ideology, and Identity in the Koryŏ Dynasty.* Leiden: Brill.

Brown, Lucien. 2011. "Korean Honorifics and 'Revealed', 'Ignored' and 'Suppressed' Aspects of Korean Culture and Politeness." In *Politeness Across Cultures,* edited by Francesca Bargiela-Chiappini and Dániel Z. Kádár, 106–127. New York: Palgrave Macmillan.

Cho, Young-mee, Hyo Sang Lee, and Carol Schulz. 2000. *Integrated Korean: Beginning 1.* KLEAR Textbooks in Korean Language. Honolulu: University of Hawai'i Press.

Ch'oe Pu. 1571. *Kŭmnamjip* [Collected Writings of Southern Brocade]. "Tongguk T'onggam-non" [A theory of the comprehensive mirror of the Eastern Country]. In *Kŭmnam sŏnsaeng chip* [Collected works of Ch'oe Pu], vol. 2. Accessed June 3, 2021. http://contents.nahf.or.kr/id/NAHF.gb.d_0092_0060

Chŏng T'ae-sun. 2003. "Uri-mal ŭn ryeŭi pŏmjŏl ŭl ttokttokhi nat'anael su innŭn usuhan ŏnŏ" [Our language is a superior language capable of clearly expressing propriety]. *Kim Ilsŏng Chonghap Taehak hakpo (Ŏmunhak)* 49 (1): 19–23.

Chōsen Sōtokufu. 1936. *Chūtō Kyōiku Shūshinsho 2* [Self-Cultivation manual for middle school education 2]. Keijō: Chōsen shoseki insatsu kabushiki kaisha.

Chosŏn Ilbo. 1921. "Kyemyŏng Kurakpu kŏnŭisŏ (sang)" [The proposal of the Enlightenment Club (1)]. September 25.

Harkness, Nicholas. 2015. "Linguistic Emblems of South Korean Society." In *The Handbook of Korean Linguistics,* edited by Lucien Brown and Jaehoon Yeon, 492–508. Malden, MA: John Wiley & Sons.

Hobsbawm, Eric. 1983. "Introduction: Inventing Traditions." In *The Invention of Tradition,* edited by Eric Hobsbawm and Terence Ranger, 1–14. Cambridge: Cambridge University Press.

Hong, Jin-ok. 2006. "The Functional Notion of Korean Honorific Usages Reflecting Confucian Ideologies." *Modern English Education* 7 (1): 73–100.

Hunminjŏngŭm yŏn'guso [Hunminjŏngŭm Research Institute], ed. 2012. *(Chuhae) Hongsa han'ŭn: Tan'gun ŭi kohyang ŭl asimnikka?* [(Annotated) *Hongsa han'ŭn:* Do you know the homeland of Tan'gun?]. Seoul: Hanbaedal.

Hwang, Juck-Ryoon. 1990. "'Deference' versus 'Politeness' in Korean Speech." *International Journal of the Sociology of Language* 82 (January): 41–56.

Hwang, Kyung Moon. 2015. *Rationalizing Korea: The Rise of the Modern State, 1894–1945.* Oakland: University of California Press.

Jorgensen, John. 2004. "The Rebirth of a Marginalised Knowledge: Alternate Histories and Symbolic Analysis in Nativist Korean New Religious Movements." *Kojosŏn Tan'gun-hak* 10:329–356.

Kádár, Dániel Z., and Sara Mills. 2011. *Politeness in East Asia.* Cambridge: Cambridge University Press.

Kang Hae-su. 2008. "'Toŭi ŭi cheguk' kwa singminji Chosŏn ŭi naesyŏnŏl aident'it'i" [Rhetoric of "morality and righteousness" and the formation of national identity in colonial Korea]. *Han'guk munhwa* 41 (June): 183–203.

Kim Kye-gon. 1994. *Uri-mal, kŭl ŭn uri ŏl ŭl tamnŭn kŭrŭt ini* [Our language and writing are the vessels to hold our spirit]. Seoul: Ŏmun'gak.

Kim So-ch'un (Kim Ki-jŏn). 1920. "Changyuyusŏ ŭi malp'ye, yunyŏn namnyŏ ŭi haebang ŭl chech'ang ham" [The negative effects of elders-first hierarchy and the emancipation of youth]. *Kaebyŏk* 2 (July): 52–58.

Kim Tong-su. 1983. *Chosŏnmal ryejŏlpŏp* [Linguistic etiquette in the (North) Korean language]. Pyongyang: Kwahak paekkwa sajŏn ch'ulp'ansa.

King, Ross. 2007. "North and South Korea." In *Language and National Identity in Asia,* edited by Andrew Simpson, 200–234. Oxford: Oxford University Press.

———.2014. "Linguistic Etiquette, Women's Language, and Moral Panics in North Korean Language Planning Discourse." Unpublished manuscript.

Ko Pong-gyŏng. 1947a. "Yejŏl ŭl kajin kungmin i toeja [Let us become national people with etiquette]. *Sae Sallim* 1 (January): 38.

———. 1947b. "Yeŭi rŭl kajin kungmin i toeja [Let us become national people with etiquette]. *Sae Sallim* 1 (January): 41–42.

Koh, Young-jin. 2002. "The Civilizing Process in the West and Korea: Norbert Elias' Theory and Confucianism." *Seoul Journal of Korean Studies* 15:129–152.

Kojong Sillok [Veritable records of Kojong]. n.d. *Saryo Kojong sidae-sa,* vol. 2. Accessed September 28, 2019. http://db.history.go.kr/id/sk_002_0010_0090_0090_0030

Konghaksa Sangho. 1906. "Koa ich'ŏn man tongp'o (kisŏ)" [A word to our twenty million compatriots]. *T'aegŭkhakpo* 2 (September): 17–19.

Kongsanjuŭi ryeŭi todŏk kyoyang [Communist etiquette, morals, and culturedness]. 1964. Tokyo: Hagu sŏbang (originally published by Pyongyang kunjung munhwa ch'ulpansa).

Ku To-yŏng. 2015. "Chosŏn chŏn'gi Cho-Myŏng oegyo kwan'gye ŭi hamsu, 'yeŭi chi kuk'" [The state of propriety: The functional relations of Chosŏn-Ming diplomacy in the early Chosŏn period]. *Taedong munhwa yŏn'gu* 89:159–203.

Kŭmsŏng. 1923. "Hondon, 4-nyŏn mane koguk e torawasŏ" [Chaos upon returning to my home country after four years]. *Kaebyŏk* 39 (September): 49–60.

Kungmin toŭi kyoyuk hakhoe. 1964. *Silch'ŏn Yepŏp* [Practical decorum]. Seoul: Pŏmmun'gak.

174   LANGUAGE OF THE "NATION OF PROPRIETY IN THE EAST"

Kungmin toŭihoe. 1954. *Silch'ŏn Kungmin Yepŏp* [Practical code of decorum for national citizens]. Seoul: Mun'gyosa.

Kyŏngch'al chŏnmun hakkyo [Police College]. 1956. *Kyŏngch'al kyoyuksa* [History of police education]. Seoul: Kyŏngch'al chŏnmun hakkyo.

Mikajiri Hiroshi. 1934. "Naisengo keigohō no kongen to sono un'yō ni tsuite" [Origin of the Korean honorifics system and its operation]. *Bunkyō no Chōsen* 15 (November): 96–105.

Mun'gyobu. 1952. *Kugŏ 5–2* [National language]. Seoul: Taehan mun'gyo sŏjŏk chusik hoesa.

———. 1972. *Saenghwal yejŏl* [Life etiquette]. Seoul: Mun'gyobu.

NIKL (National Institute of the Korean Language). 1992. *P'yojun Hwapŏp haesŏl* [Explanations for Standard Speech]. Seoul: National Institute of the Korean Language.

O To-yŏl. 2015. "Kongja ŭi 'Kui 九夷' wa Han'guk minjok sasang ŭi yŏn'gwansŏng nonŭi" [On the correlation of Confucius's "Kui 九夷" with Korean national ideology]. *Tongyang Ch'ŏlhak Yŏn'gu* 81:173–208.

Pak Tong-gŭn. 2010. "Yejŏlbarŭn Han'gugŏ" [The polite Korean language]. In *Uri-mal ŭi imojŏmo: Han'gugin i araya hal uri-mal sangsik yŏsŏt madang* [This and that in Korean: 16 must-know commonsense facts about the Korean language], 81–87. Seoul: Kungnip Kugŏwon [The National Institute of the Korean Language].

Pang U-ha, ed. 1952. *Toŭi Kungmin ŭi ponghwa* [A beacon for moral national citizens]. Pusan: Kungmin kyoyang hyŏphoe.

Pŏm-gungmin yeŭi saenghwal silch'ŏn undong ponbu [Nationwide Courtesy Movement Association]. n.d. "Tongbang yeŭi chi kuk ŭn Han'guk ŭi koyu myŏngsa" ["The Nation of Propriety in the East" is a proper noun in Korean]. Accessed September 28, 2019. http://www.yejeol.or.kr/book/book_1.php

Schmid, Andre. 2002. *Korea Between Empires, 1895–1919.* New York: Columbia University Press.

Song Ho-su. 2005. *Tan'gun ŭn silchon inmul-iŏtta: Tan'gun 2,220-nyŏnsa kojŭng* [Tan'gun was a real figure: Historical investigation of the 2,220-year-old history of Tan'gun]. Seoul: Kaech'ŏn taehak ch'ulpan-bu (Hant'ŏ).

Tae Ya-bal. 1950. *Tan'gi kosa* [Ancient history of Tan'gun and Kija]. Translated by Kim Tuhwa and Yi Hwasa. Seoul: Kyŏngch'al kyoyang hyŏpchohoe.

T'onggambu munsŏ [Documents of Japanese Residency-General of Korea]. 1908. "Kak ŭmmyŏnni myŏnjang, chipkang ege kohan paeil hun'go wa puil, pan-han-ja rŭl kyut'anhan kyŏnggo hullyŏng" [Admonition announced to township and village headmen for anti-Japanism and cautionary instructions for impeaching pro-Japanists and anti-Koreanists]. T'onggambu munsŏ, vol. 9.

Toŭi han'guk-chi p'yŏnch'an wiwŏnhoe. 1962. *Kungmin Toŭi* [Morality for national citizens]. Seoul: Toŭi kungmin p'yŏnch'an wiwŏnhoe.

Yi Kŏn-bŏm et al. 2018. *Na nŭn irŏk'e pullinŭn kŏsi pulp'yŏnhamnida: Injŏng kwa sŏyŏl ŭi rit'ŭmŏsŭ, isanghan nara ŭi hoch'ing iyagi* [I am uncomfortable being addressed like this: The litmus of recognition and hierarchy, a story of terms of address in a strange country]. Seoul: Han'gyŏrye ch'ulp'an.

Yi Kwang-su (Yi Ch'un-wŏn). 1922. "Minjok Kaejoron" [A theory of national reconstruction]. *Kaebyŏk* 23 (May): 18–72.

Yi Mun-yŏng. 2010. *Mandŭrŏjin Han'guksa* [Concocted Korean history]. Seoul: P'aran midiŏ.

Yi On-gyŏn. 1996. "Nambukhan ŭi ŏnŏ yejŏl ko" [Review of linguistic politeness in North and South Korea]. *T'ong'il Nonch'ong* 13:33–67.

Yum, June Ock. 1988. "The Impact of Confucianism on Interpersonal Relationships and Communication Patterns in East Asia." *Communication Monographs* 55 (4): 374–388.

CHAPTER 5

Re-invented in Translation?

Korean Literature in Literary Chinese as One Epitome of Endangered Cultural Heritage

ANDREAS SCHIRMER

This chapter examines a specific discourse about modern (vernacular) Korean translations of *hanmun*. While *hanmun* signifies any text written in classical Chinese (Literary Sinitic), except where the term is used to refer to Literary Sinitic itself, as a medium of expression, the discourse examined here revolves specifically around writings in classical Chinese authored by Koreans. This discourse developed in parallel with, and in explicit reference to, the hangul-only policy of the late 1960s. Based on a collection of voices raised in newspapers since the mid-1960s, this investigation focuses on the rhetorical repertoire of the discourse.

The translation of *hanmun* texts into modern Korean—also referred to as *kugyŏk* (national translation) or *hangŭlhwa* (transformation into hangul)—gathered momentum during the Park Chung Hee era thanks to a government-sponsored campaign, although it was also always a grassroots effort. This impressive movement embodies an unlooked-for case in point of invented tradition. After all, *hanmun* translation was supposed to symbolically reinforce social cohesion, legitimize the state, and facilitate citizens' socialization into a system of shared values and beliefs—all in times when South Korean society experienced a breathtakingly rapid transformation.

KOREAN "CLASSICS"

The Korean term that is often used in this context, *kojŏn*, is not synonymous with the handy English term "classics." *Kojŏn* often denotes any premodern text written in *hanmun*, but it can also refer to premodern Korean literature written in hangul. It is the former meaning of the term—*kojŏn* as premodern *hanmun* texts—that is more relevant in this chapter. By connotation, *kojŏn* can also imply the meaning of a permanently established canon of texts (or a text belonging to this canon)—but this does not apply to the majority of what is in fact called *kojŏn*, as distribution and general knowledge of most of these texts have always been limited.

The concept of "classics" is often, in many national literatures, an example of invented tradition par excellence—ascribing a permanent or even eternal value, as happened, for example, when Goethe and Schiller were elevated to an Olympus of national German literature, on an imagined par with the ancient Greek literary titans. Now, as indicated, the Korean term *kojŏn* mostly does not refer to a venerated body of literature—this latter meaning being an optional semantic layer, derived from the Western concept of "classics"—but usually denotes simply an old text, be it the most marginal and unknown. Traditionally, however, if there was a Korean concept of classics in the canonical sense, then this was associated with the authoritative Confucianist canon (the Four Books and Five Classics), and thus with texts that, coincidentally, originated outside of the Korean Peninsula.[1] Then again, the semantic layer mentioned above cannot be underestimated: there is the connotation of emotional value, by which talk of *kojŏn* implies a venerable tradition bequeathed through the centuries. And it is precisely this implication that has deliberately been exploited by the promoters of *hanmun* translation since the 1960s. They could draw on the old natural reverence for *hanmun* writing, as Literary Sinitic represented the "sacred language."[2] This also explains why, in intellectual debates of the late nineteenth and twentieth centuries, many Korean scholars stubbornly adhered to *hanmun* as *chinsŏ*—the true script—trying to fend off the sudden rise of the long-despised hangul, the phonetic script that is aligned with and inherently corresponds with spoken Korean. However, by the time the discourse that forms the focus of this chapter emerged—the late 1960s—Korean nationalism had already led to "an almost cult-like respect and even worship-like reverence" for hangul (King 2007, 221).

THE DEMOTION OF *HANMUN*

It has been barely more than a century in Korea since the vernacular (*ŏnmun*) has transformed from the antithesis of cultured and literary language into the yardstick thereof.[3] *Ŏnmun* literally and precisely denotes a writing or script, *mun*, for the common spoken language, *ŏn*. However, just like "vulgar" can simply mean the common but also the coarse and gross, the connotations of *ŏnmun* included lowness and inferiority. A likewise contemptuous branding was, in the context of patriarchal culture, *amgŭl*, "women's script." As the Literary Sinitic, or classical Chinese, had, at the expense of *ŏnmun*, enjoyed the status of the standard medium of writing in Korea, any standardization, refinement, and sophistication of Korean as a written language was neglected.[4] Condensed development, so defining for many things Korean, is thus also very salient when it comes to language: Korean entered the twentieth century unstandardized, and with a history of marginalization in terms of writing culture, only to be degraded before long in favor of Japanese. Because of this extreme[5] history, language activism and language policy are quite understandably still top-priority issues. But the fierce feuds and ardent debates[6] between advocates of *ŏnmun ilch'i* (the unification or congruence of the spoken and the written[7]) on one side, and conservatives clinging to *hanmun* on the other, were settled by the 1920s at the latest. The matter—which was not simply about choice of script, but about lexicon, grammar, and orthography[8]—is clearly decided and has been for more or less a century; composing a few lines in *hanmun* now enjoys, at best, the status of an exclusive pastime or freakish hobby, only slightly more common than writing Latin poetry in Europe.[9]

The gradual demotion of Literary Sinitic[10] during the late nineteenth and early twentieth centuries met with fierce opposition in what is now summed up as *hanmun p'yeji nonjaeng*, the debate about the abolition of *hanmun*. The advocates of *ŏnmun ilch'i* deplored the debilitating disconnect between spoken and written expression brought about by *hanmun* writing; their opponents cautioned against the extinction (*somyŏl*) of traditional intellectual knowledge and the imminent rupture of present and past, between modern Koreans and their ancestors. Proponents of traditional scholarship such as Sin Ki-sŏn (1851–1909) argued that by abandoning *hanmun* man would become animal again,[11] and that all order would be overturned.[12] During these debates, progressive intellectuals identified Korean adherence to *hanmun* with slavish dependence on China.[13] They felt compelled to polemicize against learning Literary Sinitic or even merely learning Chinese characters (*hantcha*) as a waste of time—in their opinion, much useful knowledge could be acquired with the effort and energy invested in (and ultimately wasted on) learning characters[14]—and considered learning Literary Sinitic a hindrance to national self-improvement and advancement (see Kim Chin-gyun 2008).

Ever since, over the past eight decades, no advocate of reintroducing *hanmun* as the principal form of written expression has come forth in earnest. In fact, reinstating *hanmun* has become completely unthinkable; instead, English is occasionally considered as the language medium of Korea's future.[15] The current hangul-only paradigm (hangul supremacy) is only questioned by promoters of a mixed or parallel script (basically hangul, but using *hantcha* for most of the Sino-Korean vocabulary) and by partisans of *hantcha* education. In fact, their calls for the use of *hantcha* to disambiguate meaning might, in the long run, be recognized as the voice of reason.

From the radical issue of abolishing *hanmun*, the Korean debate over writing has moved on to the matter of whether hangul should be used exclusively (*chŏnyong*), or whether there should be some form of mixed use (*honyong*)—a combination of scripts like in Japan, or even a parallel use (*pyŏngyong*), in other words, a mixed script with *hantcha* provided as auxiliary glosses in parentheses for disambiguation. (Meanwhile, such disambiguation is frequently rendered by giving the English equivalent.) One peculiar motif of the contemporary debate around *hantcha*—that is, around the question of whether or not to include *hantcha* in common writing—is the leveraging of lingering anti-Americanism by *hantcha* advocates that gained momentum in the 1990s. This represents a rhetorical turning of the tables against those hangul supremacists who maintain that there is no truly Korean script beyond the "indigenous" Korean alphabet (hangul) (Kim 2005). In this line of argument, foreign missionaries (above all, the Christian Bible translators) and their Korean assistants, other estranged Koreans or Korean-Americans such as Sŏ Chae-p'il[16] (the founder and editor of Korea's first hangul-only newspaper, the *Tongnip Sinmun*), and later the Korean subsidiaries of the American military government are cast as the unholy alliance with so little regard for the true national and historical identity of Koreans that they pushed for a hangul exclusivity modeled on Western alphabetic scripts. Not patriotism but *sŏyang sadaejuŭi* (subservience to the West) is thus the alleged reason why Korean hangul supremacists were so eager to exact what, in this view, was not a vindication of a glorious Korean invention but only a poor imitation of how Latin script is used in the West.[17]

HANMUN AS (ENDANGERED) HERITAGE

Korea is famed for its condensed development, a transformation from old to new—or even hypermodern—that occurred in record time. Only seemingly a paradox: the protection of cultural heritage has become an all-the-more prominent issue in a country where nationalists were always torn between, on the one hand, criticism of a (perceived) backwardness that purportedly inhibited Korea's development into a strong nation, and, on the other, the upholding of a national pride predicating itself upon a deep-seated high civilization and culture.

In their Korean incarnations, the role and methods of preservation of heritage and state-sponsored cultural policies, and the cultivation of traditions—be they authentic or invented and constructed—have all been subjects of fruitful academic research and debate (Pai 1999; Kendall 2011). However, one seemingly natural target of heritage preservation remains absent from discussions in this context, despite being arguably the very epitome of endangered culture in Korea: Korean *hanmun*— Korea's literature in Literary Sinitic—theoretically comprising all writings in Literary Sinitic that were read by and were dear to Koreans of former generations, but especially used to refer to literature in Literary Sinitic authored by Koreans, a narrower sense that is often clandestinely applied.

This absence perhaps reflects the overall initial attitude and focus of the proponents of designating and classifying intangible cultural properties (*muhyŏng munhwajae*) when the movement came into full swing in the 1960s and 1970s: "Because it was accepted that the Korean literati and court culture, the so-called high tradition, had largely been imported from China, the more indigenous folk culture or 'low tradition' was embraced in an effort to create the iconicity that politicians and academics sought" (Howard 2014, 136).

Keith Howard here identifies a mainstream logic of preservation promoters—one that may also have been responsible for their shunning of *hanmun*, as this was synonymous with mere "high" tradition. But their discourse conflicted with an opposing one that refused to limit the status and position of *hanmun* to a matter of class.

A wider perspective reveals that the advocates of *hanmun* translation since the 1960s have drawn on the arguments of earlier apologists for the continued use of *hanmun* writing (as opposed to writing in the Korean vernacular). Korea "can no longer read the books her fathers wrote,"[18] James Scarth Gale lamented in numerous variations during the late 1910s and early 1920s (see King 2012), echoing complaints from many Koreans who opposed what came to be termed *hanmun p'yeji*, the "abolition" of *hanmun*, or *hanmun paech'ŏk*, the "ostracization" of *hanmun*. Intellectuals from the late nineteenth century onward engaged in debates over the reasons for Korea's weakness and set up guidelines for strengthening and remedying such a bad state of affairs, and many of them took aim at the amount of time erudite Koreans invested in the mere acquisition of literacy.[19] The Kabo Reforms (*kabo kaehyŏk*) of 1894 abolished the civil service examinations (*kwagŏ*) that were based on proficiency in Literary Sinitic and decreed that official records should be kept in hangul. This represented a much-disputed official break with tradition, and during the first decades of the twentieth century "a tectonic shift in the ways Koreans perceived language, identity, and culture" took place (King and Park 2016, xviii). However, the demotion of *hanmun* was a much more complex process, as a good deal of *hanmun* literature was, though increasingly marginalized, still produced during the Japanese colonial occupation and even beyond. Korea has indeed experienced a very long "hanmun hangover" (Wells 2011, 10).[20]

HANMUN AND SOUTH KOREAN
CULTURAL POLICY

The push to translate *hanmun* gained momentum against the backdrop of official cultural policy in the 1960s and 1970s. When the New Village Movement (*saemaŭl undong*)—launched in 1970—began to replace straw-thatched mud houses with new buildings and transformed the traditional rural landscape, some of the original structures were relocated and refurbished in open-air museums, as artifacts of the traditional past. At the same time, radical modernization condemned a variety of traditional handicrafts and customs to obsolescence, preserving only a few eminent masters as "living treasures." It was not only about protection for its own sake but also about the calculated political benefits of enacting protection measures. Various nomenclatures were devised to define and rank material and immaterial heritage, with the overall aim of "harnessing Korea's cultural heritage to help fuel South Korea's modernization" (Park 2010, 74).

Translation of *hanmun* was increasingly incorporated into the governmental agenda as well. The Korean Classics Research Institute (Minjok Munhwa Ch'ujinhoe) was founded in 1965 and transformed in 2007/2008 into the Institute for the Translation of Korean Classics. Stipulating the institute's purpose, the Ministry of Education declared in Article 1 that the task of "collecting, arranging and translating classical documents" should "contribute to the succession [*sic*] and development of traditional culture."[21] The campaign for the translation of *hanmun* literature claimed to prevent Koreans from becoming cut off from the cultural achievements of their past. This danger was ascribed to the impending demise of a generation with a traditional education who could read *hanmun*—synonymous with the disappearance of a core part of Korean culture that has often been described as a case of "diglossia."[22] At the beginning of this translation movement, it was considered fortuitous that many Korean fathers had cared enough to send their sons to a *sŏdang* (reading hall; private school for education in *hanmun*; K. *kŭlbang* [writing room]), despite the modern schools and their curricula.[23] These *sŏdang*-educated people were well equipped to translate *hanmun*—with the downside that some of them had not read enough in hangul, leading to a special kind of translationese (see Sŏng and Yi 2013).

THE HANGUL EXCLUSIVITY POLICY AS A TRIGGER FOR *HANMUN* TRANSLATION

Curiously, the five-year initiative for hangul exclusivity (*han'gŭl chŏn'yong 5-kaenyŏn kyehoek*), introduced in May 1968 by Park Chung Hee to eliminate the use of *hantcha* by 1972, led to increased efforts to translate *hanmun* into modern Korean. Having survived several earlier hangul-only laws that were eventually revoked, the use of *hantcha* was still standard to render Sino-Korean words. Park Chung Hee's seven-point proclamation contained a specific order to translate classic texts (*kojŏn-ŭi hangŭl pŏnyŏg-ŭl sŏdurŭl kŏt*[24]). An article published in the *Tonga Ilbo* in 1969 emphasizes the connection between the new policy and the need for *hanmun* translation, revealing that the connection was perceived as self-evident: "The enterprise of the translation of the classics . . . has gained life because the hangul exclusivity policy is pushed forward" (*Tonga Ilbo*, December 6, 1969).

But was there really a logical and obvious connection? One might argue that hangul exclusivity is simply about orthography, in other words, about abandoning one way of writing (in mixed script) in favor of another (hangul only), but not changing the language itself. *Hanmun*, by contrast, represents—strictly speaking—a different language. However, this must be put into perspective: the relinquishing of even the basic elements— the characters—with which *hanmun* literature is written must have felt like the last nail in the coffin for die-hard believers in the possibility of upholding a lifeline for original *hanmun*. This can be illustrated by the following case.

On the last but one day of 1968, the *Tonga Ilbo* reports that a professor of East Asian philosophy named Yu Chŏnggi, from Ch'ungnam National University in Taejŏn, was fired by the university's president for his agitation against the hangul exclusivity policy. In fact—as we learn from a series of articles updating readers about the case during the first half of 1969—the professor sued his employer for unfair dismissal, and half a year later had his claim upheld, only to then retire of his own volition. In the first article about his case he is quoted, amongst other statements, as saying that hangul exclusivity would turn *kojŏn* into "libraries' toilet paper" (*Tonga Ilbo*, December 30, 1968).

In fact, this statement only makes sense if we accept that there was a perceived subterranean connection between *hanmun* literacy and the use of mixed script. We still can see this linkage when Koreans use the word "*hanmun*" to mean *hantcha*, and vice versa. For example, Koreans might well say that a *hansi* (a poem in Literary Sinitic) is written in *hantcha*— while knowing perfectly well that this is a kind of understatement. After all, a text written in Literary Sinitic is not simply written with different characters; it is written in a different language. Likewise, in November 1967, Park Chung Hee was quoted in newspapers as having said: "Hangul is the most scientific and best-designed script in the world, so it is shameful that it is still mixed with *hanmun*" (*Kyŏnghyang Sinmun*, November 17, 1967, quoted in Hong 2014, 69). It is very clear that he meant not "mixed with *hanmun*" but "mixed with *hantcha*," identifying *hanmun* simply with Chinese characters. What this seeming confusion tells us is that conceiving of *hanmun* as writings in a totally different language from Korean may be theoretically correct, but at the same time, this was (and is) sometimes too abstract and pedantic for Koreans themselves. A sound basis of familiarity with two to three thousand unsimplified characters, some basic grammatical knowledge ingrained in proverbs and the common four-character idioms, plus those odd little bits of haphazardly picked-up rudimentary skills usually sufficed to prevent "modern" Koreans from being completely clueless in regard to Literary Sinitic. Ultimately, a *hanmun* text may have been largely incomprehensible, but nevertheless it did not look completely impenetrable.

In short, when *hanmun* and *hantcha* are equated with one other, it is not always through blatant ignorance but should be regarded as a telling simplification. Not least, failing to distinguish between *hanmun* and *hantcha* can serve the purpose of "othering" *hantcha* that was so vigorously pursued by hangul purists (see Park 1989). It is in this vein that the director of the Hangul Society ridicules, in a polemic published by the *Korea Journal*, the concerns of opponents of the hangul-only policy: "there are men who are greatly afraid that we will be isolated from the Oriental cultural tradition if we continue to use *han-gŭl* exclusively, inasmuch as our cultural heritage is recorded in Chinese characters" (Huh 1972, 45). Of course, the suggestion that Korean cultural heritage "is recorded in Chinese characters" misses the mark, there being much more to Literary Sinitic than its use of *hantcha*—but from the perspective of those agitating against any use of *hantcha*, it makes sense to avoid differentiation. And as seen in the case of the unfairly dismissed professor, this equation of *hanmun* and *hantcha* was made by the other side as well.

An evident underlying rationale for the hangul exclusivity policy was nation building, an attempt to cement a sense of shared cultural identity, in line with the rhetoric of national homogeneity that was so characteristic of Park Chung Hee's developmental dictatorship. *Taejungsŏng* (mass appeal) and *kongdongch'e* (community, communality) are relevant keywords in this context: the hangul exclusivity policy was meant to invoke a politics of inclusion, because it renounced a demanding writing regime that was bound to be perceived as discriminatory or even exclusive, and associated with feudalism.[25] After all, not knowing the meaning of a word is different from not even being able to recognize the characters in which it is written. Following this logic of inclusion, one corollary was the move to appropriate *hanmun* for the masses and transform it, via translation, into a common good—in a way that historically was not the case. The merit of hangul in helping Koreans achieve full literacy within a short time is widely acknowledged; on the other hand, the frequent claim by partisans of mixed script that the widespread ignorance of *hantcha* is meanwhile responsible for secondary illiteracy[26] is not unfounded, as the meaning of a Sino-Korean word is very precisely conveyed by its Chinese characters, while hangul only represents the (often) extremely ambiguous sound—a consequence of the limited number of actively used phonemes and the large stock of homophones this created.

Another rationale for the hangul exclusivity policy must be mentioned. While the dictator in fact normalized relations with Japan, he was eager to convey via symbolic politics (above all, a ban on Japanese popular culture that was only lifted near the end of the millennium) an unrelenting "patriotic" stance, to satisfy the strong critics who saw many issues closed off that—in their eyes—needed to be rectified. Now, as (Korean) "mixed script" was strongly associated with Japanese "mixed script" (the Japanese writing system that combines *kanji* with *kana*), the move for hangul exclusivity served to signal intransigence toward hated remnants of colonial rule.

The hangul-only policy was hotly contested. Not only did it meet fierce opposition in parliament[27] but there was also a public backlash, with emotional appeals published in newspapers.[28] All this forced the government to placate the dissidents.[29] Thus, the policy was not pursued consistently, but was characterized by "frequent flip-flops" (Taylor and Taylor 2014, 179), especially regarding the use of *hantcha* in school. In any case, many of those who made intensive use of language, such as publishers and academics, were unwilling to implement the new rules. This was most evident in the media, where a hangul-only newspaper (the *Han'gyŏre*) did not emerge until 1988. But eventually all other newspapers switched to an almost exclusively hangul-only style. Even if the pendulum is now moving back again in favor of more *hantcha*, this is only happening in extremely small stages, despite being occasionally heralded as signs of a resurrection. A relatively big step came in 1999, with the reintroduction of street signs showing the *hantcha* behind the names written in hangul (and thus also giving back an etymology and the flair of meaning to otherwise bland-sounding or near-nonsensical designations). Additionally, *hantcha* education is slowly regaining ground, as seen in the recent decision to introduce *hantcha* from the third grade of elementary school from 2018 onward—a benchmark decision that drew much attention.

MOTIFS OF THE DISCOURSE

As shown above, the push for mass translation of "the classics" was triggered by special circumstances: the announcement of the hangul-only policy and the parallel start of government-sponsored translation of *hanmun*. A close reading of public discussion—for example, newspaper editorials and other opinion pieces—reveals that over the years since then, a striking number of arguments (or discourse motifs, i.e., patterns of arguing) from the arsenal of late nineteenth- and early twentieth-century *hanmun* apologists was taken over in the 1960s and onward, but now in the cause of *hanmun* translation. At the same time, advocacy for *hanmun* translation displayed overlaps with the defense of *hantcha* (in practical terms: the defense of mixed script). The following identifies the main discourse motifs and rhetorical moves involved, and explores both their historical underpinnings and the roles they play in a web of interrelated arguments.

Continuity of Tradition versus Being Cut off from the Ancestors

Whatever the purpose of a particular contribution to the discourse about *hanmun* translation, it typically includes a more general argument regarding the fundamental necessity of translations: the contention that translations bridge the cultural gap between present-day Koreans and their ancestors. Typically, this includes the idea that it is the present generation's duty to pass their inheritance on to their descendants (*huson*) by translating *hanmun* texts into modern Korean, *uri kŭl* (our script) (*Sŏul Kyŏngje*, May 30, 2016). Of course, this argument only works if this inheritance is seen in a positive light like a birthright—or at least as something that can neither be refuted nor negated because it is simply an inescapable condition. "Whether you want it or not—our culture and *hanmun* are by destiny inseparable," declares one contributor to the discussion, who opines that "*hanmun* culture" (*hanmun munhwa*) is in the first place an overpowered victim of "Western culture" (*sŏgu munhwa*)—and not, interestingly, of indigenous vernacular Korean (*Tonga Ilbo*, September 18, 1969). "Classical literature is now withering and [we are terrified by the worry that] the purity of Korean ethnicity will follow the same path," the Association for the Glorious Literature of Korea (Chosŏn kwangmunhoe) warned in a public appeal in 1910 (*Sonyŏn* 1910, 56–57; quoted in Ro 2012, 195).

During the decades of Korea's increasing modernization, from the end of the nineteenth century, many a learned man felt haunted by the specter of bonds with the past and the ancestors being severed if generations to come were unable to read *hanmun*. This fear inspired fierce opposition to writing in the vernacular (or simply: in Korean). Such worries over disconnection from the past seem more justified if we consider that in the early twentieth century, even a foreigner like James Scarth Gale repeatedly deplored the abolition of the *kwagŏ* exams, referring to their demise as a disaster that would divide father and son, with the father educated in the traditions of Sinitic cosmopolitism, the son under Japanese and Western curricula.[30] However, it must also be remembered that some intellectuals during those formative decades made reconciliatory efforts to interpret the modern development of literature and writing not as a rupture but instead as a continuation of progressive trends from the premodern era.[31] The same approach was of course applied to many other fields in order to identify an indigenous pedigree for enlightenment and all kinds of modern developments. Not by coincidence, this reminds us of how Japan's successful modernization was ascribed "to the utility of premodern values and institutions" (Vlastos 1997, 1).

The rift between fathers and sons, separated by drastic historical changes, is also depicted in a number of novels from the 1930s, such as Yŏm Sang-sŏp's *Samdae* (1931) and Ch'ae Man-sik's *T'aep'yŏng ch'ŏnha* (1938).[32] In a very famous poem by Yi Sang from 1934, the poetic persona asks why he has to play—all at once—his own role together with that of his father, his grandfather, and his great-grandfather.[33] It might sound somewhat overstated but if we accept, for heuristic reasons, the bold proposition that an "unbridgeable emotional gap between fathers and sons" exists as an integral aspect of Korea's traditional "father culture" (De Mente 2012; s.v. *aboji*), then the big changes in the wake of modernization in Korea only exacerbated a perennial generational conflict and perpetual frustration in a new way. The extreme development of hangul exclusivity under Park Chung Hee was bound to rub salt in old wounds about severed bonds with the past—under circumstances that were already totally different, as *ŏnmun il'chi* (i.e., writing in the vernacular) had become unchallengeable.

The warning that links with the past would be severed is one of the key and striking tropes in the discourse on *hanmun* translation, resurfacing regularly ever since the 1960s. Unless *hanmun* is translated, worries one contributor (Chŏng 2007, 257), there is no transition (*ihaeng*) from past to present, and the past will remain buried (*maemol toeŏ pŏrigo*).

Koreans younger than forty are cut off (*tanjŏl*) from what came before, despite *hantcha* being absolutely necessary for the development of future culture, one contributor to the discussion laments in 1985 (*Tonga Ilbo*, July 15, 1985), using a metaphor that had already lasted for roughly nine decades and is still in use today. Likewise, a former director of the Institute for Translation of Korean Classics comments in a column for the *Han'gyŏre* (November 28, 2008): "Except for the decipherers of *hanmun*, who are an extreme minority, our people are in the majority total ignoramuses [*kkamangnun*] in front of the *hanmun* classics. Being unable to read the *hanmun* classics of premodern times, this naturally means being cut off from our history and traditional culture."

The metaphor of being cut off is encountered in many variations. As the branches have to maintain their connection to the "roots" (see above), Koreans have to keep themselves grounded; their identity needs a "foundation" and has to be "anchored" in order not be dragged away "during an era of rapid globalization" (Chŏng 2007, 252); Koreans are declared in need of "communication with the past" (*Han'guk Ilbo*, July 28, 2006) and are called upon, in a dramatic congestion of images, to set free a "tradition that is enclosed in the walls of Chinese characters" (*hantcha-ŭi pyŏg-e kach'in chŏnt'ong*) and to extricate the classics from the "swamp of oblivion" (*manggag-ŭi nup*) (*Han'guk Ilbo*, July 28, 2006). The notion of modern Koreans being cut off from their past is frequently illustrated by the fact that they prefer reading foreign classics, rather than their own. They read—as one commentator sums it up—Shakespeare but not Korea's eighteenth-century cultural hero Chŏng Yak-yong (*Han'gyŏre*, November 28, 2008). For advocates of *hanmun* translation this is a perfect proof of *tanjŏl*, an estrangement from what was one's own. Koreans should embrace their duty to overcome this state in order to know themselves again. *Hanmun* is identified with *ppuri* (the roots),[34] with *ponjil* (the essence),[35] with *chinsu* (quintessence),[36] with *chŏngch'esŏng* (identity),[37] and with *chuch'esŏng* (autonomy).[38]

Such reasoning obviously responds to the "othering" of *hantcha* and *hanmun*—the objection that they both have foreign (Chinese) origins and that Literary Sinitic is "a foreign language," as Korea's linguistic pioneer Chu Si-gyŏng audaciously claimed (1907, 32; cf. An 2015, 13). It is in answer to such still-lingering views that the advocates of *hanmun* translation feel the urge to insist that Koreans fully appropriated this script and literature, just as Confucianism and Buddhism underwent a perfect "acclimatization" (*sunhwa*) in Korea (see *Tonga Ilbo*, November 21, 1968). In other words, all these reminders to Koreans that *hanmun* is the very epitome of their heritage are not merely belaboring the obvious, but represent a deliberate antithesis to a rival pattern of reasoning. One *locus classicus* in this regard is Yi Kwang-su's *Munhak iran hao* (What is literature?), first published in 1916, where Yi speaks of the damage done to Koreans by Confucianism as a foreign influence detrimental to indigenous tradition (the ultimate implication being that this made Koreans less fit for survival, and susceptible to colonization by the Japanese): "Korea should

possess its own unique spiritual civilization. Sadly, however, our ancestors' great achievement—their literature—is lost to us . . . their inability
and idleness led them to fail to preserve their spiritual civilization for
future generations. . . . [T]he intrusion of Chinese ways of thinking into
Korea also weakened Korean culture (Yi 2011, 301). This idea that Chinese
influence has led to an arrogant or ignorant unwillingness to preserve
indigenous culture, causing it to become lost (or, in the case of vernacular
Korean language, at least neglected)[39] can be seen as the original thesis
against which the bold equation of Korean identity with *hanmun* reacts
as an antithesis. However, it is sometimes wiser to posit an antithesis as
if it were an original thesis. The simple equation of *hanmun* with true
Koreanness is a case in point.

Globalization and Hallyu

Globalization (*segyehwa*) has been a ubiquitous buzzword in Korea—and
still is, despite being increasingly taken for granted. President Kim Young
Sam is credited with having put globalization at the top of his agenda
when he came to power in 1993. His explicit association of globalization with Koreanness is remarkable: "we should march out in the world
on the strength of our unique culture and traditional values" (Kim 1996,
273, quoted in Finch and Kim 2009, 125). It is striking to see how regularly globalization surfaces as a keyword in the discourse about *hanmun*
translation. What is not globalized "does not exist," and therein lies the
importance of translating the classics, asserts one translator (*Han'guk
Kyŏngje Ilbo*, June 12, 2014). Rather than striving to win at the Olympic
Games, opines another contributor to the discussion, Korea's ambition
should be to make its "history and soul" known to the world (Yu 2000,
244). These examples illustrate the close link that is generally established
in Korea between the concepts of heritage preservation and globalization.
This is consistent with the logic of the World Heritage Convention, which
suggests that the most worthy and genuine local heritage is intrinsically
and ultimately also global heritage, a mirror of mankind and a witness
to humanity's spirit.[40] Consequently, South Korea has been very adept
in using the UNESCO Convention Concerning the Protection of the
World's Cultural and Natural Heritage, and has also managed to include
more materials (most of them in *hanmun*) in the UNESCO Memory of

the World Programme than any other country in Asia to this point in time.[41] Naturally, translation is seen as a means to back claims of Korean literature's global value, or at least as an indispensable prerequisite for its eligibility as world literature.

Now, it is easy to accept the notion that a global age entails the need for English translations of *hanmun*. But under such circumstances, what is the justification for the purported need for translations into Korean? This obviously begs explanation, but typically the exact nexus is not made explicit. The underlying reasoning can be inferred, however: if the globalized Koreans of today are busy enough developing proficiency in English, they can no longer be asked to bother with acquiring the ability to read the classics in the original version. Rendering Korean *hanmun* directly into the global language (English)[42] might in fact be the logical next step, but the production of translations into the vernacular—into readily accessible contemporary Korean—can plausibly be considered a recognition of globally valid standards as well. A "communion" (*kyogam*) with the classics, made possible by translations that are "customized for the era of globalization" (*segyehwa sidae-e matke*), will prove that "the past can even be a much more advanced future" (*kwagŏ-ga hwŏlssin tŏ apsŏn mirae-ga toel su itta*)—so boasts a representative of the publisher Akanet in an interview (*Han'gyŏre*, November 10, 2013).

A related issue is the possible role and involvement of foreigners.[43] Would foreigners be best served with *hanmun* (the original text), Korean translations, or English renderings? And as for Western translators, would their translations be better based on the originals or on modern Korean translations? Are good Korean translations prerequisites for good English translations, or are such intermediaries unnecessary? Occasionally, English translations of *hanmun* are welcomed as a possible stimulus for Korean humanities, since international scholars might contribute alternative interpretations and viewpoints (see *Kyosu Sinmun*, May 28, 2014).

One particular claim that reflects what may be a distinctively Korean belief[44] is that Koreans themselves should translate their quintessential classics for the outside world (into English and other languages). They should do this by having an expert on premodern literature (a Korean) cooperate with an expert on foreign literature (another Korean)—there would be "no other way" (*Yŏnhap Nyusŭ*, October 5, 2008). Tellingly, this reasoning does not even consider the inclusion of non-Koreans in the process of translating *hanmun* into foreign languages (*Yŏnhap Nyusŭ*, October 5, 2008).

One might expect some natural distance between advocates of *hanmun* translations and promoters of *hallyu* (the "Korean Wave," or the growing popularity of products of the Korean cultural industry, especially television dramas and pop music, since the late 1990s). However, in fact, affirmative rhetorical connections between *hallyu* and *hanmun* are not uncommonly drawn. Even a "kojŏn *hallyu*" is proclaimed occasionally; that is, a Korean wave based on Korean premodern (classical) literature (*Han'guk Kyŏngje Ilbo*, June 12, 2014). If *hanmun* translations are expected to form part of "K-literature," which is promoted as a high-quality (*ko'gŭp*) *hallyu* phenomenon, this invites the logical objection that even contemporary Korean literature faces significant barriers abroad. But rhetoric is sometimes little more than a game of fearless one-upmanship, and thus one contributor declares that as long as Korean premodern literature is not introduced to the outside world, contemporary literature will not find acceptance—a reasoning that is not backed up with any specific evidence or logic, but is obviously meant to be persuasive simply by force of the apodictic gesture itself (Chŏng 2007, 259). A certain jealousy is also apparent in the faulting of a perceived inequality in attention (*p'yŏnjung*) that favors the translation of modern literature (*Yŏnhap Nyusŭ*, October 5, 2008).

The most prominent way in which translations from *hanmun* into contemporary Korean supposedly exert a stimulating influence on *hallyu* is by serving as an input for historical dramas (*sagŭk*). For example, one contributor to the discussion contends that without a translation of the *Annals of the Chosŏn Dynasty* into modern Korean, there would be no *Wang-ŭi namja* (the movie *The King and the Clown*, a hugely successful historical drama from 2005), highlighting the immense potential for *hanmun* as source material for drama (*Kyŏnghyang Sinmun*, April 3, 2006). If enough translators of classics are trained, another contributor calculates, there will be "ten million more movies" (*Han'guk Ilbo*, August 6, 2014). The purported logic here is that Korean classics can be exploited for their "cultural content"—*k'ont'ench'ŭ* being an *en vogue* keyword in Korea,[45] mirroring the attention given to the culture industry (*Han'guk Ilbo*, July 28, 2006). A concise formula to sum up this point is the demand to abandon mere "conservation" (*pojon*) and concentrate on "usage" (*hwaryong*) as an agenda that is even more important (*Segye Ilbo*,

May 30, 2007). Translation, ventures the current head of the Institute for the Translation of Korean Classics, is therefore like the "production of flour," which can later serve as the basis "for bread as well as cake" (YTN radio, *Sudogwŏn t'udei*, April 28, 2017).

However, there is also an anti-*hallyu* thread in the *hallyu*-related discourse on *hanmun* translation: in the eyes of those for whom literature in *hanmun* represents the most worthy and faithful expression of true Koreanness (*Kyosu Sinmun*, May 28, 2014), a "globalization" of *hanmun* would serve Korea's image more than the worldwide popularity of K-pop—or at least it would reflect authentic Koreanness more correctly.

Despite such disagreements, it is generally welcomed that translations of the classics can provide rich "content" for dramas and movies. Another highly lauded form of representation and popularization of the classics is their "translation" into cartoons (*manhwa*, akin to graphic novels) (*Munhwa Ilbo*, June 10, 2007). This has now been augmented by webtoons, *Imgŭm-ŭi koyangi* (The king's cat) from the series *T'ammyo in'gan* (Cat-crazy human) being a flagship example of a successful outlet for translated content (*Yŏsŏng Tonga*, October 5, 2016). While the popularization (*taejunghwa*) of Korean classics is recognized as reliant on translation, these two are not simply equated with each other: "Popularization of classics is divided into two categories: producing translated contents and putting the translated content to use" (Ha 2015, 68).

Looking to Japan, China, and North Korea

Drawing on a discourse motif that will ring a bell with anyone familiar with discussions on the abolition of Latin from high school curricula in Europe, the reading of the classics and the translation of *hanmun* is advocated as a "humanist education for youth" (*ch'ŏngsonyŏn-ŭi inmun kyoyuk*)—diametrically opposed to the cramming of encyclopedic knowledge for the sake of exams (*Tonga Ilbo*, August 16, 1966).

The European situation is often jealously mentioned: "In the West, all sources and documents, not only of Greece and the Roman Empire but also of medieval Latinity, are translated into all the various European languages, so that a person without knowledge of the old languages can also freely read and study them" (*Tonga Ilbo*, July 15, 1985). In contrast to this purported situation in the West, and also in contrast to neighboring Japan, students in Korea—because of the prevailing disregard (*musi*) for *hantcha* and *hanmun* and with nobody teaching them—could become blind to their own country's invaluable classics, so the argument goes. A repeated complaint sees Koreans as "lagging a hundred years behind" Japan and China (*Chosŏn Ilbo*, May 14, 2014), which translated their classic texts into the modern vernacular more quickly, whereas *hanmun* translation activities only began to flourish on a larger scale in South Korea from the 1970s. Accordingly, problems with translation quality are often attributed to the brevity of that history of professionalism.[46]

For some time, it was routinely acknowledged that North Korea had attained better development in the field of *hanmun* translation. After all, North Korea had already published a full translation of the *Annals of the Chosŏn Dynasty* in 1981 (under the title *Yijo sillok* [Annals of the Yi-dynasty]). References to North Korea's advancement became a standard theme. Readers of the *Segye Ilbo* of May 30, 2007, learned that North Koreans were "clearly one step ahead" (*punmyŏng uri-poda hanbal apsŏtta*), both in terms of hangulization (*hangŭlhwa*), or the translation into modern Korean, and in terms of *yongŏ chŏngni*, or the standardization of terminology. The fact that ideology and political agendas color these translations is admitted, but this does not substantially alter the overall judgment. North Korean translations are respected for their ability to unpack *hanmun* sentences so that they are easily understood by a general readership, as well as for sticking to a standard usage of vocabulary (*Segye Ilbo*, May 30, 2007). The specific North Korean approach to "hanguliza-tion of premodern texts" (*komunhŏn hangŭlhwa*) is acknowledged as having grown in the 1970s and 1980s "to a dazzling degree" (*nunbusige*) (*Segye Ilbo*, May 30, 2007). Of course, it is noted that North Koreans instrumentalize this old literature to strengthen inner cohesion, but this is not automatically accompanied by criticism. (These commentators probably consider inner cohesion simply as desirable for any state, and not precariously double-edged.) These days, South Korean respect for North Korean *hangŭlhwa* seems to have cooled, with more attention being paid to flaws in the North Korean translation and arbitrary interpretations, and greater appreciation for the typically more academic approach of South Korean translators (see *Yŏnhap Nyusŭ*, January 26, 2017; see also An 2012 and Yi 2007).

Nevertheless, the translation of *hanmun* was one area in which new agreements on exchange remained possible, during times when many other projects had come to a standstill. In 2014, the South Korean Institute for the Translation of Korean Classics and its North Korean counterpart, the *Minjok Kojŏn Yŏn'guso*, signed an understanding on cooperation (albeit of limited scope), which was well covered in the media (*Mŏni t'udei*, September 18, 2014).

Rhetorical Maneuvers

Translation of *hanmun* is often a highly emotional topic that involves a rhetoric overflowing with pathos and rich in metaphors. At the same time, its promoters tend to employ an accusatory, incriminating voice, typically using embarrassing rhetorical questions that function as gestures of utter exasperation in the face of unacceptable conditions: "As our classics are all recorded in *hanmun*, how can it be tolerated that translation is making no progress?" (*Tonga Ilbo*, July 15, 1985). "Has there ever been a country which has neglected its traditions and treated its classics with contempt but still managed to fulfill its role?" exclaims a deputy director of the Tasan Yŏn'guso in a newspaper column in 2006 (*Naeil Sinmun*, August 3, 2006). "Doesn't one commit a crime against the ancestors by neglect of the classics?" goes a variation of fundamentally the same accusation, clad as a rhetorical question, which again targets a whole nation as the perpetrator (*Han'guk Ilbo*, July 28, 2006). The classics are regularly declared a "common good" (*minjok kongyu*) (e.g., *Tonga Ilbo*, November 6, 1985). Thus, the *Annals of the Chosŏn Dynasty* (Chosŏn wangjo sillok) are revalued, not to say upgraded and ennobled, as a *kungmin sillok*, meaning that the annals of the dynasty and the king turn into annals (*sillok*) of the citizens (*kungmin*), disseminated via the internet to the common people of Korea (*Munhwa Ilbo*, October 5, 2010).

This selling of *hanmun* as a common good of Koreans was certainly quite a bold maneuver, if we only look at all those later Chosŏn-period satires and mocking of literati (*sŏnbi*) arrogance, indulging in schadenfreude at their mishaps. A hilarious example is the fictitious anecdote of a learned man having become immersed in his *hanmun* studies to the absurd degree of being unable to communicate with the commoners of his village in the worst possible emergency imaginable: the scholar's father being dragged away by a tiger.[47] In other words, given that true mastery of Literary Sinitic—requiring hard training of cognitive reflexes from early childhood onward in order not to miss intertextual references, implicit subtexts, and intricate allusions—had always been confined to an elite few, the blatant appropriation of *hanmun* as a shared heritage is tantamount to a denial of historical realities.

The emphatic appeal to regard translation as a "patriotic movement" (*aeguk undong*) (*Tonga Ilbo*, July 15, 1985) and as "enhancing national prestige" (*kugwi sŏnyang*) (*Tonga Ilbo*, November 24, 1966)—and thus as a national enterprise and collective responsibility—is a major thread of the discourse on *hanmun* translation, and one that spans decades. In 2016, the head of the Institute for the Translation of Korean Classics harangues in a column contributed to the *Chosŏn Ilbo*: "That the citizens of a country cannot read their own country's history is really a disgrace. It is a problem for the dignity of the nation. All over the world, is there another country of that kind?" (August 16, 2016). We also find mention of occasional initiatives and financial support from the private sector, but in such cases the reliance on donations is bemoaned (*Tonga Ilbo*, July 15, 1985; *Segye Ilbo*, May 30, 2007). State and government are regularly reminded that it is their responsibility to carry out the task systematically (Chŏng 2007, 258).

Korea's reputation, claims one contributor in 1985, is based more soundly on the classics than on visible new wealth: "The world will respect a people that lives in straw-huts but reads its classics" (*Tonga Ilbo*, July 15, 1985). This comment is reminiscent of a remark by Henri Zuber that has become famous in Korea, suggesting that the French painter (who in 1866 took part in the punitive campaign undertaken by France against Korea in retaliation for the Koreans' execution of Catholic missionaries) felt ashamed upon observing the presence of books in even the poorest Korean house.[48] The point made is that the translation of *hanmun* may not be profitable but has nevertheless the potential to enhance South Korea's international standing, albeit not as directly and evidently as other measures of development (but rather as a form of "soft power," as it would be called today).

Another striking rhetorical maneuver is the deliberate inversion of established semantic and conceptual associations. Thus, the linkage of the agenda of *hanmun* translation with, of all things, "democratization" (*minjuhwa*) represents a bold move. After all, *hanmun* is more readily associated with the elitist *yangban* class[49] and is generally considered to have been an instrumental factor in a system of social exclusion, standing at odds to the masses. However, the counterargument can be made—as, indeed, the advocates of *hanmun* translation propose—that if the general public can now read and understand what in the past was reserved for a privileged minority, then this can be justly perceived as a kind of democratization (*Han'guk Ilbo*, July 28, 2006).

In the same vein, even though *hanmun* translations clearly seem to be, by definition, backward-oriented and devoted to the past, a simple rhetorical maneuver can turn the tables and make sure that in the end Koreans are cast as backward precisely for *not* translating. The trick here is to brand the objection against a preoccupation with *kojŏn* (as indulging in something old and backward) as backward itself—in other words, to blame the objectors for their failure to recognize the signs of the times, which point to a new demand for *kojŏn*, at least in translation.

Finally, a gesture that is close to the rhetorical question is the imperative. The advocates of *hanmun* translation make ample use of it in declamatory demands: bring the books that are "buried in libraries" back to the "living rooms" (*anbang*) (*Han'gyŏre*, November 4, 2013) to "save the tradition" (*chŏnt'ong ŭl kuhara*), and so on (*Han'guk Ilbo*, July 28, 2006).

Practical Issues

The matter of *hanmun* translation is mainly kept alive in public discourse by those involved professionally in the business of translating (or equivalent nonprofit endeavors), or by people who enjoy rank and position in institutions devoted to the translation of *hanmun*. It therefore comes as no surprise that their discussions mostly revolve around funding and sponsorship, and aim at inducing additional support. Many of the complaints dwell on what is perceived as a lack of governmental responsibility. Despite various masterplans, there are regular calls for a longer-term outlook. One contributor claims in 2007 that no medium- or long-term plan had ever been implemented during more than forty years of *hanmun* translation (*Kyosu Sinmun*, February 5, 2007).

Lamentations over the shortage of translators, and how to educate and foster more of them, are very common, as well as complaints that so many texts still await translation due to the dearth of talented, able people (*injae*). This alleged lack exacerbates the perceived crisis. As the seasoned translators who are currently in charge grow older, the need for a new generation of experts is becoming ever more vital, according to an oft-repeated mantra (*Tonga Ilbo*, November 6, 1985). Yi Tong-hwan, a former director of the Institute for the Translation of Korean Classics, complains in 2011 that no more than twenty to thirty sufficiently skilled people exist (*Han'guk Ilbo*, January 3, 2011)—an astonishingly low estimate (or high standard) that seems to disavow the skills of many more translators who in fact are doing *hanmun* translations. The purpose of painting such a bleak picture might be that it serves to underscore the director's call for a specialized graduate school, although he envisions that it will take ten years of training to produce capable translators (*Kyosu Sinmun*, May 28, 2014).

At the same time, the grassroots origins of translation work are a source of pride. According to a column in the *Tonga Ilbo* (July 15, 1985), some scholars were providing free accommodation and meals for people willing to learn the tools of the trade. Such scholars deserve respect, not noisy politicians, rants the columnist (probably knowing full well that the authoritarian incumbents did not need to be as "noisy" as those clamoring for democracy) (*Tonga Ilbo*, July 15, 1985). In the same vein, veterans of *hanmun* translation would be proud of their self-made education, in the heroic and sacrificial tradition of the *chu-gyŏng-ya-dok* ideal: farm by day, study by night (see Sŏng and Yi 2013, 332).

Compilation, Preservation, and Editing of Originals

It is peculiar and telling that the discourse about *hanmun* as heritage (and thus about securing continuity of cultural transmission) revolves so much around translation. But given the paucity of critical editions that compare—consistent with standards of textual criticism—all the various printed versions (plus the sometimes very numerous handwritten manuscripts, or *p'ilsabon*), the editing of originals should play a much more central role, and not be treated as a subsidiary matter of *hanmun* translation.[50] Thus, the task of establishing a reputable text edition to work from should precede the task of translation (Yun Chae-min et al., 2009). *Han'gŭlhwa* should go hand in hand with *chŏngbonhwa*, the creation of authoritative critical editions of the originals (Sŏ 2010). This means that translation should not simply be undertaken in order to replace the originals.

Conservation—in the most literal sense—is another related, and compelling, concern. Unique books, *yuilbon*, are bound to rot away, as an article in the *Tonga Ilbo* laments on December 7, 1970. A related practical issue is that large numbers of original and precious texts are located in libraries and private collections outside of South Korea,[51] which may have inhibited access and translation work in the past (such claims have naturally waned in times of scanners and smartphone cameras, however). If *hanmun* is considered a legacy, the most obvious measure in terms of preservation would not be translation but collection, compilation, reproduction in facsimile, and editing. The physical damage to originals, let alone the disappearance of unique copies of old books (*kosŏ*), had already become a concern by the beginning of the twentieth century. In 1910, a literary club warned in a public appeal that old books, "an expression of Korean wisdom and talent," were "about to disappear" (*Sonyŏn* 1910, 56–57; also quoted in Ro 2012, 195). Whilst such alarms have echoed through the decades, compilation work has in fact been pursued on a grand scale, with ambitious masterplans and an enormous output achieved since the mid-1980s.[52]

In this regard, a recent variant of this discourse motif can be seen in the attempt to put pressure on Korean efforts to record and digitize all *hanmun* sources, by pointing to the urgency to do so in the face of Chinese projects that are accused of appropriating all Korean materials written in Literary Sinitic, on the basis of *hanmun*'s assumed transnationality. Worries have been raised that materials are simply brought to China—via private actors or via university exchange—which have not even been photocopied in Korea. The implication (and the concern of South Korean commentators) is that North Korea is especially vulnerable in that regard (*Munhwa Ilbo*, April 26, 2017). These purported goings-on and the call to take action against the danger and unfair competition they represent are reminiscent of previous "history wars" (Ahn 2007, 2008; for more on these conflicts see Andrew Logie's chapter in this volume).[53]

Reception and Target Audience

The scope of reception is a big concern in the discourse about *hanmun* translation: should the target audience be narrowly confined to the academic community, or should the translation be broadly accessible to the general public? There are complaints about certain translations being overly *hanmun*-like in style (*hanmunt'u*), containing translationese (*pŏnyŏkt'u*) formulations that resonate strongly with the Literary Sinitic of the original, which makes reading awkward for the general public.

One recurring admonition is the demand to tailor translations to the needs of the "hangul generation" (*hangŭl sedae*)—even though this expression was originally coined for a generation (first enrolled in school after the Liberation) that in fact still possessed a very thorough training in reading and writing *hantcha*. The term *hangul sedae* has now become a common formula, reminding translators of the changed linguistic environment and the needs of their contemporary readers.

Calls for "readability" (*kadoksŏng*) are often aimed at "*hanmun*-ish" style; translators are reminded to consistently stick to the grammar of the vernacular and to avoid becoming over-influenced by the source text's *hanmun* grammar and mannerisms. Alternatively, translators are exhorted to aim at a single target audience: either erudite scholars or the general public. It is now generally accepted that scholars are not best served simply with old books just as they are, but that they need processed (annotated, digitized) or even translated texts.[54] However, there is considerable dissent and a broad range of opinion regarding the degree to which the original language should be retained in translations, whether in the form of *hanmun* phrases or special Sino-Korean terms (*hantchaŏ*) (see An 2012; Nam 2011; Sŏ 2008; Sŏng and Yi 2013).

In the face of seemingly irreconcilable opposites, Solomonic arguments to moderation are offered every now and then. One simple example of this is the proposal for freer, more readable translations for beginners, alongside more faithful ones for advanced readers (*Kyŏnghyang Sinmun*, December 2, 2007). Less trivial is the following example: As noted above, North Korea is often lauded for outdoing the South in "hangulization"— a *hangŭlhwa* in the proper sense, making the most of the possibilities of vernacular language. The reconciliatory formula, which some like to apply here, accentuates positives on both sides: the translators from the North are commended for catering well to general readers, those from the South for striving to preserve flair by letting the original wording shine through (*Segye Ilbo*, May 30, 2007).

Discourse on Mistakes

"Re-invention" is always innate to the idea of translation, particularly when it is about the translation of a text from a so-called dead language. The old text has to be revived and re-invented, in a metaphorical sense of the word. Translation of *hanmun* also (re)invents tradition in this trivial yet fundamental way. That said, the fact that any translation is necessarily a re-invention conflicts with the demand for fidelity to the original.[55] It has become a commonplace to say that "hangul versions" (*han'gŭlbon*) of *hanmun* are full of mistakes (*oryu t'usŏngi*) (*Han'gyŏre*, November 8, 2005), or blemished by flaws in the crystal, or, literally, in the jade (*og-e t'i*) (*Kungmin Ilbo*, October 11, 2010). Most evaluations are heavily subservient to the conventional paradigm of loss. Losses as well as decisions that are perceived as praiseworthy are mostly identified in relation to vocabulary (see O 2008). A culture of quick fixes and shortcuts, otherwise valorized in Korean society, is often blamed for this: translators share the work of translating a specific text to meet deadlines, exacerbating the risk of incoherence (Chŏng 2007, 255).[56] When the North completed its translation of the *Annals of the Chosŏn Dynasty*, the South raced to finish its own version, a haste that is said to have led to many errors (*Segye Ilbo*, February 15, 2007).

A very particular phenomenon is the involvement of netizens (or, previously, CD-ROM-users) in the detection of mistakes—giving a very concrete idea of how the promoters of *hanmun* translation have perhaps managed, indeed, to turn *hanmun* into a kind of "common good," something that was certainly not the case traditionally. In this respect, the translation of the *Annals of the Chosŏn Dynasty* is declared a national mission, a truly collective society-wide enterprise (*Yŏnhap Nyusŭ*, February 14, 2007; *Segye Ilbo*, February 15, 2007). Likewise, when amateur users of the online digitized translation of the *Annals* were encouraged to report mistakes, a monthly average of 177 clear mistakes was found, according to the *Kyŏnghyang Sinmun* (October 1, 2010; see also *Kungmin Ilbo*, October 11, 2010)—an example of open-source intelligence gathering that is ongoing and seems to befit the participatory culture of South Korean netizen engagement especially well. In the face of the sheer quantity of mistakes in the Korean *kugyŏk* translations, some contributors are skeptical about any translation into English (*Kyŏnghyang Sinmun*, February 6, 2012)—the logic, of course, being the even greater distance between the original and target languages in this case.

Recently, the discourse about *hanmun* translation has begun to mention the advantages of automatic translation, that is, the potential of neural machine technology to speed up translation work, by taking a computer-generated rough draft as the starting point for reworking and counterchecking it against the original (*Tonga Ilbo*, March 7, 2017).

Since the 1960s, numerous voices have continually urged and promoted modern Korean translations (*kugyŏk*) of premodern Korean literature written in classical Chinese (*hanmun*)—in principle, all works previously read by Koreans, but more specifically and more fervently those authored by Koreans themselves—as a form of heritage conservation. This chapter has outlined a discourse that was, and still is, mostly perpetuated by researchers, directors of related organizations, and scholars involved in translation of *hanmun*, who raise their voices on behalf of their work and rehearse a repertoire of arguments that has displayed a striking consistency over the decades.

Even more intriguingly, arguments (or discourse motifs, patterns of arguing) originally used by apologists of *hanmun* from the late nineteenth century onward were taken over in the 1960s and thereafter both by those who pushed for translation of *hanmun* into modern Korean, as well as by the apologists of *hantcha* (practically spoken: the public use of mixed script or at least classes for teaching Chinese characters in school). The most striking example of such a motif is the warning that Koreans get cut off from their fathers and their cultural past due to the ongoing changes in terms of script and writing. It is very peculiar that this premonition could persist for such a long time, from the late nineteenth century into the 1960s and even up to our days, over several generations—and despite all the transformations that have taken place. In other words, either the prophesied catastrophe never materialized, or standards of connection to the past were constantly lowered, so that the writing on the wall could remain without any updating. It is astonishing that the matter of preservation of *hanmun*—which at first sight ought to be a matter of conservation and editing—gets so regularly linked to translation. It is also surprising that translation is linked in turn with a proclaimed necessity for further popularization (*taejunghwa*), with zest being added by the proven potential of translated *hanmun* to provide useful content for the culture and entertainment industries of South Korea. However, the understanding of translation as being for those who cannot read the original means that those who are at least partly able to read the originals are not considered (and thus not catered to) as a possible target audience, and are also not sufficiently in the field of vision of the contributors to the discourse. But originals that count—texts that have canonical status, or are intrinsically important—should not simply be dispensed with and replaced by translations. Translations of classics should form a bridge back to the authentic words, and should also enable those who are not experts to connect, at least to some degree, with the original text. One way of guaranteeing this is by producing bilingual editions (in parallel print), a format that is currently well used in Korean editions of *hanmun* poetry but not usually for prose (at best, the text is provided after the translation, at the back in the book). It seems safe to predict that the future will see the increasing emergence of state-of-the-art critical editions of important *hanmun* classics, together with masterful contemporary translations printed in parallel for synoptic reading, richly annotated and imbued with all previously accumulated philological scholarship. Whether this serves a historical re-enactment of literati scholarship or the retrogressive utopia of Korea as the "Nation of Propriety in the East" (*Tongbang yeŭi chi kuk*) is a different matter (see chapter 4).

Clearly, *hanmun* texts are an epitome of Korea's endangered heritage, firstly because books were or are still in danger of disappearing (i.e., being physically lost and not surfacing again), and secondly because of waning readership. Now, if readership and attention is secured by translation and popularization, the concept of invented tradition comes into play. The physical texts themselves—the books—do not readily lend themselves to this concept, but the roles assigned to them can certainly do so.

The authoritarian regime of Park Chung Hee in South Korea aimed at social and national cohesion and sought to legitimize itself by laying claim to a continuity with the past—perhaps not seamless, but gloriously restored. The translation of *hanmun* texts into hangul also satisfied the imperatives of that nationalist modernity metanarrative that cast Korea as one of a kind in a world of very distinct nations. Originally, this narrative had emerged during the opening of Korea in the last quarter of the nineteenth century, when progressive intellectuals called for an emancipation from the "big brother" China. It was no coincidence that they aligned their cause with some significant symbolic values associated with hangul: cultural independence, an assertion of national identity, and egalitarianism (the latter by representing a script for the masses, the *minjung*—in contrast to *hanmun* and *hantcha* that were associated with feudalism). At the same time, however, the enshrining of *hanmun* texts no doubt appealed to conservative elements in society, many of whom were part of Park Chung Hee's base of political support. The translation of *hanmun* into hangul was a cultural-political measure toward the objective of inclusion, offering ideological meaning for the constructed imagined community, and implying a national social harmonization of something that historically, in fact, was not "one" but a very disparate social fabric riddled with conflict and fracture lines. The message of the authoritarian ruler was that his move for radical innovation (hangul exclusivity) did not constitute modern Koreans becoming different from their ancestors. However, the suggested continuity was, of course, fictitious because many Koreans had illiterate or barely literate ancestors for whom any text composed of Chinese characters, in classical Chinese, surely amounted to a riddle wrapped up in an enigma, a closed book of incomprehensible hieroglyphs.

The move for translation was suggestive of granting access to high culture to all, by rendering *hanmun* into the "national" language (Korean, by contrast to Literary Sinitic) and into the national script (hangul, instead of *hanmun*, but also instead of mixed script). At the same time, many promotors justified their call for even more governmental support for translation efforts with the claim that *hanmun* was a kernel of national identity. But the construction of these "old classics" as the centerpiece of original Koreanness is extremely daring and, at best, one-sided. And while *hanmun* translations do not concoct something that was not there at all, they still create a new, re-invented tradition. Likewise, the concept of a whole nation united in reading the "old classics" (in modern translation) is, of course, imagining a community that historically never existed in this form.

GLOSSARY

aeguk undong 愛國運動

amgŭl 암글

chinsŏ 眞書

chinsu 眞髓

chŏngbonhwa 正本化

chŏngch'esŏng 正體性

Chosŏn kwangmunhoe 朝鮮光文會

Chosŏn wangjo sillok 朝鮮王朝實錄

chuch'esŏng 主體性

chu-gyŏng-ya-dok 晝耕夜讀

hallyu 韓流

hangŭl chŏn'yong 한글專用

hangŭl sedae 한글世代

hangŭlhwa 한글化

hanmun 漢文

hanmun paech'ŏk 漢文排斥

hanmun p'yeji 漢文廢止

hanmun p'yeji nonjaeng 漢文廢止論爭

hanmunt'u 漢文套

hantcha 漢字

hantchaŏ 漢字語

honyong 混用

huson 後孫

ihaeng 移行

injae 人材

inmun kyoyuk 人文敎育

kabo kaehyŏk 甲午改革

kadoksŏng 可讀性

kojŏn 古典

komunhŏn 古文獻

kongdongch'e 共同體

kosŏ 古書

kugwi sŏnyang 國威宣揚

kugyŏk 國譯

kŭlbang 글방

kungmin 國民

kwagŏ 科擧

kyogam 校勘 a critical edition

kyogam 交感 communion

manhwa 漫畫

minjok kongyu 民族共有

minjuhwa 民主化

muhyŏng munhwajae 無形文化財

ŏnmun 諺文

ŏnmun ilch'i 言文一致

oryu 誤謬

p'ilsabon 筆寫本

pojon 保存

ponjil 本質

pŏnyŏkt'u 飜譯套

pyŏngyong 竝用

saemaŭl undong 새마을運動

sagŭk 史劇

segyehwa 世界化

sŏdang 書堂

sŏgu munhwa 西歐文化

somyŏl 消滅

sŏnbi 선비

sŏyang sadaejuŭi 西洋事大主義

taejunghwa 大衆化

taejungsŏng 大衆性

tanjŏl 斷絕

Tongbang yeŭi chi kuk 東方禮儀之國

uri kŭl 우리 글
yangban 兩班

yongŏ chŏngni 用語古典
yuilbon 唯一本

NOTES

Work on this chapter was supported by a SEED grant from the Korean Studies Promotion Service (Academy of Korean Studies), no. AKS-2017-INC-2220002.

1. "Compared to texts composed in China, Classical Chinese writings of Chosŏn were marginalized" (Jung 2011, 21).
2. This term is frequently used by Anderson (1983); see also Oh (2003, 188).
3. For a concise history of language reform in Korea, see King (1998).
4. It is possible to interpret several vernacular royal edicts deployed during the Imjin War (1592–1598) as the "inauguration of a vernacular national communicative space" (Kim Haboush 2016, 76), but ultimately such communication by the Korean ruler with his people in vernacular Korean was exceptional and obviously not sustainable.
5. Quite probably, modern Korean constitutes an even more drastic example than those European languages that Hobsbawm presumably had in mind when he wrote: "Standard national languages, to be learned in schools and written, let alone spoken, by more than a smallish élite, are largely constructs of varying, but often brief, age" (Hobsbawm 1983, 14).
6. For overviews of the feuds, see Kang (1985), King (1998), and Pak (2011).
7. For the many ways to translate this term and its history, see King (2015, 12–13).
8. See Pieper (2017, 252).
9. Regarding the idea of congruence between speaking and writing, there is an objection that has a special relevance to Korea: "putting to one side the question whether perfect *ŏnmun ilch'i* is even possible, the sort of literary Korean one could write in such a style would be nothing more than low-level idle chitchat" (Koh 2014, 158). In a very strict sense, writing can, indeed, never fully convey speech. As for Koh's harsh judgment concerning "chitchat," this is probably accounted for by the familiar contention that spoken Korean is underdeveloped, or has not lived up to its full potential, due to a historically inherited lack of regard for rhetoric and eloquence. In any case, if we think of a conventional transcription of a good story told by a naturally gifted narrator, we have, in practice, a perfectly functional instance of congruence between speaking and writing. Digging deeper into the history of debate about *ŏnmun ilch'i*, we would find much complaint

about *hanmunt'u*, "hanmunish" style, and about translationese, mostly with a Japanese flair—the point being that during the process of developing standard written Korean, the reservoir of actual spoken Korean and regional dialect was neglected and should have been more extensively exploited.

10. See Wells (2011).

11. Sin Ki-sŏn in a submission to King Kojong in April 1896. See Sin (1981, 244). Quoted in Kang (1985, 213).

12. This reminds us of the memorial by Ch'oe Mal-li that was submitted in 1444 in protest against the new script (immediately after its promulgation). A translation of this famous text, which was recorded in the *Sejong sillok*, is given in Lee (1993, 519–520).

13. See Andre Schmid's *Korea Between Empires, 1895–1919* on the "decentering of the Middle Kingdom," that is, the re-evaluation of Korea's dependence on China that took place concomitantly with the intellectual struggle to define Korea as "part of the new global ecumene" (Schmid 2002, 9).

14. A *locus classicus* for this argumentation is Chu Si-gyŏng's "Kungmunnon" [On the national script], *Tongnip Sinmun* 1897, April 22–24. See Kang (1985, 206) and Pieper (2011, 51).

15. Author and public intellectual Pok Kŏ-il became (in)famous in the late 1990s with his demand to supplant Korean with English as Korea's official language. See Pok (1998), Si et al. (2003).

16. Aka Soh Jaipil or Philip Jaison. For an example of how this cultural hero is under attack from strong opponents of hangul exclusivity see, for example, Son and Yang (2007).

17. *Sadaejuŭi* is the ideology of "serving the great": a term describing the relationship between tributary state (for example, Korea) and suzerain (China). For a representative example for this thread of discourse, see Kim Ch'angjin (2013). See also Silva (2002).

18. Unpublished typewritten report (no date) to the Christian Literature Society, quoted in King (2012, 244).

19. For "probably the earliest public petition for government-led translation and vernacular education" (Pieper 2017, 271), see the editorial in the *Hansŏng Chubo* (Weekly Gazette of Seoul), February 15, 1886 (quoted in Pieper 2017, 271–272): "We must translate everything into *ŏnmun*, from the books of the sages Confucius and Mencius to the commercial and technical works . . . of Europeans."

20. "The use of Literary Sinitic, though increasingly marginalized, continued well into the colonial era and in some ways beyond. Korea has indeed experienced a very long 'hanmun hangover'" (Wells 2011, 10). For years after the Korean War, Korean newspapers—which were otherwise written in the

vernacular, in mixed script—encouraged the submission of classical Chinese poetry, with the chosen poems published regularly in a special section. Even today, an annual national *hansi* contest (*chŏn'guk hansi paegilchang*) is a major event attracting hundreds of competitors. The past decade has seen pioneering research (Kim 2015) on "modern *hanmun*," a body of literature produced in the shadow of the vernacular. An anthology of poetry in classical Chinese composed during the colonial period (Han Yŏng-gyu et al. 2009) drew attention to what was even dubbed a "*hansi* renaissance." Recently, there has also been an emerging recognition that the formation of modern Korean poetry took place in a "*hanmun* context" (Chŏng 2017) that cannot be discarded.

21. Institute for the Translation of Korean Classics Act, Act No. 8852, February 29, 2008, Ministry of Education, Science and Technology (Humanities and Social Sciences Research Division).

22. Basically, diglossia means that two language varieties are used in one and the same language community, with a prestigious, highly codified variety that has no native speakers and a low variety that is used in everyday conversation. The problematic aspects of applying this term to the historical situation in Korea have been exposed in recent scholarship. Some critics rightly point to the "multiple intermediate inscriptional varieties" (King 2015, 11). Thus, "the problem of 'diglossia' is its fundamental 'twoness'—its need for two distinct poles" (King 2015, 11). See also Yu Cho (2002), Wang (2014), and Strnad (2016).

23. According to contemporaneous Japanese statistics, 1.2 million Koreans attended a *sŏdang* in 1942 (Tsurumi 1984, 307). The Japanese government fostered classical learning and endorsed Korean Confucianists, trying to capitalize politically on basic Confucian values such as loyalty to the center of authority.

24. "Kojŏn-ŭi hangŭl pŏnyŏg-ŭl sŏdurŭl kŏt." For the full text see https://www.hanmalgeul.org/70 (accessed June 30, 2019).

25. "The history of struggle between hangul and Chinese characters is precisely the history of the struggle between democracy and feudalism. We Koreans should use hangul not because it is Korean but because using hangul accords with democratic values" (Koh 2014, 241).

26. The inability to read and write well enough to meet the requirements of daily life.

27. See the chapter devoted to "Han'gŭl chŏnyong, kŭ orae toen nollan" (Hangul exclusivity, that old controversy) in a book on humanities-related topics discussed in the Korean parliament (Hong 2014).

28. Hating *hantcha* is misguided patriotism (*aeguksim*), claims one commentator, while those opposed to the abolition of *hantcha* may rightfully invoke patriotism (*Tonga Ilbo*, October 14, 1968). Someone else solemnly implores the president not to turn Koreans into a people of commerce (*sangŏp minjok*) but into a people of high culture (*kodo munhwa minjok*) (*Tonga Ilbo*, October 31, 1968).
29. For example, the Ministry of Education announced that publishers and media will not be forced to enact the change (Hong 2014, 70). More generally, the level of public opposition during the times of dictatorship is often underestimated. For the little-known tale of the dissident intelligentsia (*chaeya*, literally "out of office" or "out of power") and its remarkable power during Park Chung Hee's authoritarian rule, see Park (2011).
30. This is a recurring motif in several unpublished essays and missionary reports by Gale, quoted in King (2012, 243–244).
31. For example, An Cha-san, author of the first history of Korean literature (1922). See Yi (2013). Generally speaking, this is about the fundamental conflict between *chŏn'tong kyesŭngnon* (the theory of tradition succession) and *chŏnt'ong tanjŏllon* (the theory of tradition rupture), competing as leading paradigms for interpreting Korean history.
32. Both novels are translated into English. See Yŏm (2005) and Ch'ae (2015).
33. Yi Sang's *Ogamdo* (Crow's eye view) poems are frequently anthologized. This one, no. 2, is printed in translation, among others, in McCann (2004, 66).
34. *Tonga Ilbo*, November 21, 1968.
35. *Tonga Ilbo*, November 24, 1966.
36. *Sŏul Kyŏngje*, May 30, 2016.
37. Chŏng 2007, 257.
38. *Tonga Ilbo*, November 21, 1968.
39. In the preface to his *Sinjajŏn* (New dictionary), published 1915 (Seoul: Sinmungwan), Ch'oe Nam-sŏn states: "We completely abandoned our own words and imitated the foreign language." For a discussion see Ro (2012, 201). Of course, one bigger picture, or wider context, that is relevant here is the vernacular movement in China itself (see Zhou 2011).
40. See for example the second paragraph of the World Heritage Convention, which states: "deterioration or disappearance of any item of the cultural or natural heritage constitutes a harmful impoverishment of the heritage of all the nations of the world" (http://whc.unesco.org/en/conventiontext/). Of course, there is an alternative logic conflicting with this view: the most genuine heritage is often considered to be inaccessible for outsiders.

41. The register allows access by region and country, http://www.unesco.org/new
    /en/communication-and-information/memory-of-the-world/register/
42. See Kim Chin-gyun (2008).
43. In contrast to the efforts to coordinate support for the translation of Korean
    classics into Korean, translation of Korean classics into Western languages
    was not made a target in its own right. This has changed with the ambi-
    tious English Translation of 100 Korean Classics Project, initiated by the
    Academy of Korean Studies (AKS), which aims at state-of-the-art anno-
    tated translations, partly replacing previous translations.
44. See King (2003, 214): "It strikes me as rather odd that what passes as
    common sense virtually everywhere else in the world—namely, that the
    very best literary translation is always accomplished by 'inbound' transla-
    tors translating into their mother tongue—is viewed almost as a revelation
    in Korean academic and funding circles."
45. "Munhwa k'ont'enchǔ is an openly trade-oriented conception of culture
    that was adopted after South Korea's inclusion in the Uruguay Round Trade
    talks . . . in 1993" (Wang Medina 2018, 397).
46. For a comprehensive history of the translation of Korean classics, see two
    recent publications by the Kojŏn Pŏnyŏkhak Sent'ŏ (2013–2015, 2017). In
    terms of quantitative proportions, progress until now is difficult to gauge
    because the usual counts of books, volumes, and titles are heterogeneous
    and incompatible. While many notable works are translated, the untrans-
    lated texts (of all kinds and genres) still seem to outweigh by far the texts
    already translated. Sceptics used to hold the view that "it is quite impossible
    to translate the enormous body of classics" (Lee 1972, 52), but the poten-
    tial of digitization is beginning to change the game.
47. However, this story was really only funny for the learned elite, who would
    understand at least some of the ridiculous *hanmun*-loaded gibberish that
    the agitated scholar screams to the villagers in order to make them assist
    and chase the tiger to save his father. The story is anthologized in Kim
    (2000, 341). See Jung (2011, 20).
48. In fact, Zuber did not only attribute this to Korea: "A fact that one cannot
    help but admire throughout the Far East, one which does not flatter our
    self-esteem, is the presence of books in even the poorest homes. Those
    who cannot read are very rare, and incur the scorn of their fellow citizens.
    We would have a lot of people to despise in France if public opinion against
    the illiterate were as severe here" (Zuber 1873, 414; rendered here after
    the complete translation provided by Brother Anthony on his homepage,
    http://anthony.sogang.ac.kr/ZuberEnglish.html).

49. The *yangban* were Korean scholarly officials; and the term also represented their family and descendants and their social class. For a discussion of this seemingly self-evident concept, see Lee (2003, 191–192).

50. One magisterial example of a state-of-the-art *chŏngbon*, a definitive edition based on textual criticism, is the emended and annotated text redaction of the *Yŏyudang Chŏnsŏ* by Tasan Chŏng Yak-yong, published in 2012. Pak Hŭi-byŏng's critical edition of selected Korean fiction in Classical Chinese (2005) is considered among philologists as unsurpassed in terms of academic rigor applied to provide a *kyogam*, an authoritative scholarly curated text version based on painstaking comparison of variants, all of them made available to the reader in footnotes. But the production of critical editions is undergoing massive changes now thanks to the development of efficient digital tools, and the South Korean penchant for cutting-edge electronic text processing might come in handy to make up for, compared to Western standards, a late kickoff. The boost for digital humanities is visible in the "DB of Korean Classics" that offers access to original text images, electronically processes (searchable) texts, and also translations, with the offer of materials growing at high speed.

51. For a time, the "80,000 volumes" claimed to be located outside of Korea (*Tonga Ilbo*, December 25, 1975) enjoyed almost mythical status. The archetypical example of such assiduously repeated semi-apocryphal numbers is the notorious invocation of "5,000 years of Korean history."

52. See Pak (2013). See also Institute for the Translation of Korean Classics (2010).

53. Bitter disputes have flared up during the first decade of the new millennium over the overlapping histories in early periods of Northeast Asia, most notably over the correct portrayal of Koguryŏ, conventionally considered to have been one of Korea's ancient kingdoms. A revisionist Chinese campaign tried to frame this kingdom as a Tungusic ethnic state—and thus, in the end, just part of China's diverse regional history. The ensuing controversy represents the paradigmatic case of what became known as the "Northeast Asia history wars."

54. This is not self-evident, because it is possible to argue that a true expert should be able to rely on originals alone; however, it seems perfectly normal even in present-day European university programs in classical (Latin and ancient Greek) philology to acquire a broad basis and a wide hermeneutical horizon on the basis of translations, counterchecking the originals by reading in parallel.

55. South Korea is a "standout country in the realm of translation" (Kim

Chi-wŏn 2013, 50)—and this is true also in terms of its obsession with translation mistakes (see Schirmer 2020). This is epitomized by large volumes that are basically mere compendiums of translation errors (see, for example, An 2013; Kang 2004; *Kyosu Sinmun* 2006, 2007), which nevertheless manage to garner a lot of public attention. Scrutiny is mostly devoted to Korean translations of Western literature, while translations of Korean literature (including *hanmun*) into Western languages or translations of *hanmun* into modern Korean usually spend much less time in the spotlight. Gradually, however, this marginalization is lessening, although attention does not often transcend the confines of academic circles and peer critique. For example, in 2009 Kim Hyŏl-cho managed to garner much public attention for his rendering in modern Korean of one of the proudest examples of "classical" literature, Pak Chi-wŏn's *Yŏrha ilgi*, a translation that he justified by pointing out many previous mistranslations as well as the stubborn persistence of mistakes because of the habit of "plagiarizing" earlier translations. See Heo (2009) and Kim Hyŏl-cho (2008).

56. One might suspect that it is not only a problem of rushing to meet deadlines but also a deeply ingrained culture of exploitative subcontracting or of passing on tasks to subordinates without proper attribution or credit.

REFERENCES

All links were last verified on July 31, 2017.

Ahn, Yonson. 2007. "China and the Two Koreas Clash Over Mount Paekdu/Changbai: Memory Wars Threaten Regional Accommodation." *The Asia-Pacific Journal / Japan Focus* 5 (7): [unpaginated]. http://apjjf.org/-Yonson-Ahn/2483 /article.html

———.2008. "The Contested Heritage of Koguryo/Gaogouli and China-Korea Conflict." *The Asia-Pacific Journal / Japan Focus* 6 (1): [unpaginated]. http://apjjf .org/-Yonson-Ahn/2631/article.html

An Chŏng-hyo. 2013. *Oyŏk sajŏn: Tangsin-ŭl choŭn pŏnyŏkka-ro mandŭnŭn kkankkanhan pŏnyŏk killajabi* [Dictionary of mistranslations: A meticulous guide to make you a good translator]. P'aju: Yŏllin ch'aektŭl.

An Tae-hoe. 2012. "Han'guk hanmunhag-ŭi han'gŭl pŏnyŏk-kwa munhaksŏng." *Nara sarang* 121:116–126.

An, Yelee. 2015. "Generality and Distinctiveness of Korean Language Modernization." *HYI Working Paper Series*. https://www.harvard-yenching.org/features/hyi -working-paper-series-yelee

Anderson, Benedict. 1983. *Imagined Communities: Reflections on the Origin and Spread of Nationalism*. New York: Verso.

Ch'ae, Man-Sik. 2015. *Peace Under Heaven: A Modern Korean Novel*. Translated by Chun Kyung-Ja. London: Routledge.

Chŏng Hae-ch'ul. 2007. "Hanmun kojŏn pŏnyŏg-ŭi munjejŏm-gwa kaesŏn pangan" [Issues and ways for improvement in the translation of *hanmun* classics]. *Han'guk ŏmunhak kukje haksul p'orŭm che 2-ch'a kukje haksul taehoe*. Conference proceedings: 252–260.

Chŏng Ki-in. 2017. *Han'guk kŭndaesi hyŏngsŏng-gwa hanmunmaek* [The formation of modern Korean poetry in the context of *hanmun* literacy]. PhD diss., Seoul National University.

Chu Si-gyŏng. 1907. "Kugŏ-wa kungmun-ŭi p'ilyo" [The necessity of national language and national script]. *Sŏu* 2:31–34. http://db.history.go.kr/id/ma_003_0020_0140

De Mente, Boye Lafayette. 2012. *The Korean Mind: Understanding Contemporary Korean Culture*. Clarendon, VT: Tuttle.

Finch, John, and Seung-kyung Kim. 2009. "Thinking Locally, Acting Globally: Redefining Traditions at the Korean Minjok Leadership Academy." *Korean Studies* 33:124–149.

Ha Sŭng-hyŏn. 2015. "Hanmun Kojŏn Pŏnyŏkwŏn kojŏn taejunghwa saŏb-ŭi hyŏnhwang-gwa kwaje" [Current state and tasks in regard to the popularization of classics project undertaken by the Institute for the Translation of Korean Classics]. *Minjok munhwa* 45:35–68.

Han Yŏng-gyu et al., eds. 2009. *Singminji sigi hansi charyojip* [Collected materials on *hansi* in the times of colonial rule over Korea]. Seoul: Sŏnggyungwan taehakyo taedong munhwa yŏn'guwŏn.

Heo, Mi-gyeong. 2009. "A Complete Translation of the Great Work of Yeonam." *Korea Focus*, September 25. http://www.koreafocus.or.kr/design2/layout/content_print.asp?group_id=102737

Hobsbawm, Eric. 1983. "Introduction: Inventing Traditions." In *The Invention of Tradition*, edited by Eric Hobsbawm and Terence Ranger, 1–14. Cambridge: Cambridge University Press.

Hong Il-p'yo. 2014. *Kukhoe sog-ŭi inmunhak: Uri-rŭl hana-ro mukkŭn "Taehan min'guk" iran kukho-nŭn ŏdisŏ pirot toen kŏsilkka* [Humanities in the parliament: Where does the name of our country that unites us as one, *taehan min'guk*, stem from?]. Seoul: Chŏun ttang.

Howard, Keith. 2014. "Preserving Korean Identity through Intangible Cultural Heritage." In *The Oxford Handbook of Music Revival*, edited by Caroline Bithell and Juniper Hill, 135–159. New York: Oxford University Press.

Huh, Woong. 1972. "Exclusive Use of Han-gul and Hanmun Education." *Korea Journal* 12 (4): 45–48.

Institute for the Translation of Korean Classics, ed. 2010. *A Compendium for the Comprehensive Publication of Korean Literary Collections in Classical Chinese.* Seoul: Institute for the Translation of Korean Classics.

Jung, Byungsul. 2011. "The Status and Characteristics of Classical Chinese and Vernacular Korean in Chosŏn Korea: A Comparative Study of Fables of Mind and Body." *Horizons* 2 (1): 1–30.

Kang Myŏng-gwan. 1985. "Hanmun p'yaejinon-gwa aeguk kyemonggi-ŭi kuk-hanmun nonjaeng" [The debate about the abolition of *hanmun* and the debate about mixed script in the patriotic enlightenment movement]. *Han'guk hanmunhak yŏn'gu* 8:195–252.

Kang Tae-jin. 2004. *Chanhokhan ch'aek ilkki* [No mercy when reading translated books]. Seoul: Chagŭn iyagi.

Kendall, Laurel. 2011. *Consuming Korean Tradition in Early and Late Modernity: Commodification, Tourism, and Performance.* Honolulu: University of Hawai'i Press.

Kim, Ch'ang-jin. 2013. *Han'gŭl chŏnyong-ŭn wihŏnida* [Hangul exclusivity is against the constitution]. Seoul: Ŏmun Chŏngch'aek Chŏngdanghwa Ch'ujinhoe.

Kim, Chi-wŏn. 2013. "Korean Tradition of Translation: From the Gabo Reform to the Present." *Pŏnyŏkhak yŏn'gu* 14 (3): 41–63.

Kim Chin-gyun. 2008. "20-segi ch'oban-ŭi kyemong tamnon-gwa hanmun" [The enlightenment discourse in the beginning of the twentieth century and *hanmun*]. *Chŏngsin munhwa yŏn'gu* 31 (4): 275–299.

———.2015. *Modŏn hanmunhak* [Modern *hanmun*]. Seoul: Hakchawŏn.

Kim Hyŏl-cho. 2008. "'Yŏlha ilgi' pŏnyŏg-ŭi yŏrŏ munjedŭl" [Various problems concerning the translation of the *Yŏlha Diary*]. *Hanmun hakpo* 19:679–718.

Kim Hyŏn-nyong, ed. 2000. *Han'guk munhŏn sŏlhwa* 7 [Korean written folktales]. Seoul: Kŏn'gukdae ch'ulp'anbu.

Kim Haboush, JaHyun. 2016. *The Great East Asian War and the Birth of the Korean Nation.* New York: Columbia University Press.

Kim, Jeongsu. 2005. *The History and Future of Hangeul: Korea's Indigenous Script.* Translated by Ross King. Folkestone: Global Oriental.

Kim, Young Sam. 1996. *Korea's Reform and Globalization: President Kim Young Sam Prepares the Nation for the Challenges of the 21st Century.* Seoul: Korean Overseas Information Service.

King, Ross. 1998. "Nationalism and Language Reform in Korea." In *Nationalism and the Construction of Korean Identity*, edited by Hyung Il Pai and Timothy R. Tangherlini, 33–72. Berkeley: Institute of East Asian Studies.

———. 2003. "Can Korean-to-English Literary Translation Be Taught? Some Recommendations for Korean Funding Agencies." In *2002 Seoul Symposium on Literature and Translation*, edited by Korea Literature Translation Institute, 211–225. Seoul: Korea Literature Translation Institute.

———. 2007. "North and South Korea." In *Language and National Identity in Asia*, edited by Andrew Simpson, 200–234. Oxford: Oxford University Press.

———. 2012. "James Scarth Gale, Korean Literature in Hanmun, and Korean Books." In *Haeoe han'gukpon komunhŏn charyo-ŭi t'amsaek-kwa kŏmt'o*, edited by Kyujanggak Han'gukhak Yŏn'guwŏn, 237–264. Seoul: Samgyŏng Munhwasa.

———. 2015. "Ditching 'Diglossia': Describing Ecologies of the Spoken and Inscribed in Premodern Korea." *Sungkyun Journal of East Asian Studies* 15 (1): 1–19.

King, Ross, and Si Nae Park. 2016. *Score One for the Dancing Girl, and Other Selections from the "Kimun ch'onghwa": A Story Collection from Nineteenth-century Korea*. Toronto: University of Toronto Press.

Koh, Jongsok. 2014. *Infected Korean Language, Purity vs. Hybridity: From the Sinographic Cosmopolis to Japanese Colonialism to Global English*. Translated with a critical introduction by Ross King. Amherst, NY: Cambria Press.

Kojŏn Pŏnyŏkhak Sent'ŏ, Chŏmp'ilchae Yŏn'guso, ed. 2013–2015. *Han'guk kojŏn pŏnyŏkhag-ŭi kusŏng-gwa mosaek* [Translation studies applied to the translation of Korean classics: Setup and outlook]. Vols. 1–2. P'aju: Chŏmp'ilchae.

———. 2017. *Han'guk kojŏn pŏnyŏksa-ŭi chŏn'gae-wa chip'yŏng* [History of the translation of Korean classics: Development and prospects]. P'aju: Chŏmp'ilchae.

Kyosu Sinmun, ed. 2006, 2007. *Ch'oego-ŭi kojŏn pŏnyŏg-ŭl ch'ajasŏ* [On the lookout for the best translation of the classics]. 2 vols. Seoul: Saenggak ŭi Namu.

Lee, Jee Sun Elizabeth. 2003. "In Search of the Present: Language, Space, and Time in the Construction of Korean Nationhood, 1894–1926." PhD diss., Cornell University.

Lee, Peter H., ed. 1993. *Sourcebook of Korean Civilization* 1. New York: Columbia University Press.

Lee, Sung-nyong. 1972. "On the Need of Teaching Chinese Characters." *Korea Journal* 12 (4): 49–52.

McCann, David Richard, ed. 2004. *Columbia Anthology of Modern Korean Poetry*. New York: Columbia University Press.

Nam Ch'ŏl-jin. 2011. "Han'guk kojŏn pŏnyŏg-e poineun pŏnyŏkt'u (translationese)-ŭi yuhyŏng koch'al: *Tang-Song p'alga mun* pŏnyŏg-ŭl chungsim-ŭro" [A typological investigation of translationese that can be observed in translations of classical literature: With a focus on translations of *The Selected Prose of Eight Masters of the Tang and Song Dynasty*]. *Chungguk ŏmunhak nonjip* 68:189–213.

O Yun-sŏn. 2008. *Han'guk kososŏl yŏngyŏkbon-ŭro-ŭi ch'odae* [Invitation to English translations of Korean premodern novels]. Seoul: Chimundang.

Oh, Young Kyun. 2003. "The Translation of Chinese Philosophical Literature in Korea: The Next Generation." In *One into Many: Translation and the Dissemination of Classical Chinese Literature*, edited by Leo Tak-hung Chan. Amsterdam: John Benjamins.

Pai, Hyung Il. 1999. "Nationalism and Preserving Korea's Buried Past: The Office of Cultural Properties and Archaeological Heritage Management in South Korea." *Antiquity* 73 (281): 619–625.

Pak Chae-yŏng. 2013. "Kojŏnjŏk chŏngni-ŭi ch'ŭngmŏn-esŏ pon *Han'guk munjip ch'onggan* p'yŏnch'an-ŭi ŭiŭi-wa hyanghu kwaje" [Significance and future challenges of editing the *Printed collectanea of Korean literary anthologies* from the perspective of the Korean classics compilation project]. *Minjok munhwa* 42:253–285.

Pak Chin-su. 2011. "Han'gug-ŭi hanmun p'yaeji nonjaeng-ŭi sajŏk koch'al" [A historical review of the controversies over the abolition of *hanmun* in Korea]. *Tongbang hanmunhak* 47:175–255.

Pak Hŭi-byŏng. 2005. "Han'guk hanmun sosŏl kyohap kuhae" [A critical edition of selected Korean fiction in Classical Chinese]. Seoul: Somyŏng.

Park, Myung-Lim. 2011. "The *Chaeya*." In *The Park Chung Hee Era: The Transformation of South Korea*, edited by Kim Byung-Kook and Ezra F. Vogel, 373–400. Cambridge, MA: Harvard University Press.

Park, Nahm-Sheik. 1989. "Language Purism in Korea Today." In *The Politics of Language Purism*, edited by Björn H. Jernudd and Michael J. Shapiro, 113–140. Contributions to the Sociology of Language 54. Berlin: De Gruyter.

Park, Sang Mi. 2010. "The Paradox of Postcolonial Korean Nationalism: State-Sponsored Cultural Policy in South Korea, 1965–Present." *Journal of Korean Studies* 15 (1): 67–93.

Pieper, Daniel Olivier. 2011. "Han'gŭl for the Nation, The Nation for Han'gŭl: The Korean Language Movement 1894–1945." MA thesis, Washington University in St. Louis.

———.2017. "Korean as a Transitional Literacy: Language Education, Curricularization, and the Vernacular-Cosmopolitan Interface in Early Modern Korea, 1895–1925." PhD diss., University of British Columbia.

Pok, Kŏ-il. 1998. *Kukcheŏ sidae-ŭi minjog-e* [The national language in the age of the international language]. Seoul: Munhak kwa Chisŏngsa.

Ro, Sang-ho. 2012. "Print Culture in the Imagination of Modern Korea, 1880–1931: Knowledge, Literature, and Classics." PhD diss., Princeton University.

Schirmer, Andreas. 2020. "Aspects of the Never-Ending Translation Wars in South Korea: A Cultural Phenomenon and its Reasons." *Lebende Sprachen* 65 (2): 390–410.

Schmid, Andre. 2002. *Korea Between Empires, 1895–1919.* New York: Columbia University Press.

Si Chŏng-gon, Chŏng Chu-ri, Chang Yŏng-jun, Pak Yŏng-jun, and Ch'oe Kyŏng-bong. 2003. *Han'gugŏ-ga sarajindamyŏn: 2023-yŏn, yŏngŏ singminji Taehan Min'guk ŭl kada* [What if Korean were to disappear?]. Seoul: Han'gyŏre sinmunsa.

Silva, David J. 2002. "Western Attitudes toward the Korean Language: An Overview of Late Nineteenth- and Early Twentieth-Century Mission Literature." *Korean Studies* 26 (2): 270–286.

Sin Ki-sŏn. 1981. *Sin Ki-sŏn chŏnjip sang* [Collected works by Sin Ki-sŏn 1]. Seoul: Asea munhwasa.

Sŏ Chŏng-mun. 2008. "Hanmun kojŏn pŏnyŏk sajŏk maengnag-esŏ pon pimun munje" [The problem of ungrammatical sentences in translations of classical *hanmun* literature, from a historical perspective]. *Minjok munhwa* 32:43–74.

———.2010. "Kojŏn pŏnyŏk saŏb-ŭi chonghapchŏk mokp'yo sŏlchŏng-ŭl wihan siron" [An essay on the comprehensive target setting for the task of translating the Korean classics]. *Kojŏn pŏnyok yŏn'gu* 1:97–128.

Son Tong-u and Yang Kwŏn-mo. 2007. *Chayu-ŭi chong-ŭl nant'a hara: Tonghak hyŏkmyŏng esŏ che 2 konghwaguk kkaji 1894~1960* [Ring the bell of freedom: From the Tonghak Peasant Revolution to the Second Republic 1894–1960]. Seoul: Tŭlnyŏk.

Sŏng Paek-hyo, and Yi Yŏng-jin. 2013. "Hanmun kojŏn pŏnyŏg-ŭi wŏllo-rŭl chaja—3" [Let us meet veterans of the translation of Korean classics]. *Kojŏn pŏnyok yŏn'gu* 4:325–341.

Sonyŏn [The boys] 9. 1910. "Chosŏn kosŏ sujip palhaeng Chosŏn kwangmunhoe kwanggo" [Collecting and reprinting old books from Korea: An announcement by the Association for the Glorious Literature of Korea].

Strnad, William. 2016. "On Shadow and Form: Korean Nationalism's Digraphic Conflict." *International Journal of Korean Humanities and Social Sciences* 2:87–121.

Taylor, Insup, and M. Martin Taylor. 2014. *Writing and Literacy in Chinese, Korean and Japanese.* Rev. ed. Amsterdam: John Benjamins.

Tsurumi, Patricia. 1984. "Colonial Education in Korea and Taiwan." In *The Japanese Colonial Empire*, edited by Ramon H. Myers and Mark R. Peattie, 275–311. Princeton, NJ: Princeton University Press.

Vlastos, Stephen. 1997. "Tradition: Past/Present Culture and Modern Japanese History." In *Mirror of Modernity: Invented Traditions of Modern Japan*, edited by Stephen Vlastos, 1–16. Berkeley: University of California Press.

Wang Medina, Jenny. 2018. "At the Gates of Babel: The Globalization of Korean Literature as World Literature." *Acta Koreana* 21 (2): 395–422.

Wang, Sixiang. 2014. "The Sounds of Our Country: Interpreters, Linguistic Knowledge, and the Politics of Language in Early Chosŏn Korea." In *Rethinking East Asian Languages, Vernaculars, and Literacies, 1000–1919*, edited by Benjamin A. Elman, 58–95. Leiden: Brill.

Wells, William Scott. 2011. "From Center to Periphery: The Demotion of Literary Sinitic and the Beginnings of *Hanmunkwa*—Korea, 1876–1910." MA thesis, University of British Columbia.

Yi, Kwang-su. 2011. "What Is Literature?" Translated by Jooyeon Rhee. *Azalea* 4:293–313.

Yi Sang-ha. 2007. "Kojŏn ŏnhae mit nambukhan kojŏn kugyŏg-ŭi pigyo kŏmt'o-wa kojŏn yŏkchu-ŭi han pangan" [A comparative investigation of vernacular translations of the classics in North and South Korea and premodern vernacular explications, and a plan for annotation]. *Minju munhwa* 30:93–136.

Yi Sang-hyŏn. 2013. "Kojŏnŏ-wa kŭndaeŏ-ŭi pun'gi kŭrigo pulganŭnghan taehwa-ŭi chijŏmdŭl: *Chosŏn munhaksa* (1922) ch'ulhyŏn-ŭi kŭndae haksulsajŏk munmaek, Tak'ahasi/Gale-ŭi han'gug(ŏ) munhangnon" [The watershed of classical language and modern language and points of impossible communication]. *K'ogit'o* 73:56–113.

Yŏm, Sang-sŏp (Yom Sang-seop). 2005. *Three Generations*. Translated by Yu Young-nan. Brooklyn, NY: Archipelago Books.

Yu Cho, Young-mee. 2002. "Diglossia in Korean Language in Literature: A Historical Perspective." *East Asia* 20 (1): 3–23.

Yu Myŏng-u. 2000. "Han'gug-ŭi pŏnyŏk-kwa pŏnyŏkhak" [Translation and translation studies in Korea]. *Pŏnyŏkhak yŏn'gu* 1 (1): 229–248.

Yun Chae-min, Yi Tong-ch'ŏl, Song Hyŏk-ki, Chŏn Pyŏng-uk, Kim Chŏng-suk, and Paek Chin-u. 2009. "Hanmun kojŏn chŏngni pŏnyŏk sisŭt'em yŏn'gu" [A system of collecting and translating Korean classics written in classical Chinese]. *Minjok munhwa* 33:237–276.

Zhou, Gang. 2011. *Placing the Modern Chinese Vernacular in Transnational Literature*. New York: Palgrave Macmillan.

Zuber, Henri. 1873. "Une expédition en Corée: Par M. H. Zuber, ancien officier de marine, 1866" [An expedition in Corea]. *Le Tour du monde illustré* 25:401–416. Original available at http://gallica.bnf.fr/ark:/12148/bpt6k34400n/f404

PART III

Consuming and Performing Tradition

Music, Food, and Crafts

Introduction

CEDARBOUGH SAEJI

I have been thinking about the issue of "invention of tradition" since I first read Hobsbawm's introduction to his collection. To accept Hobsbawm's compelling arguments shook me—no longer could I simply believe that traditions emerged naturally from the mists of history as an evolving expression of cultural values and aesthetic desire. I realized that even defining tradition was difficult. What is tradition? Is it a thing that is of the past? Is it the "past reborn in a shifting context?" (Park 2003, 20). How much pastness is needed to call something tradition? We want to believe in the connection between the past and what we see today, and we want that connection to be authentic not artificial, but authenticity is no easier to define than tradition. Our human desire to believe in the authenticity of traditions has been explored by various scholars; in the Republic of Korea (ROK) the dominant understanding came to be what the anthropologist Edward Bruner calls "original (not copy)" (1994, 399). Is any of the past that we consume today as tradition actually the original, not a copy? Did it pass through the colonial era unscathed? Ethnomusicologist Keila Diehl explains that tradition is "an interpretive process embodying both continuity and discontinuity, rendering it symbolically constituted rather than natural" (2002, 3). Why go to the effort? Why constitute something called "tradition"? Who benefits? What are these symbols for?

The symbolism in invented traditions is convenient. The political leadership of a state or an individual can establish a "tradition" through linking a new practice with a longer history, or advance a new ideological meaning for an older practice in a way that dovetails with immediate goals. If this invented tradition is convincingly cloaked in a feeling of pastness, its inventedness will probably be unnoticed to all but the most astute observer. If the invented tradition continues to fulfill a need or desire in society, it may continue long after the specific reasons for its origin have disappeared. For example, eating frog in the Democratic People's Republic of Korea (DPRK) supports the narrative of the nation as scrappy and self-sufficient. Eating frog, even when it is not needed for protein symbolically connects the eater to the scrappy freedom fighters, Kim Il Sung, and the nation.

As Maria Osetrova clarifies in her chapter, the same invented traditions, or as she calls them in the context of the DPRK, propaganda, can also be delivered in two different ways: for the domestic audience and for the foreign audience. Traditions presented for the consumption of foreign audiences are intimately tied to political discourses about the desired image of the country. In the ROK this discourse shifts and changes frequently as successive five-year single-term presidents call for new initiatives and fresh campaigns. This has often become mired in a conflation of destination marketing and national branding, where consistency is given a pass and the ROK is treated as a playground or backdrop. The surface-level engagement prompted by such campaigns is driven by financial imperatives, visions of a foreign and exotic past, and *hallyu* (pop culture) tourism—such as donning a rental *hanbok* (Korean clothing) to pose for photos in a reconstructed Kyŏngbok Palace, or purchasing a (Chinese-made) bamboo comb in a shop in Insadong as a Korean tourist trinket, not to dress long, straight hair or pick lice. In the present-day tradition has been reduced to a series of symbolic items and moments—Instagram backdrops for the *selca* (selfie) generation, accessories to differentiate the Koreascape from other regions, or the setting for a pseudo-nostalgic historical drama. In the DPRK, however, the government has been run by three members of the same family, and since the 1960s it has been unified under the same driving ideology of self-reliance, called Juche. This has led to a more consistent projected image—the traditional North Korea conveyed to the visitor has shifted since the 1948 national founding, but in a way that is more internally consistent than in the South.

Tradition, for the foreign eye, is necessarily about historical rootedness and national identity, but for the domestic audience how differently are invented traditions leveraged? Sociologist John Lie explains, "tradition, annihilated, is reconstructed as an imagined past imperfect; the rhetoric of tradition and continuity casts a powerful spell on contemporary

South Korea even as substantive and organic links to the past are largely expunged" (2015, 92). Although locals in the South may engage with tradition in the same ways as outsiders, having become tourists of their own culture, some interface with tradition at a more substantial level, perhaps captivated by the very rhetoric of tradition and continuity Lie identifies. As Laurel Kendall's chapter shows, bamboo combs are still being made, but her interlocutors demonstrated profound generational differences in their understanding of this material culture. Deeper engagement with tradition often only continues with significant state-level support, as Laurel Kendall, Keith Howard, and Jan Creutzenberg touch on in their chapters. The ROK has established various legal supports for Korean tradition, including the Cultural Property Protection Law (CPPL), and the Intangible Cultural Heritage Safeguarding and Promotion Law (ICH-SPL). These official lists of protected heritage were made as various anthropologists and folklorists "were encouraged to mount or even invent cultural events loaded with symbols of antiquity, originality, uniqueness, and authenticity" (Kim 2004, 256). The government in the South has also invested heavily in museums and other cultural institutions, and has expended a great deal of funds to reconstruct palaces and various structures, excavate archaeological sites, and promote Korea through organizations like the Korea Foundation and Korea Creative Contents Association. The invocation of nostalgia for a vanished past, a romanticized ideal premodern society represented by *sanjo*, *p'ansori*, and bamboo combs may be losing practical effect in a South where the population that emotionally connects to the premodern is growing smaller every day. Modern performers and artisans must develop new approaches to interest a population that cannot understand the sung phrases in *p'ansori*, aesthetically evaluate the quality of a *sanjo* performance, or see a need for a bamboo comb. Yet the very government policies that promote heritage also act to curtail natural change. The justification for preserving heritage is its claim to the mantle of tradition, therefore change undermines preservation agendas at the same time that lack of change endangers cultural viability.

The tension to preserve an unchanging tradition in the South exists in sharp contrast with the approach taken by the northern neighbors, who romanticize a more perfect future under the guidance of successive Kim dynasty leaders, in particular the founder, Kim Il Sung. The linkage between Kim Il Sung's early years and valorized traditions meant that the romanticized past of the North became not the precolonial united country, but the time of Kim's rise, leading to, among other things, food traditions purportedly begun over guerrilla campfires. Because the goal is a more perfect future, in the DPRK the population is expected to engage with traditions that are constantly being developed and improved upon. Despite changes to the foodways and cultural elements inherited from the precolonial past (such as musical instruments with different tuning and construction and even entirely new sounds), the changes are portrayed as completely indigenous and deeply connected to the nation and its leaders. Furthermore, for propagandistic purposes food is almost unrivaled as every person must constantly engage with it—a far cry from *kugak* or Korean traditional music, which is ignored by much of the southern population.

The four stories of invented tradition in this section present very different cases partially because the DPRK has continued to use its supposed autonomy to build nationalism, while today the ROK relies more heavily on success in fields such as the economy, popular culture, and sports to stimulate pride in the nation. Laurel Kendall's chapter explores the institutionalization of vernacular aestheticism. Kendall traces the path through which the split-bamboo comb, once a ubiquitous object, has become a Korean icon and the focus of local heritage agendas. The transformation of a humble object into a heritage item is the result of Ye Yong-hae's enduring romanticized discourse about the bamboo comb in the 1960s, and also present-day cultural management. Ye's romanticized image of the past created enough aura around what was a common utilitarian object to raise it to the status of provincial, if not national, heritage. Yet Ye's evocation of a beautiful raven-tressed woman combing her hair is far from the memories of dirt, deprivation, and nit picking related to Kendall. This case demonstrates how agentive framing contributes to the process through which an ordinary object achieves new life as heritage. In this chapter Kendall examines how an object as ordinary as a comb can evoke memories of a past era, and simultaneously the separation from that same past that allows Koreans to openly chuckle about a time when picking nits was commonplace.

Keith Howard explains that the meaning of *kugak*, considered national music, has been intentionally reimagined. Originally *kugak* described elite court music with heavy Chinese influence. To brand *p'ansori* (epic song) and *sanjo* (solo instrumental music), the two genres at the focus of his chapter, as representative sounds of traditional Korea meant that proponents of these two genres had to convince the public that *p'ansori* and *sanjo* were *kugak*. Howard lays out the process through which *p'ansori* and *sanjo* emerged not only as *kugak* but as representative musical forms. These genres lack the shiny patina of elite culture, and have few legitimacy-granting historical records, but as unique sounds of Korea that developed independent of other regional musical traditions they can more easily claim to be Korean representative culture than court forms like *tang'ak* and *aak*, which originated in the Sinosphere.[1] Although real artistic practices of the past, they could have been forgotten until they were granted new life through the CPPL, becoming in the process, in Hobsbawm's sense, invented traditions. Although governments have been complicit in the invention of tradition for nationalistic purposes on countless occasions in recent years, the Korean example is particularly deliberate. The anthropologist Hyung Il Pai calls the Cultural Heritage Administration "the main institution responsible for the invention of 'Korean' culture and tradition" (2001, 73). The existence of a support system for the preservation of tradition is to Hobsbawm a clear mark of the inventedness of that tradition (1983, 8), and other scholars have reached similar conclusions (for example, Kirshenblatt-Gimblett 1995, 2006; Killick 2001). In this vein, every item covered by the CPPL could be considered "invented." Bringing the chapter through to the present moment, Howard discusses the tension between the fixed canonical versions of national heritage, and the creative impulses of musicians. He leaves us pondering whether it is the very pressures of the present day that produce creativity, rather than inhibit it.

Jan Creutzenberg's chapter narrows the focus still more. Starting from the assumption that the reader knows that *p'ansori* is a premier heritage item, he explains how a specific type of performance, the *wanch'ang* or full-length rendition, became highly celebrated. Here tradition is invented to accrue immediate benefit to a certain type of performer. Although the actual performance of *wanch'ang* was not a practice in the premodern era, the CPPL heritage system transitioned from one based on succession primarily through genealogical relationships between teachers and students, to include succession based on performance capability. The most important indication of mastery became a *wanch'ang* performance. Then (as now) the idea of performing, from memory, a five-hour (or longer) epic was so impressive that this athletic feat eclipsed performances of excerpts performed with greater finesse. Only recently, as Creutzenberg shows, have members of the *p'ansori* scene pushed for other interpretations and measures of mastery.

Maria Osetrova's chapter feels like a classic explanation of the concept of invented tradition (or what the introduction to this volume refers to as a "monumental" invented tradition). As Osetrova discusses, food in the DPRK, the ideological links, and benefit to the government of constructing these links is clearly demonstrated. The ways that the story of Korean food—a pure food unsullied by foreign influences—is used to shore up Juche ideology in the North are intriguing. Through these invented links between ideology and food the attitudes toward practical and available items such as potatoes, frog, and even roots and pine pitch have been changed from disdain—due to the association with poverty—to pride.

In Osetrova's chapter the DPRK achieves a distinctive culinary tradition, and with it demonstrates cultural distance from the South—unlike bamboo combs, *sanjo*, and *p'ansori*, which are all presumed to be shared traditions of Koreans as an ethnic group—these special dishes are linked to a unique northern history. Through the differential framing the South's insistence on traditions originating before the Japanese colonial era, and the relative lack of concern with everyday exposure to or practice of tradition, is brought to the fore. Unlike the elderly interviewees Kendall found, youth in the South have no emotional tie to the combs, or for that matter, the performing arts. The heritage protected under the CPPL and ICH-SPL is remote from them, the daily repetitions of combing and ritualized performances of heritage arts has receded to become old-fashioned remnants of a past culture held up to young people as heritage as if its status as heritage alone was enough to justify emotional attachment—a premise clearly denied as audiences shrink (Saeji 2016).

The four chapters in this section demonstrate how heritage practices are framed as tradition for the viewer or client who consumes, observes, and purchases without ever considering issues such as when a tradition arose, and why, if it is being presented in a new way, and if it is less utilitarian than symbolic of an aesthetic, romantic past.

GLOSSARY

aak 雅樂
tangak 唐樂

NOTE

1. *Tangak* is a genre of court music imported from Tang dynasty China; *aak* is court music imported from China and played for the rites for the royal ancestors and the Confucian sages.

REFERENCES

Bruner, Edward M. 1994. "Abraham Lincoln as Authentic Reproduction: A Critique of Postmodernism." *American Anthropologist* 96 (2): 397–415.

Diehl, Keila. 2002. *Echoes from Dharamsala: Music in the Life of a Tibetan Refugee Community*. Berkeley: University of California Press.

Hobsbawm, Eric. 1983. "Introduction: Inventing Traditions." In *The Invention of Tradition*, edited by Eric Hobsbawm and Terence Ranger, 1–14. Cambridge: Cambridge University Press.

Killick, Andrew. 2001. "Ch'anggŭk Opera and the Category of the 'Traditionesque.'" *Korean Studies* 25 (1): 51–71.

Kim, Kwangok. 2004. "The Making and Indigenization of Anthropology in Korea." In *The Making of Anthropology in East and Southeast Asia*, 253–285. New York: Berghahn Books.

Kirshenblatt-Gimblett, Barbara. 1995. "Theorizing Heritage." *Ethnomusicology* 39 (3): 367–380.

———. 2006. "World Heritage and Cultural Economics." In *Museum Frictions: Public Cultures/Global Transformations*, 161–202. Durham, NC: Duke University Press.

Lie, John. 2015. *K-Pop: Popular Music, Cultural Amnesia, and Economic Innovation in South Korea*. Oakland: University of California Press.

Pai, Hyung Il. 2001. "The Creation of National Treasures and Monuments: The 1916 Japanese Laws on the Preservation of Korean Remains and Relics and Their Colonial Legacies." *Korean Studies* 25 (1): 72–93.

Park, Chan E. 2003. *Voices from the Straw Mat: Toward an Ethnography of Korean Story Singing.* Honolulu: University of Hawai'i Press.

Saeji, CedarBough T. 2016. "The Audience as a Force for Preservation: A Typology of Audiences for the Traditional Performing Arts." *Korea Journal* 56 (2): 5–31.

CHAPTER 6

Split-Bamboo Comb

Heritage, Memory, and the Space In-between

LAUREL KENDALL

Sitting in front of her mirror box, her luxuriant black hair all unbound, she secures the flowing strands with a bit of string and combs it out over her shoulder in one long tress that dangles above the lustrous white of her padded socks. She combs it with practiced strokes, first with a sturdy wooden comb, then the fine-toothed bamboo comb, then a meticulous coiling, and finally, the chignon securely fastened with a bird's head pin. Thus, does a Korean woman begin her day. With a piece of fine mulberry paper dipped in perilla oil and folded into a rectangle she carefully polishes the large and small combs that fill the drawer of her mirror box. When the drawer is opened and closed it exudes a whiff of the fragrant camellia oil that she uses to dress her hair. These small acts thread through the fading memories of times gone by. These days, short haircuts require only a few swipes with a western hairbrush and it is difficult to even find a comb, much less a fine-toothed bamboo comb.

—Ye Yong-hae, *Human Cultural Treasures*
(Ye [1963, 409] 2016, 236–237)

In the 1960s, Ye Yong-hae's *Human Cultural Treasures*, a compendium of his popular newspaper columns on this same theme, encouraged a cohort of urban South Korean readers to look at traditional performing arts and handicraft with new eyes, to regard what many saw as old-fashioned or rustic products as, instead, beautiful and nostalgia-inducing *Korean* things made visible through the skill of Korean hands, limbs, and voices transmitted over many generations, in effect to see them as "tradition" or "heritage" (Kendall 2016; Howard 2006, 2014).[1] The evocative power of Ye's writing brought the humble split-bamboo comb (*ch'ambit*), still made for a shrinking market of quotidian users at the time of his study, into the domain of Korean tradition. Ye begins his essay on bamboo comb making with the passage cited above, a near-erotic portrait of a Korean woman combing out her long black hair, deploying a split-bamboo comb in a once common practice that the author likely observed as a child. He evokes the scent of camellia oil as a memory cue that might likewise be stirred in his 1960s readers as he leads them into a more conventionally factual report on his investigation of the comb industry in South Chŏlla Province bracketed by his encounter with an elderly combmaker. If, at the time of Ye's writing, split-bamboo combs were being produced, sold, and sometimes still used, his image of a genteel woman in Korean dress down to her lustrous white padded socks and seated on the floor in front of a traditional mirror box linked possible sensate memories to a spectral Korean authenticity that was already beyond most lived experience, even when Ye wrote. One finds his opening image in museum presentations, the *yangban* (noble) woman posed beside her mirror box as a counterpoint to the scholarly *yangban* gentleman in his study, cultural memory authorized and idealized by national museum protocols. This was precisely the exhibitry that the Korean Cultural Service provided the American Museum of Natural History in 1986, its prototype found in the National Folk Museum of Korea and at that time replicated in virtually every regional museum in South Korea. These exhibits situated Korean authenticity in the Chosŏn period and positioned the combs within the time frame of that authenticity, before the rupture of colonial modernity, national division, and post–Korean War industrialization, Korea unviolated.

Objects like the split-bamboo comb migrate between signifying contexts, moving from daily use or sacred use to new identities as museum artifacts and collectables. They are miniaturized and mass produced as souvenirs, and are sometimes reimagined as gallery art. They enter the category of "traditional object" via modernity's backward glance combined with modernity's capacity for multiple replications in various media. Through such processes they become signifiers of national or ethnic pasts (Adams 1997; Kendall 2011a; Sand 2001, following Appadurai

1986; Kopytoff 1986). In Korea, such things as masks, village guardian poles, bits of celadon, and dolls in Korean dress have become iconic of the historical collectivity, but with respect to any given object, the process is neither uniform nor inevitable. This is where the idea of "invented traditions" becomes interesting (Hobsbawm and Ranger 1983). Much of the criticism of the Hobsbawm and Ranger volume has focused on the false dichotomy of "invented" versus "authentic" traditions. Critics have rightly argued for the mutability of all human projects (Plant 2008), rightly recognized that some groups are better situated to advocate for the authenticity and importance of their own cultural practices than others, and rightly noted that processes of invention or re-invention have multiple players with different stakes in the game (Beiner 2001). What these critiques generally overlook is the degree to which any self-conscious awareness of "tradition" cannot exist outside modernity. As succinctly stated by Nicholas Dirks, "The modern not only invented tradition, it depends upon it. The modern has liberated us from tradition and constantly conceives itself in relation to it" (1990, 27–28). Scottish kilts invented by an English industrialist aside, the durable value of Hobsbawm's own essay and the sum of the articles in that pathbreaking work is not in recognizing that some "traditions," like the kilt, are made out of whole cloth. It is rather in a heightened awareness of the ways that "tradition" and "heritage" have come to be named, shaped, and transformed in the service of constructing nationally remembered and collectively accessible pasts (Hobsbawm 1983). In Korea, such recognitions are the products of intellectual projects, many of them carried out under the banner of folklore studies (*minsokhak*), journalism, government certification, and in multiple contexts of modern popular consumption. Traditions become accessible to modern life through processes and institutions that are necessarily transformative and usually involve some manner of commodification; in Korea, as elsewhere, these adaptations tilt with the specter of inauthenticity, asserting claims to the contrary. In my own writing about Korea, I have considered tradition inside modernity with respect to the revival of "traditional" Korean weddings, heritage performances of shaman rituals, and in an edited volume on all manner of consumable heritage presentations, from theme parks to cuisine (Kendall 1996, 2009, xxii–33; 2011b). Ye was a significant shaper who helped to make "intangible heritage" (*muhyŏng munhwa*) a conscious category in Korean thinking about a reimagined

Korean past, a body of practices through which modern Koreans, beyond a small group of folklore scholars and collectors, might seek and celebrate tradition. His handicraft legacy is present in both museum collections and sleek gallery projects dedicated to the marketability of craft products (Kendall 2015). In South Korea today, it is not remarkable to find an interview with the practitioner of some precarious Korean craft, an article on the model of Ye's *Human Cultural Treasures*, in the pages of a glossy lifestyle magazine otherwise devoted to fashion, food, and travel.

The split-bamboo comb is not, strictly speaking, a recent fakeloric "invention." As Ye described them, split-bamboo combs were once intimate Korean "objects of daily life" (*saenghwal yongp'um*). "There was a time when the only real combs were fine-toothed bamboo combs," Ye wrote ([1963, 409] 2016, 237). One of my own interlocutors, a woman now in her eighties, affirmed this with some passion, "Even though they were expensive, even in households that had nothing, they had to have a bamboo comb." This chapter is not concerned with questions of invention or authenticity but rather with how these once-quotidian objects have become resonant icons of Korean tradition in the afterlife of their practical use. With a helpful nudge from Ye's essay, the split-bamboo comb has become an icon of past time, seemingly well anchored in "tradition." Old split-bamboo combs appear in museums and private collections of Korean handicraft. Inexpensive contemporary versions are a common souvenir commodity in Seoul's Insadong tourist district. Larger combs are made into wall decorations suspended from the knots and tassels of Korean *maedŭp*. Split-bamboo comb making is an officially recognized Intangible Heritage Property of South Chŏlla Province (Chŏnnam Muhyŏng Munhwajae) and there are whispers that this craft might be considered for possible recognition as Intangible Heritage at the national level. None of this was self-evident or even imaginable when Ye first wrote about split-bamboo combs.

My discussion draws on a variety of Korean talk and writing, a mix of popular journalism, investigative reports, and conversations. I was able to interview two combmakers and learn more about the bamboo craft industry in South Chŏlla Province by accompanying a research and planning team from the Seoul Craft Museum in June 2017. I also garnered the memories of several old friends on the prompt of a souvenir bamboo comb that I carried with me during this same trip to Korea and extracted whenever I was asked, "and what are you working on now?" For most of my conversation partners, the bamboo comb elicited a brief smiling acknowledgment: yes, we used to use them; yes, they used to be everywhere; they disappeared in the 1970s or 1980s; grandmothers used them to fix a chignon; now everyone has short hair, people have permanents, bamboo combs don't work with permanent-waved hair; split-bamboo combs were good for catching lice. But for five of my conversation partners, my tiny bamboo comb became a memory key unlocking different experiences and associations, powerful personal memories none so aesthetic as Ye's portrait, some distinctly unpleasant, and all linked to the vertiginous experience of South Korea's compressed modernity (cf. Abelmann 2003, 31–32). I learned from these conversations that the split-bamboo comb is not quite yet a frozen *lieux de mémoire*, an official monument or memory site embodying an officially authorized vision of the past that elides personal and popular memory (cf. Nora 1989) in the manner of a mannequin posed behind museum glass. While the invention of tradition is an agentive and generally conservative process, the agents themselves may change, as well as their intentions. As David Lowenthal reminds us in his counter to the notion that invented tradition is simply bad history, "heritage is not an inquiry into the past but a celebration of it, not an effort to know what actually happened but a profession of faith in a past tailored to present-day purposes" (1998, x). And the purposes themselves change within the crucible of history.

MAKING INTANGIBLE HERITAGE

Ye wrote in an atmosphere of crisis for all manner of folk traditions. An impoverished and war-battered nation, South Korea in the 1960s marched in the direction of industrial development and rapid urbanization, broadly perceived and experienced as "modern" and "Western." The engine of change promised new lifestyles and new material goods for a growing swath of the population. Ye was not alone in highlighting the value and endangerment of old performing arts and craft traditions. Intellectuals from the colonial period forward had regarded Korean vernacular culture as both precious and precarious and at the time of Ye's research, South Korean folklore scholars were also actively documenting rural traditions and lobbying hard for their preservation (Janelli 1986; Robinson 1988, 35–36; Yang 2003). But Ye's work, disseminated via the popular press, was significant in articulating how late twentieth- and early twenty-first-century South Koreans would think about what is now extolled as "intangible heritage" (*muhyŏng munhwa*) (Howard 2006, 4–6; 2014, 135–136).

South Korea's ambitious Cultural Properties Protection Law (enacted in 1962) includes provisions for the preservation of vernacular traditions in performing arts, folkloric rituals and celebrations, and handicraft production as "important intangible cultural property" (*chungyo muhyŏng munhwajae*). Designations are made following a rigorous examination of each genre with only the most accomplished and certifiably authentic examples recognized as national cultural property. The directive includes provisions for designating Human Cultural Treasures (*poyuja*),[2] vesting these performers and craftsmen with a title and a monthly stipend on the provision that they instruct the next generation in the practice of their craft. Some forms of heritage, after due deliberation, do not receive the national title but may receive less prestigious provincial or community-level designations (Yang 2003; Janelli and Yim Janelli 2013). Although "human cultural treasure" was never an official title, many heritage bearers, including the combmaker who carries a provincial-level heritage-bearer title, proudly use it in self-reference, claiming the respect that Ye intended for them. Most of the crafts that appeared in Ye's study subsequently received heritage designations, either nationally or locally, and many of the subjects of his portraits became government-designated national heritage bearers. A government official who investigated candidates early on has described how he went about his work with copies of Ye's articles in his pockets (Choi 2012; Howard 2006, 4–6; 2014, 135–136; Soul 2012; Yang 2003). In Ye's inscription, the bamboo comb is a proper heritage object, carefully crafted through traditional means in village family workshops and vested with deeply Korean associations. Fueling the urgent nationalism of Ye's project, he lamented that bamboo combs were being supplanted by plastic combs and hairbrushes, material agents of a modernity that came from somewhere else and were deployed in decidedly un-Korean modes of grooming. Even so, and unlike many of Ye's subjects, split-bamboo combs, though in decline, were still being produced in volume and marketed throughout South Korea at the time of his writing. A quarter century later, they would reach the point of near erasure and receive provincial-level heritage recognition.

THE BAMBOO COMB INDUSTRY

Split-bamboo combs have a long history in Korea. In the sixteenth century, select combmakers in different regions were officially commissioned to produce them for the court and for the households of officials (Yŏngam Munhwawŏn 2016, 4–5, 29). Beyond the elite, split-bamboo combs were a quotidian presence in Chosŏn-period life. Kim Hong-do's (1745–1806) eighteenth-century genre painting of women bathing includes a split-bamboo comb and its wooden counterpart spread on a stone beside a woman grooming her luxuriant and freshly washed hair (Yŏngam Munhwawŏn 2016, 29). Split-bamboo combs have been found in the wrecks of nearly all ships excavated off the Korean coast where they are assumed to have been the personal accoutrements of sailors (NRIMCH 2016). They appear in American museum collections from the very moment of US contact with Korea and were described as an innately Korean thing: "All classes give great attention to the care of hair. Every man and boy carries a comb in the small bag hung at the waist" (Board of Regents, Smithsonian Institution 1891). By the early twentieth century, Yŏngam and Tamyang counties in Southwest Korea were the best-known sources of bamboo combs. Tamyang had an active specialty market in bamboo products and produced combs in greater volume than Yŏngam where demand exceeded the local capacity to supply eager middlemen. Yŏngam combs, from the village of Mangho-ri, were considered particularly well-made products. Combs from Mangho-ri carried the distinction that the local combmakers, and nearly all of the village households, were members of an impoverished branch of the *yangban* Kyŏngju Yi lineage (Ye 2016, 237 [1963, 410]; Yŏngam Munhawŏn 2016, 28–29). Comb making, as a cottage industry, was particularly vigorous in the agricultural slack season. In the early 1960s, when Ye made his study, Yŏngam comb makers turned out roughly three thousand combs every five-day market cycle during the winter slack season and a thousand during seasons of sowing and harvesting (Ye [1963, 411] 2016, 244; MCIBCPP 1969, 414–415). From the early twentieth century, improved transportation networks enabled middlemen to supply markets throughout Korea, a distribution circuit that continued after Liberation (1945) and was active at the time of Ye's work. In the 1930s, combs from Yŏngam and Tamyang fed an export market to Japan and other markets in the Empire, China, and the United States. Both Yŏngam and Tamyang established mutual aid associations of combmakers during the colonial period, in part to protect the integrity of their products (Ch'ŏng 2012, 278–279; Chung 2006, 107–110; Yŏngam Munhwawŏn 2016, 30–32).

Far from an example of colonial erasure, comb making reached a high point in Korea in the early to mid-twentieth century. In 2017, Tamyang combmaker Ko Haeng-ju and his son described how local comb-making techniques had developed from around 1916, "when the Japanese were here." A stripe, incised on the comb's end piece, near the teeth, added a more finished look, a feature now also found on Yŏngam combs. From Chosŏn times, combmakers used dyes from China to color the teeth and may have first encountered colorfast German chemical dyes in the colonial period. After 1945, when dye sources were cut off, combmakers used natural dyes made of bark and berries, something their ancestors had probably also done, but used German dye when it became available. In Tamyang, the angled finish on the comb teeth comes from a practiced rub against a sandpaper strip affixed to a block of wood; in the absence of sandpaper, combmakers had used dried sharkskin until sometime in the mid-twentieth century. The Yŏngam combmaker that Ye studied around 1960 finished his combs with a knife, but Yŏngam combmakers would also adopt sandpaper. For the last few years, Yŏngam combmaker Yi Sang-p'yŏng has been finishing his combs on a simple electric belt sander, which some from the Seoul Craft Museum team considered "inauthentic" despite the manual skill required to effect a good finish.

In the early 1960s, Ye reported that Tamyang and Yŏngam counties were still primary centers of comb production but the industry was in decline. About forty households, roughly a quarter of the total in Mangho-ri, were still actively engaged in making bamboo combs either as a specialty or as a secondary occupation. According to Ye, all Kyŏngju Yi families in Mangho-ri were familiar with the techniques of comb making and respected the craft; many were inactive owing only to a decrease in the demand for bamboo combs. Tamyang combmakers had adopted more expeditious production techniques and a production sequence that involved fewer steps: twenty-two for a Tamyang comb, a full thirty-five for a Yŏngam comb. Although similar, techniques, materials, and even the workshop vocabulary varied between these two communities (Ye [1963, 409–413] 2016, 239–240; MCIBCPP 1969, 414–415). The Yŏngam combmaker and the Tamyang combmaker interviewed by the Seoul Craft Museum team each claimed ignorance of the comb-making craft in the other community.

The two communities decorated the spines of their combs to two distinctive looks. Yŏngam combmakers used a bamboo brush to inscribe the final decoration, using a chemical substance to penetrate the bamboo. Tamyang combmakers took their finished combs to a specialist in branding bamboo who inscribed a design of flowers, birds, script, or mountain landscape into the spine. At the time of Ye's research, Yi Tong-nyŏn, the only active brander in Tamyang, claimed to be barely surviving on his earnings from branding bamboo and had forbidden his son from touching a branding tool (Ye 1963, 43). Mr. Yi's skills were recognized, probably on the strength of Ye's writing (Ministry of Culture and Information 1970, 219), and at the end of his life, Yi Tong-nyŏn would become the first designated national heritage bearer for bamboo branding (nakchuk), Important Intangible Heritage Property #31 (Lee 1994). While he praised the beauty and variety of the brander's work, Ye considered Yŏngam combs the more accomplished products owing both to the integrity of their complex production and likely also because Yŏngam carvers produced completed, decorated combs within a single craftsman's workshop rather than by outsourcing the decoration. By the late 1980s, Yŏngam combmakers were also outsourcing the spine decoration, carrying their combs to a print shop that offered a silk-screening process.

Ye felt that if a larger market for bamboo combs could be stimulated, the local output would easily exceed the estimated 260,000 combs then produced annually in Yŏngam County, sentiments echoed in a comprehensive survey of rural folk culture published by the Bureau of Cultural Properties preservation a few years later (Ye [1963, 411] 2016, 239; MCIBCPP 1969, 414).[3] But it was not to be. In 1970, a Ministry of Culture and Information publication described bamboo work, including split-bamboo combs, as still "thriving" in Tamyang: "These assets of intangible culture are not old things but are living in the heart of today's machine industry, and they will surely help promote our progress towards a better tomorrow." This idealism was followed by the more sober assessment, in this same text, that the local craftsmen working on such crafts "are probably the last craftsmen manufacturing traditional items in Korea" (Ministry of Culture and Information 1970, 219). By 1981, a feature on the "disappearing Yŏngam bamboo comb" appeared in the *Tonga Ilbo*, quoting local combmakers who claimed that it was impossible to make a living this way when their products were so thoroughly undersold by plastic combs. Comb-making households were giving up the craft and, as in other rural communities in that era, were seeking better-paying jobs in the cities (Yŏngam Munhwawŏn 2016, 18–19, 34–35). The Tamyang bamboo market suffered from diminished needs for traditional products, plastic replacements, and new competition from cheaper bamboo wares produced in China and Vietnam (Chŏng 2012; Chung 2006, 110–111). According to a guide at Tamyang's Bamboo Museum of Korea, the bamboo market closed completely in 2000. "They used to make bamboo combs in every house," the Tamyang combmaker Ko Haeng-ju told a journalist in 2005, "but now they've become a useless thing" (Kim 2005, 99). In 1986, the government of South Chŏlla Province made a positive intervention to protect the region's disappearing bamboo crafts, appointing several provincial-level heritage bearers, including a Yŏngam combmaker, the late Yi Sik-u, and Tamyang combmaker, Ko Haeng-ju who is still active. Yŏngam County provides exhibition space where combmaker Yi Sang-p'yŏng sets out his tools for each stage of the comb-making process and provides a lecture demonstration, bringing his audience outside where he finishes the combs on his electric belt sander. Mr. Ko, the provincial National Treasure in Tamyang, no stranger to interviews (e.g., Kim 2005), was less obviously performative. He told the Seoul Craft Museum team that rather than demonstrating each stage of the comb-making process as Mr. Yi had, he would prepare bamboo teeth at his own pace, a process that would consume the better part of the day. Each approach was instructive in its way.

In designating comb making as local heritage, provincial-level cultural officials necessarily accepted the use of modern (i.e., post-Chosŏn) methods in comb production: stylistic elaborations, chemical dyes, sandpaper. Heritage recognition conferred value on the distinctive skills involved in the craftsman's nimble and knowing hands shaping the comb's uniform bamboo teeth, threading them with string to a firm and precise alignment, and fixing them with end pieces and spine into a sturdy and practical object (e.g., Yŏngam Munhwawŏn 2016, 76–99). Bamboo comb craft also gained an official nod when the combs were selected as one of the official handicraft souvenir items promoted during the 1988 Olympics (Yŏngam Munhwawŏn 2016, 35). Today combs in both Tamyang and Yŏngam are inscribed by a computer laser process that brands Yi Sangp'yŏng's combs as a "Yŏngam Specialty Product," and provincial-level heritage bearer Ko Haeng-ju's as "Work of Intangible Heritage Property #15." Arguably, contemporary laser inscriptions function as authenticating labels that witness but are distinct from the craft itself. These labels, the equivalent of the maker's signature, are not inconsequential. A line of shops outside Tamyang's Bamboo Museum of Korea advertises authentic local products, and Mr. Ko's works are sold there alongside cheaper combs of dubious quality identical to those offered as souvenirs in Seoul's Insadong tourist district. One Insadong shop displayed the latter in wrappers bearing the legend "made in China." When I asked the friendly proprietress about Tamyang combs, she told me frankly that they were simply too expensive for the souvenir market. Up the street, the proprietress of another shop insisted that identical combs, the telltale wrappers removed, were authentic Korean-made combs from South Chŏlla Province. Other souvenir salesmen claimed ignorance of the source of merchandise that arrives in bulk and is fairly uniform all along Insadong's main street. The split-bamboo comb is sufficiently iconic to be a souvenir, but even with the interventions described above, Korean-made combs remain a precarious craft.

As a product once produced in volume and marketed widely along modern nodes of transportation, the split-bamboo comb carries the traces of its most recent history in the chemical dyes, sandpaper, belt sander, and new techniques for finishing the spine. The split-bamboo comb pushes standard understandings of Korean heritage as something from the Chosŏn period. South Korean heritage law calls for the preservation of "original forms" (*wŏnhyŏng*) before they were "affected by Japanese or other foreign influence," but the term has been applied with some flexibility (Janelli and Yim Janelli 2013, 75; Yang 2003). The minor deployment of more efficient tools described here is not unique, either in Korea or in the larger global handicraft sphere; heritage potters use electric wheels and

kilns, traditional papermakers have power-driven pulping machines in the
back room, and other shortcuts are taken in the name of maintaining an
otherwise unsustainable craft. Recent and critical writing on handicraft
disputes the notion of pre-industrial purity, privileging instead the craftsman's ability to judge the machine's power and fashion its uses according to his own limits (Sennett 2008, 105; also Adamson 2010; Nakashima
[1981] 2010, 222). Some social critics in South Korea are also critical of
what they characterize as the "taxidermizing" of tradition (e.g., Kweon
[1998] 2017). Should the split-bamboo comb fall under investigation for
possible national intangible heritage recognition, as it might, the process
will likely provoke interesting discussions along these lines of argument.

COMBING MEMORIES

The vanishing of the split-bamboo comb, as described by Ye and in virtually all subsequent human interest writing about bamboo combs, was a
consequence of profound changes in lifestyle and consumption patterns in
late twentieth-century South Korea. Both the combmakers and the friends
with whom I discussed bamboo combs noted how new products and new
styles of grooming eclipsed the utility of the bamboo comb sometime
between 1960 and 1980. The short cuts and permanent waves sported by
a small urban middle class in the colonial period were now worn by rich
and poor, rural and rapidly expanding urban. Most men had discarded the
bound top-knot for short cuts earlier in the twentieth century, a requirement for students from the colonial period forward, and South Korea's
near universal male conscription would make short hair all but inevitable
for young South Korean men in the Republic. By the 1970s, even rural
women were wearing permanent-waved hair and small country towns
had beauty shops near the public bathhouse to service them. Bamboo
combs intended to untangle long tresses, make a sharp straight part to
the center of the forehead, and bind hair combed smooth with camellia
oil into a tight chignon would be deployed primarily by old women and
by those very few men, exotic even to Korean eyes, who held to the traditional top-knot even past the mid-twentieth century. But the combs had
a second use, which probably accounted for their continued visibility in
markets into the 1970s when I first encountered them, described to me

as a tool for catching lice. The lice do not appear in Ye's account, but they are prominent in the memories of my interlocutors to whom we now turn.

My friend Mr. P., born in the late 1940s, offers a memory of a woman combing her hair, a reprise of Ye Yong-hae's opening image, but in a different key:

> The bamboo comb, what I remember about the bamboo comb, I remember, my grandmother, if she were living today, she would be about 110 years old. She wore her hair in a *tchok* (a tight chignon at the nape of the neck), and because she wore a *tchok* she would use this (the comb) to untangle her hair, long hair [he pantomimes drawing a comb through a long tress of hair]. You don't usually use a bamboo comb for short hair, but you need it for long hair. In those days, you could only wash your hair at the pump. That was where you got water, you couldn't wash your hair in the shower the way we do now [pantomimes vigorously scrubbing his scalp]. So, from time to time, they would comb out their hair (to clean it). My grandmother would set paper on the floor, newspaper or some other paper, and set it down on the floor just so, perfectly angled like the panels of laminated floor paper. When she had carefully arranged herself on the paper, she would comb out her hair [gestures more long strokes]. And then the dirt (*ttae*) came out, clumps of dirt from the matted hair. After that, the hair and scalp would feel so refreshed! I would laugh and give it a try like this [pantomimes combing through short locks of hair; assumes the grin of a mischievous child just for a moment]. The strands had to be combed out smooth and sleek because it had all become tangled, it all had to be unsnarled, made clean and tidy, just so. And with the dirt removed and the combing, then you can imagine how good the hair and scalp would feel. The hair became beautiful, all clean and tidy, with the dirt combed out. And then, like so . . . [he pantomimes rolling up the hair in a chignon and combing back the sides]. And then she would carefully brush all the residue together, every last bit, and throw it away down the drain. It was powdery, hair dandruff (*mori ŭi ttae*) that would fly out of the trash bin, it had to be washed away in running water. [. . .] Dr. Kendall, to write your report, what you really ought to do is go without washing your hair for a couple of days and then you'll understand how good it feels to comb it out [chuckles].

Like Ye, Mr. P. finds aesthetic appeal in the image of a woman combing her hair but where Ye offers a romanticized portrait of a black-haired woman in immaculate traditional Korean dress, Mr. P.'s memories of his grandmother are more immediate and visceral. The aesthetic appeal is in the exacting precision of his grandmother's remembered actions, from carefully aligning the paper on the floor to gathering up and disposing of every last bit of the combings, the sum of these acts resulting in a tight and tidy chignon and a feeling of profound cleansing and refreshment, nearly a spiritual exercise. Dirt and snarls are integral to the memory of an old woman deploying a split-bamboo comb. A knowledgeable scholar of Korean material culture who, as a student, attended Ye's lectures, Mr. P. appreciates the technical properties of a well-made bamboo comb as integral to the process he describes, a well-crafted tool deployed by a knowing hand:

> The dirt, it catches here between the teeth of the comb, close to the spine, you have to hold the comb at a slight angle to catch the dirt and bring it out [he grabs my bamboo comb from the tabletop], not like this [straight] but like so [at a slant]. The dirt collects right here in the middle [against the spine] so you pull it through the hair just so. . . . If you rub the teeth it gives out a sound, maybe if the bamboo is good it gives out a good sound [he produces a slight tweet by rubbing his fingers along the teeth]. This one doesn't have such a good sound [chuckles]. Here, see the teeth should be flexible, bamboo should be flexible, but this one has hardly any flexibility, it's weak.

He concludes by demonstrating the proper method of cleaning a comb with a stiff piece of paper pulled between the teeth, emphasizing that the paper should be worked all the way to the spine through each aperture between the closely placed teeth, the act of a meticulous grandmother as precise in the cleaning of her comb and the binding of her hair as she was in aligning paper in exact right angles and consistent seams to cover the walls and floor of her home.

My bamboo comb evoked less pleasant childhood associations for two other friends who, as elementary schoolchildren in the 1960s, remembered rigorous maternal applications of the bamboo comb to their own scalps and hair. As a child, Professor E. was shy about exposing her naked body in the public bathhouse and said that protesting children such as herself had to be carried by force into the tank of unpleasantly hot water.

As part of the bathing ritual, her mother would carefully work through her hair with a bamboo comb. For Professor E. the comb and the bathhouse brought memories of the arrival of American shampoo as something totally new. She also recalled old women parting their hair and smoothing it back with combs dipped in camellia oil to make a well-groomed *tchok*, the bamboo comb as a hinge between past times and future possibilities.

I showed my friend Professor S. my comb and we chatted over some predictable ground about old women wearing *tchok*, short hair, and lice prevention, and then the conversation veered in another direction. Professor S. began to describe how she had been a wild, misbehaving child, often slapped on the palms of her hands and the bottoms of her feet. "I ran away from the bath and hid. I was naked, can you imagine? [. . .] I used to twist my head when my mother was trying to comb out my hair [illustrates]. When I saw that thing [she points to the comb on the coffee shop table] the memories all came pouring out. [chuckles . . .] I always had lice [grins]." She hated the bathhouse ordeal and the attendant delousing with a bamboo comb and would avoid bathing for a month at a time. In her 1960s childhood, she recalled, the children all had lice in school and used to playfully pick them off of each other's skin and hair. As part of the school physical examination, the children were spritzed with DDT. "We thought of it as a modern smell"; more chuckles followed by a reverie about her first childhood taste of butter, white bread sandwiches and mayonnaise, congealed powdered milk, oranges, and later, an enduring appetite for maple syrup.

For these two friends, the bamboo comb was a memory key, a prompt to visceral recollections of mothers, now deceased, who zealously groomed their reluctant, protesting childhood selves. Memories of split-bamboo combs, the bathhouse, and head lice were also flooded with recollections of new, "modern," foreign products, tastes, and scents. As an artifact of childhood experiences, the comb led them back to a time when products now taken for granted were novel and exotic experiences while split-bamboo combs were commonplace. The comb is a memory key but in these instances, as in Mr. P.'s memories of his grandmother, the memories are deeply personal rather than collective and they jump well beyond the pretty imagery of a woman in traditional dress combing out her long black hair.

Yongsu's Mother, a retired shaman in her eighties, was amused when I brought out my bamboo comb. Her own mother had used one to comb her hair into a *tchok* slicked with camellia oil for most of her long life, and Yongsu's Mother performed the familiar pantomime of parting, combing back the hair, and twisting a chignon. But Yongsu's Mother also has vivid memories of head lice:

> There was 6.25 [the Korean War]. There wasn't any medicine [for head lice]. There were so many lice. [She gestures to suggest lice jumping out all over her scalp.] So, we combed them all right out with this [points to the comb], they just fell out. We used the bamboo comb constantly. If you hold it like this [she holds the comb at an angle and pantomimes a stroke] *sak*! The lice fall out and their nits come out too.

Here the conversation takes a new turn as the comb leads her to reflect on long hair and politics in the contemporary moment, a linking of moral character and proper personal appearance as was once enabled by bamboo combs:

> Even now it would be good for people with long hair to use these to make the hair sleek, bright, glossy. [. . .] These days, both men and women go around with long, disheveled hair flying. The entire world is in a state of chaos, unsettled, nothing but sound and fury, right? The country is a mess. Isn't that so? In the past, they used to comb their hair tidily, even young women were brought up that way. These days young women, boys, housewives, bachelors, married men, they all go around with long, disheveled hair flying around, it's so unsettling. I think of these things as I grow old. They behave this way and the whole country is unsettled. The government is all in turmoil. Every day it's the same thing, every day. Remember President Park Chung Hee [the military dictator sometimes nostalgically associated with a time of imagined political stability]. [. . .] And now isn't the country all in a mess? Girls with their unbound hair flying around, I mean really, if they did that in the past, they would have been in for it. Even adults are unstable. They fight at home too. Long hair should be bound up [she pantomimes pulling it back for a *tchok*] or braided [gestures braiding]. This is awful! They leave it all unbound. All of them, the hair all disheveled. It unsettles the whole country. Men used to look so nice with their close-cropped hair. Why do men have to go around with their hair flying, acting crazy?

She has been flapping her arms comically to indicate the flapping hair, chuckling, amused with the images she is evoking, but she becomes more serious and heated when she turns to recent events:

> The state of the world follows upon human behavior. In the past, would men have gone around with unbound hair? It's ugly, shabby, and it puts the world out of joint, that's what I say. Look at Park Geun-hye [daughter of Park Chung Hee and discredited former president of South Korea], they took her away in handcuffs in front of everyone. She had been the [recently deposed] President, what did she do to deserve that? This was wrong. This was excessive.

In Yongsu's Mother's logic, long, disheveled hair leads to a moral climate where the former president could be defamed and disgraced. Yongsu's Mother speaks of bound hair and braids but she also evokes the close-cropped hair enjoined on men by the Park Chung Hee regime, which she recalls as a better, more stable time. If, in the early twentieth century, short permanent-waved hair suggested a racy modern style, for Youngsu's Mother, so groomed for more than sixty years, short hair and tightly bound hair have reached a point of equivalency in decorum and restraint relative to loose—in her eyes louche—contemporary styles. Yongsu's Mother's tirade evokes a persistent Confucian strain in Korean thinking, a link between appearance, character, and social order that once caused even impoverished families to maintain a bamboo comb and impressed early foreign observers with the care given to grooming the hair. But one need not be "Confucian" to equate radical changes in grooming with moral disarray. Yongsu's Mother's tirade against the chaotic state of a world in which both men and women sport long, disordered hair sounded eerily similar to voices heard in my late 1960s American coming-of-age. Suffice it to say that the bamboo comb, and the moral qualities associated with careful grooming that it facilitated, gave Yongsu's Mother an anchor for her commentary on the very different contemporary moment.

My fictive sister Suk-cha also used the comb to unlock a vision of the past, but it was not the same past. The second youngest child in a rural family in the 1970s, her family was poor but she was always aware of the even greater deprivations her parents had experienced from the end of the colonial period through the Korean War. After my trip to Yŏngam and Tamyang, I gifted Suk-cha with a pair of Yŏngam combs tied with colorful silk cords. She smiled over the gift and took one of the combs in her hands, but then she said with a quiet smile "They remind me of a sad story." I asked her for the story and brought out my tape recorder, which she is used to:

> My parents, in the past, when we were sitting together eating dinner, this was something they often talked about with us, about the bamboo comb. In the past in Korea after dinner we had a lot of time on our hands. We didn't have TV, we didn't have anything else to do, so they would talk to us about the past. When people had long hair, they used to comb through it looking for lice (she pantomimes combing a long tress). The lice were in their clothing too. They would bite and tickle so in those days, at night, they didn't have electricity, so they would catch lice by candlelight, combing out their hair with a bamboo comb. The lice were tiny and the teeth of the comb have only a tiny space between them. If you combed through like this and like this [pantomimes] the lice would come out and die, "*dak, dak,*" the sound of lice being pinched to death. My parents would talk about this, about how they lived in the past.
>   *Why do you say it's a sad story?*
>   Because in the past, not now, now people are very clean, they know a lot, they're educated. In the past, they didn't know anything about hygiene. People are more educated now, they have enough to eat, they live well, clean. In the past they were hungry, they didn't know anything about hygiene, so they had lice. Life was hard then and that's why I said it was sad. The bamboo comb wasn't just for a woman to comb her hair to be beautiful, it was for catching lice. The combs we use now, the teeth are wide apart, you can't catch lice with that. You need a bamboo comb. *Ahyuuu!*

This was not the first time that Suk-cha had expressed sorrow about her parents' hard lives. The comb as key opened a double set of memories, Suk-cha's own of a time before television when her parents spent the evening talking about the past, and her parents' memories, told on those occasions, of a time before electricity when they spent evenings hunting lice by the light of a candle. She was too young to have known routine lice combings in her own childhood although as we both acknowledged, head lice flare up periodically among elementary schoolchildren in both South Korea and New York. Inexpensive bamboo combs, like the one I was using as an interview prompt, are sold on the internet for $7.50 US as a device for spotting lice on the scalp.

Small and humble, the split-bamboo comb has yet been an actant in Bruno Latour's sense ([1991] 1993) precipitating various activities intended to move it from obsolete object of daily use to celebrated heritage product through the work of different human agents. Ye Yong-hae journeyed to the mountain hamlet of Mangho-ri to sit with an elderly combmaker whose fingers never paused from working strips of bamboo to make a comb. Ye wrote about his experiences, linking the work of the rural combmaker to the toilette of a woman inhabiting an elegant Korean past time. Other studies followed and official reports were written. News and human-interest stories were posted. Combs were collected and exhibited and craft demonstrations hosted. The administration of South Chŏlla Province took steps to preserve comb making and other bamboo crafts. If rumors are correct, bamboo comb making may soon be at the center of an extended investigation for possible promotion to the status of a national Important Intangible Cultural Property—a process of committees, subcommittees, reports, and deliberations. As my hostess on the trip to Yŏngan and Tamyang observed in the van that was carrying us due south, "we are traveling the length of Korea (*sam cholli*) all because of a split-bamboo comb."

Ye made his case for the split-bamboo comb by linking it to an evocative image of classical Korean femininity. In my friend Mr. P.'s own memories, the elegant black-haired gentlewoman is replaced by a grandmother, her hair no longer black, but no less precise in her performance of grooming, meticulously engaged in the extraction of dirt and dandruff from her scalp. And as my sister Suk-cha noted, "The bamboo comb wasn't just for a woman to comb her hair to be beautiful, it was for catching lice," the lice she attributes to the poor hygiene of uneducated people. Yongsu's Mother described her own lice, jumping out all over her scalp, as a consequence of wartime deprivation; she knew very well how to treat them, but the medicine was unavailable. For Suk-cha and Yongsu's Mother and for my other interlocutors, the past is another country, not always the same country but close enough to offer a sharp contrast with both Ye's opening imagery and with the present South Korean moment. In the early

1960s, when Ye wrote, the lice, dirty scalps, and naughty children in the bathhouse would not have furthered the cause of a vanishing handicraft, any more than had he chosen to emphasize, rather than elide, twentieth-century innovations in the production of combs. More than a half century on, the lice, dirt, and reliance on public bathhouses have become the stuff of nostalgia, as recounted above. These living memories, personal and idiosyncratic, resist the finalization of the split-bamboo comb's (re)invention as a *lieu de memoire* signifying heritage according to Ye's inscription. In Hoskins's (1998) sense and for my five interlocutors, the comb is a biographical object, participating in the construction of selves through narrative, Korean selves who have migrated from poorer times to a place of seemingly unbridled consumerism. As the work of Nancy Abelmann (2003), Cho Han Haejoang (2002), and Laura Nelson (2000) suggests, this precipitous transformation has provoked both moral questioning and a concern for the future of Korean identity itself. In this ambivalent regard for the contemporary moment, we find intimations of a remembered "tradition" that might just possibly accommodate the still-living memories contained in split-bamboo combs.

Authorized presentations of the past are not immutable; sometimes they topple as dramatically as Lenin's statues with the fall of communism, sometimes the shifts are subtle. Ye's work was agentive, written at a time when folk heritage was best legitimized and valorized by linking it to a precolonial specter of cultural authenticity. Fast-forward half a century. Label texts in national, local, and city-sponsored South Korean museums now present, in nostalgic evocation, the material culture of a history that extends though the twentieth century and into the twenty-first. This move is most monumentally explicit in the new National Museum of Korean Contemporary History (opened 2012) but change was already evident when the Seoul Museum of History (opened 2002) included artifacts of colonial modernity among its exhibits. This was soon followed by colonial-era exhibits in the National Folk Museum of Korea and in some regional museums in the national system. Appealing to the nostalgias of my cohort of conversation partners, the grounds of the National Folk Museum of Korea now house a vintage modern streetscape with a tearoom, comic book rental shop, neighborhood tailor, and other memory-inducing sites. Such histories are not necessarily prettified. The Seoul City Museum reproduced a c. 1960s sweatshop, the Cheonggyecheon

[Chŏnggye chŏn] Museum (opened 2005) re-created the squalid tenements that once stood beside an open sewage ditch. The War Memorial Museum marked the Republic of Korea's sixtieth anniversary (2005) by devoting most of a large gallery to the fabrication of a post–Korean War hillside squatters' settlement inhabited by mannequins in baggy clothing and with windburned faces, huddling to get warm. These exhibits are, in Lowenthal's sense, "celebratory," marking the distance from poor and grubby times to South Korea's relatively affluent and comfortable present tense, a reminder to a younger generation of what their parents and grandparents endured. As contexts of heritage commemoration, these authorized versions of the recent past share the nostalgic distance that enabled my conversation partners, no longer young, to speak of dirt and head lice with chuckles animated by pantomimes of combs in motion. It is also just possible that, with the problematic twentieth century as a now-acknowledged part of the South Korean past, the craftsmen's innovations could be seen as acts of handicraft heritage that are also historical in their way. It is just possible, although by no means certain at the time of this writing, that unruly memories of small bamboo combs could become part of an officially authorized story about the strides the South Korean nation has taken into its glittering present. In some interesting ways, the comb's (re)invention remains incomplete and its direction as open to speculation as is the continuing re-inscription of what constitutes the South Korean past.

GLOSSARY

Chŏnnam Muhyŏng Munhwajae 全南 無形 文化財

Chosŏn 朝鮮

chungyo muhyŏng munhwajae 重要 無形 文化財

Insadong 仁寺洞

Kim Hong-do 金弘道

Ko Haeng-ju 高行柱

Kyŏngju Yi 慶州 李

Mangho-ri 望湖里

minsokhak 民俗學

muhyŏng munhwa 無形 文化

nakchuk 烙竹

Park Chung Hee 朴正熙

Park Geun-hye 朴槿惠

poyuja 保有者

saenghwal yongp'um 生活 用品

Tamyang 潭陽

Tonga Ilbo (Dong-a Ilbo) 東亞日報

wŏnhyŏng 原形
yangban 兩班
Ye Yong-hae 芮庸海
Yi Sang-p'yŏng 李相評

Yi Sik-u 李植雨
Yi Tong-nyŏn 李同年
Yŏngam 靈岩

NOTES

Research in Korea was supported by the Jane Belo-Tanenbaum Fund, American Museum of Natural History. I am grateful to Young-Kyu Park for invaluable information, Hong Nam Kim for inviting me to travel with the Seoul Craft Museum team, and Homer Williams for all manner of research support and technical assistance. Thanks to many others who appear here in different degrees of anonymity. All shortcomings are my own.

1. *Munhwa* is usually translated as "culture" or "civilization" but is now also widely used to signify "heritage," as in "intangible heritage" (*muhyŏng munhwa*).
2. Literally "[title] possessor" or "[title] holder."
3. The report's section on Yŏngam County bamboo comb production adds four years to the age of its key informant but otherwise summarizes Ye's account.

REFERENCES

Abelmann, Nancy. 2003. *The Melodrama of Modernity: Women, Talk, and Class in Contemporary South Korea*. Honolulu: University of Hawai'i Press.

Adams, Kathleen. 1997. "Nationalizing the Local and Localizing the Nation: Ceremonials, Monumental Displays and National Memory-Making in Upland Sulawesi, Indonesia." *Museum Anthropology* 33 (3): 113–130.

Adamson, Glenn. 2010. Introduction to *The Craft Reader*, edited by Glenn Adamson, 1–5. Oxford, New York: Berg.

Appadurai, Arjun, ed. 1986. *The Social Life of Things: Commodities in Cultural Perspective*. Cambridge: Cambridge University Press.

Beiner, Guy. 2001. "The Invention of Tradition?" *History Review* 22:1–10.

Board of Regents, Smithsonian Institution. 1891. *Annual Report of the Board of Regents, Smithsonian Institution*. Washington, DC: Government Printing Office. Accessed June 2, 2017. https://library.si.edu/digital-library/book/annualreportofbo1891smit

Cho Han, Haejoang. 2002. "Living With Conflicting Subjectivities: Mother, Motherly Wife, and Sexy Woman in the Transition from Colonial-Modern to Postmodern Korea." In *Under Construction: The Gendering of Modernity, Class, and Consumption in the Republic of Korea*, edited by Laurel Kendall, 165–196. Honolulu: University of Hawai'i Press.

Choi, Sung-ja. 2012. "Fifty Years of Endeavor for Preservation and Transmission." *Koreana: Korean Arts and Culture* 26 (3): 18–21.

Chŏng Yŏng-sin. 2012. *Han'gugŭi changt'ŏ* [Korean marketplaces]. Seoul: Nunbit Ch'ulp'ansa.

Chung, Seung-mo. 2006. *Markets: Traditional Korean Society*. Seoul: Ewha Womans University Press.

Dirks, Nicholas B. 1990. "History as a Sign of the Modern." *Public Culture* 2 (2): 25–32.

Hobsbawm, Eric. 1983. "Introduction: Inventing Traditions." In *The Invention of Tradition*, edited by Eric Hobsbawm and Terence Ranger, 1–15. Cambridge: Cambridge University Press.

Hobsbawm, Eric, and Terence Ranger, eds. 1983. *The Invention of Tradition*. Cambridge: Cambridge University Press.

Hoskins, Janet. 1998. *Biographical Objects: How Things Tell the Stories of People's Lives*. New York: Routledge.

Howard, Keith. 2006. *Preserving Korean Music: Intangible Cultural Properties as Icons of Identity*. Burlington, VT: Ashgate.

———. 2014. "Reviving Korean Identity through Intangible Cultural Heritage." In *The Oxford Handbook of Music Revival*, edited by Caroline Bithell and Juniper Hill, 135–159. Oxford: Oxford University Press.

Janelli, Roger L. 1986. "The Origins of Korean Folklore Scholarship." *Journal of American Folklore* 99/391:24–49.

Janelli, Roger L., and Dawnhee Yim Janelli. 2013. "Safeguarding Intangible Heritage: The Role of Folklore Scholarship in the Republic of Korea." *Anais do Museu Histórico Nacional* 45:69–79.

Kendall, Laurel. 1996. *Getting Married in Korea: Of Gender, Morality, and Modernity*. Berkeley: University of California Press.

———. 2009. *Shamans, Nostalgias and the IMF: South Korean Popular Religion in Motion*. Honolulu: University of Hawai'i Press.

———. 2011a. "The *Changsŭng* Defanged: The Curious Recent History of a Korean Cultural Symbol." In *Consuming Korean Tradition in Early and Late Modernity: Commodification, Tourism, and Performance*, edited by Laurel Kendall, 129–148. Honolulu: University of Hawai'i Press.

———, ed. 2011b. *Consuming Korean Tradition in Early and Late Modernity:*

Commodification, Tourism, and Performance, edited by Laurel Kendall, 129–148. Honolulu: University of Hawai'i Press.

———.2015. "Intangible Traces and Material Things: The Performance of Heritage Handicraft." *Acta Koreana* 17 (2): 537–555.

———.2016. "Primary Text: Commentary." *Modern Craft* 9 (2): 227–233.

Kim Eun-sik. 2005 "Mŏritsogŭro punŭn shiwŏnhan taebaram: ch'ambitchang Ko Haeng-ju" [A refreshing bamboo breeze in one's hair: Bamboo comb master Ko Haeng-ju]. *Chungdŭng urigyoyuk* [Our general education] 4:96–101. Accessed May 25, 2017. http://www.dbpia.co.kr/Article/NODE00586330

Kopytoff, Igor. 1986. "The Cultural Biography of Things: Commoditization as Process." In *The Social Life of Things: Commodities in Cultural Perspective*, edited by Arjun Appadurai, 64–91. Cambridge: Cambridge University Press.

Kweon, Sug-In. (1998) 2017. "Discourses of Korean Culture amid the Expansion of Consumer Society and the Global Order." *Korean Anthropology Review* 1(1): 131–159. Originally published in *Pigyo Munhwa Yŏn'gu* [Korean cultural studies] 4:181–214.

Latour, Bruno. (1991) 1993. *We Have Never Been Modern*. Translated by Catherine Porter. Cambridge, MA: Harvard University Press.

Lee, Kyong-hee. 1994. "Kuk Yang-mun and Kim Ki-chan: Lonely Heirs to a Vanishing Art." *Koreana* 8 (2): 1–2. Accessed April 9, 2020. https://koreana.or.kr/user/action/backIssueView.do

Lowenthal, David. 1998. *The Heritage Crusade and the Spoils of History*. Cambridge: Cambridge University Press.

MCIBCPP (Ministry of Culture and Information, Bureau of Cultural Properties Preservation). 1969. *Han'guk minsin chonghap chosa pogosŏ, Chŏnnam* [Report of the comprehensive investigation of Korean folk beliefs, South Chŏlla Province]. Seoul: Munhwajae Kwalliguk, Munhwa Kongbobu.

Ministry of Culture and Information. 1970. *The Ancient Arts of Korea*. Seoul: Ministry of Culture and Information, Republic of Korea.

Nakashima, George. (1981) 2010. The Soul of a Tree. In *The Craft Reader*, edited by Glenn Adamson, 219–225. New York: Berg.

Nelson, Laura C. 2000. *Measured Excess: Status, Gender, and Consumer Nationalism in South Korea*. New York: Columbia University Press.

Nora, Pierre. 1989. "Between Memory and History: Les Lieux de Mémoire." *Representations* 26 (Spring): 7–25.

NRIMCH (National Research Institute of Maritime Cultural Heritage). 2016. *Underwater Archeology of Korea*. Seoul: Gongmyong. Accessed June 2, 2017. https://books.google.com/books?id=JfLKDQAAQBAJ

Plant, Byron King. 2008. "Secret, Powerful, and the Stuff of Legends: Revisiting

Theories of Invented Tradition." *The Canadian Journal of Native Studies* 27 (1): 175–194.

Robinson, Michael Edson. 1988. *Cultural Nationalism in Colonial Korea, 1920–1925*. Seattle: University of Washington Press.

Sand, Jordan. 2001. "Monumentalizing the Everyday: The Edo-Tokyo Museum." *Critical Asian Studies* 33 (3): 251–378.

Sennett, Richard. 2008. *The Craftsman*. New Haven, CT: Yale University Press.

Soul, Ho-jeong. 2012. "The Hidden Friends of Living Treasures." *Koreana: Korean Culture and Arts* 26 (3): 22–25.

Yang, Jongsung. 2003. *Cultural Protection Policy in Korea: Intangible Cultural Properties and Living National Treasures*. Seoul: Jimundang.

Ye Yong-hae. 1963. *In'gan Munhwajae* [Masters of Cultural Heritage of Korea]. Summary translation by Soh E. Ton. Seoul: Eomungag Publishing Company.

———.2016. "Primary Text: Selections from Human Cultural Treasures." Translated by Laurel Kendall. *The Journal of Modern Craft* 9 (2): 235–244.

Yŏngam Munhwawŏn [Yŏngam Cultural Service]. 2016. *Yongam Ch'ambit* [Split-bamboo Combs of Yŏngam]. Yŏngam chŏnt'ong minye p'um pogosŏ (Investigation of traditional folk handicrafts of Yŏngam). Yŏngam, ROK: Yŏngam Munhwawŏn.

CHAPTER 7

Tradition as Construction

Embedding Form in Two Korean Music Genres

KEITH HOWARD

Most cultural forms that assume the moniker "traditional" are constructions. They are, to cite Marshall Sahlins, "neo-traditional," with "exogenous elements" that are "culturally indigenized." For the owners of a tradition there is no "radical disconformity, let alone inauthenticity" in the construction (Sahlins 1999, xi). If so, then Hobsbawm and Ranger's (1983) distinction between "genuine" and "invented" traditions is wide of the mark; it imposes a false "contrast between real continuity and a constructed sense of permanence" (Otto and Pedersen 2005, 14), potentially undermining innate flexibility and adaptability in cultural production. Killick's (2010) concept of the "traditionesque," a cultural product sitting somewhere between old and new, or between genuine and invented, is equally troublesome, since it does little to reconcile the untraceable past inherent in the old with observable changes in the present. Ultimately, such notions reveal the position of the author (much as, for example, has been revealed in critiques of an earlier generation of anthropologists), and can be argued to be imperialistic, since they impose Enlightenment ideas that once seemed relevant to the Global North on to the rest of the world.[1] Traditions embed symbolic actions; they are "discursive" (in the sense of symbolic anthropology, after Geertz 1973, as taken up by many others, including Beeman 1981; Schechner 2002, 28–29) and "entextualized" (in the sense of making discourse extractable; Bauman and Briggs 1990; Silverstein and Urban 1996). They involve individual and institutional agency, both planned and improvised. They are emerging rather than static entities, in which layers accrete over time, disguising the scaffolding and at times substituting new building blocks for old frames. But understanding the agency within tradition is essential to inform the planning and operation of the contemporary local and global movements that seek to preserve and sustain the intangible cultural heritage.

In a recent article (Howard 2016), I looked at the agencies involved in the construction of *kugak*, Korean traditional music. Briefly stated, *kugak* is a constructed tradition centered on the Republic of Korea (South Korea). If it is considered to mark an inherited tradition, and to mark a soundworld that sets South Korea apart from its immediate neighbors on the Chinese mainland and in the Japanese archipelago, it does so because we have bought into the aural component of a nationalistic discourse developed largely since 1945, when liberation from Japanese colonialization was marked by the emergence of the two rival Korean states. In the 1920s, the loose grouping of writers, scholars, and activists often known as the "cultural nationalists" (*munhwa undong*) had interpreted Korea's failure to remain independent in terms of an unwillingness to modernize. Cultural nationalists were indebted, much as Benedict Anderson observes of the West, to the growth of print capitalism (Shin 2006, 46). They criticized backward-facing Confucianist thinking, and China, as the source of so much in old Korea, was replaced by a version of the West filtered through a reformed Japan. Nationalism, though, floundered by the late 1930s, as artists and writers struggled with a disappearing future (Poole 2014), and many looked to Japan for a way forward. At the time, few Koreans saw any future in *kugak*, as music inherited from the past.

To normalize *kugak* as the national soundworld after 1945 demanded agents—whether promoters, scholars, or musicians—and this required the few who had stuck with it during the colonial period to join a coalition of scholars, journalists, and educators to set and influence policies that would promote it. Much has centered on a single state-sponsored institution that in recent years has been known in English as the National Gugak Center—the successor to the colonial-era Court Music Bureau (Aakpu or, including a reference to the king, the Yiwangjik aakpu) set up by government decree as the Korean War began. The Center is promoted as the successor to court offices stretching back 1200 years to the Unified Silla dynasty, compressing together various offices named in annals and other historical documentation at specific times into a unitary and continuous list. From the 1960s, promotion was aided by what is now a well-established state heritage preservation system. In this, performance arts, including *kugak* genres, were elevated to the status of National Intangible Cultural Properties (*Kukka muhyŏng munhwajae*).[2] The result has been that "Korean music" has become synonymous with *kugak*; the parallel to Scotland, where iconicity is embedded in bagpipes but also in kilts and associated tartans, with influence from the Low Countries and English mills—to cite Hugh Trevor-Roper's contribution to *The Invention of Tradition* (1983, 15–41)—is intriguing.

The association of *kugak* in former times was, however, with a court culture, both ritual *aak* (Ch. *yayue*) and secular *chŏngak*, supplemented by music favored by the literati and, as a broader category of *chŏngak*, the "middle class" (*chungin*)—a small urban, professional elite that emerged from the eighteenth century onward. Confucianism kept the court separated from the masses, and *kugak* must have been known to only a small minority of the total population, since an early 1900s Japanese census identifies less than 3 percent of the population as belonging to literati/professional circles. Significantly, the first appearance of the term "*kugak*" in modern times applied to this music, and dates to 1907, when it was introduced in opposition to *ŭmak* music (i.e., Western music; No 1989, 13); this parallels a distinction in Japan between *Nihon gaku* and *ongaku* made as music entered the school curriculum. Narrowly defined, *kugak* was, to vamp on Michael Church's (2015) title, an *Other* classical music, giving a watermark that could justify its maintenance. Hence, when the National Gugak Center opened during the Korean War, and until the 1980s, it was known in English as the National Classical Music Institute. However, unlike Western classical music, where the decline of court patronage was offset by a public concert culture that grew with industrialization at the end of the eighteenth century, *kugak* never became a commercial proposition. *Kugak* continues to occupy only a minor place in domestic musical activity, confined primarily to education, subsidized performance activities, and broadcasting. In other words, *kugak* moved straight from court to state in terms of sponsorship, and, unlike Western classical music, never enjoyed support from coalitions of the wealthy.

Here, I extend my discussion by revisiting two key genres that were once exogenous to the narrow court and literati former remit of *kugak*, but that have today become central to it: *sanjo* (scattered melodies for solo melodic instrument and drum accompaniment) and *p'ansori* (epic storytelling through song). *Sanjo* and *p'ansori* occupy territories at the professionalized end of what Koreans, following the East Asian practice of distinguishing the Great from the Little tradition, consider to be "folk" music—as music of the people (*min'gan ŭmak³*), rather than music of the court, aristocracy, and literati. *Sanjo* and *p'ansori* illustrate how those steering *kugak* have broadened its narrow compass, incorporating repertoires to appeal to domestic and international audiences, and habituating these into the total *kugak* canon. Indeed, *kugak* has recently been defined as "multiple court and folk genres as well as new music inspired by court and folk aesthetics" (Finchum-Sung 2017, 12). *Kugak*, then, has not been a static entity in post-Liberation South Korea, and *sanjo* and *p'ansori* illustrate how the construction of tradition has, necessarily, taken more than one route.

There is more than one way to argue a history, and thereby to justify a tradition through transmission, and its emergence over time as layers are sedimented and as the scaffolding is added to. Court and literati *kugak* benefits from an abundance of historical source materials. It enjoys continuity in its forces, in that musicians who performed or trained at the colonial-era court music bureau became the senior *kugak* musicians in post-Liberation South Korea. This, though, illustrates two distinct and often conflicting approaches to tradition: For a music tradition to have iconicity—or validity—should the yardstick for authenticity be historical texts or the memories and practices of elder practitioners? If transmission typically relies on those who pass things down from the past to the present, and taking from Thomas Kuhn's (1962) argument that history is little more than an interpretation of the past for the present, how can musicology influence—or in an extreme case, dictate—performance practice? This question has considerable salience in contemporary South Korea, since as musicology has offered ever-closer readings of historical sources, some have questioned the reliability of elder musicians from the court and literati tradition within the National Gugak Center who trained at the court bureau during the colonial period and who were potentially influenced by the colonial power. The most notable recent dispute has concerned the ritual dance (*ilmu*) of sacrificial rites, at the Rite to Royal Ancestors (*Chongmyo cheryeak*), National Intangible Cultural Property 1, and at the Confucian shrine (*Munmyo*) for which the rite, *Sŏkchŏn taeje*, is Property 85.[4] In contrast to court and literati music, to make *p'ansori* and *sanjo* part of the *kugak* canon, compensation for relatively weak historical source materials has been demanded. As I discuss below, compensation has been found by emphasizing largely aural/oral knowledge supplemented by analyses of the early twentieth-century recordings of past masters. The construction of both genres, as traditions, is thereby made apparent, since musicologists have sought to apply a methodology developed for court and literati music to both "folk" genres.

INTRODUCING *SANJO* AND *P'ANSORI*

Sanjo and *p'ansori* are two of the most popular *kugak* genres today. They are taught to performance majors in schools and universities, and are staples of national and international performance tours. Many *sanjo* "schools" (*ryu*, borrowing a term from Japan) are recognized, each based on the performance style of a master musician from an earlier generation. Although *sanjo* was first introduced for the twelve-stringed plucked zither, *kayagŭm*, versions are played on all major Korean instruments. In recent decades, composers have written *sanjo* for piano, cello, and other Western instruments, and the pop-musician-turned-film-composer Kim Soo-chul has even recorded an electric guitar *sanjo* (Living Sound, 2002). The gloss, "scattered melodies," translates the two Sino-Korean characters that comprise the name *sanjo*, but hardly does justice to the complexity, since a single piece can last an hour, progressing in a series of conjoined movements each using a single rhythmic cycle, gradually increasing in tempo.

P'ansori is a composite art form that combines song (*sori*), narration and dialogue (*aniri*), and dramatic action (*pallim*). Five core repertoires or stories (*madang*) survive, four popular folk/morality tales with Confucian overtones and one a Chinese-originating battle story. Each repertoire, given in its entirety, lasts between four and eight hours, hence my admittedly controversial gloss of the genre as "epic storytelling through song" (see Creutzenberg's chapter in this volume). Although *p'ansori* schools or styles are distinguished, such as the western school (*sŏp'yŏnje*) and eastern school (*tongp'yŏnje*), lineages or forms for each repertoire or story, tracked back to eighteenth- and nineteenth-century master-singers (*myŏngch'ang*) have taken on increasing importance as scholarship has developed and as the preservation system has formalized transmission.

Sanjo and *p'ansori*, in contrast to court and literati music, are genres where historical texts and scores tend to be sparse and/or require critical analysis—not least when written by literati rather than by the largely illiterate musicians themselves. Hence, to argue for "deep roots" (*ppuri kip'ŭn*)—to use a phrase known to all Koreans from the first, fifteenth-century, poem that celebrated the invention of the Korean alphabet—within the tradition is problematic. Texts must be supplemented by other materials, hence oral histories and performances are collected from senior musicians, and recordings are analyzed. The three data sets (texts, recordings, and the memories and performances of living musicians) used to justify a tradition need to be weighed against each other, and this, as I have discussed elsewhere (Howard 2016), introduces agency in the form of individual and institutional motivations.

RECORDING KOREAN MUSIC:
CONSIDERATIONS

Music is sound, so written records as well as oral history are always inadequate, since they are selective and insufficient to prove constancy over time. As the late ethnomusicologist Frank Harrison once succinctly told me (Belfast, 1986), we cannot know with certainty what music sounded like before the advent of recordings. A single 1899 advertisement published in a Korean newspaper, the *Hwangsŏng Sinmun* of March 13, 1899, marks the earliest reference to music recordings (in this case, Western music) for sale in Korea (reproduced, with modern Korean transliteration, in No 1995, 657), although the first known recordings of Korean music had actually been made by Alice Cunningham Fletcher in Washington in 1896. Fletcher, though, recorded three students who likely left Korea during the post–Sino-Japanese War turbulence, and was not intending her recordings to be for distribution and sale (Provine 2012). The first known commercial Korean music recordings were of popular folk songs[5] sung by Han In-o, made in Japan by the Columbia Graphophone Company in 1907 and released early in 1908.[6]

Sometime after 1908 but before 1911, the Victor Talking Machine Company of New Jersey published three recordings—the labels state they were recorded in East Asia but, since prices are printed on their labels in dollars, they were distributed in the United States. Of these, Victor 13510 has a trio of *kisaeng* courtesans singing the southwestern popular folk song, "*Yukchabaegi*," Victor 13528 has an excerpt from the *p'ansori* repertory of "*Chŏkpyŏkka*/Song of the Battle at the Red Cliff," and Victor 13530 has a vocal duet with drum accompaniment, "*Yusan'ga*." More vocal recordings followed, featuring *p'ansori* excerpts ("*Simch'ŏngga*/Song of the Filial Daughter" on Victor 49286, "*Ch'unhyangga*/Song of Spring Fragrance" on Victor 42988, and "*Hŭngboga*/Song of Two Brothers" on Victor 43226), as well as popular folk songs such as "*Sŏngjup'uri*" on Victor 42971 and the *p'ansori* episode "*Ibyŏlga*" on Victor 42984. The Japanese label Nipponophone released its first Korean recordings in 1911: the popular folk songs "*Kase t'aryŏng*," "*Kyŏngsan t'aryŏng*," "*Chebiga*," "*Sŏngjup'uri*," and so on. Most likely, these early releases were intended primarily for the Japanese market;[7] they were recorded in Japan rather than Korea, and Japanese-based companies exerted a monopoly over Korea after Korea was formally incorporated into the Japanese Empire in 1910. Recordings of vocal music remained dominant, reflecting taste but also technical matters: the process of acoustic recording, which was only replaced by electrical amplification around 1925, favored the voice, since a concentration of sound-wave energy was needed to actuate the sapphire cutter that made grooves in a disc, and the easiest way to achieve this was if a vocalist sang directly into a horn. We should also remember that acoustic recording captured frequencies up to 2,000 Hz, an octave above the soprano range but below many of the subtle harmonics that create the timbral distinctiveness of Korean instruments.

The first recordings of *kugak* as court and literati music were produced after electrical amplification arrived, and were issued on nineteen SP recordings made by Victor in June 1928 and released in January 1929 (Victor 49801–49820; there is no record of 49814 being released; see Pae 1994, 288–290). These featured members of the colonial-era court music bureau. By 1945, more than five thousand discs of Korean music had been produced,[8] the majority being popular songs. The catalogue continues to provide a treasure trove for researchers. And, since the Korean musicology methodology that emerged in South Korea following Liberation was both historical and comparative (Howard 2002), seeking the earliest version of repertoire as documented in texts or—more importantly for *p'ansori* and *sanjo*—on recordings, has proved an important exercise. As musicology developed, then, its scholars compared different SP recordings, or compared SP recordings with post-1945 performances, one example being Lee Hye-ku's (Yi Hye-gu, 1909–2010) exploration of the popular folk song "*Yukchabaegi*"—the pertinent fact being that he compares commercial recordings rather than live performances or contemporary field recordings (Lee 1981, 177–191).

Commercial recordings involved decisions relating to selection or compression. Hence compromises were made, with the result that SP recordings provide only partial accounts of the music being performed at their time. The reason is because, prior to World War II (when imports were disrupted), discs were made from shellac, a tree insect resin native to India, and this yielded best results where grooves were given adequate space and when discs were spun at speed (i.e., at 78rpm). A single recording, a "side" on the SP, then, was limited to roughly four minutes. Today's aficionados, in contrast, want to possess a recording of a full *sanjo* performance, lasting an hour, or a full *p'ansori* performance, in which a story can last up to eight hours.

Sanjo

Korean texts routinely assert, taking their lead from Ham Hwa-jin's *Chosŏn ŭmak t'ongnon* (1948), that *sanjo* was first performed by Kim Ch'ang-jo (1865–1919)[9] in the 1890s. Some claim that Kim invented the genre, though our knowledge of other earlier and late nineteenth-century zither musicians indicates an arrangement of existing materials was more likely involved. No recording exists of Kim, although his granddaughter, celebrated in later life under the name Kim Chuk-p'a (1911–1989), studied with him for a few months before he died and, subsequently, with several of his immediate students. Kim Chuk-p'a recorded a number of SPs under the stage name Kim Un-sŏn ("Angel from the Clouds";[10] "Chuk-p'a" combines characters for "bamboo" and "fidelity"). Documentation for Kim Chuk-p'a's early radio broadcasts also exists, but in 1932 she married a government official, Yi Min-t'aek, and abandoned her professional career, emerging back on to the public stage only after the death of her second husband forty-five years later, on Christmas Eve, 1977.

SP recordings also survive of Kim Ch'ang-jo's students, the so-called second generation of players, which have been reissued on CDs in a manner that reinforces the notion of there being a set of *sanjo* schools: *Kayagŭm sanjo myŏngindŭl* (*The Legendary Artists of Korean Kayagŭm Sanjo* [King Records, SYNCD-059B–063B, 1993]) and *Kayago sanjo ŭi myŏngindŭl 1* (Cantabile, SRCD-1101, 1993)—"*myŏngin*" literally translates as "great person," a "star." SYNCD-060B, for example, gives a twenty-one-minute *sanjo* by Sim Sang-gŏn (1889–1965) taken from Columbia recordings (40040, 40049, 40060, 40280) that offers a short, four-minute first movement, *chinyangjo* (today this is normally the longest movement of a *sanjo* piece), and intriguingly gives this as the "A" side before a "B" side containing a section described as *sasŏl* (the tuning section, *tasŭrŭm*, that today would normally precede *chinyangjo*, since, of course, one tunes the instrument at the beginning of a performance). This is followed by a six-minute *sanjo* by Kang T'ae-hong (1894–1968) from the A and B sides of Victor 49244.[11] So, two of the six recognized schools. Across the set of five King Records releases we hear remastered SPs of Chŏng Nam-hŭi (twenty-one minutes) coupled to longer, post-1945 mono recordings that give the remaining schools and their key variants, by Kim Chuk-p'a, Sŏ Kong-ch'ŏl, Wŏn Ok-hwa, Kim Yun-dŏk, Ham Tongjŏng-wŏl, Kim Pyŏng-ho, Sŏng Kŭm-yŏn, and Kim Sam-t'ae. Sim also features on SRCD-1101, along with two *sanjo* specialists who later settled in North Korea, An Ki-ok (1894–1974) and his disciple Chŏng Nam-hŭi (1910–1984)—that is, the third recognized school—plus two lesser colonial-era performers, Kim Chong-gi (1902–1940[12]) and Kim Hae-sŏn (dates unknown). *Chinyangjo* is the longest movement in this reissue, but at its maximum was originally recorded on two SP sides lasting seven minutes, whereas today's *chinyangjo* will last twenty minutes or longer.

Although early recordings do not substantiate the notion of the hour-long performance familiar today, common material recorded by different performers is taken to indicate what was taught by a common, earlier teacher. This practice develops a Korean musicological method that compares historical scores to isolate the earliest version of a piece (see Hahn 1990, chapters 3 and 4). Hence, common elements in the recordings of two second-generation players, Han Sŏng-gi (1889–1950) and An Ki-ok, and in Kim Chuk-p'a's later performances, have been isolated to define what Kim Ch'ang-jo's piece must have been (Mun 2000, 13–30; Yang 2001). Although pedantic, some details illustrate: An performed 24 measures (or bars) of Kim Ch'ang-jo's *chungmori* (12/4, medium paced movement) in a movement comprising 39 measures, 19 of his *chungjungmori* (12/8, moderately fast movement) measures in a movement of 51 measures, and 101 *chajinmori* (12/8, fast movement) measures in a movement of 241 measures total; Chŏng's 29-measure *chungmori* uses 24 of Kim's measures, and his 88-measure *chajinmori* preserves 64 of Kim's.

Second- and third-generation *sanjo* performers who survived into the 1960s were, as musicology developed and as the state preservation system was activated, consulted to complement the data recoverable from recordings. But, there were complications. An had moved to North Korea in the 1940s, and strict censorship in place until the late 1980s meant that South Koreans could not mention his name. Again, access to North Korean materials was banned until the early 1990s, so although An's student, the Chinese Korean Kim Chin (1926–2007), had in the 1970s notated An's later performance practice, this could not be cited in South Korea. Again, An's earlier student, Chŏng Nam-hŭi, had recorded multiple SPs before he too settled in North Korea, so he could not be mentioned. But Chŏng, before moving to Pyongyang, had taught Kim Yun-dŏk (1918–1980), who remained in South Korea. Because second-generation players had died by the time of the appointment of *sanjo* as a Cultural Property, in 1968 Kim became one of the first "holders" (*poyuja*) of *kayagŭm sanjo* as National Intangible Cultural Property 23. The result was that An's or Chŏng's school was, by necessity, labeled as Kim's in South Korean texts and recordings. Kim's disciple and successor as holder of Property 23, Yi Yŏng-hŭi (b. 1938), in August 1991 told me that the basic form of her teacher's piece, the *pat'ang*, was Chŏng Nam-hŭi's, but Kim "added some melodies of Kang and a little more that was his own."[13] A further disciple of Kim, Byungki Hwang (Hwang Pyŏng-gi, 1936–2018), links Kim primarily back to Chŏng (Hwang 1998), as does Lee Chae-suk (1998; but not in her 1971 notation of what she terms the "Kim Yun-dŏk *sanjo*"). Many years later, Hwang served as head of the South Korean delegation that visited Pyongyang in 1990, where he obtained recordings of Chŏng's *sanjo* made during the latter's later life. Hwang then claimed what he regarded as his proper inheritance, in a published notation (1998) and recording (Sung Eum DE-0234, 1998) that documented his own version of *sanjo* based on the Chŏng Nam-hŭi *pat'ang*.

Sanjo had been taught by rote until notations in 1960s South Korea marked both the move of the genre into institutionalized training and the development of musicology. Notations were needed for the first degree program in *kugak*, set up at Seoul National University in 1959.[14] This used grade examinations for Western instruments as a model when devising a curriculum for performers. So, where, say, a Western pianist must learn repertoire from the Baroque and Classical periods as well as twentieth-century or more recent "modern" pieces,[15] *kugak* performers were required to master court, folk, and contemporary repertoires. Note that *kugak* was now a much broader animal than just court and literati music; not only was folk music embraced, but also a demand was created for composers to begin to write new music for traditional instruments— in so doing generating neologisms such as "creative traditional music" (*ch'angjak kugak*) and "new traditional music" (*sin kugak*). *Sanjo* fitted the folk component for performance majors, although it can be argued that it became normative by displacing other—lesser?—folk instrumental forms.[16] At the same time, regular examinations were instituted, much as the Western conservatoire model, and the resulting need to show progression lent itself to the use of notations. Notations, however, create fixed forms, and the still commonly heard statement that "*sanjo* is improvised" should be interpreted as a reflection of its pre-1960s, pre-institutionalized form. Byungki Hwang, incidentally, became one of the first lecturers for the Seoul National degree—he had graduated in law, but unlike most musicians, he actually had a degree, and it was a requirement that lecturers be graduates.

Tertiary education, notations and the preservation movement made lineage central. Hence, the key texts that attempt to define Kim Ch'ang-jo's *sanjo* are by two of Kim Chuk-p'a's former students now appointed holders of *kayagŭm sanjo* as Property 23: Mun Chae-suk (b. 1953; 1989, 2000, 2001) and Yang Sŭng-hŭi (b. 1948; 2001, 54–143). Comparing their accounts with Kim Chuk-p'a's recordings demonstrates that Kim, among other additions, expanded her grandfather's first movement, *chinyangjo*, and added a final movement of her own, *sesanjosi*. Kim Chuk-p'a had been allowed by her second husband, Yi Wan-gyu, to teach *kayagŭm* to a few women in the Pusan enclave during the Korean War, and around that time it is thought she introduced this new movement to match what other *sanjo* performers were doing. Kim began to come back into view in the 1960s, when she became (because of the recommendation of the former radio presenter and then musicologist Lee Hye-ku, and because of a lineage connection to her husband) teacher to Lee (Yi) Chae-suk (b. 1942). Only once widowed did Kim reappear on the public stage, and she then set about expanding her *sanjo*, generating her own *sanjo* school. The development is charted in four published notations (Lee 1971, 1983; Mun 1989, 2000, 37–103). In summary, SP recordings do not substantiate the contemporary view that *sanjo* has long existed in its current format, while more recent recordings, when analyzed, show some of the ways it has evolved and developed, becoming the discrete schools that are today celebrated as Cultural Properties.

P'ansori

Although transmission is commonly discussed in *p'ansori* literature, here I explore how the authorized account reflects relatively recent discourse. In respect to the first of the three documentary source types identified above, there are two undisputed primary texts for *p'ansori*. The first is Chŏng No-sik's *Chosŏn ch'anggŭksa* (1940), which gives biographies and stories about master singers and is generally read uncritically as factual by Korean scholars—by Pak Hwang (1974, 1976, 1987), for example, and in the many subsequent texts that quote Pak. The second is a set of late nineteenth-century texts complemented by a narrative poem, *Kwangdaega*, compiled by the local government official (*ajŏn*) Sin Chae-hyo (1812–1884). Sin promoted *p'ansori* to the regent, the Taewŏn'gun, and to higher echelons of society. He trained and championed the first female singer and, most importantly, wrote out and revised complete versions of today's five core *p'ansori* repertoires. His texts were protected by his family, and published by his descendant Kang Han-yŏng in 1977; Kang was director of the state-funded body performing staged versions of *p'ansori*, the National Traditional Opera Company (Kungnip ch'anggŭk tan; Killick 2010). Taken together, these two sources enshrine both lineage and the architecture of the full stories for the repertoires. These sources have, then, long guided reports, publications, and the appointment of holders for *p'ansori* as National Intangible Cultural Property 5.

Recordings offer additional documentation, but recording an extended *p'ansori* performance was never a priority for the SP market. Excerpts, of a single song or a compressed episode, were more commonly recorded, a natural consequence of an SP being able to record around four minutes per side (in other words, a four-hour repertoire would require about thirty double-sided SPs). Nipponophone was one of the earliest labels to release multiple discs featuring extended performances, and the daily newspaper *Maeil sinbo* announced in September 1925 that a second Japanese label, Nitto, had recorded extended excerpts from two of the five repertoires, "*Simch'ŏngga*" and "*Ch'unhyangga*" (Pae 1993). In 1988, three enthusiasts, Pae Yŏn-hyŏng, Yang Chŏng-hwan, and Chŏng Ch'ang-gwan, reissued a compilation of SPs on LP that featured a handful of short excerpts by five star singers, *P'ansori 5 myŏngch'ang* (LP, Sung Eum SEL-RO 135, 1988; reissued on CD, Synnara SYNCD-004, 1992). The singers were Song Man-gap (1865–1939), Kim Ch'ang-hwan (1854–1927), Yi Tong-baek (1866–1947), Chŏng Chŏng-nyŏl (1876–1938), and Kim Ch'ang-nyong (1872–1935), four of whom had featured in Chŏng No-sik's publication (Sheen 2001; Yi 2003, 28).

Interest in early *p'ansori* recordings led to the formation of the Society for Korean Discology (Han'guk ko ŭmban yŏn'guhoe). This society, with the three who had put together *P'ansori 5 myŏngch'ang* as founders, was inaugurated in March 1989 at the home of the folk music scholar Yi Po-hyŏng. Yi had collected many SPs, sourcing them during many years traveling the countryside conducting fieldwork for the government body responsible for cultural preservation. The society began to compile SPs by other singers. Two featured Yi Hwajung-sŏn, regarded by many as the foremost female *p'ansori* singer of the early twentieth century (first, Sung Eum SEL-RO 0219, 1989, and second, King Records KO-002, 1992 [LPs], both reissued on CD as Synnara SYNCD-012, 1992); Kim So-hŭi (1917–1994), who in many ways inherited Yi's crown and who as a young girl sang alongside her, provides a heartfelt tribute in the booklet accompanying the first re-release. One featured Yi's elder, Kim Ch'ang-hwan (LP, Sung Eum SELRO 598, 1990, and on CD, King SYNCD-103), adding two songs from "*Ch'unhyangga*" and two *chapka* (miscellaneous songs). More SPs by others featured on *P'ansori 5 myŏngch'ang* such as Chŏng Chŏng-nyŏl (King SYNCD-080 had thirteen SP sides from *"Ch'unhyangga," "Simch'ŏngga,"* and more) and Kim Ch'ang-nyong (King SYNCD-082 featured songs from four of the five repertoires, *"Ch'unhyangga," "Simch'ŏngga," "Sugungga/*Song of the Underwater Palace," and *"Hŭngboga"*). A younger singer, Im Pang-ul (1905–1961), who fronted a traveling performance group and achieved a somewhat legendary status in his later years (Chŏn 1986), had many songs from his renditions of all five core repertoires reissued (e.g., LP, Sung Eum SEL-RO 597, 1990, and CD, Synnara SYNCD-010, 1992; Synnara SYNCD-150, 1996; Seoul Records/Kungnip kugagwŏn SRCD-5103, 2003). Synnara, a company attached to a new religion, featured strongly in this activity. They took the rights to Sung Eum releases and bought the King company, and published many more *p'ansori* SP compilations (e.g., SYNCD-007, -009, -013, -066, -067, -068, -069, -081, -082, -106). By the turn of the millennium, they owned one of the largest archive collections of *kugak* recordings at their headquarters in Yongin, south of Seoul.

Based on recordings, on newspaper documentation, and on the accounts of Chŏng No-sik, it is clear that singers in the nineteenth and early to mid-twentieth century were celebrated for specific episodes in *p'ansori* repertoires. Chan E. Park, on the basis of an interview with the singer Sŏng U-hyang (1935–2014), notes that the norm earlier in the century had been "segmental episodic singing," much as in Japanese *kabuki* or Peking opera (2003, 107). Certainly, most of the extended multi-SP recordings that were made featured a number of singers, each offering one or more episodes, and the late Kim So-hŭi recalled that this was the standard way that *p'ansori* had been performed when she came to prominence in the 1930s (Pihl 1984, 1994). However, the Property system and recent scholarship concentrate on the totality of a repertoire—the full version (*wanch'ang*) of a story. While not denying that this has historical merit, it is of note that it was only in 1968 that Pak Tong-jin (1917–2003) (re-)established the notion of presenting a *wanch'ang*, when he performed a five-hour version of one of the five repertoires, *"Hŭngboga,"* at the school then attached to the successor to the National Gugak Center. The next year, he gave an eight-hour version of a second repertoire, *"Ch'unhyangga,"* at the National Theater, following this up with complete performances of the remaining three core repertoires over the next three years (Yu et al.

1985, 10; Kim 1993, 58; Chŏng 2001, 233). It is generally stated that there were twelve repertoires in Sin's time, and he left some additional texts for, for example, *P'yŏn'gangsoega* (recorded by Pak Tong-jin on Synnara SYNCD-005, 3 CDs, 1990).

Texts are able to give length to epic poetry, and this leads to accounts of, say, Homer's *Iliad*, the Kyrgyz *Manas*, or the South Asian *Ramayana* where the totality of a story, and the number of verse lines it contains, is celebrated. However, reciters—or *p'ansori* singers—will often lift an episode out of the larger corpus in performance. Do performers need to be able to relate the full story in its entirety? This question is rarely asked, and is antithetical to much of the literature on epic poetry (although explored in Howard and Kasmambetov 2011). Although the jury is out as to whether *p'ansori* can be equated with epic poetry, we should not ignore the influence of scholars of epic poetry such as Milman Parry and Albert B. Lord on those who study *p'ansori*, including Marshall Pihl and Pihl's student, Chan E. Park. Indeed, in performing full versions, Pak was responding to scholars and aficionados who were looking for ways to stem the decline of *p'ansori*. While decline has become a standard commentary on Korean cultural production during the Japanese colonial period, decline undoubtedly accelerated post-Liberation as Korea struggled to rebuild itself following the Korean War and began to modernize. There were few concerts devoted to traditional music, and *p'ansori* also suffered as theatrical versions featuring multiple actors took away much of its audience. Korea's cultural tradition—and threats to its continued existence—had been explored by the journalist Ye Yong-hae in columns for the *Han'guk Ilbo* (Korea daily news) from 1958 onward that were collected together in 1963 in his book *In'gan Munhwajae*/Human Cultural Treasures.[17] Ye's intervention was timely, and was particularly influential. He rediscovered artists struggling to feed themselves, but he was also aware of pockets of discussion among academics: "Those who studied music were only concerned with music; those concerned with dance were only concerned with dance. Among them, there was very little interest to keep things that had once been common or popular [only court and literati forms]," he told me in an interview in August 1991.

Once legislation for state preservation had been enacted, *p'ansori* was duly appointed in 1964 as National Intangible Cultural Property 5. In fact, "*Simch'ŏngga*" was given its own appointment, as Property 36, between

1970 and 1973, to accommodate a specific lineage, and *P'ansori kobŏp* (drum accompaniment for *p'ansori*) was appointed Property 59 from 1978 until 1991, when it was absorbed into Property 5 after the death, during an eighteen-month period, of three drummers successively nominated as holders, one being the great Kim Myŏng-hwan (1913–1989). Research was ordered prior to the appointment of Property 5, and continued after the appointment, as senior singers were nominated as holders. Selections enshrined lineages for each of the five core repertoires and, over time, the five repertoires or stories (*tasŏt madang*) began to be conflated with, arguably somewhat uncomfortably, five forms (*tasŏt pat'ang*), with these then divided into a notion of crops grown from seeds (*pat'i*). Creating an entity for each repertoire/form happened contemporaneously with the move toward complete *wanch'ang*, and from autumn 1973 the agenda was pushed by a group who founded a new association, the P'ansori Hakhoe, led by Chŏng Pyŏn-guk, Kang Han-yŏng, Yi Po-hyŏng, and Ko Hyŏn-guk. Kang and Yi have been introduced above; Chŏng was a Korean literature professor at Seoul National University, remembered for his book, *Han'guk ŭi p'ansori* (1981), and still respected by singers, because "Chŏng listened to *p'ansori* from the time he was seven years old. He would sit on his grandfather's knee and listen. Singing and playing the drum accompaniment became his hobby" (Cho Sang-hyŏn, interview, August 1992). The fourth individual, Ko, was at the time President of North Chŏlla National University, which has its main campus in the city considered the heartland of *p'ansori*, Chŏnju, where the primary *p'ansori* festival, the *Chŏnju segye sori ch'ukch'e*, is held.

The P'ansori Hakhoe promoted complete performances, holding about one hundred events within five years. They began with a single monthly performance, but increased their activities once sponsorship was secured from The Deep-Rooted Tree (Ppuri kip'ŭn namu), a journal and associated company over which the Chŏlla native Han Ch'ang-gi (1930–1997) presided, and from the *Han'guk Ilbo*, where Ye Yong-hae remained a journalist. However, success also heralded eventual collapse, because singers raised their fees to the point where they were demanding more than could be paid.[18] The immediate legacy, beyond making *wanch'ang* full performances common, was a set of 23 LPs under the title *Ppuri kip'ŭn namu p'ansori* (*The Deep-Rooted Tree P'ansori Collection*; Korea Britannica/ Jigu JLS120162–JLS120167, 1982), supplemented by a book (Ppuri kip'ŭn namu, eds., 1982), and a further collection on twenty-two LPs, *Ppuri kip'ŭn namu p'ansori tasŏt pat'ang* (*The Deep-Rooted Tree P'ansori Five Forms*; The Deep-Rooted Tree, SELRO593, -596, -668, and OL-3225 and OL-3241, 1989–1992). Assuming each LP is around an hour in length, the number of discs gives a good indication of the length of each of the five repertoires recorded.

As the most celebrated singers recorded full *wanch'ang*, so *p'ansori* became fixed. This is discussed by Jan Creutzenberg in this volume, but to add to his account it is useful to see how this happened in respect to one singer, Kim So-hŭi. She recorded a full version of *"Simch'ŏngga"* in 1974. Released on four LPs by Sung Eum, and re-released twenty years later on Seoul Records (SRCD-1299–1302, 1995), Kim was accompanied by the drummer Kim Myŏng-hwan. Two years later, again accompanied by Kim Myŏng-hwan, she recorded a full *"Ch'unhyangga"* on five LPs, again issued by Sung Eum. This second recording was reissued on seven discs in the fifty LP set *Han'guk chŏnt'ong ŭmak taejŏnjip* (Great collection of traditional Korean music) in 1980 (vols. 30–36), re-released again in 1988 on the *Kugak ŭi hyangyŏn* (Scent of Korean traditional music) set published by the *Chungang Ilbo* newspaper, and re-released yet again as six CDs in 1995 (Seoul Records SRCD-1293–1298). Because of her lineage—from Kim Ch'aeman to Song Man-gap to Chŏng Chŏng-nyŏl to Kim—her recording was then notated by the composer, scholar, and educator Kim Ki-su (1917–1986) and issued within the National Gugak Center's seminal series, *Han'guk ŭmak*/Anthology of Korean Music (vol. 15, 1977). This series used Western staff notation, so Kim Ki-su then produced a trans-notated version in an updated Korean-style *chŏngganbo* notation in the Center's second seminal series, *Kugak chŏnjip/Collection of Traditional Music*. By the 1970s, *p'ansori* had been brought into the National Gugak Center, and today, *p'ansori* performers train in Korea's universities, taught by students of holders of Property 5. Thus, the construction of *p'ansori* as tradition is, like that of *sanjo*, complete.

RITORNELLO

In sum, the authoritative versions of full *p'ansori* repertoires, based on lineage and on texts stretching back only to the late nineteenth century, reflect discourses and practices that belong primarily to the twentieth century. Seen within the state preservation system, in the concert, broadcasting, and other promotional activities of the National Gugak Center, and as established within university musicology and performance education, these are discourses and practices pursued from above that set boundaries and limits on musicians while also authenticating particular performance styles and forms. But we should not lose sight of discourse being creative, in that practitioners were and remain active agents who seek to satisfy their audiences. The discourses from above establish and perpetuate a strong sense of canon, found in the maintenance of five *p'ansori* repertoires within the Intangible Cultural Property mechanism. This canon creates a scaffolding, the use of which allows "lost" *p'ansori* repertoires to be restored and new repertoires established. *Sanjo*, likewise, has gained authoritative versions of six schools for the *kayagŭm* zither, and additional schools for other instruments. These are today notated and taught in a manner that memorializes fixed, complete forms. And these, too, form a scaffolding to facilitate attempts to create new forms and new schools. The preservation system of which the Property mechanism is a part is by necessity, and without any chance of adequate resolution, inadequate, since there can never be sufficient resources to protect all schools and lineages. But this is the way it must be, since fixing musical genres results in inflexibility, in which reconsideration of what is appointed for preservation after the appointment is first made becomes difficult, and where sunk costs limit the capacity and motivation to entertain change. But, at the same time, the Property system, the promotion of *kugak* at the National Gugak Center, and the teaching of *kugak* as musicology and performance, is a necessity. Without these agents, the construction of *kugak* would crumble.

Creativity and development involve making the exogenous indigenous and allowing conceptions of authenticity to shift. This is a necessity if *kugak* is to be anything other than the sonic equivalent of a museum display case. And *kugak* relies on musicians to give the construction life. Musicians are resilient. They jockey for position. They claim lineage and distinction, with an eye to what might prove personally beneficial. But, at the same time, they segment and re-arrange components of a repertoire. To paraphrase Paul Ricoeur (1984, 68), they mix sediments transmitted from earlier times with innovations demanded by their audiences today or added simply because they appeal. The British social anthropologist Paul Connerton (1989, 75) has discussed resilience in respect to collective memory, describing how fixed sediments provide springs that release innovation. His perspective has been adapted for ethnomusicology by Jeff Todd Titon (2015, 192), who argues that adaptations are made when stress points force change in systems.

This chapter, ultimately, is a story of invention but also tradition, where adaptability and flexibility (as Beiner 2001 and Plant 2008 argue for) has over time, enabled by the advent of the recording industry, the rise of local musicology, and by commendable preservationist ambitions, subsided to leave standardized, unchanging forms. But it is not a story of "invented traditions," since the fixity of today is considered authoritative, stretching back into history and being faithful to music inherited across many generations.

GLOSSARY

aak (Ch. *yayue*) 雅樂
ajŏn 衙前
aniri 아니리
chajinmori 1 자진모리 (자즌모리)
chinyangjo 진양조
chŏngak 正樂
Chongmyo cheryeak 宗廟 祭禮樂
Chosŏn ch'anggŭksa 朝鮮唱劇史
chungin 中人
chungmori 중모리
Ibyŏlga 이별가
ilmu 佾舞
kayagŭm 伽倻琴
kisaeng 妓生
Kukka muhyŏng munhwajae 國家無形文化財
Kungnip ch'anggŭk tan 國立唱劇團
madang 마당
min'gan ŭmak 民間 音樂
Munmyo 文廟
myŏngch'ang 名唱
myŏngin 名人
pallim 발림
p'at'ang 바탕
ppuri kip'ŭn 뿌리 깊은
ryu 류
sanjo 散調
sasŏl 사설
Silla 新羅
Sŏkchŏn taeje 釋奠大祭
Sŏngjup'uri 성주풀이
sŏp'yŏnje 西便制
tasŭrŭm 다스름

tongp'yŏnje 東便制
ŭmak 音樂
Yiwangjik Aakpu 李王職雅樂部

Yukchabaegi 六字배기
Yusan'ga 遊山歌

NOTES

1. Eric Wolf (1982) explores such matters.
2. In 2015, "Important" (*Chungyo*) officially became "National" (*Kukka*). Although the prefix "national" has been used interchangeably for several decades, earlier publications tend to give "Important" rather than "National." See Howard (2006) for an account of the system up to the first years of the new millennium.
3. Some use *minsok* (folk) in place of *min'gan*, but the former term implies the local, agrarian, and supposedly less specialized folklore that has concerned collectors from Johann Gottfried Herder to Cecil Sharp and the founders of the International Folk Music Council, rather than the professional forms that *sanjo* and *p'ansori* represent.
4. I explore this in Howard (2012).
5. I distinguish popular folk songs (*t'ongsok minyo* or, in some accounts, *sin minyo*) as "songs for the people" recorded by professional singers, from local folk songs, "songs of the people" (*t'osok minyo, yennal sori/norae*).
6. Kim Chŏm-do (2000, 444) lists additional early and undated Columbia recordings.
7. Pae (1991, 98–100) states these appeared in autumn 1911, but Kim Chŏm-do (2000) dates them to 1912.
8. This is the number given in the first volume of *Korean Discology* (*Han'guk ŭmbanhak*) by Chŏng (1991, 243).
9. Some texts give 1856 as Kim's birth date and 1918 as the year of his death. Accounts of *sanjo* in English include Song (1986), Howard, Lee, and Casswell (2008), and Lee (2009).
10. A list of the recordings that were issued with this name given for Kim has been compiled elsewhere (http://www.sparchive.co.kr; last accessed May 15, 2019).
11. A final track of this album, lasting thirty-four minutes, is a more recent recording by Kang's disciple from the Tongnae *kwŏnbŏn* (a courtesan training institute), Wŏn Okhwa (1928–1971).

12. Kim's dates are uncertain; some publications have suggested 1904/1905–1937/1938.
13. Demonstrated in analysis by Kim Hee-sun (2000).
14. Musicology predated this time, of course, for which Ham Hwa-jin's 1948 volume is often cited as the most significant early text. Ham (1884–1949) was director of the colonial-era court music bureau, and prior to this volume had published four books on court music, its instruments, and its scores. Provine (1993) offers an overview of early Korean musicology.
15. See the Associated Board of the Royal Schools of Music in the UK website: http://us.abrsm.org/en/our-exams/piano (accessed August 7, 2017).
16. Considering the forty-six known SP recordings of the *taegŭm* transverse flute player Pak Chong-gi (1879–1947; some texts give other dates), *taegŭm sanjo* only features on four, Okeh 30014 (1935, *chinyangjo* movement), 30015 (1936, *chungmori*), 30016 (1936, *kutkŏri*), and 12121 (K648; 1938), while many more feature other instrumental music, including solo repertory on four Columbia 40041 (1929), Chosŏn sorip'an K804 (1929), and Million CM821 (1936) (listed in Yi 2007, 255–281).
17. Trevor-Roper (1983), likewise, identifies authors and journalists involved in the promotion of Scottish identity.
18. Although this was how Han Ch'ang-gi related the collapse to me, the journal had been forced to close in 1980, along with many other media operations, by the military government led by Chun Doo Hwan, leaving the company with very reduced income.

REFERENCES

Bauman, Richard, and Charles Briggs. 1990. "Poetics and Performance as Critical Perspectives on Language and Social Life." *Annual Review of Anthropology* 19:59–88.

Beeman, William O. 1981. "A Full Arena: The Development and Meaning of Popular Performance Traditions in Iran." In *Modern Iran: The Dialectics of Continuity and Change*, edited by Michael E. Bonine and Nikki Keddie, 361–381. Albany: State University of New York Press.

Beiner, Guy. 2001. "The Invention of Tradition?" *The History Review* 12:1–10.

Chŏn I-du. 1986. *Im Pan-gul: P'ansori myŏngch'ang* [Im Pan-gul: P'ansori mastersinger]. Seoul: Hyŏndae munhaksa.

Chŏng Ch'ang-gwan. 1991. "Han'guk ko ŭmban yŏn'gu hoe yŏksa." [History of the Korean Old Records' Research Society]. *Han'guk ŭmbanhak* [Korean Discology] 1:243–253.

Chŏng No-sik. 1940. *Chosŏn ch'anggŭksa* [History of Korea's staged *p'ansori*]. Seoul: Chosŏn Ilbosa.

Chŏng Pŏm-t'ae. 2001. *Myŏngin myŏngch'ang*. [Famous master-singers]. Seoul: Kip'ŭnsaem.

Chŏng Pyŏn-guk. 1981. *Han'guk ŭi p'ansori*. [Korea's *P'ansori*]. Seoul: Chimmundang.

Church, Michael. 2015. *The Other Classical Musics: Fifteen Great Traditions*. Woodbridge: Boydell Press.

Connerton, Paul. 1989. *How Societies Remember*. Cambridge: Cambridge University Press.

Finchum-Sung, Hilary. 2017. "Foreword: Aesthetics of Interculturality in East Asian Contemporary Music." *The World of Music*, n.s., 6 (2): 7–21.

Geertz, Clifford. 1973. *The Interpretation of Culture*. New York: Basic Books.

Hahn, Man-young. 1990. *Kugak: Studies in Korean Traditional Music*. Seoul: Tamgu Dang.

Ham Hwa-jin. 1948. *Chosŏn ŭmak t'ongnon* [An introduction to Korean music]. Seoul: Ŭryu munhwasa.

Hobsbawm, Eric, and Terence Ranger, eds. 1983. *The Invention of Tradition*. Cambridge: Cambridge University Press.

Howard, Keith. 2002. "Lee Hye-Ku and the Development of Korean Musicology." *Acta Koreana* 5 (1) (January): 77–99.

———.2006. *Preserving Korean Music: Intangible Cultural Properties as Icons of Identity*. Aldershot: Ashgate.

———.2012. "Authenticity and Authority: Conflicting Agendas in the Preservation of Music and Dance at Korea's State Sacrificial Rituals." In *Music as Intangible Cultural Heritage: Policy, Ideology, and Practice in the Preservation of East Asian Traditions*, edited by Keith Howard, 113–139. Farnham: Ashgate.

———.2016. "The Institutionalization of Korean Traditional Music (*gugak*)." *Asian Pacific Business Review* 22 (3): 452–467.

Howard, Keith, and Saparbek Kasmambetov. 2011. *Singing the Kyrgyz Manas: Saparbek Kasmambetov's Recitations of Epic Poetry*. Folkestone: Global Oriental.

Howard, Keith, Chaesuk Lee, and Nicholas Casswell. 2008. *Korean Kayagŭm Sanjo: A Traditional Instrumental Genre*. Aldershot: Ashgate.

Hwang Pyŏng-gi. 1998. *Tchalbŭn kayagŭm sanjo moŭm, Chŏng Namhŭi-je Hwang Pyŏng-gi ryu* [Collected shorter zither *sanjo*, Chŏng Nam-hŭi style, Hwang Byungki school]. Seoul: Ihwa yŏja taehakkyo ch'ulp'anbu.

Kang Han-yŏng. 1977. *Sin Chae-hyo p'ansori sasŏl chip* [An edited collection of Sin Chae-hyo's *p'ansori* texts]. Seoul: Posŏng munhwasa.

Killick, Andrew. 2010. *In Search of Korean Traditional Opera: Discourses of Ch'anggŭk*. Honolulu: University of Hawai'i Press.

Kim Chŏm-do, ed. 2000. *Yusŏng ki ŭmban ch'ongnam charyojip: 1907-nyŏn put'ŏ 1943-nyŏn kkaji* [The complete listing of released SP gramophone records: from the year 1907 to 1943]. Seoul: Synnara.

Kim, Hee-sun. 2000. "The Development of a *Sanjo* School: A Case Study of the Kim Yun-duk Kayagum Sanjo." Unpublished paper given at the annual conference of the Society for Ethnomusicology, University of Pittsburgh.

Kim Ki-su. 1977. *Han'guk ŭmak* [Anthology of Korean music] 15. Seoul: Kungnip kugagwŏn.

Kim Myŏng-gon. 1993. *Han. Kim Myŏng-gon ŭi kwangdae kihaeng* [The aesthetic, *han*. Kim Myŏng-gon's travels as a musician]. Seoul: Tosŏ ch'ulp'ansa.

Kuhn, Thomas. 1962. *The Structure of Scientific Revolutions*. Chicago: University of Chicago Press.

Lee (Yi) Chae-suk. 1971. *Kayagŭm sanjo*. Seoul: Unha ch'ulp'ansa.

Lee Chae-suk. 1983. *Kayagŭm sanjo, Kim Chuk-p'a ryu* (Kayagum Sanjo of Kim, Chuk-Pa School with Changgo accompaniment). Seoul: Susŏwŏn.

———. 1998. "Kayagŭm ŭi kujo wa chubŏp ŭi pyŏnch'ŏn" [The development of the construction and performance techniques of the *kayagŭm*]. In *Yi Hyegu paksa kusun kinyŏm ŭmakhak nonch'ong* (Essays in Musicology, an Offering in Celebration of Lee Hye-ku on His Ninetieth Birthday), 345–376. Seoul: Seoul National University.

Lee, Hye-Ku (Yi Hye-gu). 1981. *Essays on Korean Traditional Music*. Translated by Robert C. Provine. Seoul: Korea Branch of the Royal Asiatic Society.

Lee (Yi), Yong-Shik, ed. 2009. *Sanjo: Korean Musicology Series 3*. Seoul: National Gugak Center.

Mun Chae-suk. 1989. *Kim Chuk-p'a. Kayagŭm kokchip* [A collection of Kim Chuk-p'a's music for the *kayagŭm*]. Seoul: Segwang ŭmak ch'ulp'ansa.

———. 2000. *Kim Chuk-p'a kayagŭm sanjo yŏn'gu* [A study of Kim Chuk-p'a's *kayagum sanjo*]. Seoul: Hyŏndae ŭmak ch'ulp'ansa.

———. 2001. *Yŏngsan hoesang. Yi Wan-gyu Kim Chuk-p'a sojang akpo ch'ungsŏ 1* [*Yŏngsan hoesang*: Collected manuscript notations by Yi Wan-gyu of Kim Chuk-p'a]. Seoul: Minsogwŏn.

No Tong-ŭn. 1989. *Han'guk minjok ŭmak hyŏndan'gye* [Korean folk music in modern times]. Seoul: Segwang ŭmak ch'ulp'ansa.

———. 1995. *Han'guk kŭndae ŭmaksa 1* [A history of modern Korean music 1]. Seoul: Han'gilsa.

Otto, Ton, and Poul Pedersen. 2005. "Disentangling Traditions: Culture, Agency and Power." In *Tradition and Agency: Tracing Cultural Continuity and*

Invention, edited by Ton Otto and Poul Pedersen, 11–49. Aarhus, Denmark: Aarhus University Press.

Pae Yŏn-hyŏng. 1991. "Ilbon Chosŏn sori (Nipponophone) yŏn'gu 1" [A study of Nipponophone's sounds of colonial Korea]. *Han'guk ŭmbanhak* [Korean Discology] 1:91–154.

———. 1993. "Chebiga Chosŏn rek'odŭ (Nitto Record) yŏn'gu" [A study of "Swallow" on Korea Records (Nitto Records)]. *Han'guk ŭmbanhak* [Korean Discology] 3:15–76.

———. 1994. "Pikt'ŏ (Victor) rek'odŭ ŭi Han'guk ŭmban yŏn'gu" [A study of Victor Records' Korean discs]. *Han'guk ŭmbanhak* [Korean Discology] 4:283–434.

Pak Hwang. 1974. *P'ansori sosa*. [A brief history of *p'ansori*]. Seoul: Sin'gu munhwasa.

———. 1976. *Ch'anggŭksa yŏn'gu*. [A study of the history of Korea's staged *p'ansori*]. Seoul: Paengnok ch'ulp'ansa.

———. 1987. *P'ansori ibaengnyŏnsa* [Two hundred years of *p'ansori*]. Seoul: Sasayŏn.

Park, Chan E. 2003. *Voices from the Straw Mat: Toward an Ethnography of Korean Story Singing*. Hawai'i Studies on Korea. Honolulu: University of Hawai'i Press.

Pihl, Marshall, R. 1984. "The Korean Singer of Tales." *Korea Journal* 24 (10): 21–31.

———. 1994. *The Korean Singer of Tales*. Cambridge, MA: Harvard University Press.

Plant, Byron King. 2008. "Secret, Powerful, and the Stuff of Legends: Revisiting Theories of Invented Tradition." *The Canadian Journal of Native Studies* 28 (1): 175–184.

Poole, Janet. 2014. *When the Future Disappears: The Modernist Imagination in Late Colonial Korea*. New York: Columbia University Press.

Ppuri kip'ŭn namu, eds. 1982. *P'ansori tasŏt madang* (Annotated *p'ansori* Text with English Introductions). Seoul: Han'guk Pŭrit'aenik'ŏ.

Provine, Robert C. 1993. "Korea." In *Ethnomusicology: Historical and Regional Studies*, edited by Helen Myers, 363–376. London: Macmillan.

———. 2012. "The Earliest Recordings of Korean Music." Unpublished paper given at the symposium *Past, Present and Future: The Diversity and Distinctiveness of Korean Music and Dance*, SOAS, University of London, April 13.

Ricoeur, Paul. 1984. *Time and Narrative*, vol. 1. Chicago: University of Chicago Press.

Sahlins, Marshall. 1999. "What Is Anthropological Enlightenment? Some Lessons of the Twentieth Century." *Annual Review of Anthropology* 28:i–xxiii.

Schechner, Richard. 2002. *Performance Studies: An Introduction.* New York: Routledge.

Sheen, Dae-Cheol. 2001. "The Advent of Korean Discology: A New Branch of Korean Musicology." *Han'guk ŭmbanhak* 11:167–179.

Shin, Gi-Wook. 2006. *Ethnic Nationalism in Korea: Genealogy, Politics, and Legacy.* Palo Alto: Stanford University Press.

Silverstein, Michael, and Greg Urban. 1996. *Natural Histories of Discourse.* Chicago: University of Chicago Press.

Song, Bang-song. 1986. *The Sanjo Tradition of Korean Kŏmun'go Music.* Seoul: Jung Eum Sa.

Titon, Jeff Todd. 2015. "Sustainability, Resilience, and Adaptive Management for Applied Ethnomusicology." In *The Oxford Handbook of Applied Ethnomusicology,* edited by Svanibor Pettan and Jeff Todd Titon, 157–195. New York: Oxford University Press.

Trevor-Roper, Hugh. 1983. "The Invention of Tradition: The Highland Tradition of Scotland." In *The Invention of Tradition,* edited by Eric Hobsbawm and Terence Ranger, 15–41. Cambridge: Cambridge University Press.

Wolf, Eric. 1982. *Europe and the Peoples Without History.* Berkeley: University of California Press.

Yang Sŭng-hŭi. 2001. "Kim Ch'ang-jo-e kwanhan nambukhan charyo mit munhŏnkoch'are ŭihan kojŭng" [Study of Kim Ch'ang-jo using documents and literature found in North and South Korea]. In *Sanjo yŏn'gu. Sanjo ch'angsija aksa Kim Ch'ang-jo kinyŏm nonmun t'ŭkchip* 1 [Studies on *sanjo.* Collected memorial articles on the *sanjo* creator and musician, Kim Ch'angjo], edited by Kayagŭm sanjo hyŏnjang saŏp ch'ujin wiwŏnhoe, 54–143. Seoul: Ŭnha ch'ulp'ansa.

Ye Yong-hae. 1963. *In'gan Munhwajae* [Human cultural treasures]. Seoul: Han'guk Ilbosa.

Yi Chin-wŏn. 2007. *Taegŭm sanjo ch'angsija Pak Chong-gi p'yŏngjŏn* [A critical biography of the *taegŭm sanjo* creator, Pak Chong-gi]. Seoul: Minsogwŏn.

Yi T'ae-gyu. 2003. *Han'guk ŭi sori* [The sounds of Korea]. Seoul: Synnara Music.

Yu Ik-sŏ, Kim Myŏng-gon, Han Myŏng-hŭi, Yi Sang-nyong, Sŏl Ho-jŏng, and Han Im-hwa. 1985. *Myŏngin myŏngch'ang* [Famous master-singers]. Seoul: Tonga Ilbosa.

CHAPTER 8

Making Masters, Staging Genealogy

Full-Length P'ansori *as an Invented Tradition*

JAN CREUTZENBERG

When people in South Korea think of *p'ansori*, they think of affective vocals and old-fashioned stories. When they think of *p'ansori* performances, they think of events going on for half a day. The full-length (*wanch'ang*) format—one singer presenting a complete story in one sitting, resulting in performances of up to eight hours—dominates the general perception of this traditional singing-storytelling art, one of the most distinct Korean "icons of national identity" (Howard 2006, 49).[1] More accessible ways of performing *p'ansori* are common today, most prominently potpourris of excerpts from various works, often including other genres of traditional music or dance. Nevertheless, a typical *wanch'ang* performance, complete with an academic introduction, a complimentary textbook, and traditional stage design, decoration, and costumes, represents the prime league of the art (Ch'oe 2014, 337–338).

In fact, *wanch'ang p'ansori* is a fairly recent invention: Pak Tong-jin's five-hour full-length presentation of the piece *Hŭngboga* in 1968 is generally considered the "birth" of the *wanch'ang* format.[2] Although often implicitly assumed as the standard style of performance, the historicity of the format is rarely acknowledged or discussed in the abundant scholarship on *p'ansori*.[3] While singers of the past certainly may have told complete stories, for example on invitation at an upper-class party in a private setting over the course of an extended banquet, the casual context, proceedings, and length of such events were radically different from a modern performance environment (Ch'oe 2014, 340–341). Today's *wanch'ang p'ansori*, presented on a theater stage with assigned seats and only a short intermission, resembles "staging the leisurely duration of 'back porch music' without the leisurely reality of the back porch"—over-length performances that do not fit the expectations of contemporary audiences (Park 2003, 107). Despite earlier cases of full pieces performed by one singer, modern *wanch'ang p'ansori* emerged in the wake of the heritage legislation enacted in South Korea, the "Cultural Property Protection Law" (Munhwajae Poho bŏp, CPPL) of 1962. A standard of skillfulness in the 1970s, with more and more singers performing *wanch'ang* at an increasingly early age, the format soon became an obligatory "rite of passage" for aspiring *p'ansori* performers (Chŏng 2014, 52).

In other words: *Wanch'ang p'ansori* is an "invented tradition," defined by Hobsbawm as "a set of practices . . . which seek to inculcate certain values and norms of behaviour by repetition . . . to establish continuity with a suitable historic past" (1983, 1). The practices associated with *wanch'ang p'ansori* today, not exclusive but obligatory, go beyond the full-length format. In particular, the typical stage design (folding screen, straw mat), decoration (traditional furniture), and costumes (*hanbok* and, for men, a wide-brimmed horse-hair *kat*) suggest an upper-class (*yangban*) house concert in premodern Korea. In its staging, *wanch'ang p'ansori* privileges a specific place in time, the nineteenth-century "heydays" (*chŏnsŏng-gi*) of *p'ansori*, when an increasing number of audiences and sponsors from the upper- and middle-class led to its spread throughout the peninsula, accompanied by rapid aesthetic development (Ch'oe 2011, 431; cf. Um 2013, 45). This "suitable historic past" thus represents the lowest common denominator of nationwide exposure and artistic refinement, legitimating *p'ansori* as an iconic national heritage, a uniquely Korean high art.

In this chapter, I argue that *wanch'ang p'ansori* was invented in response to the CPPL but, while retaining a link to the late nineteenth century, transformed from an external mechanism of differentiation to an occasion for the *p'ansori* scene to both consolidate its members inside, and promote its foundational essence to the outside world. Differently put, once a means of individual ranking, *wanch'ang p'ansori* has become an occasion for collectively staging community. Between preservation and promotion, artistic practice and nation branding, *p'ansori* retains its ties to the past while facing the future.

In the following, I trace the development of the modern *wanch'ang* format, from a novel method of qualification to an obligatory rite of passage: First, I assess its "invention" and specific function in the preservation system. Then I discuss its role in the expansion of *p'ansori* audiences. Finally, focusing on contemporary full-length presentations, I analyze the performative potential in the staging of genealogies and its audience appeal. The incidental invention of the *wanch'ang* format shows that an invented tradition, while serving an ideological goal, can also be re-interpreted by flexible artists to solve internal issues of their art.

INVENTING *WANCH'ANG*

On Monday, September 30, 1968, at noon at the National Gugak Center:[4] After months of preparation, Pak Tong-jin is about to perform the traditional *p'ansori* piece *Hŭngboga*. Five hours and twenty minutes later, he has written history. On October 2, a full recording of the event is broadcast on the Voice of the United Nations Command (VUNC, K. Yu En Kun Ch'ongsaryŏngbu Pangsong)—an unprecedented event both in the world of *p'ansori* and in Korean broadcasting history, as the *Sŏul Sinmun* (Seoul Newspaper) predicted on September 28, 1968. The immediate impact of Pak's performance on professional circles (the *p'ansori* scene) and the wider public is difficult to determine in retrospect.[5] But his full-length rendering, a format later referred to as *wanch'ang*, certainly had lasting consequences, both on how *p'ansori* is performed and imagined: long and strenuous.

The act of presenting a story from beginning to end was not previously unheard of, yet the event stood out in several ways from similar attempts. First, Pak was not an established master singer but a relatively unknown musician employed at the National Gugak Center; second, although performed for the radio, the live event became the center of attention, not least due to its sheer duration, which the broadcast replicated; third, as part of an effort by the Gugak Center, the main venue for traditional music (*kugak*) in Korea, to establish authoritative versions of the five canonical pieces, the performance inaugurated a series of full-length performances by Pak (1968–1971). In this section, I discuss how Pak's *wanch'ang* complemented the formal and ideological characteristics of the heritage legislation. This is exemplified by two earlier cases of full-length performances by more established singers that failed to attract the same amount of attention, further pinpointing how Pak's approach fit the ideologies of preservation under the CPPL.

Conceived as a policy to preserve transmitted art in its "original form" (*wŏnhyŏng*), the CPPL was theoretically centered on a fixed repertory of transmitted works.[6] Yet it relied on practitioners who could perform the art in question. To safeguard the continuing existence of the various registered "Important Intangible Cultural Properties" *(Chungyo Muhyŏng Munhwa)*, skilled individuals were designated as "holders of talent" (*yenŭng poyuja*), more commonly known as "Human Cultural Treasures" *(In'gan Munhwajae)*.[7] In the case of *p'ansori*, designated Important Intangible Cultural Property No. 5 on December 24, 1964, determining an original form worthy of preservation proved difficult. The canon of *p'ansori* consists of five pieces, each one in various versions, which were orally handed down from teachers to students in different schools of transmission (*yup'a*) that had formed in the early nineteenth century (Yu 2013, 355).[8] Performances in the colonial era and the early post-Liberation period commonly featured several singers who performed various unrelated excerpts from different pieces in the version they had learned from their respective teachers. These events were referred to as *myŏngch'ang taehoe* (famous singers' festival; Killick 2010, 85), *pubun-ch'ang* (segmental episodic singing), or later *t'omak sori* (piecemeal song; Park 2003, 107).[9]

Among the two pillars of preservation envisioned by the CPPL—works in their original form and singers capable of performing them—only the latter appeared viable in 1964. Hence being taught by esteemed teachers became the most important criterion for selection. The designation of *p'ansori* was consequently followed by the nomination of five singers from esteemed genealogies as "holders," each one covering one section of *Ch'unhyangga*, the most famous of the five canonical pieces of *p'ansori*.[10] This application of the CPPL effectively conserved the status quo by acknowledging well-established master singers for doing what they used to do. The schools of transmission they were affiliated with rose in prominence, while others were excluded from governmental support, at least on a national level.[11]

Pak Tong-jin's 1968 performance of *Hŭngboga* had broken with the common performance format of the time, *t'omak sori*, by presenting a whole piece in its entirety, resulting in an unprecedented length of more than five hours. However, despite his undisputed role as the "originator" (*ch'angan-ja*) of *wanch'ang* performances, Pak was not the first to present a *p'ansori* piece in full-length (Ch'oe 2014, 351). Apart from possibly undocumented full-length performances in premodern Korea, other singers successfully presented *p'ansori* pieces in their entirety during the years preceding Pak's invention of the *wanch'ang* format. Two particular cases help to understand why Pak Tong-jin's five-hour *wanch'ang* performance was generally considered a singularity at that time.

Im Pang-ul (1904–1961) was one of the earliest *p'ansori* stars in the modern sense. His 1930 recording of the song "Ssuktae Mŏri" (Disheveled hair, from the piece *Ch'unhyangga*) was sold in huge numbers (Jang 2014, 103) and he attracted large audiences as a performer of *ch'anggŭk* (literally "singing drama," or staged *p'ansori*).[12] In the mid-1950s, shortly before his death, he made three live recordings (*silhwang nogŭm*) of full works,[13] two of which were later issued on LP.[14] Pak Nok-chu (1905–1979), trained by several eminent masters in the early twentieth century, had likewise enjoyed success during the colonial period and continued her career as a member of a popular *yŏsŏng kukkŭk* (female-only *ch'anggŭk*) ensemble in the 1950s. Her 1963 recording of *Ch'unhyangga* (in full-length) was broadcast on the Christian radio station CBS (kidokkyo Pangsong) from April to May 1964 in serialized form (Song 2014, 391).

Why did the full-length performances by Im Pang-ul and Pak Nok-chu fail to gain as much notoriety as Pak Tong-jin's? First, quantity. In order to accommodate the capacity of a long play album, Im Pang-ul had selected rather short pieces (or short versions of them) that did not take much more than two hours each. Pak Nok-chu's performance of *Ch'unhyangga*, while about six hours long in total, was broadcast in twelve segments of about twenty-five minutes each within the existing program structure of CBS, with added comments and conversations on the themes of the piece (Song 2014, 381). Second, the focus on the excessive live event. Im's and Pak's recordings were aimed at a sellable (or broadcastable) product rather than a memorable performance. As the integrity of the work was second-ary to accessibility, the segmentation of Pak Nok-chu's performance of *Ch'unhyangga* was not only acceptable but beneficial for consumption.

Pak Tong-jin's 1968 performance of *Hǔngboga*, in contrast, seems to have caught the attention of the *p'ansori* scene and the media with its then unprecedented duration of over five hours. The fact that Pak performed without a rest was highlighted in most press articles and announcements of *Hǔngboga* and subsequent events.[15] The broadcast, just two days later, followed the same nonstop format, stressing the integrity of the original work, which in this case had been edited to fit Pak's needs. His version of *Hǔngboga* toned down the tragic scenes while bringing comical situa-tions to the fore, also cutting references to Confucian morality or chang-ing them "to adequately fit the changed values of contemporary *p'ansori* audiences" (Kang 2003, 25–26). While earlier *t'omak sori* performances had led to increased attention on musical elaboration and decoration, such as vibrato (Jang 2014, 105–106), and allowed master singers to show-case their superior singing skills, a full-length performance offered Pak, due to his improvisational attitude known as a *chaedam kwangdae* (joke entertainer; Kim 2001, 88), the chance to shine as a humorous storyteller. Finally, Pak's performance of *Hǔngboga* set off a whole series of events that included *wanch'ang* versions of all five canonical *p'ansori* pieces, as well as several restored "lost" works and new compositions. Ostensibly in the name of the art and, different from the 1968 broadcast, these well-attended stand-alone live events brought Pak continual attention through-out the following years.

The novelty of the way Pak presented full-length *p'ansori* is also reflected in the ambiguous terminology used to describe his perfor-mances, which changed as his series proceeded. *Hǔngboga*, his first full-length performance, was announced in the *Kyŏnghyang Sinmun* (Kyŏnghyang Newspaper) on September 30, 1968, as well as in other newspapers, as *kyech'ang*, meaning "continuous singing," differentiating the new format from then common performances of excerpts. The des-ignation used prominently throughout the pamphlets of the series was *yŏnch'ang-hoe* (consecutive singing events), which likewise stressed the difference compared with earlier formats. *Chŏnp'an* (full piece), men-tioned as an alternative term in the pamphlets, was also used in other contexts, where it could include full-length recordings or full-length performances in several sittings (for example, the "Deep-Rooted Tree" series; see next section). *Tokch'ang-hoe*, the common term for a "[sung] solo recital" of classical (Western) music, was also used on occasion, for example in the announcement of Pak Ch'o-wŏl's full-length performance of *Sugungga* in the *Tonga Ilbo* (Tonga Daily News) on October 31, 1970.[16]

These different terms, which stress either one of the two primary characteristics of the modern full-length format—one complete piece, performed by one singer alone—were soon replaced by *wanch'ang*, maybe first used in the announcement of Pak Tong-jin's *Ch'unhyangga* in the *Tonga Ilbo* on May 13, 1969. In a later preview of Pak's *Sugungga* in the *Tonga Ilbo* on October 26, 1971, *wanch'ang* was defined as "one piece of [*p'an*-]*sori* from beginning to end [sung] alone," and contrasted with *t'omak sori*, until then the common format.[17] From then on, *wanch'ang* became the regular term for this newly invented format, commonly accepted and widely used in the media.

Various explanations of Pak Tong-jin's motives for performing *p'ansori* works in full-length have been offered. Pak himself noted in an interview more than thirty years later that his aim was "to find out how far my talent would go" (Kim 2001, 91), while others suspect that Pak and those who would follow his example were motivated by the desire "to present themselves as hard-training singers and achieve a nomination as a 'holder' [*poyuja*]," the highest rank within the official system of preservation (Jang 2014, 138; see Ch'oe 2014, 349–350).[18] While Pak's individual motives remain open to debate, the results speak for themselves: previously "close to an unknown [*mumyŏng*]" in the *p'ansori* scene (Kim Ki-hyŏng 2014, 56), Pak first received the newly inaugurated "Korea Culture Prize" for traditional singing (known as the Han'guk Munhwa Taesang, Kugak Pumun Sŏngak-sang). Surprisingly, he was awarded specifically for "mastering [all] five *p'ansori* pieces," as noted in the *Sŏul Sinmun* on November 16, 1968, even though the proposed performance series had just begun at that time and would take almost three years to complete. More importantly, within five years Pak was appointed a Human Cultural Treasure (Howard 2006, 62–64). His designation in 1973 was preceded by a reform of the preservation system in 1970 that reshuffled responsibilities. Every registered "holder" was now assigned a full piece, according to the respective schools of transmission, allowing Pak to fill in for the vacant piece *Chŏkpyŏkka*, which he had performed in full-length in 1971.[19]

Whether intentional or not, Pak Tong-jin's full-length performance of *Hŭngboga*, followed by a whole series of *wanch'ang*, was a well-timed intervention in the early development of governmental heritage preservation. His institutional recognition, as well as his popular and critical success, inspired other singers to perform *wanch'ang* and led to lasting changes in the *p'ansori* scene.

MAKING MASTERS

Wanch'ang p'ansori transformed from a pioneering spectacle to common practice in the course of the 1970s, a decade that proved crucial for the development of performance styles and the inner structure of the *p'ansori* scene. Genealogical teacher-student relations still remained important with regard to training. But despite persisting continuities between the traditional process of succession and the official system of recognition, soon the ability of performing *wanch'ang* became a new standard for designation as a Human Cultural Treasure, the highest honor a *p'ansori* singer could possibly achieve. The evaluation of a singer through the teacher-student system, long predating the introduction of governmental support, began to be replaced by a performance-based criterion, epitomized by the *wanch'ang* format.

Numerous singers who had come of age amidst the turmoil of the postwar years, now in their thirties and forties, embraced the new format. First in individual "full-length presentations" (*wanch'ang palp'yo-hoe*), then also in series dedicated to audience appreciation (*kamsang-hoe*), not always in full-length, they presented their singing skills.[20] Measurement of singing skills, until then mostly focused on *tŏnŭm*, "individual innovations" added in the process of transmission (Park 2003, 178; see Um 2013, 106), or abstract categories like *tŭg'ŭm* (high level of expressive vocal skills; see Kim 2001, 88), expanded to include the full repertory of five canonical pieces, preferably performed in full-length. Proficiency in *wanch'ang* became essential to being a master singer, not unlike the "Presidential Prize" (Taet'ongnyŏng Sang), awarded at selected national competitions.[21] Some singers of the older generation, maybe most pronouncedly Kim So-hŭi, who allegedly never sang a *wanch'ang*, tended to abstain from the new format, which they considered a showcase of duration over aesthetics (Kim 2005, 60; Ch'oe 2014, 375–376).[22]

Nevertheless, when the first generation of Human Cultural Treasures passed away or stepped back in the 1990s and early 2000s, they were succeeded by members of what I call the "generation *wanch'ang*," singers like Sŏng Ch'ang-sun, O Chŏng-suk, and Cho Sang-hyŏn (who became Human Cultural Treasures in 1991; Cho later had this title revoked over a bribery affair), and Pak Song-hŭi, Sŏng U-hyang, and Song Sun-sŏp (2002) who had extensively performed in full-length in their mid-career. Even beyond their deaths, they dominate the *p'ansori* scene until today as crucial members in a professional network of dependencies (see O 2017), while their students, for whom *wanch'ang* performances have become an inevitable stepping-stone in their career, compete against each other for the next open spot. It is pointless to ponder whether these well-trained and highly talented performers would not have been nominated anyway, even if they had not presented *wanch'ang* performances, that is. Without a doubt, however, their performance practice contributed to the close association of *wanch'ang p'ansori* and mastery of the art.

Following Pak Tong-jin's invention of *wanch'ang*, scholars of *p'ansori* got more involved in the planning of performances. The P'ansori Research Society (P'ansori Hakhoe), founded by like-minded academics in 1973, cooperated with Korea Britannica, publisher of the Korean edition of the Encyclopedia Britannica, whose director Han Ch'ang-gi shared a personal interest in popularizing traditional arts, to initiate a regular series of *p'ansori* performances, the monthly "Britannica P'ansori Kamsang-hoe" (Pŭrit'aenik'ŏ P'ansori Kamsang-hoe, 1974–1975). After a hiatus of almost one year the series continued for one hundred more installments from 1976, now in a weekly rhythm (Friday, 7 p.m.), as the "Deep-Rooted Tree P'ansori Kamsang-hoe" (Ppuri Kip'ŭn Namu P'ansori Kamsang-hoe, 1976–1978), matching the title of Britannica's new magazine. The performances of the "Deep-Rooted Tree" series were about one hour long, followed by a discussion. As "real" *wanch'ang* performances were impossible under these time constraints, pieces were performed in segments and stretched over several weeks, a format referred to as *chŏnp'an* (full piece).[23]

The popular impact of these events, held at Britannica headquarters located in central Seoul for audiences of up to a hundred spectators, might seem arguable. Their importance for the consolidation of the *p'ansori* scene, however, by providing paid performance opportunities beyond self-sponsored *palp'yo-hoe*, cannot be overstated. While singers of the generation *wanch'ang* were frequent guests at the "Deep-Rooted Tree" series, another achievement of the research- and preservation-focused program was the "re-discovery" of well-trained singers who, for economic reasons, had left the active scene in Seoul behind (Kim Sŏk-pae 2014, 23). As a gathering place for practitioners and scholars outside of the practice room with an audience of aficionados and academics, post-performance discussions, and a presumably salon-like atmosphere (Kungnip Kugagwŏn 2011, 76–77), the "Deep-Rooted Tree" series furthermore contributed to the opening of the *p'ansori* scene and the expansion of general audiences.

Although not *wanch'ang* in the literal sense, the *chŏnp'an* performance style of the "Deep-Rooted Tree" series matched the work-centered perspective on *p'ansori* that Pak Tong-jin (who was a regular contributor) had introduced, and shared the same academic spirit and preservationist agenda. The series presented a wide variety of schools and singing styles, enriched with printed full lyrics and scholarly comments, features that would soon become standard procedure of *wanch'ang* practice. A comprehensive album set with full-length recordings of the canon and extensive liner notes by experts was issued by Britannica Korea under the title "Deep-Rooted Tree" in 1982 after the series had concluded (see Kim Sŏk-pae 2014). Now a collector's item, the set further contributed to the status of *p'ansori* as a traditional high art and remains a lasting testimony of the series' role in the acculturation of the invented tradition *wanch'ang p'ansori*.

Maybe inspired by the success of the "Deep-Rooted Tree" series, other *p'ansori* performance formats emerged, often in serialized form and supported by the media, drawing an increasing number of younger spectators. Some attempts were short-lived, such as the monthly "P'ansori Kamsang-hoe" at the Samillo Ch'anggo Sogŭkchang, a small theater that otherwise showed experimental drama (see Yang 2002, 96). The efforts of the National Changguk Company (Kungnip Ch'anggŭk-tan), however, a resident ensemble at the National Theater composed mostly of high-skilled *p'ansori* singers, had more lasting effects. After some experiments with serial formats, the "P'ansori Chŏnggi Kamsang-hoe" (1977–1984) was established as a regular event. Once a month, on the last Saturday at 3 p.m., three to four singers, mostly members of the ensemble, would present one short excerpt each. After the series had changed its format several times, the success of a special event in honor of the 200th anniversary of the death of early *p'ansori* scholar and sponsor Sin Chae-hyo (1812–1884), four full-length performances on consecutive days (December 18 to 21, 1984), paved the way to a *wanch'ang*-only series. As the name indicates, the "Wanch'ang P'ansori" series (first called "Wanch'ang Presentation [Palp'yo-hoe]"), sponsored by the *Tonga Ilbo* Publishing Company, and during the first year also by the national television service KBS, was exclusively dedicated to *wanch'ang* performances and began in March 1985 with Sŏng Ch'ang-sun's performance of *Simch'ŏngga*.[24] Sŏng Ch'ang-sun would perform eight more times until her demise in 2017 and singers like Pak Tong-jin, An Suk-sŏn, and Song Sun-sŏp also regularly contributed to the series.

Until today, acknowledged singers present full-length performances at the National Theater several times a year. The series draws from a relatively large pool of possible singers, including members of the hosting ensemble as well as winners of the Presidential Prize, and many singers of the generation *wanch'ang* perform regularly once a year.[25] From the beginning, full lyrics were provided to the audience, first in three-month volumes, later also in books for the whole year, and invited scholars of *p'ansori* gave introductions.

Besides the normalization of the term *wanch'ang*, another change in designation that followed swiftly is noteworthy. While early *palp'yo-hoe* (presentations) or *tokch'ang-hoe* (solo vocal recitals) implied singer-focused events, the term *kamsang-hoe* (appreciation event) that became prominent in the 1970s takes an audience perspective (Ch'oe 2014, 360–361).[26] This new terminology testifies to the expansion of the functions of *wanch'ang p'ansori*, from a means for singers to present their skills, to an occasion for spectators to appreciate their cultural heritage. The expanded prominence of the audience also heralded the declining importance of *wanch'ang* performances as a measurement of skill (Cho 2016, 133). Paralleling the increasing number of national competitions that awarded the Presidential Prize, the inflation of *wanch'ang* performances transformed this format into an obligatory rite of passage for professional singers, rather than a special qualification. From the 1990s the age of *wanch'ang* performers decreased more and more, as young singers like

Lee Jaram (Yi Cha-ram) (*Ch'unhyangga* at the age of twenty in 1998) or Yu T'ae-p'yŏng-yang (*Sugungga* at the age of eleven in 2003) hit records (Ch'oe 2014, 368–372). Rather than a mere presentation of artistic skills, *wanch'ang* performances were now conceived as a form of social interaction with lasting effects, adding to their importance for the inner workings of the *p'ansori* scene.

STAGING GENEALOGY

In full-length performances of *p'ansori*, unlike at premodern communal events where *p'ansori* may have been part of a diverse side-program, possibly background music to more important leisurely activities, the art takes center stage. They are "a challenge for singer and audience alike," as a pamphlet for the "Wanch'ang P'ansori" series at the National Theater notes. Now with its own tradition of over thirty years, the series symbolizes "a dream stage for younger singers . . . and a stage of pride for veteran masters."[27] But even more important for the *p'ansori* scene than these public and prestigious performances are individually organized "full-length presentations" (*wanch'ang palp'yo-hoe*) that take place in semi-private settings. Usually free of admission and sponsored by regionally organized preservation societies (*pojon-hoe*), these events are thus without a commercial incentive and rarely employ professional promotion. Relying on "circular networks of exchange" (Howard 2011, 198), the attendants are mostly limited to members of the *p'ansori* scene, a phenomenon that also exists in other traditional performing arts (Saeji 2012, 459). Through the cooperative efforts and face-to-face meetings among teachers, students, and other members, full-length presentations not only transform the status of the singer in the scene, but also re-affirm and strengthen social bonds within the professional community in general. They are occasions to "stage genealogy": to performatively re-enact the process of transmission.

The *p'ansori* scene, consisting of various *yup'a* led by senior singers, constitutes what Kay Kaufman Shelemay calls a "descent community" that is based on "shared identities, whether they are grounded in historical fact, are newly invented, or emerge from some combination of historical circumstance and creative transformation" (2011, 367). In contrast to premodern times, with *p'ansori* education provided at schools and universities and membership in the scene being largely a matter of choice and skills (and their recognition), features of "affinity communities" come to the fore, which "derive their strength from the presence and proximity of a sizeable group and for the sense of belonging and prestige that this affiliation offers" (Shelemay 2011, 373). In *p'ansori* performances, on the one hand processes of descent highlight the historical roots of the respective genealogy—the lineage of past teachers and students—, while on the other hand processes of affinity stress the contemporaneity and future prospects of the lineage and the genre at large. Lineage appears in its most tangible form in the pamphlets that are handed out at *wanch'ang* presentations. A far cry from the folded leaflets that introduced the singer and the piece within the restrictions of four pages in Pak Tong-jin's early *wanch'ang* performances, today these pamphlets—of *p'ansori* as well as other *kugak* performances—are often glossy brochures with more than a dozen pages. In the following, I will first discuss discursive and visual depictions of lineage in the pamphlets of *wanch'ang* presentations and then consider their realization in performance by acts of affinity.

At full-length presentations, the pamphlet has to mediate between the performing singer, obviously the star of the event, and the school of transmission he or she represents. These two aspects are closely intermingled and appear most prominently in the title of the event. For example, Ko Hyang-im's presentation of *Sugungga* is announced on the poster, the pamphlet, and other promotional material as follows: 2011 Ko Hyang-im Myŏngch'ang Tongch'o-je P'ansori. In compressed form, this title locates the event in the here-and-now (exact date, time, and venue are mentioned below on the poster) and provides the singer's name and rank ("master singer," *myŏngch'ang*). Presentation titles rarely fail to mention the *yup'a*, in this case "Tongch'o-je," the school affiliated with singer Kim Yŏn-su (1907–1974) who used the pen name "Tongch'o."[28]

Pamphlets of presentations tend to be conservative in content and design, reflecting both the hermetic structure of the *p'ansori* scene and the preservationist agenda of these events. A typical pamphlet offers additional information on the singer, the *yup'a*, and the piece performed. A congratulatory remark by the teacher and the singer's introductory address usually express praise and pride, or gratitude, respectively. Scholarly texts that reference famous singers of the past and transmitted aesthetic characteristics, together with visual aids such as photos or diagrams, clarify the genealogy and stress the historicity of the *yup'a*. In addition, some pamphlets provide full lyrics (if not, at least the general structure or a synopsis of the piece), which not only represent the integrity of the work, but also serve as a practical means to follow along with the singer's performance, and to offer assistance when needed, thus showing dedication and support.

Besides textual references, visual means strongly contribute to the framing of the singer as an agent between tradition and innovation, the link between past glories and future prospects of the lineage. A typical cover image shows the singer in a full-body shot, striking a stark pose. Gestures and props, such as an opened mouth, spread-out arms, and a fan in hand, can suggest a performance scene. More recent pamphlets, in particular those of younger singers, feature staged studio shots of the protagonist posing in a *hanbok* outside of any performance context.[29] Favoring more reflective or meditative poses, sometimes bordering on "romantic" clichés, the images of a new generation of singers attempt to satisfy both the requirements of a traditional community and an individual artistic identity.[30] In contrast to the cover image, the photos that identify the authors of texts in the pamphlet, usually passport-format portraits, suggest a function within a system, rather than individual expression. Similar formal images are occasionally employed in diagrams that depict connections between past masters and the performing singer, ranging from simple succession of singers connected by direct lines to more elaborate image galleries. These diagrams visualize the historicity of the *yup'a* through a complex network of singer-student relations and thus supplement the texts by scholars and teachers.

While the pamphlet recognizes the mutual relations between singer, teacher, and their predecessors—past and present of the *yup'a*—the performance itself extends them into the future. The event proceeds as a collaboration between various agents, including the teacher, the students, and possibly friends and family of the singer. Besides well-timed calls of encouragement (*ch'uimsae*), a concrete and audible proof of proficiency with the conventions of *p'ansori*, this collaboration also includes practical acts of support and symbolic acts of affiliation that all relate in one way or another to the process of transmission (Cho 2016, 125–126). With regard to the genealogy and the teacher-student hierarchy it is based upon, the most striking acts are performances of gratitude and recognition that evoke reciprocal behavior. For example, when introducing the singer, the announcer also points out the teacher in the auditorium, if present, who then stands up to receive the applause and delivers a brief informal speech that acknowledges the singer's skills, diligence, and endurance.

The most iconic way of expressing gratitude, the "deep bow" (*k'ŭn chŏl*), performed by the singer kneeling on the floor before or after the presentation, likewise evokes a reciprocal gesture of recognition by the teacher. When Han Sŭng-sŏk got down on his knees and bowed for his teacher An Suk-sŏn after finishing the version of *Simch'ŏngga* that he had learned from her, she came on stage only reluctantly. Nevertheless, she offered a short speech in praise of her prodigy student's skill and determination, her eyes filled with tears (Namsan Kugak-tang, December 12, 2012). Besides creating strongly emotional moments, both master and disciple, through their reciprocal acts of gratitude and recognition, re-affirm their individual relation and respective position in the *p'ansori* scene.

Apart from their practical support in the preparation and active participation with *ch'uimsae*, students play a likewise important role in their teacher's full-length presentation. Closely following the lyrics and helping out the singer with some words when needed, they can be seen in almost every full-length presentation, usually sitting in the first rows. They perform a double-act: offering their support to the singer and showing dedication in learning themselves. Thanks to them, momentary memory lapses on part of the singer are not perceived as mistakes but can turn into highly energizing scenes of communality, once again attesting that the whole event is a collective effort and accomplishment.

These various displays of gratitude and recognition, support and dedication to continual study give concrete meaning to the genealogical relations among singer, teacher, and students that are described and depicted in the pamphlet. Text and visual print material on the one hand, the performative affirmation of relationships on the other, provide the necessary conditions for the common cause: the transmission of *p'ansori* from past masters to future generations.

Lineage in *p'ansori*, like in many other traditional performance genres, is conceptualized as a community of descent in retrospect and, looking forward, as a community of affinity. Rite of passage for the singer and communal meeting for the *p'ansori* scene, a full-length presentation is

positioned at the center of this traditional trajectory, connecting the past
with the present and extending it to the future. The pamphlet, which puts
the singer in a line with his or her predecessors and the current presentation at the end of a long series of (imagined) similar events, contributes to
the discursive creation of the transmission process. The performance of a
given piece in a specific version in full-length then becomes a site of communal knowledge transfer that guarantees the continuity of this process,
in which the attendants, by enacting a specific role and thus performatively actualizing mutual relations, become a part of dwelling in a shared
past and together taking steps toward a shared future.

Wanch'ang p'ansori was invented in the context of governmental heritage
legislation as a measure of mastership by singers like Pak Tong-jin and
other members of the generation *wanch'ang*. It was then established and
expanded as a high-profile performance format that attests to the artistic uniqueness and aesthetic force of *p'ansori* by the combined efforts of
scholars and practitioners. Increasingly conceived as a rite of passage
that, based on staged genealogies and shared outlooks, consolidates the
p'ansori scene, the *wanch'ang* format is at a crossroads today.

On May 31, 2014, the National Theater hosted a memorial event on
the occasion of the 30th anniversary of its "Wanch'ang P'ansori" series.
From the early afternoon until late at night, some of the best singers and
drummers of the country appeared onstage, including six Human Cultural Treasures. Nobody performed a piece in full-length, though, as this
potpourri-style gala consisted of a series of short excerpts. Ironically,
wanch'ang p'ansori was celebrated with *t'omak sori*. Even more piquant,
the series itself had been put on hold that year but, presumably due to
negative audience reactions, later continued in the established fashion. An
increase of the entrance fee by 50 percent (from 20,000 to 30,000 Korean
wŏn) was soon revoked.

A symposium that accompanied the anniversary gathered some of
the most prolific scholars of *p'ansori* as well as senior singers who related
some of their experiences (Kungnip Ch'angguk-tan 2014). In their talks
and the following discussions, they suggested that *wanch'ang*, despite its
importance in establishing *p'ansori* as a proper (and, at times, popular) art
in the 1960s, 1970s, and 1980s, has lost much of its thrust—as well as its

audience. Most suggestions for reforming the (arguably) outworn format involved shortening the overlong duration. In fact, some changes from what many South Korean audiences consider to be the orthodox way of performing *wanch'ang* (one singer, one piece, in one sitting) have developed in recent years, replacing enduring performances by a solo singer with ensemble solutions. For example, since the 2010s the traditional end-of-year performance (*cheya kongyŏn*) of the "Wanch'ang P'ansori" series features not only An Suk-sŏn (then principal singer of the National Changguk Company), but also some of her students. One piece is presented from beginning to end, but separated in segments performed by different singers. On another occasion, three students of the same teacher consecutively presented parts of the work they had learned together, resulting in a full-length performance by three singers.[31] The "shared" performance of Tongp'yŏn-je *Hŭngboga* by Lee Jaram and her teacher Song Sun-sŏp (National Gugak Center, November 8, 2015), where each singer performed one half of the piece, is another example of this trend.

Besides adding a twist to the common *wanch'ang* format, conjoint performances by several students and their teacher put the communal bonds that are otherwise evoked between stage and auditorium even more on display. While in "traditional" presentations the result of transmission is staged and acknowledged by members of the *p'ansori* scene gathered in the auditorium, in these new formats the actual process of transmission is re-enacted on stage. Aimed at an unrelated public, this way of staging genealogy does not only offer more diversity, but also reduces the spectators' responsibilities. Whether this turn toward general audiences will prove profitable for the symbolic preservation of *p'ansori* remains to be seen.

With regard to individually organized *wanch'ang* presentations, financial burdens for the hosting singer are also a concern. Sŏng Ch'ang-sun notes that taking an entrance fee of 3,000 Korean wŏn (1,000 wŏn for students and senior citizens) for her presentation of *Simch'ŏngga* in 1977, a decision made after much pondering, was unusual (Sŏng 1995, 228). Today, the majority of presentations are still free of charge (Cho 2016, 126), while a considerable number of events (five out of thirteen presentations that I attended between 2011 and 2016) take a modest fee of 20,000 wŏn, similar to the "Wanch'ang P'ansori" series at the National Theater and equivalent to inexpensive seats in a theater performance. Catering to general audiences with more diverse—although rarely much shorter—performances appears to be an attempt to integrate the hitherto semi-private presentations into the logics of a performance environment where governmental subsidies are supplemented by entrance fees.

By combining an excessive performance format with the preservationist heritage policies of the time, Pak Tong-jin managed to "re-invent" *p'ansori* as a high art. That *wanch'ang p'ansori* did not remain a one-time sensation but developed into a mandatory rite of passage despite not being embraced by everyone may be due to its function of keeping the genre exclusive, not only out of reach for amateur singers (who tend to learn small parts only), but also for those professional singers who lack the resources and institutional support necessary for a presentation. The physical hardship showcased in long performances, associated with dedication and integrity, may also be a way for mid-career singers to distinguish themselves from earlier generations of well-established masters, some of whom publicly denounced the practice, though notably not for historical but for aesthetic reasons. The subsequent use of the invented format is shaped by singers' concerns as well as prospective audience reactions, ranging from academic scholars to a wider public. Besides the differentiation and the consolidation of the *p'ansori* scene, *wanch'ang* performances fulfill various functions. The close examination of the conventions and contexts that influence this constant process of re-invention indicates that the various predicaments faced by a traditional art today—such as changing audience appeal, modern practices that challenge authenticity, and problems of marketing—play out both on an institutional level and for the individual performer. *Wanch'ang p'ansori*, with its extended focus on the solo singer and the supporting audience, shows both the triumph of individual dedication and the limits of personal agency. Different from traditions invented by elites that idealize past practices for contemporary cultural capital,[32] in this case performers seeking to define their unique place and rank as traditional artists in modern social and cultural milieu, incidentally invented a new tradition in reaction to concrete problems. A by-product of larger transformations of the *p'ansori* scene, *wanch'ang* performances continue to sustain the genre and keep its singular, eccentric imagery alive.

GLOSSARY

ch'anggŭk 唱劇
Chŏkpyŏkka 赤壁歌
chungyo muhyŏng munhwa 重要無形文化財
Ch'unhyangga 春香歌
hanbok 한복
Hŭngboga 興甫歌
In'gan Munhwajae 人間文化財
kamsang-hoe 鑑賞會
kat 갓
kugak 國樂
kukka muhyŏng munhwa 國家無形文化財
Kungnip Kugagwŏn 國立國樂院
Munhwajae Poho pŏp 文化財保護法
p'ansori 판소리

pojon-hoe 保存會
pubun-ch'ang 部分唱
Simch'ŏngga 沈淸歌
Sugungga 水宮歌
Taesasŭp Nori 大私習 놀이
Taet'ongnyŏng Sang 大統領 賞
tokch'ang-hoe 獨唱會
t'omak sori 토막 소리
tŏnŭm 더늠
tŭg'ŭm 得音
wanch'ang 完唱
wanch'ang palp'yo-hoe 完唱 發表會
wŏnhyŏng 原形
yangban 兩班
yenŭng poyuja 藝能 保有者
yup'a 流派

NOTES

1. The long duration of *p'ansori* stories and performances also features prominently on popular online resources such as Wikipedia (https://en.wikipedia.org/wiki/Pansori), as well as on websites of UNESCO (http://www.unesco.org/culture/ich/en/RL/pansori-epic-chant-00070) and the Korean Cultural Heritage Administration (http://www.heritage.go.kr/heri/cul/culSelectDetail.do?ccbaCpno=2221100320000), all accessed June 12, 2021.

2. *Hŭngboga* (sometimes spelled *Hŭngbuga*) or the "Song of Hŭngbo" is a canonical *p'ansori* piece about poor Hŭngbo and his rich brother.

3. While some scholars mention the *wanch'ang* format as one among many forms of performing, for example, Um (2013, 11, 17), the only in-depth historization of *wanch'ang p'ansori* is Ch'oe (2014).

4. While the Korean name of this major public institution in the preservation and promotion of traditional music (*kugak*) has been Kungnip kugagwŏn since its establishment in 1950 as the "National Classical Music Institute" (it opened in 1951 in Busan) its location and political affiliation, as well as

its official English name have changed several times. At the time of Pak's performance, the Center was located on the slopes of Mt. Namsan, the current location of the National Theater of Korea. On the role of the National Gugak Center (its current English name, which I use throughout this chapter), see Howard (2016).

5. In a fictionalized biography of Pak Tong-jin, aimed at young adults and told from the protagonist's perspective, Song Ŏn imagines that "not one of the two hundred seats was empty" (1999, 155), transferring the event into the realm of legend.

6. The *wŏnhyŏng* is the form supposed to be preserved and transmitted, according to the CPPL. However, since the last revision of the CPPL in 2016, the term "*wŏnhyŏng*" is not used anymore. On this change from "archetype to model," see Sŏ (2016).

7. *Yenŭng poyuja* is the highest rank within the system of preservation established by the CPPL. The 2016 revision of the CPPL adopted "Human Cultural Treasure" as an official term and formerly "important" intangible properties were renamed to "National Intangible Cultural Properties" (*kukka muhyŏng munhwa*).

8. *Yup'a* can be thought of as groups of artists who preserve and transmit a specific style of singing; the term is also used to refer to such a style.

9. *Pubun-ch'ang* or *t'omak sori* are *p'ansori* stories performed in excerpted form, presumably the most common practice until the twentieth century.

10. These were Kim Yŏn-su, Kim So-hŭi, Kim Yŏ-ran, Pak Nok-chu, Chŏng Kwang-su, and Pak Ch'o-wol. For a full list, see Yu (2013, 361–362). *Ch'unhyangga* or the "Song of Ch'unhyang" is a canonical *p'ansori* piece about a young couple whose class-transcending romance is put to the test.

11. On local preservation efforts and their results, see Yu (2013).

12. *Ch'anggŭk* are often stage adaptations of *p'ansori* with an ensemble cast, minimalist in its beginnings in the early twentieth century, nowadays usually involving a large cast, elaborate stage design, and costumes.

13. *Chŏkpyŏkka* on April 28, 1956, and on September 21, 1957, as well as *Sugungga* on November 23, 1956. For detailed transcripts and descriptions of the recordings and pamphlets, see Pae (2001, 182–200).

14. Like Pak Tong-jin's performance of *Hŭngboga*, Im Pang-ul's recording sessions took place at the National Gugak Center, presumably with an audience of aficionados. As preserved on the reel tapes of these events, the announcer Sŏng Kyŏng-rin, head of the Gugak Center's music division, notes that "as you know, *p'ansori* has to be listened to in full-length [*chŏnp'an*]" (*Chokpyŏk-ka*, April 28, 1956). Im Pang-ul himself, on another

occasion, asks for understanding that he has often performed *"tomak, tomak,"* only parts, as "nowadays there are no guests that listen [to these] long [performances]" (*Chokpyŏk-ka,* September 21, 1957). See partial transcripts in Pae (2001, 183, 198).

15. The *Kyŏnghyang Sinmun* on April 15, 1970, for example, notes that Pak will not rest (*shwiji ankʻo*) throughout his performance of *Simchʻŏngga.* However, the pamphlet of Pak's full-length performance of *Chʻunhyangga* (May 20, 1969), which also mentions the "astonishing attempt of performing *Chʻunhyangga* as an eight-hour performance without a break [*hyusik ŏmnŭn yŏnchʻang*]," nevertheless indicates an intermission between the first and the second half of the performance proceedings.

16. *Sugungga* or the "Song of the Underwater Palace" is a canonical *pʻansori* piece about a Dragon King fallen ill who sends a tortoise out to find help in the form of a rabbit.

17. The pamphlet for *Sugungga* (November 3, 1971), while retaining *yŏnchʻanghoe* in the title, also mentions the term *wanchʻang.*

18. Yi Po-hyŏng mentions the possible influence of Sŏng Kyŏng-rin, director of the National Gugak Center from 1961 to 1972, who allegedly "held *chŏnpʻan* performances in the old days," as head of the Gugak Center's music division (*aksajang*) from 1950 to 1961, in other words, when Im Pang-ul performed his full-length recording sessions in 1956 and 1957 (Kungnip kugagwŏn 2011, 86).

19. *Chŏkpyŏkka* or the "Song of the Red Cliff" is a canonical *pʻansori* piece about war between three generals, based on the Chinese *Romance of the Three Kingdoms.*

20. A *wanchʻang palpʻyo-hoe* is a performance of a complete *pʻansori* story by one singer, and often take place in semi-private settings, sponsored by a preservation society, free of admission.

21. This is the highest award in the fields of culture and society, in the case of *pʻansori* commonly considered the defining attribute of a master singer.

22. Kim So-hŭi is quoted by one of her students, saying that "Nowadays, people [like Pak Tong-jin] foolishly perform for six or seven hours with their noses at the grindstone, draining all their energy" (Yi 1996, 56).

23. For a list of performances, see Yi (2015, 222–225). On the historical development of the "Deep-Rooted Tree" series, see also co-host Yi Po-hyŏng's memories (Kungnip kugagwŏn 2011, 68–78), as well as reminiscences by Kim Myŏng-gon, who briefly worked at Britannica Korea in the late 1970s (2008, 231).

24. *Simchʻŏngga* or the "Song of Simchʻŏng" is a canonical *pʻansori* piece about

the girl Simch'ŏng who sacrifices her life for her father to regain his eyesight, showcasing her exemplary filial piety

25. The "Wanch'ang P'ansori" series and the Presidential Prize are two criteria of mastership intrinsically connected in a closed circuit, as most contests demand *wanch'ang* experience as a necessary condition for participation in the relevant section. See, for instance, a current application for the Taesasŭp Nori, literally the "great study play," a major *p'ansori* contest held in Chŏnju, South Chŏlla Province, that awards the Taet'ongnyŏng Sang; also Ch'oe (2014, 365).

26. *Kamsang-hoe* are performances of *p'ansori* (or other arts) that can feature one or several singers. The term *tokch'ang-hoe* is used for vocal recitals in classical (Western) music, but in the late 1960s and early 1970s also for *wanch'ang p'ansori* performances.

27. The first quote is from the 2012–2013 season program of the National Theater, the second from the 2014 pamphlet of the "Wanch'ang P'ansori" series.

28. Broadly speaking, *yup'a* are indicated by the suffix "-je" or "-badi" and either reference geographical styles (for example, Sŏp'yŏn-je, "Western style") or lineages inaugurated by a famous master, such as Chŏng Kwang-su-badi, the "style of Chŏng Kwang-su"; see Um (2013, 101–106), and Jang (2014, 147).

29. *Hanbok* are usually worn by the singer and the drummer in traditional *p'ansori* performances.

30. A cover-image of Yu T'ae-p'yŏng-yang (b. 1992) stages this dilemma most concretely, by showing him two times: facing the camera and wearing full *hanbok* including the *kat* on the left, dressed in a casual shirt looking at his other "traditional" self on the right (pamphlet, Kangsan-je *Simch'ŏngga*, October 18, 2014). For other examples of young *kugak* performers who tackle this dilemma by combining different visual codes, see Finchum-Sung 2012.

31. Pak Tong-sil-je *Simch'ŏngga* Wanch'ang Palp'yo-hoe, Buam Art Hall, January 4, 2014, with Kim Su-mi, Yi Sŏn-hŭi, and No Hae-hyŏn.

32. See Howard and Jackson in this volume for discussion of these kinds of tradition.

REFERENCES

Cho Se-hun. 2016. *Han'guk p'ansori-ŭi chŏnsŭng-gwa toje kwan'gye* [The transmission of Korean *p'ansori* and the master-apprentice relation]. Seoul: Minsok-wŏn.

Ch'oe Tong-hyŏn. 2011. "Munhwa pyŏndong-gwa p'ansori" [Cultural change and *p'ansori*]. *P'ansori Yŏn'gu* 31:423–454.

———. 2014. "P'ansori wanch'ang-ŭi t'ansaeng-gwa pyŏnhwa" [Birth and transformation of full-length *p'ansori*]. *P'ansori Yŏn'gu* 38:373–383.

Chŏng Hoe-ch'ŏn. 2014. "Wanch'ang-i issŏ myŏngch'ang-gwa myŏng-gosu, kwimyŏngch'ang-do issŏtda" [Because of *wanch'ang*, there are master singers, master drummers, and master listeners]. In Kungnip Ch'anggŭk-tan 2014, 43–52.

Finchum-Sung, Hilary Vanessa. 2012. "Visual Excess: The Visuality of Traditional Music Performance in South Korea." *Ethnomusicology* 56 (3): 397–425.

Hobsbawm, Eric. 1983. "Introduction: Inventing Traditions." In *The Invention of Tradition*, edited by Eric Hobsbawm and Terence Ranger, 1–14. Cambridge: Cambridge University Press.

Howard, Keith. 2006. *Creating Korean Music: Tradition, Innovation and the Discourse of Identity*. Aldershot, UK: Ashgate.

———. 2011. "Kugak Fusion and the Politics of Korean Musical Consumption." In *Consuming Korean Tradition in Early and Late Modernity: Commodification, Tourism, and Performance*, edited by Laurel Kendall, 195–215. Honolulu: University of Hawai'i Press.

———. 2016. "The Institutionalization of Korean Traditional Music: Problematic Business Ethics in the Construction of Genre and Place." *Asia Pacific Business Review* 22 (3): 452–467.

Jang, Yeonok. 2014. *Korean P'ansori Singing Tradition: Development, Authenticity, and Performance History*. Plymouth, UK: Scarecrow Press.

Kang Yun-jŏng. 2003. "Pak Tong-jin bon Hŭngbuga sasŏl-ŭi t'ŭkching" [Characteristics of Pak Tong-jin's version of *Hŭngbuga*]. *P'ansori Yŏn'gu* 5:5–29.

Killick, Andrew. 2010. *In Search of Korean Traditional Opera: Discourses of Ch'anggŭk*. Honolulu: University of Hawai'i Press.

Kim Ki-hyŏng. 2001. "Uri sidae-ŭi chinjŏng-han sorikkun Pak Tong-jin-ŭi sori-ŭi segye" [The world of sound of our era's genuine *p'ansori* singer Pak Tong-jin]. *Munhwa Yesul* 5:88–99.

———. 2005. "P'ansori, taejung-sŏng hoebok wi-hae sae p'an tchal ttaeda: wanch'ang p'ansori kongyŏn-e tae-han pansŏng-jŏk chŏmgŏm" [Making a new *p'an* to restore the popularity of *p'ansori*: A reflective examination about full-length *p'ansori* performances]. *Munhwa Yesul* (January): 58–61.

———. 2014. "Wanch'ang p'ansori-ui hyŏnjae-wa mirae" [Present and future of full-length *p'ansori*]. In Kungnip Ch'anggŭk-tan 2014, 55–63.

Kim Myŏng-gon. 2008. "'Kwak-ssi buin sangyŏ naga-nŭn taemok'-ŭl ŏnje tasi pullŏrina" [When will [I] sing again the [*p'ansori*] part about 'wife Kwak leaving the bier' [from *Simch'ŏngga*]. In *T'ŭkchip! Han Ch'ang-gi* [Special edition! Han Ch'ang-gi], edited by Ko Se-hyŏn, 230–234. P'aju: Ch'angbi.

Kim Sŏk-pae. 2014. "Ppuri Kip'ŭn Namu p'ansori ŭmban chŏnjip-ŭi hyŏnhwang-gwa kach'i" [Current state and value of the "Deep-Rooted Tree" collection of *p'ansori* records]. *Yŏlsang Kojŏn Yŏn'gu* 41:15–49.

Kungnip Ch'anggŭk-tan [National Changguk Company]. 2014. *Wanch'ang p'ansori 30nyŏn maji t'ŭkpyŏl kongyŏn* [Special performance on the occasion of 30 Years of *wanch'ang p'ansori*]. Program book, including proceedings of the seminar "*Wanch'ang p'ansori 30nyŏn hoego-wa chŏnmang*" [Thirty years of *wanch'ang p'ansori*: Remembrance and outlook]. National Theater of Korea, May 31.

Kungnip kugagwŏn [National Gugak Center]. 2011. *Kusul ch'ongsŏ 3* [Oral History Series 3]. Interview with Yi Po-hyŏng.

O Chŏng-sim. 2017. "Sahoe yŏn'gyŏl-mang punsŏk-ŭl tong-han muhyŏng yusan kongdong-ch'e yŏn'gu" [Research on intangible heritage communities through the analysis of social networks]. *Munhwa Chŏngch'aek Nonch'ong* 31 (1): 158–183.

Pae Yŏn-hyŏng. 2001. "Im Pang-ul ŭmban yŏn'gu 2" [A study of Im Pang-ul's records 2]. *Han'guk Ŭmban-hak* 11:181–230.

Park, Chan E. 2003. *Voices from the Straw Mat: Toward an Ethnography of Korean Story Singing*. Honolulu: University of Hawai'i Press.

Saeji, CedarBough Tam. 2012. "Transmission and Performance: Memory, Heritage, and Authenticity in Korean Mask Dance Dramas." PhD diss., University of California, Los Angeles.

Shelemay, Kay Kaufman. 2011. "Musical Communities: Rethinking the Collective in Music." *Journal of the American Musicological Society* 64 (2): 349–390.

Sŏ Yu-sŏk. 2016. "Wŏnhyŏng-esŏ chŏnhyŏng-ŭro: muhyŏng munhwajae chedo-ŭi pyŏnhwa-wa p'ansori" [From archetype to model: Changes in the intangible cultural heritage system and *p'ansori*]. *P'ansori Yŏn'gu* 41:135–168.

Sŏng Ch'ang-sun. 1995. *Nŏn sori toduk nyŏn-iyŏ: sori-kkun Sŏng Ch'ang-sun-ŭi sori insaeng-gwa chinghŏn sarang iyagi* [You're a vocal thief: *P'ansori* singer Sŏng Ch'ang-sun's singing life and love story]. Seoul: Ŏnŏ Munhwa.

Song Mi-gyŏng. 2014. "Kidokkyo Pangsong nogŭm Pak Nok-chu 'Ch'unhyangga' (1963)-ŭi t'ŭkching-gwa p'ansori-sa-jŏk ŭiŭi" [Characteristics and significance of Pak Nok-chu's recording of *Ch'unhyangga* (1963) for Christian Broadcasting System]. *Kongyŏn Munhwa Yŏn'gu* 29:379–423.

Song Ŏn. 1999. *K'ŭn sorikkun Pak Tong-jin Iyagi* [The story of the great *p'ansori* singer Pak Tong-jin]. Illustrations by Kim Se-hyŏn. Seoul: Uri Kyoyuk.

Um, Haekyung. 2013. *Korean Musical Drama: P'ansori and the Making of Tradition in Modernity*. Farnham, UK: Ashgate.

Yang Kyŏng-mo. 2002. "Ch'anggo Kŭkchang yŏn'gu [Research on the Ch'anggo [Warehouse] Theatre]." MA thesis, Dongguk University.

Yi Myŏng-hŭi. 1996. "Manjŏng Kim So-hŭi sŏnsaeng-ŭi p'ansori kyoyuk-kwa na-ŭi p'ansori suŏp-ki" [Manjŏng Kim So-hŭi's *p'ansori* education and my *p'ansori* studies records]. *Dongni Yŏn'gu* 3:47–58.

Yi T'ae-hwa. 2015. "'Ppuri Kip'ŭn Namu P'ansori Kamsang-hoe' kaech'oe-ŭi ŭimi-wa p'ansori puhŭng-e kkich'in yŏnghyang" [Significance of the "Deep-Rooted Tree *P'ansori* Appreciation Event" and its influence on the revival of *p'ansori*]. *Han'guk Ŏnŏ Munhak* 95:207–236.

Yu Yŏng-dae. 2013. "P'ansori chŏnsŭng hyŏnhwang-gwa pojon pangan: chungyo muhyŏng munhwajae chijŏng hyŏnhwang-ŭl chungsim-ŭro" [Current status of the transmission of *P'ansori* and methods of preservation: On the situation of appointed important intangible cultural properties]. *P'ansori Yŏn'gu* 36:351–387.

CHAPTER 9

The State Leader as Inventor of Food Traditions in the DPRK

MARIA OSETROVA

Food tradition is an important part of national identity and can be an effective instrument in a state's cultural politics and its global image construction. The Korean Peninsula presents a particular and rare example of a food tradition, shared for centuries, but now developing separately (since the division of the Peninsula in 1945 and formation of two independent states in 1948). Today, two variations of Korean cuisine exist, differing not only in their official names (in the South *hansik*, in the North *Chosŏn ryori*) but also in their transmission of varied cultural and ideological messages both within and outside the two states. This difference suggests that understanding and representing a society's national food tradition primarily depends on the understanding of a national identity, the meaning of national culture and a nation's position on the global stage (the explanation and examples of this idea will be introduced below). Thus, the study of national food ideology and imagery can contribute to our comprehension of national cultural politics, its evolution, and the process of cultural identity construction.

This chapter seeks to examine how the narrative of a national food tradition is constructed in the DPRK and how it is built into the country's ideology. In order to do this, it will explore the role of the leader in this process. I argue that the specifics of North Korean invented traditions lie in the almost mandatory linking of any cultural practice to the leader—his words, images, writings, or biography. This is how practices become institutionalized and legitimized in the North Korean social reality. I use the term "invented" here in two senses. First, there are precedents when a North Korean leader himself suggests a new custom—thereby literally inventing it. For example, it is well known that it was Kim Il Sung who in 1985 suggested calling dog meat—a popular food product in Korea—*tan'gogi* (sweet meat). Since then it has become the official name of the dish in the DPRK, and is even included in dictionaries (Chosŏnmal taesajŏn 1992, vol. 1, 688) and culinary encyclopedias (Kim, Chŏng, and Ch'ŏn 1985, 336). The second usage of the term is closer to Eric Hobsbawm's definition. Hobsbawm identified invented traditions as those in which continuity with the historic past is "largely factitious" (Hobsbawm 1983, 2); in other words, they are traditions that are strategically employing a link to the past. Hobsbawm pointed out: "The historic past into which the new tradition is inserted need not be lengthy, stretching back into the assumed mists of time. Revolutions and 'progressive movements' which break with the past, by definition, have their own relevant past" (1983, 2). This statement can be perfectly applied to the case of North Korea, where many "invented" traditions tend to find their origin in Kim Il Sung's guerrilla era (between the end of the 1930s and 1945), according to his official biography.

This chapter focuses on invented traditions within the food sphere because food—despite being an extremely mundane part of every individual's life—is inextricably linked to everyday life. Due to its repeatability and omnipresent nature, food contributes greatly to the formation of an individual's worldview, value system, and cultural and national identity. Access to food also plays a role in defining an individual's social status, which is why authorities, especially in socialist states with centrally planned economies, regulate this sphere strictly. The most obvious proof of this statement in a North Korean context is the country's Public Distribution System (PDS)—an institution that has been supplying staple foods to the urban population on a monthly basis almost since the DPRK was founded. Despite the fact that the PDS has failed to execute its functions properly since the 1990s, the authorities do not seem to have any plans to abandon it in the near future (Cwiertka 2012, 156–163).

To explore the specifics of the construction of a national food narrative and its relation to DPRK ideology, this chapter starts by describing the narrative's basic characteristics before examining specific cases to show the actual mechanics of the invention process in food traditions and the role the leader plays in it. This examination will be undertaken via the analysis of a range of North Korean culinary literature from different periods (the 1980s, 1990s, 2000s, and present), state leaders' writings on food issues, official propaganda resources, evidence provided by defectors and others who have experience of living and working in the DPRK on a long-term basis, and materials collected by the author during a research trip to Pyongyang in October 2017. It is important to distinguish the North Korean propaganda resources oriented at domestic and at foreign audiences as the first type aims at indoctrination of the DPRK population while the second one works to create the international image of the country. The two types can coincide at certain times but basically go different ways. To better comprehend the specifics of the North Korean invented traditions it is reasonable to explore both types in parallel as far as the resources are available.

FATHER FEEDING HIS CHILDREN

The basic feature underlying the North Korean national food narrative is its strong political and ideological background. Any source related to food issues, whether it is an article in the main newspaper the *Rodong Sinmun*, a multi-volume culinary encyclopedia, or a simple recipe book, inevitably underscores the connection between the DPRK's national cuisine and the socialist way of life, Juche (the main North Korean ideological principle asserting independence and self-reliance in every aspect of social life) or *sŏn'gun* (the military-first political course introduced in 1996) ideas, not to mention the ubiquitous quotations of the leaders. Perhaps the best example is the classic maxim of Kim Il Sung that "rice is communism" (*ssar-ŭn kot kongsanjuŭi-ida*)—meaning that the quickest way to achieve communism is by feeding the people properly (Kim 1991, 130).[1] Kim Jong Il in his turn stated that "the advantages of socialism are to be seen first of all in the people's diet" (Kim 2010, 14).

Most importantly, however, the national food narrative always emphasizes the fact that the improvement of the people's diet and the development of national cuisine is primarily defined by the will of the leader. In fact, the leader is presented as a "father feeding his children." This metaphor is very popular in North Korean food narratives and finds its reflection not only in textual propaganda but also in North Korean visual art. The images of the leader sharing food with his compatriots or managing the food production process are ubiquitous throughout North Korean mass culture.

We can also trace the representation of the leader as a nourisher of the nation through the popular North Korean practice of distributing special food rations referred to as "the leader's gifts." They are distributed on the main national holidays, which are Kim Il Sung or Kim Jong Il's birthdays or the day that celebrates the foundation of the Workers' Party of Korea. Historian Andrei Lankov notes that in the 1980s such gifts could be half a kilo of sugar or some fruit (1995, 219–220). A similar practice was spread through schools and kindergartens, and in Pyongyang, elementary schoolchildren used to also receive a cup of milk every day—along with the idea that it was to be perceived as a token of the leader's care and love (Lankov 1995, 219–220). Many of these practices are still common today. For example, it is possible to see menu boards declaring that the food on offer has been "sent by the leader" (today Kim Jong Un, fig. 9.1). Honey is usually sent on behalf of the leader to maternity hospitals for women who

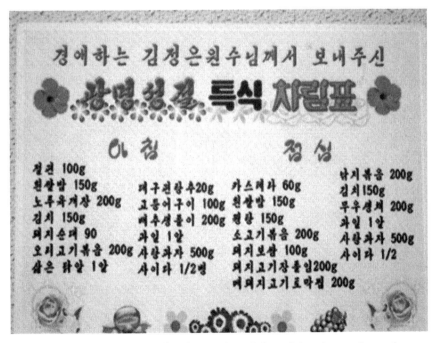

FIGURE 9.1.   Pyongyang school menu board describing the meal, sent by Kim Jong Un on the occasion of the birthday of Kim Jong Il (photo, Konstantin Asmolov). Courtesy of Konstantin Asmolov.

have just given birth because in the DPRK this food product is regarded to be a strong recovery remedy.

In addition, propaganda often promotes images of the lavishly laid tables, also referred to as "presents from the leader," claiming that it is one of the ways the leader recognizes a distinguished worker or any other honored person in the DPRK (fig. 9.2).

These examples show how the DPRK propaganda places the leader at the center of the national food narrative to present him as nourisher of the nation in both literal and figurative terms. This provides the background for another role for the leader—as creator of food traditions.

Because the North Korean national food narrative reflects the basic ideological principles of the state, it generally embodies the dual standpoints of cultural independence and self-reliance. Therefore, no foreign influence or cultural exchange is discussed or even mentioned in official food narratives. Instead, the history of food traditions is always presented as the progressive development of authentic national food patterns dating back to ancient times that has never been swayed by external influences but could nevertheless have a beneficial effect on neighboring countries' food cultures (Kim, Chŏng, and Chŏn 1985, 13–20). For example, *miso*

FIGURE 9.2.   A birthday table feast sent by Kim Jong Un to a Japanese repatriate on the occasion of his hundredth birthday (*Korea Magazine* 2014 [9]). Courtesy of *Korea Magazine*.

paste is considered to be a Japanese variation of traditional Korean soy paste, or *chang*, which was adopted by the Japanese during the Koryŏ era (Kim, Chŏng, and Ch'ŏn 1985, 16). Admitting a foreign influence on Korean culture or admiring foreign cultural practices is regarded as a sign of national servility and that is why such discourses contradict the major line of the DPRK ideology that assigns primary importance to stressing autonomous national subjectivity (Person 2016, 212). In this respect, every North Korean tradition is supposed to be indigenous, free from alien borrowings in its development.

What is more, national cuisine is also presented as an expression of the superior character of Korean culture in general. A typical passage that can be found in many types of culinary text at least since the 1980s goes like this:

> Chosŏn cuisine is an outstanding national cuisine that reflects long-standing traditions. By living harmoniously as an ethnically homogeneous nation for a period of five thousand years in our beautiful land, our people have created a unique national cuisine and continue its successful development.
>
> Our unique national cuisine is enriched by its long history, and strongly reflects national characteristics such as creative wisdom and abilities of our wise and diligent people, their discerning tastes and sophisticated palates.
>
> The active promotion and development of our national cuisine by discovering all unique national dishes created since ancient times is necessary not only so that we can independently develop the cooking techniques of our nation, making people's nutrition even more important and refined, but also for invoking in our people feelings of national pride, national self-confidence and patriotism. (Chosŏn ryori hyŏphoe 1994, Vol. 2, 3)

Sources continually stress the importance of national food as an integral part of national culture that deserves admiration and praise, strongly support it against cuisines from elsewhere, and emphasize its superiority over other national food traditions. However, all these things are possible only thanks to the leader's will. In the DPRK no tradition—either real or invented—can exist without the leader's symbolic blessing. Typically, the *Handbook on Regional Dishes* points out that, "thanks to benevolent interest and enormous care of our beloved and respected leader, our national cuisine today is developing in diverse ways on the basis of traditional regional cookery and in accordance with the socialist way of life and contemporary tastes, contributing to the development of world gastronomy" (Cho 2010, 3). It is therefore the leader who decides which part of the national food tradition is the most representative and which aspect of tradition to pursue. The leader gives instructions on cooking technologies, ingredients, and even the material the utensils are made of. For example, in his well-known speech *We Must Actively Promote and Develop National Cuisine* addressed to the party central committee's members after visiting a national food exhibition on June 20, 2004, Kim Jong Il begins by pointing out that "our nation's outstanding cuisine could develop and become famous around the world due to the great leader (Kim Il Sung), who has devoted much effort to it and to cultivating patriotic feelings with the help of national food" (2006, 238). Kim Jong Il names in the speech two of the most important North Korean national dishes—*sinsŏllo* (a Korean variety of hotpot) and Pyongyang *raengmyŏn* (Pyongyang-style cold noodles) (Kim 2006, 238)—and describes in detail how *sinsŏllo* is to be cooked, what ingredients should be used (according to Kim Jong Il, the must-have items are sea cucumber and shrimp) in order to produce the classic dish. Below he adds that tableware should not be made of brass, which looks "reactionary" (*pokkojuŭi*) stating that porcelain is preferable (Kim 2006, 240).

In this respect, it is interesting to point out another noteworthy detail of the North Korean national food narrative—persistently emphasizing the need to "develop" (*palchŏn-sik'igi*) or "develop and enrich" (*palchŏn-p'ungbuhwa sik'igi*) the traditional dishes in accordance with the socialist way of life, contemporary tastes/demands, and/or Juche ideas. The party has elaborated the whole complex of ideology (*sasang*) and guiding directives (*ryŏngdo*) for this development (see *Chosŏn minjok-ryori-palchŏn-ŭl wihan uri tang-ŭi widaehan ryŏngdo* 2013; *Chosŏn minjok-ryori-rŭl kyesŭng-palchŏn-sik'il-te taehan uri tang-ŭi sasang* 2014). This shows that the North Korean leadership values not so much the originality and antiquity of the national traditions but their correspondence with the basic ideological principles of the state. That is why, if necessary, the traditions can be altered. This fact is openly acknowledged by the authorities and demonstrates the leadership autonomy over cultural heritage that in these cases use the formula—"national in form, socialist in contents" (Kim 1982).

FOOD TRADITIONS INVENTED IN THE ERA OF KIM JONG IL

Kim Jong Il occupies a special place among the three North Korean leaders of the modern era in terms of the invention of food traditions. Until now he was the most active of the three in his participation in the construction of North Korean food narratives for several reasons. First, beginning in the 1960s he was responsible for agitprop in the artistic and cultural spheres, so it was his job to manage and control the process of building official discourse on national culture, tradition, and heritage issues. It is accepted that he was very energetic in this role. Second, the start of his leadership coincided with a devastating famine that lasted from 1994 until 1998 (also known as *konan-ŭi haenggun* or Arduous March), so he had no choice but to become deeply involved in addressing food-related problems. Third, as many observers attested, Kim Jong Il was a gourmet himself, so cuisine had a special personal meaning for him (Fujimoto 2003, 143–144; Pulikovskiy 2002, 59–62). There is a famous portrait photo of Kim Jong Il that can be seen in several public places in Pyongyang today, including the prominent Ongnyugwan restaurant and the top-end Haemaji restaurant complex located on Ch'angjŏn Street. The photo depicts the leader in the kitchen in a very informal outfit cooking chicken breasts. The text below the portrait says: "Cooking is a science and an art" (*ryori-nŭn kwahag-igo yesul-ida*)—a phrase attributed to Kim himself. All these factors support my argument that Kim Jong Il was the most influential leader in terms of the development of the North Korean food tradition narrative—an assertion that can also be indirectly confirmed by looking at North Korean paintings: the majority of the artworks featuring food-related topics together with a leader's image shows Kim Jong Il rather than the other two North Korean leaders.

A distinctive feature of the national food narrative during the Kim Jong Il era (1994–2011) was the invention of what I call "guerrilla cuisine," reflecting official descriptions of eating practices that occurred during Kim Il Sung's anti-Japanese guerrilla struggle. For obvious reasons, these

practices are nothing like haute cuisine; the term applies to very unso-
phisticated cooking techniques and humble, low-status, readily accessible ingredients such as wild herbs, grass roots, tree bark, rice bran, and
residue left over from brewing. Reasonably enough, the guerrilla cuisine
rhetoric often goes hand in hand with references to Kim Il Sung's memoir
Segiwa tŏburŏ [With the century] published in the 1990s.

One of the lesser known North Korean eating practices, which can
be regarded as an example of guerrilla cuisine, is frog meat consumption. Nowadays it is possible to find this unusual product on the menu of
some North Korean restaurants as well as in food stores in Pyongyang.
The price of frog is sometimes higher than chicken, clearly indicating that
this is not a food for those deprived of other sources of nutrition (fig. 9.3).

Today North Korean edible frogs are reared at the Taedonggang terrapin farm (*Taedonggang chara kongjang*), constructed in 2011 under
the direct supervision of Kim Jong Il, who treated it as a personal project
with the official goal of feeding the nation with the most nutritional food.
Kim Jong Il personally inspected the farm on October 13, 2011 (*Chosŏn
Sinbo*, October 14, 2011).

It is important to add here that frogs have never been a part of the
mainstream culinary tradition of premodern Korea, although they were

FIGURE 9.3.   Kwangbok Street Pyongyang restaurant price board advertising
a dish prepared of fresh bullfrogs (*san sogeguri*). Photo by author, 2017.

완공된 료리전문식당

도마도튀각   련어회

위대한 장군님께서는 주체99 (2010) 년 10월 17일 료리전문식당에서 세계적으로
이름난 료리들을 봉사할데 대하여 교시하시였다.

FIGURE 9.4. Pyongyang's Ongnyugwan Restaurant poster featuring Kim
Jong Il's praise for world-famous dishes like frogmeat and pizza. Photo by author,
2017.

a minor local custom in northern areas of the Peninsula.[2] Apparently, the
practice came to Korea from China, where frog is historically considered
a delicacy (Chang 1977, 30, 131, 169). There is also oral evidence to the
effect that at the beginning of the twentieth century Korean children
in the countryside used to catch frogs in the rice paddies and fry them.
However, they usually did it mainly for their own amusement rather than
as a famine-relief measure.[3] However it is also possible to find accounts
of eating frogs as a sign of severe food shortages in the mid-1990s (see
Demick 2009, 137, 164).

Nevertheless, dishes prepared from frog are offered today not only in
Pyongyang but also in some North Korean restaurants located abroad. For
instance, the Moscow restaurant *Koryo*, which positions itself as a specialist in traditional Korean cuisine, serves *kaeguri-twidari-t'wigi* (deep-fried
frogs' legs). According to the manager of *Koryo*, the dish was included in

the menu due to its rich nutritional qualities and high gastronomic status that is well recognized even in prestigious French cuisine.[4]

There is also evidence that in the 2000s it was possible to sample frog dishes in several restaurants for foreigners (*oehwa-siktang*) in Pyongyang, where frog was referred to as *hanŭltak*.[5] This Korean word translates literally as "heaven chicken" (an inaccurate translation of the Chinese name for the dish[6]). The same name can be found in one of the main North Korean online propaganda resources, *Uri minjok-kkiri* that in the second part of the 2000s tells an anecdote in its "Literature for the young" (*chŏngnyŏn munhak*) and "Revolutionary legends" (*hyŏngmyŏng chŏnsŏl*) sections. The anecdote tells of a time in 1940 when Kim Il Sung and an unnamed Soviet intelligence officer had drinks together, and due to wartime food shortages they had nothing but frog as a side dish. Talking about this later, Kim Il Sung called the dish *hanŭltak* in order to save face for the Soviet officer who had asked him not to tell anyone (especially the officer's wife) about this embarrassing episode. At first, the leader explains that *hanŭltak* is "a rare and expensive dish offered only to special guests," but later reveals its true origin, making the audience laugh and admire his tactfulness, outstanding wit, and sense of humor (Uri minjok-kkiri 2007/2009).

Interestingly, there is no mention of this episode or the *hanŭltak* dish in Kim Il Sung's memoir, but in the eighth volume published in 1998 (four years after Kim's death) suddenly a passage appears about the Great Leader's experience of eating frogs. According to the memoir, the episode took place on May Day (May 1), 1940 (same year quoted in the "revolutionary legend") when he was fighting with his guerrilla unit against Japanese troops:

> We were so hard up that we ate frog legs on May Day that year. In some countries, fashionable restaurants serve frog legs as gourmet food, but in our country no restaurant serves frog legs. It is true that children catch frogs in rice fields or in brooks and broil them skewered on sticks. But they do this not for the taste of the meat but mostly for fun. . . . Although guerrilla life was arduous, we had never gone hungry on a May Day before. On the May Day of 1939 on the Xiaodeshui plateau, we even served liquor to our fighters. On the May Day of 1940, however, liquor was out of question; we had nothing to eat at all. So we caught frogs in brooks to allay our hunger. (Kim 1992–1998, vol. 8, 12–13)[7]

It is important to mention here that in the memoir the leader openly admits that he would have preferred other food if he'd had a choice, and only the severe shortages made him offer such an ignoble dish to his soldiers. Kim Il Sung encourages them by saying: "Comrades, although we celebrate May Day by eating frog meat today, we will defeat Japanese imperialism and celebrate the liberation of our homeland in Pyongyang by feasting on cold noodles and the soup of mullet caught in the Taedong River" (Kim 1992–1998, vol. 8, 12–13). However, in the secondary sources published in the 2000s (for example, the abovementioned *Uri minjok-kkiri*) this story is presented as an example of the heroic overcoming of hardships and the leader's optimism and lack of pretention, and this is how the anecdote and the frog dishes gain their positive connotations. Thus, in the 2000s, guerrilla cuisine is intended to evoke in North Koreans a warm feeling of nostalgia for the years of the supreme leader's youth, his heroic struggle against the imperialists and the harsh but romantic days of the Korean revolution. According to North Korean propaganda, the frog dish consumption (though in a contemporary civilized form) can contribute to this sense of nostalgia.

This is not to say that today frog is a popular and ubiquitous food product in the DPRK, and it is doubtful that North Koreans eat it on a regular basis. Recipe books do not include the dish in their contents and the *hanŭltak* word is not in the dictionaries yet. Of course, it is still an exotic dish for ordinary North Koreans and for diners in any North Korean restaurants that serve this delicacy. Nevertheless, this case is a good example of an attempt (although not a particularly successful one) to artificially construct a food tradition in the DPRK. We can see all the elements of such a construction: appealing to the glorious past, utilizing the figure of the leader, evoking nostalgia, and a sense of national pride. All these contribute to the creation of a certain emotional mixture that is necessary to help a new cultural practice be more easily implemented in North Korean society.

Frog is not the only example of the guerrilla cuisine rhetoric in Kim Jong Il's DPRK. Another example can be seen in the potato revolution campaign (*kamja nongsa hyŏngmyŏng*), which was launched in the late 1990s with the aim of turning the potato into a symbol of prosperity. Historically the potato had been unknown for Koreans for many centuries and was introduced into Korea as an agricultural crop only in the middle of the nineteenth century mainly as a famine relief food and thus for a long time was regarded as a low-status food product (Siegmund 2010, 64). To elevate the symbolic status of potato North Korean propaganda again refers to Kim Il Sung's guerrilla past. In her detailed analysis of the campaign Tatiana Gabroussenko draws attention to the way propaganda utilizes Kim Il Sung's reminiscences about potatoes in promoting a re-evaluation of the staple (2016). Though the leader himself considered potatoes inferior to more nutritious food products such as rice or meat, North Korean ideologists of the 2000s downplayed connections between the potato and poverty. Instead they stressed its symbolic meaning associated with the leader's memory of the "warmth of the people's hearts, the generosity of the poor toward guerrillas, and the inventiveness of Korean mothers, who managed to cook nutritious dishes for their families despite very limited resources" (Gabroussenko 2016, 131–132).

As far as the potato was concerned, the aim of the propaganda was to invent a new food tradition for quite pragmatic reasons. It was an attempt to feed the army as well as ordinary people with lower farming costs. Unfortunately, these agricultural perspectives failed to materialize, although the ideological effect of the campaign was tangible. The potato has not overtaken rice in the Korean symbolic food hierarchy, but its cultural meaning has become much more established. Even defectors, who are usually highly critical of their former government's initiatives, admit that North Korean potatoes can become an effective food resource for a future united Korea (Yi 2012, 126–127).

There is another example of a national dish invention from Kim Jong Il's era—*kogi-chaengban-kuksu* (meat noodles on a tray)—that was developed by the leader in 1999. The story goes that during times of severe food hardship Kim expressed the desire to feed his people with *eobuk kuksu* (noodles with high-quality beef) that was known as a royal family delicacy back in premodern Korea. In order to adjust the recipe so the dish can be cooked on a large scale for the masses the leader suggested using chicken instead of beef and explained what kind of seasoning should be applied so the taste and nutritional value would be even higher than in the original recipe. The official sources describe this historical event as the "birth of a new national dish" (*Chosŏnŭi Onŭl*, November 7, 2017). Here we can see the immediate example of the "development and enrichment" of the national food tradition made by the leader himself "in accordance with the contemporary demands" as well as the leader in the role of the nation's nourisher.

These examples demonstrate that during the era of Kim Jong Il the North Korean national food narrative developed quite dynamically due to the personal interest and active involvement of the state leader. This development was determined in the first place by external events like the natural calamities of the 1990s and successive famine, as well as political conditions of the time. The highlighting of the relations between guerrilla experience and overcoming hunger can be seen as the ideological response to *konan-ŭi haenggun* or Arduous March. As a matter of fact, the term *konan-ŭi haenggun* itself, used in the DPRK to metaphorically indicate the period of extreme scarcity since the second part of the 1990s, also refers to the long march of survival of the Kim Il Sung–led guerrilla unit at the end of 1938 (fig. 9.5). Thus, the guerrilla discourse was an approved method of interpreting the immediate social realities. Cultural anthropologists Heonik Kwon and Byung-Ho Chung (2012) in their analysis of the North Korean leadership continuity also point out the role of the partisan state idea, military-first politics, and the politics of longing in understanding the mechanics of personality cult and power succession in the DPRK today. Marking the change in the cultural politics in North Korea in recent years, they observe:

> In the mid-1990s the North Korean literature and media tended to emphasize the inventiveness of military-first politics as associated with the genius of Kim Jong Il and his distinctive style of rule. The emphasis has shifted from originality to heritage since the mid-2000s, and the argument has since focused on military-first politics' deep historical and genealogical connections to the origin of the North Korean revolution and the early biographical history of Kim Il Sung. . . . Broadly speaking, the contemporary narrative aims to situate the idea of military-first politics in a sublime family heritage of supremely exemplary revolutionary merit, the progression of which is being crystallized in the persona of Kim Jong Il. (Kwon and Chung 2012, 84–85)

The argument of guerrilla cuisine can be understood within the same conceptual framework. As it was shown above, the tendency to relate the national food narrative to the guerrilla past of Kim Il Sung emerged

FIGURE 9.5.   Revolution Museum photo showing dishes developed during
the 1990s famine that resemble food allegedly eaten by Kim Il Sung during the
1938 Arduous March. Photo by author, 2017.

mostly since the end of the 1990s and throughout the 2000s. Thus, it is
possible to view the trend of referring to guerrilla cuisine as one of the
elements of the large-scale ideological campaign of legitimizing of Kim
Jong Il as a political successor by connecting *sŏn'gun* ideas with the early
history of the DPRK.

FOOD TRADITIONS CONNECTED TO PRECEPTS FROM THE LEADER

Inventions of culinary traditions are also quite effective for constructing
the rhetoric of the leaders' precepts (*yuhun*) and their fulfillment. In this
regard it is interesting to look at the example of *ŭnjŏngch'a*—North Korean
tea, a name that literally translates as "tea of benevolent care." The name
was coined in 2000 by Kim Jong Il himself as a tribute to his father and
his decision to cultivate tea in the DPRK. As the name suggests, the tea
is a symbolic expression of the leader's endless care and love toward his
people. Here again the leader appears in the role of nourisher of a nation,
and guardian of its health and well-being.

The contemporary sources report that Kim Il Sung ordered the cultivation of tea in North Korea after his visit to Shandong Province in China in September 1982. There, the leader visited the tea plantations and decided to grow tea in Kangnyŏng-gun County, South Hwanghae Province, and in Kosŏng-gun County, Gangwon Province—locations that were situated at the same latitude as Shandong (*Chosŏnŭi Onŭl*, April 23, 2015). That is why until the 2000s, those North Korean tea brands were called Kangnyŏng-ch'a and Kosŏng-ch'a.

Kim Jong Il visited the plantations several times after 2000, and in 2011 ordered a special tearoom (*ŭnjŏngch'a-jip*) to be opened on the prestigious Ch'angjŏn Street in Pyongyang. This happened shortly before his death, so then it fell to Kim Jong Un to fulfill his father's last precept. Kim Jong Un visited the *ŭnjŏngch'a* tearoom in May 2012, where he emphasized the special cultural and symbolic meaning of the tea as the legacy of the two previous North Korean father-leaders and ordered the renovation of the tearoom (Cho 2015).

The North Korean media have covered the tea topic extensively since 2012 describing the Kims' contribution to the tea production industry in the DPRK as a new chapter in the history of Korean tea culture. North Korean television has featured several documentaries about Korean tea

FIGURE 9.6.   One of the places serving *ŭnjŏngch'a* on the streets of Pyongyang. Photo by author, October 2017.

traditions.[8] New academic research on the history of Korean tea culture was published in 2012 and republished in 2014 due to its significance (as explained above [Cho 2012; 2014, 2]). The research was authored by none other than the head of the North Korean Academy of Social Sciences, Professor Cho Hŭi-sŭng, showing the level of importance attributed to the topic.

The narrative of the history of Korean tea culture in the book possesses all the typical features of the general national food narrative that were discussed above. First, it is described as "outstanding" (usuhan) tea culture created by "our wise nation" (sŭlgiroun uri minjok). Second, it is called "unique" (koyuhan) though the author mentions that originally tea came to Korea from China (Cho 2014, 33), and there were many cultural exchanges between these two countries (174). It is also stressed that the national tea culture is an important subject for national pride and patriotic feelings (Cho 2014, 2). A separate chapter is devoted to the idea that Japanese tea culture developed under the direct influence of that of Korea (Cho 2014, 178–195). For the examination of the premodern period of tea history in Korea Cho utilizes a class approach arguing that the reason for the decline of tea drinking in Chosŏn was the sadaejuŭi ideology of the ruling class who preferred foreign types of tea while neglecting the domestic ones of a better quality. On the other hand, common people could not afford to drink tea due to the extreme poverty and exploitation (Cho 2014, 153–156). The colonial period is presented as the time when the Japanese were exploiting Korean resources and inculcating their own tea culture among Koreans (Cho 2014, 160–162). Finally, it is explained that the North Korean tea renaissance came thanks to the leaders' direct will and their personal efforts (Cho 2014, 209–212). In other words, the leaders are presented as the re-creators of tea culture in Korea, and it is the duty of their offspring and the Korean people to keep and develop the tradition.

In this narrative of tea history, we can observe not simply the strong nationalistic discourse so typical for the DPRK ideology but also the North Korean way of imagining its historic past and experience of modernity. The colonial period is always presented as the time when the national cultural identity was on the verge of total elimination and was saved and restored exclusively by the leader's wisdom and efforts. That is why the narrative stresses the importance of following his teachings and fulfilling his precepts in order not to jeopardize the cultural identity again.

Besides this, in the example of *ŭnjŏngch'a* and the (re)invention of tea-drinking culture in the DPRK we can also see another functional side of the invention of food traditions—the aspiration to elevate the country's cultural status both on the internal and external level. Tea is recognized worldwide as a powerful cultural symbol of Far East civilizations (for example, Chinese tea-drinking traditions, the Japanese tea ceremony). Thus, the availability of tea-drinking culture can contribute not only to the gentrification of the general cultural image of the country but also (more pragmatically) to the stimulation of food exports and tourism. In this respect, both Koreas are trying hard to re-establish tea-drinking traditions, each according to its specific ideology. Curiously enough, in the ROK the surge of interest in traditional tea culture also came at the beginning of the 1980s (Lankov 2006, 421), suggesting the North's attempt to re-create its tea industry might have been a response to the South's resurrection of its tea culture. However, in both Koreas contemporary tea-drinking customs are clearly an invented tradition because historically the majority of the population did not drink green or black tea on a regular basis (Kim 2008).

THE CURRENT SITUATION

At first glance, the third North Korean leader, Kim Jong Un, who came to power in 2011, adheres to his father's line as far as national food discourse is concerned. He provides on-the-spot guidance at farms, food factories, and places of public catering, where he continues to emphasize the key role of his father and grandfather in national food security, calling for the fulfillment of their precepts. Like his predecessors, Kim Jong Un stresses the need to encourage preparing national dishes among other tasks in the development of a national culture (Kim 2015, 5–6). Kim Jong Il's speech of 2004 about the need to develop a national cuisine is still regarded as the main guiding line in this respect.[9] However, it is possible to trace certain minor shifts in the North Korean foodscape and food narrative that reflect the general trends in Kim Jong Un's Korea.

First, there is a trend toward the liberalization of the restaurant business. This began slowly under Kim Jong Il (Lankov 2007, 93) but today it is developing more actively and is enthusiastically celebrated in the North

Korean press. Nowadays restaurants and cafes are openly presented in the official discourse as places of leisure and forms of public entertainment. This is quite a recent trend as historically the economic model of the DPRK emphasized primarily heavy industry and the militarization of the economy. Tatiana Gabroussenko points out that within this model consumption was understandably discouraged while altruism and asceticism were endorsed as the core values of the North Korean mentality (2015, 120). In Kim Il Sung's time, eating out was never promoted in the official sources as an appropriate form of entertainment for a worker, the focus being on food production rather than consumption. However, today eating-out practices are officially promoted and have been elevated in status. The media strongly advocates the popularity of restaurants, bars, and coffee shops among ordinary North Koreans as places of recreation and healthy entertainment for workers. It is also possible to observe such modern elements of consumption culture as street food, food blogs, TV food shows, and even food e-shopping in the DPRK (though still at a comparatively elementary level compared to international standards) (Gabroussenko 2017).

Second, Kim Jong Un's propaganda has also gradually started to enlist food topics for the construction of the DPRK's international image. There are considerably more articles introducing national food, reports on culinary contests and food festivals held in the DPRK than there used to be in the external propaganda sources of the DPRK. In 2016 the National Association of Korean Cuisine (Chosŏn ryori hyŏp'oe, founded in 1988) launched its website, which can be visited even from abroad.[10] Periodicals oriented at the foreign public, as well as reference books on North Korea published after 2011, offer more space than before to stories and images of national dishes as symbols of the DPRK (see Kang, Han, and Kim 2013, 140–142). However, it should be noted that these types of resources stress the high nutritional values and/or the (pseudo)historic aspects of national food traditions (*The Pyongyang Times*, March 5, 2016),[11] while the role of the leader is usually mentioned less and tends to be saved for domestic propaganda.

One of the most notable examples is the Taedonggang beer festival, inaugurated in Pyongyang in August 2016, which the foreign media dubbed "the North Korean Oktoberfest." If we compare the media coverage of the event for internal and external audiences, we can see that although the contents are almost the same, the focus is different. The main North Korean newspaper, *Rodong Sinmun*, did not report on the festival in its pages, but there are several short articles in the digital version of the newspaper. They mostly stressed the role of the party in providing the setting and conditions for the festival and pointed out that it was Kim Jong Il who had initiated the large-scale production of Taedonggang beer in the DPRK—for which the general population was grateful. The article mentions that a special video about Kim Jong Il's contribution to the beer industry in the DPRK was shown to festivalgoers on the first day of the event (*Rodong Sinmun*, August 13, 2016). However, the English-language *Pyongyang Times* (August 20, 2016) stresses the high quality of the beer and its comparability with the leading world brands such as "Heineken, Carlsberg, Tsingtao and Asahi." The article also stressed the safety of the ingredients and the beer's positive medical effects on people's health (this was even confirmed by "clinical tests" according to the article). However, much attention in both sources was given to the description of the "cheerful mood of the festival," the intention of which was supposedly to demonstrate that life in the DPRK is affluent, joyful, and relaxed despite the harsh international economic sanctions.

Another noteworthy event that took place after Kim Jong Un came to power was the inclusion of the North Korean kimchi-making tradition in the UNESCO World Intangible Culture Heritage list on December 4, 2015. Although this was not reported immediately, and was not front-page news in the DPRK, official sources proudly noted "the vitality of the DPRK's government policy on the protection of national heritage" (Pang 2015). However, reports missed the fact that the list already had a kimchi-making tradition—the one from the South, which had been included two years earlier, in December 2013. The same happened to the *Arirang* folk song, which was included in the UNESCO list from the South Korean side in 2012 and two years later from the North Korean side. The song became the first North Korean World Intangible Culture Heritage item on the list. These examples illustrate how propaganda has started to see the resource of national food traditions as a soft power mechanism and an effective instrument for constructing a positive global image. The process was apparently enabled under the indirect influence of the South Korean *hansik* globalization campaign, launched by the government in 2008, and many other recent gastronomic PR activities of the ROK (Osetrova

2016a, 105–125), as well as the recent world fashion for culinary diplomacy (Chapple-Sokol 2013). In this respect, the sphere of national food can also be seen as a space for inter-Korean cultural controversy, as both sides claim authenticity for their version of the national food tradition—especially given the fact that North Korean restaurants abroad serve not only as a source of hard currency for the regime but also as an instrument of public cultural diplomacy on behalf of the DPRK (Osetrova 2016b).

As already stated, the differences between the two versions of Korean culinary tradition can be seen in their official names—*hansik* and *Chosŏn ryori*—that relate to the proper names of the two states themselves. This means that national food tradition is incorporated into the pantheon of national cultural symbols that define Korean identity together with national costume, traditional housing, and the Korean writing system. The DPRK and ROK since the moment of their foundation sought to prove to each other as well as to the rest of the world that each is the true Korea. Of course, national cuisine was never the primary argument in this debate, but it still matters, since Korean food is an indispensable part of the life of any Korean regardless of his/her citizenship, social background, or ideological viewpoint.

Both states defend their version of the national cuisine claiming that their counterpart has failed to preserve a pure traditional taste. The North affirms that the ROK has lost it by blindly following Western (American) lifestyle and globalization trends. Also the North claims that Koreans in the South add too much chemical seasoning to their dishes and in doing so destroy original recipes.[12] The South contends that in the DPRK any cultural practice is defined by the personality cult and socialist ideas rather than historical patterns.

Such mutual accusations have tended to escalate during the periods of inter-Korean alienation and sometimes take on really absurd manifestations. For example, President Lee Myung-bak and President Park Geun-hye were notorious for their anti-DPRK positions, and during their terms in office the Ministry of Foreign Affairs officially asked ROK citizens to refrain from visiting North Korean restaurants when they were abroad. The authorities justified this measure as a part of their efforts to stem the flow of hard currency to the Kim Jong Un government and the development of its nuclear program (*The Korea Times*, February 17, 2016). On the other hand, during the periods of more amicable relations both sides demonstrate interest in each other's gastronomic cultures. There are several examples of this, notably when North Korean restaurants were opened in the South. Recently, after the historic inter-Korean summits of 2018 a joint documentary entitled *Seoul and Pyongyang: The Story of Two Cities* was filmed in both Korean capitals, with the first episode devoted to the topic of Korean cuisine. This episode ends with a scene where two young men, one South Korean and one from the North, sit and eat together. The image of a shared table became the emblem of reconciliation between the two states (*Han'guk Kyŏngje*, September 23, 2018).

All of this provides evidence that both Koreas closely monitor each other's activities in the sphere of national cuisine promotion and respond if the other side makes a move. Such a mutual influence can be seen in the case of the re-invention of tea culture, in the case of kimchi registration in the UNESCO list, and more broadly in the general elevation of the status of food as a tool of a country's global image construction. By doing so, both countries not only compete for cultural authenticity but at the same time receive commercial benefits, through the establishment of restaurants abroad, advertising, and the sale of food products. For these purposes both states invent traditions. There are also important commonalities between the South and North over their representation of their respective cuisines, especially in their stress on the health and well-being of their food culture, its ancient and exotic roots. Another similarity in the North-South national food narrative is a similar emphasis on uniqueness. Both distinguish between their cuisine and that of other countries and emphasize the qualitative superiority of their food products compared with the world beyond the Korean Peninsula. However, the North's culinary narrative omits the pronounced nostalgic connotations typical of the South's, such as references to mother's cooking or the tastes of childhood. The North replaces these familial associations with claims of technological progress, the improvement of people's nourishment, and devotion to the leader.

As shown above, the North Korean national food narrative is closely connected to the country's state ideology and is therefore often mobilized to help with its immediate tasks. To do this, certain food traditions can be invented. At first glance, the main reason for these inventions might appear to be the food shortage problem for which the DPRK was notorious, especially in the 1990s. However, a closer study of the North Korean national food narrative reveals that the actual reasons are more diverse.

Eric Hobsbawm wrote that "invented traditions seek to inculcate certain values and norms of behaviour by repetition" (1983, 1). This statement proves true in the case of food traditions. Due to their strong connection to everyday life they become one of the best tools for inculcating values and norms of behavior and so help to shape a collective identity. Eating the same things in the same way makes people feel that they belong to one community. Thus, the invention of new Korean food traditions can be seen as an instrument for unifying the North Korean people. These new elements in North Korean food culture and imagery allow the regime to construct new, Juche-styled worldviews and life patterns that contribute to the formation of the accepted national identity on a very basic and mundane level—that of dietary culture. The interweaving of the leader's image into the fabric of the country's food ideology helps to reinforce the relationship between the people and power. In this context, the analogy of the father feeding his children contributes to the creation of the sense of family bonds in North Korean society.

Invented food traditions also help in what Kwon and Chung called "legacy politics" that played a vital role in the complex process of the symbolic transfer of power in the DPRK (2012, 44, 72). The examples of guerrilla cuisine and ŭnjŏngch'a support this argument. By linking the contemporary national eating patterns to the food precepts left by Kim Il Sung, the propaganda legitimized Kim Jong Il and later Kim Jung Un as political successors of the first North Korean leader. The leader is the one who is mapping the changing boundaries of the national food tradition discourse. He has the right to decide what can be officially considered Korean traditional food and what is to be excluded from this domain. He also has the power to develop the national food tradition by including new elements in it. This is one of the most effective ways of inventing food traditions in the DPRK. This explains, for instance, why menu cards of Korean restaurants located abroad have dishes like frog legs. This is not only because Kim Il Sung consumed it back in his guerrilla days, but also because his son decided in the 2000s that Korean people should eat it because of its internationally acknowledged gastronomic reputation, as well as being an easily accessible source of protein.

The national food narrative is adjusted in the DPRK and in its state-run restaurants abroad to demarcate *Chosŏn ryori* from the *hansik* of its southern rival and to demonstrate to international audiences that *Chosŏn ryori* is the correct and authentic version of a Korean national cuisine. The invention of culinary tradition is an effective tool used by both Koreas in the formation of distinct cultural identities for both internal and external consumption. How the two states represent their respective culinary culture correlates with how they would like their values to be understood. State concepts of food also reflect official and public understandings of national self. For North Koreans their food is supposed to be infused with the love of the leader. By eating in the way the leader dictates, North Koreans articulate the importance of the teachings of the leader in their everyday life. This discourse cannot be found in the South where Koreans transmit different cultural meanings through their food practices. This is direct evidence of the connection between national cuisine and collective identity.

GLOSSARY

ch'ŏn 天
ch'ŏn 田
Chosŏn ryori 조선료리
hansik 한식
Juche (Chuch'e) 주체

kogi-chaengban-kuksu 고기쟁반
국수
Pyongyang-raengmyŏn 평양랭면
shinsŏllo 신선로
tian ji 田鸡
ŭnjŏngch'a 은정차

NOTES

1. This maxim can be found in the text of Kim Il Sung's speech at the joint session of the Workers' Party of Korea central committee and Supreme People's Assembly on April 14, 1982. However, it is also attributed to his earlier works, namely *the Letter to the Heads of P'yŏngan-namdo Party Committees* [P'yŏngannamdo-dang wiwŏnjang-ege ponaen sŏhan] dated January 28, 1956. There it appears as "rice is socialism" (*ssar-ŭn kot sahoejuŭi-ida*).
2. See the online article on local dishes (*hyangt'o ŭmsik*) in *Han'guk minjok munhwa taebaekkwa sajŏn* (n.d.).
3. From a discussion with Dr. Kim Young-woong, a leading researcher of the Center for Korean Studies, Institute of Far Eastern Studies, Russian Academy of Sciences, February 2016. Dr. Kim heard about this eating practice from his father who was born in Korea in 1914 in Hamgyŏng-namdo Province.

4. Information received through field study of North Korean restaurants located in Moscow. The field study was conducted by the author in January–February 2016 (for details see Osetrova 2016b).

5. For example, see the following entry from a personal blog of Kwŏn Hyŏn-ch'ŏl (2004).

6. The explanation of the "heaven chicken" name's etymology proves the Chinese origin of the term. The original word for frog dish in Chinese is *tian ji*, which literally means "chicken in the farmland." Due to the similar pronunciation (*ch'ŏn*) of the characters for farmland and heaven it mistakenly became "heaven chicken" in Korean.

7. The English translation of the passage is taken from the website of the Korean Friendship Association (KFA) that published the full-text translation of Kim Il Sung's memoir in 2003. Accessed June, 2017. https://www.korea-dpr.com/lib/202.pdf

8. For example, see the following video on the *Uri minjok-kkiri* YouTube channel (2014).

9. See the article in *Rodong Sinmun* written by the head of the Department of Public Services (*inmin pongsa ch'ongguk*), Kim Mi-ok, on the occasion of celebrating the ten-year anniversary of the national cuisine speech of Kim Jong Il (Kim 2014).

10. See http://cooks.org.kp/, accessed December 29, 2017. This is an official website of the DPRK national association of Korean cuisine (Chosŏn ryori hyŏp'oe).

11. One of the possible examples of such pseudo-historic narratives is the mythologized story of the origin of *sinsŏllo* (a Korean variety of hotpot). For instance, the March 5, 2016, *Pyongyang Times* (the main English-language organ of external propaganda) writes that "between the late fifteenth and early sixteenth centuries an old man who lived in a mountain boiled food in the brazier, an old document says, and he looked like a wizard, hence the name *sinsŏllo*, or "wizard's brazier."

12. Information received by the author during her meeting with the representatives of the national association of Korean cuisine (*Chosŏn ryori hyŏp'oe*) on October 23, 2017.

REFERENCES

Chang, Kwang-chih, ed. 1977. *Food in Chinese Culture: Anthropological and Historical Perspectives*. New Haven, CT: Yale University Press.

Chapple-Sokol, Sam. 2013. "Culinary Diplomacy: Breaking Bread to Win Hearts and Minds." *The Hague Journal of Diplomacy* 8:161–183.

Cho Chŏng-hun. 2015. "Kim Jong Il yuhun chung hanan-ŭn ŭnjŏngch'a" [Ŭnjŏngch'a is one of Kim Jong Il's precepts]. *Tongil News*, April 24. Accessed June 28, 2017. http://www.tongilnews.com/news/articleView.html?idxno =111768

Cho Hŭi-sŭng. 2012. *Ch'a-ŭi ryŏksa-wa munhwa* [The history and culture of tea]. Pyongyang: Kwahak-paekkwa-sajŏn ch'ulp'ansa.

————. 2014. *Ch'a-munhwa-ŭi ryŏksa* [The history of tea culture]. Pyongyang: Pyongyang ch'ulp'ansa.

Cho Tae-il. 2010. *Chibang ŭmsik p'yŏllam* [Handbook on regional dishes]. Pyongyang: Sahoe kwahak ch'ulp'ansa.

Chosŏn minjok-ryori-palchŏn-ŭl wihan uri tang-ŭi widaehan ryŏngdo [Great guidance of our party regarding the development of Korean national cuisine]. 2013. Pyongyang: Sahoe kwahak ch'ulp'ansa.

Chosŏn minjok-ryori-rŭl kyesŭng-palchŏn-sik'il-te taehan uri tang-ŭi sasang [Ideology of our party regarding inheriting and development of Korean national cuisine]. 2014. Pyongyang: Sahoe kwahak ch'ulp'ansa.

Chosŏn ryori hyŏphoe. 1994. *Chosŏn ryori chŏnjip* [Complete collection of Korean cuisine recipe]. Pyongyang: Oegukmun-jonghap ch'ulp'ansa.

Chosŏn Sinbo. 2011. "Kim Jong Il-changgunnim, Taedonggang-chara-kongjang-ŭl hyŏnji-chido" [Kim Jong Il conducted field guidance of Taedonggang terrapin farm]. October 14. Accessed June 2, 2017. http://chosonsinbo.com/2011/10 /kcna_111014

Chosŏnmal taesajŏn [Grand dictionary of Korean language]. 1992. Pyongyang: Sahoe kwahak ch'ulp'ansa.

Chosŏnŭi Onŭl [The DPRK today]. 2015. "Kŭ irŭm-do yujŏnghan chosŏn-ŭi ŭnjŏngch'a (1)" [Ŭnjŏngch'a—the Chosŏn tea with a warmhearted name (1)]. April 23. Accessed June 28, 2017. http://www.dprktoday.com/index.php?type =2&no=2971

————. 2017. "Kogi-chaengban-kuksu-e kittŭn sayŏn" [The circumstances around the kogi-chaengban-kuksu]. November 7. Accessed December 28, 2017. http://www.dprktoday.com/index.php?type=2&no=26142

Cwiertka, Katarzyna J. 2012. *Cuisine, Colonialism and Cold War: Food in Twentieth-Century Korea*. London: Reaktion Books.

Demick, Barbara. 2009. *Nothing to Envy: Ordinary Lives in North Korea*. New York: Spiegel and Grau.

Fujimoto, Kenji. 2003. *Kim Jŏng Ir-ŭi yorisa* [Kim Jong Il's chef]. Seoul: Wŏlgan-chosŏnsa.

Gabroussenko, Tatiana. 2015. "Well-Nourished Beauty: Culinary Symbolism in the Mass Culture of North Korea, 1960–2014." *Tiempo devorado* [Time devoured] 2 (2): 119–135. Accessed May 15, 2017. doi: http://revistes.uab .cat/tdevorado/article/view/v2-n2-tgabroussenko

———. 2016. "The Potato Revolution in the DPRK: A Novel Type of Political Campaign." *Korea Journal* 56 (1): 116–139.

———. 2017. "Iron and Rice: Food Culture in North Korean Movies." NKnews .org, December 21. Accessed December 28, 2017. https://www.nknews.org /2017/12/iron-and-rice-food-culture-in-north-korean-movies

Han'guk Kyŏngje. 2018. "'Seoul Pyongyang, tu tosi iyagi' Pyongyang 4 tae eumsik-kwa ch'ŏngnyugwan chubang konggae" [The story of two cities: Entering the kitchens of four Pyongyang restaurants]. September 23. Accessed October 10, 2019. https://www.hankyung.com/entertainment/article/2018092344094

Han'guk minjok munhwa taebaekkwa sajŏn [Encyclopedia of Korean culture]. N.d. Accessed May 9, 2020. http://encykorea.aks.ac.kr/Contents/Index ?contents_id=E0062997

Hobsbawm, Eric. 1983. "Introduction: Inventing Traditions." In *The Invention of Tradition,* edited by Eric Hobsbawm and Terence Ranger, 1–15. Cambridge: Cambridge University Press.

Kang Ryong-shil, Han Pong-ch'an, and Kim Chi-ho. 2013. Obzor po Koree [Overview on Korea]. Pyongyang: Izdatelstvo literatury na inostrannykh yasykakh [in Russian].

Kim Il Sung. 1991. Sochineniya [Writings] 37 (January 1982–May 1983). Pyongyang: Izdatelstvo literatury na inostrannykh yazykakh [in Russian].

———. 1992–1998. *Segiwa tŏburŏ* [With the century]. Pyongyang: Paektusan p'yŏnjippu.

Kim Jong Il. 1982. *Chuch'e sasange taehayŏ* [On the Juche idea]. Pyongyang: Chosŏn rodongdang ch'ulp'ansa.

———. 2006. "Minjok ŭmsik-ŭl chŏkkŭng changnyŏhago palchŏnsik'yŏnagaya handa" [We must actively promote and develop national cuisine]. In *Minjok munhwa yusan-gwa minjok-chŏk chŏnt'ong-e taehayŏ* [On the issue of national cultural heritage and national tradition], 237–244. Pyongyang: Chosŏn rodongdang ch'ulp'ansa.

———. 2010. *Utverdit sotsialisticheskuyu kulturu byta, kak togo trebuet epokha songun* [To strengthen socialist life culture as *seongun* era demands it]. Moscow: Obshcestvo dryzhby i razvitiya sotrudnichestva s zarubezhnymi stranami [in Russian].

Kim Jong Un. 2015. *Okhrana natsionalnogo naslediya—patrioticheskoe delo, natselennoe na proslavlenie istorii i traditsiy nashei natsii* [National heritage protection is a patriotic work aimed at glorification of history and traditions of our nation]. Moscow: Rossiyskiy pisatel [in Russian].

Kim Mi-ok. 2014. "Minjok ŭmsikŭl palchŏnsik'inŭn kŏsŭn uri tangŭi ilgwanhan chŏngch'aek" [Development of national cuisine is the consistent policy of our party]. *Rodong Sinmun,* June 29.

Kim Pok-cho, Chŏng Sun-hwa, and Ch'ŏn Sŏk-kŭn. 1985. *Sahoejuŭi saenghwal-munhwa-baekkwa* [Encyclopedia of socialist lifestyle and culture]. Vol. 1. *Chosŏn ŭmsik* [Korean food]. Pyongyang: Kŭllo tanch'e ch'ulp'ansa.

Kim Tong-myŏng. 2008. "Singminji shigi ch'a-ŭi munhwa jŏppyŏn" [A study of acculturation of green tea in colonial Korea under Japanese rule]. *Hanilgwan'gyesa yŏn'gu* [Research of the history of Korean-Japanese relations] 31 (31): 133–167.

The Korea Times. 2016. "South Koreans asked not to eat at NK restaurants." February 17. Accessed October 9, 2019. http://www.koreatimes.co.kr/www/news /nation/2016/02/485_198258.html

Kukka misul chŏllamhoe. Chosŏn minjujuŭi inmin konghwaguk ch'anggŏn 60-tol kyŏngch'uk. [Exhibition of the state fine art. On the occasion of the 60th anniversary of the foundation of the DPRK]. 2009. Pyongyang: Pyongyang yesul ch'ulp'ansa.

Kwon, Heonik, and Byung-Ho Chung. 2012. *North Korea: Beyond Charismatic Politics*. Lanham, MD: Rowman and Littlefield Publishers.

Kwŏn Hyŏn-ch'ŏl. 2004. "Puk'anmal paeugi" [Learning the North Korean language]. *Pighc's Blog*, October 6. Accessed March 17, 2017. http://blog.naver.com /pighc/40003201168

Lankov, Andrei. 1995. *Severnaya Korea: vchera i segodnya* [North Korea: yesterday and today]. Moscow: Vostochnaya literatura [in Russian].

———. 2006. *Byt' koreitsem* [To be Korean]. Moscow: AST [in Russian].

———. 2007. *North of the DMZ: Essays on Daily Life in North Korea*. Jefferson, NC: McFarland and Co.

Osetrova, Maria. 2016a. "National Food and Gastronationalism in Contemporary Korea." PhD diss., Yonsei University. Available online at http:// dcollection.yonsei.ac.kr/public_resource/pdf/000000448040_20171230201144 .pdf

———. 2016b. "Severokoreiskaya kukhnya kak sredstvo publichnoi diplomatii" [North Korean cuisine as an instrument of public diplomacy]. In *Koreiskiy poluostrov v epokhu peremen* [Korean Peninsula in the epoch of change], edited by Alexander Zhebin, 369–379. Moscow: Institute of Far Eastern Studies [in Russian].

Pang Un-ju. 2015. "Kimchi making custom inscribed as world heritage." *The Pyongyang Times*, December 24. Accessed June 20, 2017. http://www.naenara .com.kp/en/order/pytimes/?page=Culture&no=21321

Person, James F. 2016. "North Korea's Chuch'e Philosophy." In *Routledge Handbook of Modern Korean History*, edited by Michael J. Seth, 211–220. London: Routledge.

Pulikovskiy, Konstantin. 2002. *Vostochnyi express: po Rossii s Kim Chen Irom*

[Eastern express: Crossing Russia with Kim Jong Il]. Moscow: Gorodets [in Russian].

The Pyongyang Times. 2016. *"Sinsŏllo,* a Pride of Korean Food." March 5.

Rodong Sinmun. 2016. "Pyongyang Taedonggang maekchu ch'ukchŏn kaemak." [Pyongyang Taedonggang beer festival opens]. August 13. Accessed July 27, 2017. http://www.rodong.rep.kp/ko/index.php?strPageID=SF01_02_01&newsID =2016-08-13-4001

Siegmund, Felix. 2010. "Tubers in a Grain Culture: The Introduction of Sweet and White Potatoes to Chosŏn Korea and Its Cultural Implications." *Korean Histories* 2 (2): 59–74. Accessed December 28, 2017. https://koreanhistorieswebsite .files.wordpress.com/2017/04/kh2_2_siegmund_tubers.pdf

Uri minjok-kkiri. 2007/2009. "Hanŭltak-kogi" [The meat of heaven chicken]. May 14/October 27. Accessed March 25, 2017.

Uri minjok-kkiri. 2014. "Nanari chit'ŏganŭn ŭnjŏngch'a hyanggi" [The fragrance of ŭnjŏngch'a that goes stronger day by day]. September 11. Accessed June 28, 2017. https://www.youtube.com/watch?v=2mH0yMEC-RU

Yi Ae-ran. 2012. *Pukhan sikkaek* [North Korean gourmet]. Seoul: Ungjin ribing-hausŭ.

PART IV

Embodying Tradition

Spaces

Introduction

CODRUȚA SÎNTIONEAN

Some invented traditions entail a direct engagement of their consumers and performers with a specific space or landscape, in ways that are carefully constructed and regulated. The institutions and authorities that manufacture traditions deliberately anchor them in a prescribed space because of the potency of physical experience to engage, and so, to persuasively convey a message or a narrative. Some invented traditions involve the consumption of space particularly because landscapes are "a powerful medium of manipulation" (Atkins 1996, 203), endowed with "a moral or normative function" to represent the world in an "ideologically prescriptive" way (202). The production and communication of landscapes have been central themes in human and cultural geography, which conceptualize landscapes (and, more broadly, spaces and places) as dynamic cultural practices (Wylie 2007), "processes by which social and subjective identities are formed" (Mitchell 2002, 1), places constructed as much "by imagination as by their physical reality" (Tangherlini and Yea 2008, 3). A landscape and the meanings ingrained in it are never static; rather, they are constantly influenced by changing social, political, and economic conditions, such as industrialization, urbanization, mobility, or alterations in human interactions with nature. The poly-semantic nature of space enables landscapes to function as communicational tools, representations of local or national identities (Olwig 2008), and repositories of social memory (Foote and Azaryahu 2007; Wylie 2007, 191–194). Also, among the most potent functions of space is to unconsciously inculcate a behavior or create an attitude (Duncan and Duncan 1988, 123), such as the veneration of the past.

The chapters in this section examine these functions of space, and discuss the construction of orchestrated routes through South Korean historic sites (Codruța Sîntionean) and North Korean ideological landscapes (Robert Winstanley-Chesters). The spatial design of each of these paths is meant to control and guide the physical experience of visitors, in a way that acts as a journey back in time. Whether this past that is retrieved through the actual passage through space is a replica of the distant Chosŏn dynasty or the heroic time of anti-colonial guerrilla fighting (during the 1930s), the agenda inherent in landscape and itinerary design is the same: first, to create a pretense of historicity; and, second, to generate enough charisma to inculcate a feeling of respect and awe, even an attitude of worship toward the past. Both the South and the North governments have created invented traditions in order to legitimize their authoritarian regimes, and have used space and ideologized landscapes to convey their agenda, appropriate narratives about the past, and mold ideal citizens.

The significance of landscapes also originates in the fact that space (land) is owned, so the invented traditions embodied in these spaces also belong to somebody—institutions, governments. But just as visitors, tourists, and marchers often consume landscapes in an unconscious way, the agency of invented traditions and the agenda behind the making of space go unquestioned. When consuming invented traditions, tourists or citizens rarely examine their recent origins, and every form of consumption legitimates and reinforces the new practice. This can be regarded as a form of complicity that actually starts with the institutions that create traditions and ends with consumers. Those who willingly alter or create historical narratives to fit the newly invented practice, the authorities who endorse the performance of invented traditions, the performers and the consumers themselves—all of them are willingly ignoring issues of authenticity or historicity by accepting invented traditions, thus ensuring their longevity.

The chapters in this section explore various uses of space in relation to invented traditions. Codruța Sîntionean investigates the political appropriation of the vernacular and the subsequent packaging of traditional architectural forms in carefully designed heritage sites and landscapes during the 1960s and 1970s. The Park Chung Hee regime located tradition in a time that was no longer accessible (Chosŏn dynasty) and sought to revive it in objects, places, and practices easily recognizable as Korean.

His regime designed cultural policies that selected visual icons of Korean identity and eventually re-invented the notion of tradition itself. Although clearly the product of a certain sociopolitical and cultural context, this notion of tradition has proved very enduring, particularly because it relies on the visual communication of what "Koreanness" means.

Robert Winstanley-Chesters's chapter reflects how contemporary North Korea instrumentalizes the national mythology of Kim Il Sung's anti-colonial guerrilla fighting into an invented tradition, the Annual Schoolchildren's March. The re-territorialization of historical moments, whether they are real or invented, depends on the effectiveness of physicality and on the actual engagement of students with a prescribed itinerary allegedly permeated with the leader's spirit. Moreover, the success of the march as an ideological tool relies on its power to generate spectacle and spectacular images, to be consumed by the children who perform it, and, most importantly, by the citizens who watch them through the ideologically charged lens of the media. Both performers and viewers accept the convention inherent in the invented tradition: the march re-enacts the patriotic struggles of Kim Il Sung, but only to a limited degree, as no participant can actually cross the river border in search of actual or even symbolic liberation. Both chapters establish the consumers of space (tourists and the marching students) as worshippers in relation to the past events evoked by the landscape.

REFERENCES

Atkins, Peter. 1996. "A Seance with the Living: The Intelligibility of the North Korean Landscape." In *North Korea in the New World Order*, edited by Hazel Smith, Chris Rhodes, Diana Pritchard, and Kevin Magill, 196–211. London: Palgrave MacMillan.

Duncan, J., and N. Duncan. 1988. "(Re)reading the Landscape." *Environment and Planning D: Society and Space* 6:117–126.

Foote, Kenneth E., and Maoz Azaryahu. 2007. "Toward a Geography of Memory: Geographical Dimensions of Public Memory and Commemoration." *Journal of Political and Military Sociology* 35.1:125–144.

Mitchell, W. J. T. 2002. "Introduction." In *Landscape and Power* (1st ed. 1994), edited by W. J. T. Mitchell, 1–4. Chicago: The University of Chicago Press.

Olwig, Kenneth R. 2008. "'Natural' Landscapes in the Representation of National Identity." In *The Ashgate Research Companion to Heritage and Identity*, edited by Brian Graham and Peter Howard, 73–88. Burlington, VT: Ashgate.

Tangherlini, Timothy R., and Sallie Yea. 2008. "Introduction—Constructed Places, Contested Spaces: Critical Geographies and Korea." In *Sitings. Critical Approaches to Korean Geography*, edited by Timothy R. Tangherlini and Sallie Yea, 1–11. Honolulu: University of Hawai'i Press.

Wylie, John. 2007. *Landscape*. London: Routledge.

CHAPTER 10

Spatializing Tradition

The Remaking of Historic Sites
under Park Chung Hee

CODRUȚA SÎNTIONEAN

In 1962, when the authoritarian military leader Park Chung Hee paid his first official visit to Hyŏnch'ungsa, an altar dedicated to Admiral Yi Sun-sin (1545–1598), he started to envision a new, re-created site that he believed would express more accurately the identity of this hero. The Office of Cultural Properties (Munhwajae Kwalliguk, hereafter the OCP),[1] the authority in charge of the management of heritage, spent several years in the 1960s and, again, in the 1970s, carrying out the design conceptualized by President Park. By 1974, when the refashioning of Hyŏnch'ungsa was finished, the site was a far cry from the original. But most importantly, the case of Hyŏnch'ungsa established a pattern of treatment of heritage sites that the OCP employed throughout Korea in the 1970s.[2] Projects undertaken with this approach were routinely called "purification projects" (*chŏnghwa saŏp*). As the term suggests, the OCP pursued a selection of aesthetic and architectural features that the government perceived as desirable and appropriate to embody both tradition and the national identity of a modern Korea, and proceeded to discard everything that did not fit this carefully tailored vision of the past.

The present chapter examines the characteristics of purification projects and their connection to a wider discourse about tradition and identity expressed through Korean architecture. I argue that the Park regime crafted a restrictive definition of traditional Korean architecture, suitable for political use, and simultaneously proceeded to invent heritage practices in order to disseminate this sanitized notion of tradition. I refer to these practices mostly by the term used by the OCP and the media during the Park era—purification projects—but actually the phrase encompasses a wide variety of interconnected processes, such as: the construction with modern materials of buildings imitating the architecture of the past; the reconstruction of lost heritage; the refashioning of old vestiges in grandiose projects; landscape architecture; and the erection of majestic monuments dedicated to selected figures of the past. Demolition and forcible removal of displeasing architecture was just as powerful a tool as the construction of new spaces, because these were essential practices in the designation of so-called traditional architectural features. This study sets out to gain further understanding of how the purification projects altered the physical landscape of cultural spaces in South Korea, in an attempt to define a purely Korean identity. It uses archival data from various sources: the public speeches of Park Chung Hee, OCP reports about purification projects, scholarly publications authored by prominent OCP professionals in positions of power, and interviews with such professionals. These sources render the image of state-led efforts to redefine what traditional culture and Korean identity are, and top-down enforced policies that have had a long-lasting impact on the understanding of Korean traditional architecture.

For President Park Chung Hee, heritage, culture, and the arts had great educational and political value, and must contribute to the development of the state. This view explains the enormous investment in culture during the Park regime and the particular insistence on tradition and the past as the quintessential sources of national identity. These government-led practices standardized a notion of tradition that was paradoxically oriented toward the future, because it had to reflect the modernization of Korea in the 1960s–1970s. The state manifested itself not simply as an inheritor of traditions, but as an owner of traditions with the authority to invent, revive, delete, or revise traditions, as it saw fit. The political context in which the Korean government started to promote selected traditions (or a certain notion of tradition) points to the fact that the forming of tradition is a present-centered selective process. What we commonly call tradition today has been shaped over time, through a process of selection of past rituals, customs, and performances to be reproduced and continued, often redefined, reshaped, and sometimes completely invented, based on representations of the past. Hobsbawm and Ranger (1983) understood the fact that invented traditions only make a reference to the past, but are manifestations of the present. The present investigation further stresses that everything we call tradition is present-based, and uses the past as a discursive legitimizing tool. This is evident in the case of the invention of a taekwondo tradition: the discursive association with *hwarangdo* (in itself an invented term) creates the illusion of historicity, legitimacy, and prestige. The discourse promoted by taekwondo associations discredits the idea that taekwondo originated in Japanese martial arts and creates instead a powerful story about the unadulterated indigenous origins of taekwondo (Moenig and Kim 2016; Capener 2016). Similarly, businesses in the food and tourism industries, Buddhist orders, and the government have had a vested interest to promote Buddhist temple food as a cultural commodity embodying authentic Korean identity. In the context of globalization, temple food has been re-invented as "healthy" and "Korean," and the rebranding has given rise to new practices, such as cooking temple food outside temples, detached from the religious context, and the emergence of famous chefs among Buddhist clergy (Moon 2008). Invented traditions gain authenticity by reference to the past, but the process of selection and invention of traditions is always present-centered and, thus, political.

Equally political is the making of heritage landscapes, another topic considered in this chapter. Landscape, like heritage, is now understood as a social construct (O'Keeffe 2007; Harvey and Wilkinson 2019), embedded with meaning, conveying customized narratives, continuously shaping and being shaped by our interactions with space. This awareness invalidates the long-standing perception of landscape as a mere "passive, neutral setting for human activity," "another form of artefact," and "instead it encompasses material, cognitive and symbolic realizations of human-environmental relationships" (Finch 2019, 166). Since landscapes are designed to invite engagement, consumption, and interpretation, landscape studies stress their relational, communicative nature (Krauss 2008). Building on these features, geographer Denis Cosgrove has analyzed how the cultural act of seeing or gazing is inextricably connected to the appropriation of spaces and landscapes, inviting semiotic, iconographical, and aesthetic frameworks of analysis (1984, 2003). The exploration of the remaking of heritage landscapes by the Park Chung Hee government makes a fascinating case study of how these definitions of landscape were organically understood and applied in South Korea, without any evident theoretical background. The manipulation of space, giving birth to an invented notion of tradition, conveyed symbolic meanings designed to legitimize Park's policies and authoritarian government, to incorporate facets of urbanization and industrialization, and to encourage citizens to participate in the spatialization of a shared national identity. In analyzing the re-creation of historic spaces in South Korea, this chapter fills a gap in landscape studies, which have emerged from a Eurocentric perspective and have so far prioritized European and American historic and cultural landscapes.

THE REDEFINITION OF TRADITION

By October 1973, when the Ministry of Culture and Information[3] announced the "First Five-year Plan for the Promotion of Culture and Arts" (*Che 1-ch'a munye chunghǔng 5-kaenyǒn kyehoek*, 1974–1978), the government already had a clear vision about "creating a new national culture built on the foundation of the traditional culture" (Kim 1976, 19), an objective that stood as the basis of the new cultural policy. However, it was already clear that whenever referring to tradition, the government did not envision the sum of all past values, rituals, customs, or performances. The rhetorical insistence on "sound" (*kǒnjǒn han*) culture and tradition in the public speeches of the president or in the phrasing of cultural policies (Park 1977) indicates that the government was considering the revival of tradition on a very selective basis. The regime considered that some past traditions were more meaningful, representative, symbolic, or purely "Korean" than others, and fervently pursued their revival, adaptation, and promotion. At the same time, the government neglected and rejected other traditions, dismissing them as base or vulgar, no matter how meaningful and pervasive they had been in Korean society in their own time (see Laurel Kendall's chapter in this volume). Folk superstitions, governing the everyday life of the villages during the late Chosǒn period, are one such example; the campaigns to eradicate such superstitions and the presumed backwardness associated with them were one of the hallmarks of the regime. While the state-led discourse derided some folk traditions for their unrefined character, in the 1960s it also criticized the inheritance of the elite culture, mainly the influence of Confucianism. President Park Chung Hee's initial negative assessment of the Chosŏn dynasty's "limited culture" (Park 1962, 72) influenced his economic and cultural policies. In his view, development could be achieved only after overcoming the damaging legacy of the past, so ingrained in the modern national character: the laziness of the privileged *yangban*, their "lack of pioneering spirit" (Park 1962, 75), "fatalistic resignation," "negative escapism from reality" (76), and poor critical judgment.[4] This type of discourse was so influential that, by the early 1970s, the prevalent view in society was that tradition must be discarded (Lee 1972, 14–16). In this context, policy makers strived to create a more nuanced consciousness:

> A willing acceptance of change may be desirable in general, but change must be accepted or resisted on a selective basis. Likewise, willingness to depart from tradition may be desirable in most cases, but tradition must be discarded or conserved on a selective basis. In short, the critical criterion should not be whether a particular thing is traditional or new, but whether it contributes to the improvement of the quality of life. (Lee 1972, 14)

Written by the head of the Policy Research Institute in 1972, this statement reflects the prevailing practices of the time: the government selected and promoted traditions that politically benefited the regime. These included customs that mirrored the magnificent royal culture of the past (as opposed to the presumed backwardness of commoners' culture) and had the potential to represent a new, modern Korea. Another selection criterion was the ability of traditions to educate, to present heroes and models from the past that could motivate citizens to be the tools of the developmentalist, anti-communist state. Part of the then-despised Confucian tradition of the Chosŏn dynasty was redeemed in this context: in the 1970s, the state elevated loyalty and filial piety, fundamental concepts of the Confucian ethos, to the rank of national values, and by the late 1970s they were taught in schools (Chŏn 2012). To sum up, the grounds for this selective view of tradition were laid in the formative decade of the 1960s, which established the direction of the economic and cultural policies of the regime in the 1970s.[5]

344 SPATIALIZING TRADITION

KOREAN TRADITIONAL ARCHITECTURE

The OCP materialized this redefined, selective idea of tradition in distinguishable visual features and tangible places and monuments. Noticeable among visual icons, architecture labeled traditional became standardized through a careful selection of elements considered Korean. Borrowing from Judy Van Zile's discussion of Korean traditional dance, there was a certain "visually recognizable" Koreanness (2011, 170) that the OCP was looking for and, through this process, redefining: it selected sloped, tiled roofs, geometric patterns adorning fences, *tanch'ŏng* motifs decorating doors and ceilings in order to represent a distinct national identity. Interestingly, these were the very elements decorating Korean royal palaces and Buddhist temples. Japanese art historians during the colonial period had previously singled out Three Kingdoms Buddhist art and architecture as the pinnacle of Korean civilization (Pai 2001, 84). Following in their footsteps, the OCP selected components of the royal palaces and of Buddhist architecture to adorn newly built museums, refashioned historic sites, Confucian shrines, or the formerly private homes of historical figures, put under state ownership and transformed into memorial houses. It is evident that the choices made by the OCP singled out the high culture of the Chosŏn elite and the Buddhist religious culture, which the OCP equated with cultural excellence, as it still does today (Saeji 2014). These choices led to practices that neglected and erased the architecture of the common people—the ordinary houses in rural communities were demolished throughout the Park regime. This has to do with the perception of cultural managers at the time (but also today) of what represents impressive, majestic features in Korean architecture. A study authored by Kim Chŏng-gi who served as the OCP research division director in the early 1970s, narrowly defines traditional architecture as "monumental and/or public buildings [such] as Buddhist temples, palace buildings and castles" (Kim 1972, 17). The labeling of magnificent, elegant traits as "traditional" aimed to create the semblance of a long-standing, rich culture.

A visual examination of the so-called traditional architecture built during the Park era demonstrates how this selective vision of tradition was incorporated into the contemporary landscape. In 1966, the OCP invited proposals for the design of a new museum inside the Kyŏngbokkung Palace (currently, the National Folk Museum, Kungnip Minsok Pangmulgwan).

The call for applications specifically encouraged architects to imitate the outer appearance of the most representative Korean vestiges (Kim 2017, 166). Opposing the government's superficial understanding of how tradition should be interpreted in modern architecture, architects boycotted the call and defended the idea of originality in architectural design, but eventually some architects did apply and the OCP selected Kang Pongjin's plan. The museum replicates and combines the architectural features of several Buddhist temples that were already designated national treasures (*kukpo*) by 1966: the Ch'ŏngun'gyo and Paegun'gyo bridges of Pulguksa, the five-story P'alsangjŏn Hall of Pŏpchusa, the Kakhwangjŏn Hall of Hwaŏmsa, and the Mirŭkjŏn Hall of Kŭmsansa (Chang 2011, 870). Made of reinforced concrete, the museum building surpasses in height the throne hall Kŭnjŏngjŏn, the highlight of Kyŏngbokkung Palace. The architecture of the National Folk Museum reflects the belief, prevalent in the 1960s and the 1970s, about the replicability of tradition: the past could be exploited for its aura of venerability and legitimacy, and reproduced in new material forms in order to create new identities.

Equally striking are the monumental pillared gates, often designed by reputed architects, located at the entrances of sites that celebrate nationhood: the entrance gates of Pusan United Nations Memorial Cemetery (1966), Seoul National Cemetery (1969), Taegu Talsŏng Park (1969), and Taejŏn National Cemetery (finished in 1983, but planned in 1976) all have the hip-and-gable roof (*p'alchak*) common in palaces (for example, the throne hall Kŭnjŏngjŏn of Kyŏngbokkung Palace), Confucian academies, and the houses of the Chosŏn social elite (Jackson and Koehler 2012, 47).

The National Folk Museum building and these gates have something particular in common: they imitate traditional architecture, but are all made of reinforced concrete. The embodiment of old forms in new materials managed to express both tradition and modernity at the same time within the precincts of cultural and historic sites. None of the connotations associated with tradition—"premodern, unscientific, preindustrial, authentic, non-commercial" (Graburn 2001, 80)—remain valid in the re-interpretation of architectural tradition during the Park Chung Hee regime. The extensive use of concrete by cultural managers in the 1960s–1970s created a deliberate mixture of traditional forms with the modern, scientific, industrial, cosmetic, and commercial—the trademarks of the industrialization era. The OCP and local governments manifested great concern for aesthetic value, but less for historical authenticity, and adopted a rather superficial approach to building traditional architecture.

However, not all attempts to re-embody tradition in modernity went well. In 1967, architect Kim Su-gǔn (1931–1986) completed one of his early works, the Puyŏ National Museum. It was meant as a building inspired by traditional forms: the concrete frame was reminiscent of rafters, and the slightly curved roof reflected the architecture of *hanok*. These elements were supposed to give the structure an imposing, magnificent air. Despite marking the Koreanness of the building with traditional patterns and ornaments, critics of the building saw in its shape too much of a resemblance to a Japanese shintō shrine. Moreover, the likeness between the main gate and Japanese *torii* gates sparked such a controversy, that eventually the gate had to be removed. Kim Su-gǔn defended himself by saying that he had been inspired by the lines and curves of a few Paekche artifacts, such as ceramics. He also stressed that Paekche architectural techniques were imported to Japan and then reimported to Korea. Since Paekche had frequent cultural interactions with Japan in ancient times, it is only natural that some aesthetic and architectural elements are of common ancestry (Cho 2015).

The case of the Puyŏ National Museum shows that government-selected criteria about Korean aesthetics in newly built architecture aimed to create the semblance of cultural continuity and an emphasis on "us," as opposed to an alien or distant "other" (i.e., Japanese or Western). Therefore, the OCP created a sanitized version of a purely "Korean" (*Han'gukchŏgin*) identity. The OCP removed architectural elements or structures that did not fit its view of Koreanness or replaced them with a wider accepted vision of the past, tradition, and national identity. There was a widespread belief that the Japanese colonial rulers distorted and diminished the worth of the Korean tradition, culture, and history by considering them subservient to China (Kim 1976, 10). OCP managers believed that Korean history, archeological studies, and the interpretation of heritage continued to be written according to the Japanese "imperialist historical view" (*hwangguksagwan*) even after the 1945 Liberation from colonial oppression (Chŏng 1977, 16). For this reason, the OCP integrated in its discourse and practices the idea of rectification of national history, and proceeded to remove any remnants of the colonial view of the past.[6] The "establishment of national historical view" (*minjok sagwan chŏngnip*) was the main focus of the 1974–1978 "First Five-year Plan for the Promotion of Culture and Arts," as evidenced by the allocation of funds for this purpose. An impressive 70.2 percent of the total budget of the five-year plan was devoted to the redefinition of a national historical view, and 63.1 percent of the total budget was actually invested in heritage management (Ŭn 2005, 249).

However, there is little in the actual architectural form of a building that can convey the "correct historical view" (*olbarŭn yŏksagwan*) that was at the forefront of Yusin ideology (Park 1973). Rather, this view was expressed through museum displays, explanation boards, and memorial plaques, which structured the viewers' experience. This indicates that the redefinition of an architectural tradition came along with interconnected practices, like talking about the past in a very selective manner. For instance, all the great heroes promoted by the Park Chung Hee government lived in the premodern period and most of them during the Chosŏn period. The commemoration practices of the OCP created a very powerful narrative of past military victories that circumvented the recent colonial past. With very few exceptions such as the restoration of Yun Pong-gil's (1908–1932) birthplace in 1974–1977, commemorations focused on heroes and battles from the distant past, alienated from citizens' everyday life. The remembrance of colonial independence fighters could have potentially sparked public debates about the remnants of the colonial rule in Korean society, something all postwar dictatorial regimes carefully avoided, so these debates were delayed until the 1990s. Also, a focus on the heroes of the colonial period would have put the spotlight on Japan as the major enemy, further fueling the national public resentment against Japan. Since President Park did not want to antagonize its economic ally, Japan, the focus was set on Chosŏn heritage. As a consequence, our understanding of Chosŏn culture and history, today, is heavily influenced by the way the OCP has reimagined and represented Chosŏn in the last five decades through heritage.

THE "PURIFICATION" (*CHŎNGHWA*) OF HERITAGE

Nowhere is this tendency to present a tailored representation of the past as visible as in the management of built heritage. In order to materialize this narrative, the OCP, often under direct orders from the president, selected historic sites (*sajŏk*, such as battlefields, fortresses, and Confucian shrines) commemorating exemplary people and events and re-created the sites almost entirely. Many of these projects were handpicked and even closely coordinated by the president himself, who took great interest in the management of heritage throughout his mandates. Heritage managers, in cooperation with local governments, were refashioning the sites according to a new logic: they had to embody tradition—the re-aestheticized, constructed idea of tradition that had taken form—and at the same time point to the rapid modernization of South Korea.

The OCP labeled these large-scale projects "repair and restoration projects" (*posu pogwŏn saŏp*), but in reality the OCP had a very precarious understanding of the principles of architectural heritage restoration and conservation in the 1960s and the 1970s. None of these principles—minimal intervention, protection of the original fabric, unaltered preservation of the structure, respect for the original condition of a building—were actually applied at the time. The terminology used in the OCP documents and in the media is very telling in this respect: commonly, the restoration projects were called purification projects (*chŏnghwa saŏp*). The new buildings or the partly re-created, "purified" ones made use of architectural features perceived as traditional, instituting a sanitized version of a purely "Korean" identity.

When the OCP was established on October 2, 1961, it had 252 staff members,[7] who were bureaucrats working at the two institutions that merged to form the OCP: the former Royal Household Properties Office and the Cultural Preservation Department of the Ministry of Culture and Education (Munhwajaech'ŏng 2011b, 47). As a rule, the OCP employees were bureaucrats with no educational background or expertise in cultural management, although by 1961 some of them had acquired experience in dealing with the daily administration of the royal palaces and the museums set up by the Japanese authorities during the colonial period. In 1969, Chŏng Chae-hun, who played a key role in the remaking of Kyŏngju as the head of the Kyŏngju Office for Historic Sites (1973–1975),[8] was still decrying the lack of expertise in heritage management of most OCP employees. He stated that although there were trained specialists in specific fields, it was uncertain whether there were any people who could call themselves specialists in heritage management, in other words, people able to convert the scholarly knowledge of heritage researchers into practical administration principles (Chŏng 1969, 86). A competent heritage manager was expected to have a general knowledge about Korean studies, and spend at least three years training: travel through the country for field study for one year, analyze his findings for another year, and introduce oneself to general academic concepts about heritage management for the last year of training (Chŏng 1969, 86). If in 1969 there were very few qualified heritage managers, this means that the OCP bureaucrats started to get practical and theoretical training, at best, in the 1970s,[9] which is exactly the decade when they implemented most of the purification projects. All of these projects entailed vast reconstructions or considerable re-creation, with little respect for the original form and fabric of architectural heritage, their authenticity and historicity. The lack of expertise in heritage preservation accounts for massively altering "purification" practices and the apparent lack of opposition within the OCP to sweeping alterations of historic sites.

Looking at the structure of restoration reports, it is somewhat easier to grasp the phases of a purification project: field investigation, research of extant documents, preliminary report, drafting of a plan, application of plan, final report documenting the original state and the changes that were made. In order to complete a project, there was constant cooperation between members of the Cultural Properties Committee (Munhwajae Wiwŏnhoe), who were specialists in various fields, such as archaeology, history, architecture, and OCP bureaucrats and the bureaucrats working in the cultural departments of the local institutions.

However, it is difficult to know the specialists or the bureaucrats who were the actual designers or planners of each purification project. The reports occasionally mention the high-ranking bureaucrats who visited the premises of sites under reconstruction, made lists of recommendations for change, and informed the president on the evolution of the project. For instance, on May 4, 1968, the Head Secretary of the Presidential Office visited Hyŏnch'ungsa, accompanied by the OCP director, the Forestation Service director, and a deputy-chief engineer. Although none of these bureaucrats had training in heritage management, they devised a sixteen-point list of changes, aligned with the objectives set in writing by Park Chung Hee on his personal visit to Hyŏnch'ungsa a few days before. The requests vary from changes of little consequence, like the use of uniformly sized rocks adorning the alleys and the parking lot, to massive landscaping and the need to exclude the descendants of Yi Sun-sin from the management of the historic site, by asking them to move out of their private property (Munhwa Kongbobu 1975, 88). Although the OCP reports include such detailed information, they are silent on the individual role played by these bureaucrats in the remaking of heritage.

Also, the reports identify the committees who supervised the writing of the reports, and these panels always included the minister in charge of Culture and Information and a few members of the Cultural Properties Committee. But it is in no way clear whether the people writing the reports were also the ones who had masterminded the restoration plans. On Hyŏnch'ungsa, because it was such a complex, long-term project, there are two reports, dated 1969 and 1975 (Munhwa Kongbobu 1969, 1975), but none of the people involved in supervising and writing the 1969 report were involved in the subsequent one, so there might not have been any continuity between the teams entrusted with the restoration of the site over the years.

What emerges more clearly from the OCP reports is a substantial body of evidence of the direct involvement of President Park Chung Hee in the conception of purification projects. His preoccupation with heritage goes beyond the mere official visits at commemorative events, and manifests itself in personal encounters with heritage managers, handwritten notes sent to lower level members of the project teams (Yi 2011), hand-drawn landscape sketches, and his own calligraphy making its way into the actual fabric of heritage.[10] Hyŏnch'ungsa is again a meaningful example, because the historic site would eventually become the prototype that all the other purification projects replicated. The remaking of the site was essentially designed by Park himself in the four visits he paid in 1968, sending punctual lists of changes to the Ministry of Culture and Information, for the OCP (part of the Ministry) to follow through. The level of detail the president paid attention to is striking: he starts by ordering the cutting of grass and the removal of natural stones from the garden at Hyŏnch'ungsa, and continues by choosing which trees should be conserved (the large trees, kŏmok), which should be removed (the shrubs), and what species of trees should be planted (Himalayan cedar) in order to create a magnificent scenery along the main road leading to the altar ("the worship road," ch'ambaero). Moreover, Park Chung Hee urges the OCP staff to cosmeticize the area beyond the walls of the site, by restricting the presence of residential houses and by "choosing crops of scenic beauty." His wording ("remove" *chegŏ hara*, "demolish" *ch'ŏlgŏ hara*, "move" *ijŏn hara*, "rebuild" *chaegŏn hara*) is very suggestive of the radical alterations that transformed the site and reveals a lack of interest in the actual preservation of historic heritage in its original state (Munhwa Kongbobu 1975, 92). Park's imperative to "change everything to modern-style buildings, except the main historic buildings" (Munhwa Kongbobu 1975, 93) would be in later years invalidated by his other directives, and modern-style buildings would eventually receive alternative façades and roofs, expressing a perceived Koreanness and traditional flavor (155–156).[11] The constant change in instructions indicates that the Hyŏnch'ungsa purification project was a process of trial and error, an experiment with architectural forms and landscape architecture.

The pattern established at Hyŏnch'ungsa would be reproduced in similar projects in the 1970s, when the president played a personal role in the selection of sites worthy of being "purified" (Munhwajaech'ŏng 2011b, 186), with an overwhelming preference for military accomplishments and heroism. His broad interest in cultural properties, particularly historic heritage, stemmed from a remarkable understanding of the political and economic uses of heritage, which is why, twice a week, for an hour, ministers and vice-ministers had to listen to lectures about heritage. Yi Sŏn-gŭn, historian, supporter of Yusin ideology, and head of the Cultural Properties Committee (among other high-profile positions he occupied in cultural and educational institutions), and Chŏng Chae-hun, prominent figure of the OCP, were among those who gave the lectures (Yi 2011). The OCP reports abound in mentions of Park Chung Hee's visits to heritage sites and records of his instructions, echoing the Hyŏnch'ungsa case: the meeting where the purification plan of Haengju Sansŏng was designed took place at the Presidential Office, and the plan was approved by the president before being executed (Munhwa Kongbobu 1970, 41–42). Visiting Ch'ilbaek Ŭich'ong in 1970, Park "ordered the effective repair and purification of the premises, a more sublime extension" (Munhwa Kongbobu 1976, 45). The purification of Ojukhŏn closely followed sketches drawn by the president himself (Kangwŏndo Chibang Munhwajae Kwalliguk 1976, 78–79), and the configuration of the site after the remaking was over shows that the design conceived by President Park was followed literally.

Notably, most of the president's demands concern landscape architecture, and an aesthetic that would convey an imagined Koreanness. Places like Hyŏnch'ungsa and Ojukhŏn can be justly considered his own creation, and the changes he demanded reveal a surprising understanding of landscape as a cultural resource, able to embody the nation-state. Following his suggestions, the managers of the OCP experimented with the landscape's potential to express cultural values, in a way that has been theorized only recently, in studies that establish the connection between cultural identity and the way people interact with landscapes (Stephenson 2008).

Financial backing for the projects came from the Ministry of Culture and Information, through the OCP, and from local governments. The government acquired funding for cultural projects by selling state-owned properties, formerly the assets of the Imperial Household. Between 1963 and 1978, the government sold 2.73 million *pyŏng* of the land formerly owned by the last rulers of the Chosŏn dynasty (over nine million square meters) (Ŭn 2005, 249). As Ŭn Chŏng-t'ae aptly puts it, the government was "selling selected traditions in order to rediscover traditions" (Ŭn 2005, 249). The budget reserved for heritage from 1974 to 1978 according to the "First Five-year Plan for the Promotion of Culture and Arts" was spent on building museums and Sejong Institutes, but most of it was used on purification projects. Ŭn has also drawn attention to the fact that the government also used regional funds for the purification projects (funds dedicated to the New Village Movement, the reforestation movement, and road construction), so the financial data reported by the Ministry of Culture and Information does not reflect the actual amount of money invested in the purification of heritage sites (2005, 250).

I have identified four special features that distinguish these repair and restoration projects: First, the re-created sites had to embody the image of a new and modern Korea, so projects focused on the removal of old, rural architecture, perceived as backward, and the incorporation of new architecture that could be promoted as icons of modernity. Second, the refashioned historic sites presented a selection of features, convergent with the government's particular understanding of tradition and traditional architecture. Third, restoration projects claimed to assert a Korean identity that had been purified of alien elements. Finally, managers strived to create awe-inspiring features through landscape architecture.

A particular feature of the purification projects was the acquisition and clearing of land surrounding the sites. Most historic sites were surrounded by villages and farmland, but the state took ownership of it, compensated the peasants for their houses and farmland and used the newly acquired land to enlarge the precincts of the heritage sites. In 1977, Chŏng Chae-hun remarked that the "appropriate preservation and purification of historic vestiges" was an "epoch-making plan," entailing the removal of commoners' houses (*min'ga*) and the use of land for the development of cultural heritage (1977, 16). In Kyŏngju, for example, several hundred houses were demolished to make room for the landscaping of Taerŭngwŏn Tomb Complex and the preservation of the Wŏlsŏng Palace (Chŏng 1977, 16). Another OCP policy maker, Kim Chŏng-gi, considered that the disappearance of traditional dwellings in rural areas, caused by the introduction of Western architecture, was a "new trend toward improvement" (Kim 1972, 22).[12] On the cleared land, the OCP eventually designed landscapes that did not reflect the lifestyle or the beliefs of the commoners; rather, they expressed the values intended by the Park Chung Hee government—modernization, elite culture, grandeur, and a sense of awe for the past. By physically excluding villagers in order to enlarge the premises of heritage landscapes, the state unwittingly reproduced the tensions between social and economic classes from the Chosŏn dynasty and subtly integrated these tensions in the landscapes. Today rural communities or rustic architecture are regarded everywhere as sources of authenticity for heritage tourism, but in the Park era, the regime regarded thatched-roofed (*ch'oga chip*) and wooden-roofed houses (*nŏwa chip*) as an unpalatable sign of an undeveloped society in dire need of modernization.[13] Just like the use of concrete in traditional architecture, the ubiquitous practice of discarding all elements of rural, backward life surrounding heritage sites points to the most prominent agenda of the so-called repair and restoration projects: from my perspective the newly created sites had the role of reflecting the accomplishments of the developmentalist state and of creating the image of modern Korea. The regime promoted heritage tourism as a mandatory form of patriotism and of learning history, and when citizens visited the re-created sites, they experienced a new, modern Korea. This explains why the OCP replaced rural communities and paddy rice fields with modern infrastructure (for example, paved access roads, parking lots, ticket booths, souvenir shops, toilets, and other facilities) meant to attract and support a great number of tourists.

In the same vein, the OCP demolished some architectural structures, despite the fact they were buildings constructed during the Chosŏn dynasty. Clearly, the authenticity of the original fabric, which had the potential to be associated with accurate historical knowledge, was not a priority. Instead, the *impression* of the past, created through new architectural creations, was a more stringent imperative. Demolitions took place when the cultural managers considered the old buildings inappropriate, or when it was necessary to make room for new structures, designed to represent a purified version of Korean architecture and to exhibit the glory of a modernized country. The new buildings were often large, imposing monuments or memorial halls that dominated the landscape, as is the case of the 15.2-meter-tall Victory Monument situated on top of the hill at Haengju Fortress. Photographs of the era paint a striking picture: many of the new structures were made of concrete left unpainted, departing from the tradition of Korean wooden architecture.[14] Although I believe the main reason for this was ideological—to represent modernity and economic development—there are several other explanations for the use of concrete. In 1963, Japanese heritage managers had reconstructed the Shitennō-ji Temple in Ōsaka using concrete instead of wood. President Park Chung Hee sent members of the OCP to investigate this reconstruction and learn from the Japanese experience (Kim 2011, 798), particularly since China and North Korea were also using concrete in the building of cultural heritage (Yi 2011). Large wooden beams were in short supply during the Park era, because the regime conducted many construction projects throughout the country. At the same time, reinforced concrete seemed to last much longer than wood, so it appeared the most economic choice in the long run. The lack of timber could perhaps explain the OCP choice for concrete when building omnipresent architecture such as traditional entrance gates or tile-roofed memorial halls. But the use of reinforced concrete for reconstructing iconic sites such as Kwanghwamun in 1968 indicates that the government was intentionally aiming to embody modernity (i.e., cement) within traditional architectural forms, these hybrid structures being the quintessential images of the new Korea.

Of course, one can also argue that the use of concrete in heritage restorations was the consequence of an inadequate knowledge of heritage
conservation principles in Korea at the time, following a practice already
established by Japanese heritage managers during the colonial period. In
order to preserve the authenticity of historic monuments and sites, the
OCP should have applied materials very similar to the ones originally
used, a practice that started to consolidate only after the Park era. In the
early 1980s, the OCP started to gradually remove concrete from its previous restorations. Today, managers of heritage involved in these so-called
restoration projects remember the extensive use of concrete as one of the
most regrettable things (Munhwajaech'ŏng 2011a, 762), but concrete in
those days was the marker of a new, prosperous era in Korean history.
Thus, the re-created sites had to render not only Korean aesthetics and
the authentic identity of the Korean people, but also the glorified "modernization of the fatherland" (*choguk ŭi kŭndaehwa*), one of the most
prominent slogans of the Park government.

Although timber was replaced with something more convenient,
durable, and accessible, the concrete buildings replicated traditional architectural shapes—or what the government at the time defined and selected
as traditional: the structure of *hanok* houses with their elegantly curved
tiled roofs, the alternation of circular rafters and rectangular rafters,
their columns and brick walls; the so-called one-pillar gates (*ilchumun*)
that stand at the entrance of most Buddhist temples; the intricate system
of interlocking brackets of Buddhist temples; and details from the royal
palaces of the Chosŏn dynasty, such as the adorning patterns on the brick
walls of Kyŏngbokkung Palace. Replicated in concrete, these selected features of traditional architecture conferred an authentic Korean look to
newly built memorial halls, museums, the management offices of heritage sites, and sometimes even the ticket booths and the toilets adjacent
to these sites. Since the OCP did not employ any authentic materials and
techniques to re-create traditional architecture, the projects materialized into a superficial imitation of traditional forms. The application of a
selected handful of features the OCP and the government labeled traditional created the semblance of age, or an evocation of the past. In harsher
words, critics in the influential *Space* (*Konggan*) magazine called these
presumed restorations the "sort of desecration [that] gives a fake idea of

the past" (quoted in Delissen 2001, 252). The proliferation of copies of traditional architecture reflects the government agenda to "create a new national culture" based on tradition (Park 1972)—new forms of national culture that used the past as a mere reference, but were actually embedded in a discourse about modernity and economic development.

Again, it is worth stressing how restrictive this definition of traditional architecture was. It eliminated the modest architecture of the ordinary village houses and instead prioritized the culture of the social elite as typified by royal palaces, *yangban* mansions, Confucian academies, and Buddhist architecture (generally sponsored by the upper class) that became labeled "traditional." The features of royal court culture, as defined by Moon Okpyo in her study of royal court cuisine revival, easily apply to the architecture of the elite: it "display(s) distinction and exclusivity," and "epitomize(s) style, sophistication, elegance, and the utmost refinement" (2010, 53). The military heroes and soldiers that the OCP memorialized in these purified sites were not necessarily social elites, but the state appropriated their commemoration and transformed them into symbols of the nation. The state considered that the only way to commemorate them was through a representation of the past embedded in a discourse of aesthetically recognizable "tradition" and "Koreanness."

Purification projects intended to re-create space and architecture in a way that was indelibly connected to how the state envisioned the commemoration of heroes and the representation of the past. As discussed above, evidence from OCP reports shows that heritage managers acted in accordance with memos received directly from President Park Chung Hee, often in his own handwriting. It seems to have been his idea that historic sites should convey to visitors a certain "sublime atmosphere" (*changŏm han punwigi*) (Munhwa Kongbobu 1975, 88) or "refined atmosphere" (*adam han punwigi*) (Munhwa Kongbobu 1970, 54). Following his guidelines, purified historic sites gained a solemn aura that was deliberately constructed through landscape architecture, and this led to the term "sacralization projects" (*sŏngyŏkhwa saŏp*), used interchangeably with purification projects. The term sacralization projects suggests the transformation of historic sites in sanctuaries with a sublime, holy atmosphere (Ŭn 2005, 242). In his memos, Park Chung Hee referred to visitors as "worshippers" (*ch'ambaegek*) (Munhwa Kongbobu 1975, 88), not mere tourists. Therefore, the state expected visitors to behave like pilgrims who paid their respects to the national ancestors (Park 2010, 6). The regime wanted to create a tourist experience in which citizens would be awestruck or overwhelmed by powerful patriotic feelings when seeing the sites. Here the imitation of impressive, majestic architectural features referencing the culture of the social elites played an important role. But the OCP, following detailed instructions from President Park Chung Hee, devised a practice that would have a huge and long-lasting impact on the physical appearance of South Korean heritage: heavy intervention in landscape architecture. The acquisition of land surrounding sites and monuments (previously farmland or rural communities) allowed for the creation of vast terraced landscapes. In an established pattern, the ground was refashioned into different levels, connected through rows of stairs leading to the focal point of the site. The pattern became so pervasive throughout the country, that one cannot overlook its implied semiotics: visitors who climbed the stairs could admire the awe-inspiring view of the main edifice, always compelled by the ascending route to look up; they also must have felt inclined to have a dignified, respectful attitude while visiting the elegant site. The landscape, together with the reproduction of traditional architecture, provided the solemnity required for the commemoration of national heroes.

Following the pattern established at Hyŏnch'ungsa (1966–1969 and 1972–1974), the 1970s witnessed a large number of similar projects, including fortresses (Namhan Sansŏng 1970, Haengju Sansŏng 1969–1970 and 1977–1979, Suwŏn-sŏng 1975–1979, Seoul Sŏnggwak 1975–1980), tombs dedicated to the heroic soldiers who died in the Imjin War (Ch'ilbaek Ŭich'ong 1970–1971 and 1976, Namwŏn Manin Ŭich'ong 1977–1979), patriotic defenders of the country from all ages (Kyŏngju T'ongilchŏn, dedicated to King Muyŏl, General Kim Yu-sin, and King Munmu 1976–1977; Naksŏngdae, the birthplace of Koryŏ military commander Kang Kam-ch'an 1973–1974; Yesan Yun Pong-gil Ŭisa Yujŏk 1974–1977; Yu Kwan-sun Yujŏk 1975–1976), places commemorating Korean sages promoted as patriots (Tosan Sŏwŏn, dedicated to Yi Hwang 1969–1970; Kangnŭng Ojukhŏn, the birthplace of Sin Saimdang and Yi I 1975–1976), and more.[15]

These projects demonstrate that the purification of Hyŏnch'ungsa was a replicable model, and the OCP universally applied the features of sacralization projects described above. This resulted in a profound uniformization of landscape architecture and heritage sites across the country. Historic and mnemonic sites from different periods ended up looking the same, losing their local, unique, and authentic traits. The OCP during the Park era accomplished a standardization of representations of the past at public heritage sites, despite the fact that singularity and local characteristics are valuable commodities in tourism. This standardization only shows that the commodification of heritage for tourist consumption was of secondary concern. Rather, the goal of the government was to convey a coherent image of what "Korean" tradition was and to popularize a sense of a readily recognizable "Koreanness."

Toward the end of the 1970s, members of the OCP realized that there were side effects to the "zeal of worshipping ancestors" and to the "regional love of one's native place," driving massive restoration projects. This misconstrued understanding of patriotism has led to "making excessive restorations on a grand scale, for no good reason, and creating vestiges with monotonously identical shape" (Chŏng 1977, 2). Others find it regrettable, today, that there was an overemphasis on the treatment of military heroes and the heritage dedicated to them, which resulted in the neglect of other historical figures (Munhwajaech'ŏng 2011a, 762). On the other hand, the same heritage managers praise the enlargement of the territory surrounding heritage sites, the improvement of the landscape, the stimulation of citizens' interest in heritage, and the education of patriotism through the purification projects (Munhwajaech'ŏng 2011a, 762). It is evident that there is no consensual view of this era in the history of Korean heritage management. The sites that underwent major transformations during the Park regime are the products of the modernization period, perhaps even more than they are the inheritance of a distant past.

THE ENDURING LEGACY OF THE PARK CHUNG HEE ERA

Today, when we look at so-called traditional architecture, we are looking at a set of carefully selected features that the OCP and the Park government chose in order to define tradition, traditional space, or even the past. This process resembles looking through a lens that is there without us knowing we are doing so, because we have gotten so used to it. This chapter claims that the Park regime carefully constructed this lens, and it is one of Park's most enduring legacies. We now take for granted what Chosŏn dynasty architecture (especially common, repetitive structures such as entrance gates, fences, memorialization halls) should look like, without considering the transformative process heritage has gone through in the decades of the Park regime.

If further proof is needed, one should take a look at the present government guidelines for constructing new *hanok* in the urban *hanok* villages: the guidelines point to a set of exterior features that are supposed to create a traditional façade, without properly regulating preservation or interiors (Sîntionean 2015, 69). Local governments in Seoul, Chŏnju, and other cities have adopted similar guidelines in order to monitor the construction, renovation, or restoration of *hanok* in *hanok* villages, in order to preserve a coherent look and protect the areas from indiscriminate real-estate development. But the fact that these governments have deemed it necessary to regulate only the exterior look of newly constructed *hanok* is problematic, as proven by the diverse erroneous practices that have emerged: the replacement of older *hanok* with new ones, adapted for commercial use as restaurants or inns, or the construction of two-story *hanok* in protected areas, which abide by the regulation, yet fail to look traditional to a connoisseur. The result has been the creation of imposing landscapes that appear to be traditional—a superficial understanding of tradition. As Kim Ann Meejung found in her discussion of Pukch'on *Hanok* Village, there exists "the assumption that physical impressiveness will automatically translate into historicity" and a "carefree association between tradition and appearance" (2016, 151). My discussion of purification projects has shown that this assumption was deliberately created by the Park Chung Hee regime. The government, through the OCP, created memorialization sites that heritage managers and potentially tourists perceived to be more impressive: majestic monuments, elevated landscapes, larger buildings and perimeters. However, it is problematic that the government aimed to create a simulacrum of historicity by replicating monumental features in architecture and landscaping. The sites and the buildings the OCP refashioned were already historic, so it is puzzling that the government did not find them remarkable, impressive, or traditional enough to be preserved in the exact state they had inherited from the past. My chapter has highlighted the fact that the traditional features pursued by the government in heritage were not aimed at authentically reflecting the past, but focused on the ability to embody the image of a new, more developed Korea, powerful thanks to its past culture, but also its present development.

GLOSSARY

adam han punwigi 雅淡한 雰圍氣

ch'ambaegek 參拜客

changŏm han punwigi 莊嚴한 雰圍氣

Che 1-ch'a munye chunghŭng 5-kaenyŏn kyehoek 第1次 文藝中興 5個年 計劃

Ch'ilbaek Ŭich'ong 七百義塚

ch'oga chip 草家집

choguk ŭi kŭndaehwa 祖國의 近代化

Chŏng Chae-hun 鄭在鑂

chŏnghwa saŏp 淨化事業

Ch'ŏngun'gyo 靑雲橋

Chosŏn 朝鮮

Haengju Sansŏng 幸州山城

Han'gukchŏgin 韓國的인

hanok 韓屋

hwangguksagwan 皇國史觀

Hwaŏmsa 華嚴寺

hwarangdo 花郎徒

Hyŏnch'ungsa 顯忠祠

ilchumun 一柱門

Imjin (War) 壬辰倭亂

Kakhwangjŏn 覺皇殿

Kang Kam-ch'an 姜邯贊

Kang Pong-jin 姜奉辰

Kangnŭng Ojukhŏn 江陵烏竹軒

Kim Chŏng-gi 金正基

Kim Su-gŭn 金壽根

Kim Yu-sin 金庾信

kŏnjŏn han 健全한

Koryŏ 高麗

kukpo 國寶

Kŭmsansa 金山寺

Kungnip Minsok Pangmulgwan 國立民俗博物館

Kŭnjŏngjŏn 勤政殿

Kwanghwamun 光化門

Kyŏngbokkung 景福宮

Kyŏngju 慶州

Kyŏngju T'ongilchŏn 慶州統一殿

min'ga 民家

minjok sagwan chŏngnip 民族史觀定立

Mirŭkjŏn 彌勒殿

Munhwa Kongbobu 文化公報部

Munhwajae Kwalliguk 文化財管理局

Munhwajaech'ŏng 文化財廳

Munmu (King) 文武王

Muyŏl (King) 武烈王

Naksŏngdae 落星垈

Namhan Sansŏng 南漢山城

Namwŏn Manin Ŭich'ong 南原萬人義塚

nŏwa chip 너와집

Paegun'gyo 白雲橋
Paekche 百濟
p'alchak 八作
P'alsangjŏn 捌相殿
Park Chung Hee 朴正熙
Pŏpchusa 法住寺
posu pogwŏn saŏp 保守復元事業
Pulguksa 佛國寺
sajŏk 史蹟
Sin Saimdang 申師任堂
sŏngyŏkhwa saŏp 聖域化事業
Sŏul (Seoul) Sŏnggwak 서울城郭
Suwŏn-sŏng 水原城
taekwondo 跆拳道

Taerŭngwŏn 大陵園
tanch'ŏng 丹青
Tosan Sŏwŏn 陶山書院
Wŏlsŏng 月城
yangban 兩班
Yesan Yun Pong-gil Ŭisa Yujŏk 禮
山 尹奉吉 義士 遺蹟
Yi Hwang 李滉
Yi I 李珥
Yi Sŏn-gŭn 李瑄根
Yi Sun-sin 李舜臣
Yu Kwan-sun Yujŏk 柳寬順 遺蹟
Yun Pong-gil 尹奉吉
Yusin 維新

NOTES

This work was supported by a Seed Program for Korean Studies through the Ministry of Education of Republic of Korea and Korean Studies Promotion Service of The Academy of Korean Studies (AKS-2015-INC-2230006). I am grateful to Andrew David Jackson and CedarBough T. Saeji for providing insights that helped me improve my manuscript.

1. Munhwajae Kwalliguk was renamed Munhwajaech'ŏng (Cultural Heritage Administration) in 1999.

2. In this chapter, I use the general term "heritage site" to designate sites registered in the national patrimony, irrespective of their category ("historic sites" *sajŏk*, "national treasures" *kukpo*, or "treasures" *pomul*).

3. The Ministry of Culture and Information (Munhwa Kongbobu) was created in 1968 and is the precursor of today's Ministry of Culture, Sports and Tourism (Munhwa Ch'eyuk Kwan'gwangbu).

4. When discussing the positive legacy of Chosŏn, President Park singles out King Sejong (Park 1962, 83–85) and the military spirit of Yi Sun-sin (90–91), both of them later transformed into major icons of Korean culture and identity. Therefore, the 1962 book already lays the foundation of Park Chung Hee's future cultural policy—his cult for heroism and Sejong.

5. In 1976, Professor Kim Yersu (Kim Yŏ-su) of Sungkyunkwan University authored the national report to UNESCO on the state of South Korean cultural policy. The report euphemistically calls the authoritarian Yusin

regime, consolidated with the 1972 amendment of the constitution, as having "certain dirigistic tendencies" necessary for "organizing national potential and maximizing political efficiency" (Kim 1976, 14), and justifies censorship of literature, performing arts, and popular culture because some of their elements are "undermining the effective marshalling of national potential" (15). This potential can only be achieved, according to the report, through the "creation of a new national culture based on tradition and consonant with the goals of over-all national development" (Kim 1976, 19). The report goes into detail to explain what the government understood by "traditional culture," but it is clear that it was a very carefully tailored idea of tradition that supported the political and economic views of the regime.

6. Chŏng Chae-hun recalls that the first thing he did when he became director of the OCP in 1986 was to remove the Japanese-style landscape architecture from the five royal palaces in Seoul. Colonial authorities had planted cherry trees, sycamores, and boxwood trees, but the OCP removed all of them and replaced them with plants perceived as traditional and Korean, because they "grow naturally" and do not need trimming: pine and maple trees. Park Chung Hee, with his affinity for Japan and Japanese culture, had favored this kind of landscape, but for Chŏng Chae-hun, removing the cherry trees meant removing the colonial historical view (Yi 2011).

7. This represents approximately 30 percent of the number of employees the institution reported in October 2011 (857 people).

8. Between 1973 and 1986, Chŏng Chae-hun was the executive director of the Landscape Architecture Society and afterward he became the twelfth director of the OCP (1986–1993).

9. Hyung Il Pai, quoting Hanyang University Museum director Pae Ki-dong, notes that, in 1996, the OCP still lacked trained heritage managers, which suggests that the situation had not changed significantly. In 1996, the OCP had 503 employees, but only 12 held research positions, which were "notoriously hard to come by." The rest of the employees were bureaucrats rotating through the institution often enough to prevent them from acquiring meaningful expertise (Pai 2013, 27).

10. Examples of Park's calligraphy include the large Chinese characters on the 1963 Victory Monument at Haengju Sansŏng (Munhwa Kongbobu 1970, 36), the hangul engraving of the words "Ch'ilbaek ŭisa sunŭit'ap" on the eponymous monument (Munhwa Kongbobu 1976, 85), and the 1968 Kwanghwamun signboard, also in hangul. In an evident departure from tradition (because it would have been unthinkable for Chosŏn aristocrats), the OCP proceeded to change the Chinese character signboards on most historic buildings to hangul, since the Korean script evoked an

easily recognizable Korean identity. For a discussion of Park Chung Hee's hangul exclusivity policy, see Andreas Schirmer's chapter in this volume.

11. For an English language resource reproducing some of the photographs from the 1975 Hyŏnch'ungsa report, see Park (2010), particularly the exceptional evolution of the reliquary building from traditional to modern and back to a staged traditional style (the modern-style building was simply remodeled by adding painted concrete columns and a tile roof, for a seemingly traditional appearance).

12. Timothy R. Tangherlini notes that in the process of modernization of the countryside, "straw roofs were replaced by zinc ones, dirt roads were paved with asphalt, mud walls were replaced with cement blocks" (2008, 67).

13. In the United Kingdom, the heritageization of thatched cottages and log cabins is part of the so-called vernacular movement (Howard 2003, 37), while in Japan, the ubiquitous commoners' inn has been transformed into luxurious lodging and, at the same time, an icon of Japanese beauty (Guichard-Anguis 2009).

14. See, for example, the photograph taken at the inauguration of Chongyongsa, the memorial hall of Ch'ilbaek Ŭich'ong, in 1976 (Munhwajaech'ŏng 2011b, 192). The structure of the building resembles that of a Buddhist hall, but the columns, the roof and all the decorative elements of the roof, traditionally made of wood, are now made of concrete. The building looks clean and solemn, and manages to convey a sense of the past, which aptly distracts the viewer from the realization that this is not an authentic Chosŏn-era building, but a replica of it.

15. For a comprehensive list of heritage sites that underwent purification during the Park era, see Ŭn (2005, 251–252).

The OCP documented very thoroughly its purification projects in individual reports published throughout the 1960s and 1970s. Each report documents the history of the heritage site, its state before the purification and a detailed account of the reconstruction (timeline, development, budget, photographs, the memos from President Park Chung Hee). Some of these reports are available on the official website of the Cultural Heritage Administration (www.cha.go.kr), under the section Haengjŏng chŏngbo—Munhwajae tosŏ—Kanhaengmul (only in the Korean version of the website).

REFERENCES

Capener, Steven D. 2016. "The Making of a Modern Myth: Inventing a Tradition for Taekwondo." *Korea Journal* 56.1 (Spring): 61–92.

Chang Kyŏng-ho. 2011. "Kaebal kwa hwangyŏng pyŏnhwa ro put'ŏ munhwajae rŭl chik'inŭn il" [Protecting heritage against development and environmental change]. In Munhwajaech'ŏng, *Munhwajaech'ŏng 50 nyŏnsa. Charyop'yŏn* [The fifty-year history of the Cultural Heritage Administration. Materials], 870–874. Seoul: Munhwajaech'ŏng.

Cho Han. 2015. "Tu kŏnmul ŭi iyagi: Puyŏ Pangmulgwan kwa Konggan Saok" [The story of two buildings: The Puyŏ Museum and Konggan Office Building]. *ART:MU. Digital Magazine of National Museum of Modern and Contemporary Art, Korea* 87 (July 1). Accessed March 16, 2018. http://artmu.mmca.go.kr /issue/view.jsp?issueNo=87&articleNo=63

Chŏn Chae-ho. 2012. "Pak Chŏng-hŭi chŏnggwŏn ŭi.'hoguk yŏngung mandŭlgi' wa chŏnt'ong munhwa yusan chŏngch'aek" ["The making of national defense heroes" and government policy towards traditional cultural heritage during the Park Chung Hee Regime]. *Yŏksa pip'yŏng* 99 (Summer): 113–140.

Chŏng Chae-hun. 1969. "Munhwajae kwalli haengjŏng ŭi kibon panghyang–hyŏn munhwajae kwalli ŭi silmu rŭl chungsim ŭro" [The fundamental directions of heritage management: Focusing on present practical aspects of heritage management]. *Munhwajae* 4:86–122.

———. 1977. "Hoguk, sŏnhyŏn yujŏk kwa chŏnt'ong munhwa yujŏk ŭi pojon kyesŭng e taehayŏ" [On the preservation of vestiges of heroes, sages, and traditional culture]. *Munhwajae* 11. Accessed October 20, 2017. http://portal.nrich.go.kr/kor/originalUsrView.do?menuIdx=680&info _idx=11&bunya_cd=2825&report_cd=2827#link

Cosgrove, Denis. 1984. *Social Formation and Symbolic Landscape.* London: Croom Helm.

———. 2003. "Landscape and the European Sense of Sight—Eyeing Nature." In *Handbook of Cultural Geography*, edited by Kay Anderson, Mona Domosh, Steve Pile, and Nigel Thrift, 249–268. London: Sage Publications.

Delissen, Alain. 2001. "The Aesthetic Pasts of Space (1960–1990)." *Korean Studies* 25 (2): 243–260.

Finch, Jonathan. 2019. "Historic Landscapes." In *The Routledge Companion to Landscape Studies*, 2nd ed., edited by Peter Howard, Ian Thompson, Emma Waterton, and Mick Atha, 166–175. London: Routledge.

Graburn, Nelson H. H. 2001. "Learning to Consume: What Is Heritage and When Is It Traditional?" In *Consuming Tradition, Manufacturing Heritage. Global Norms and Urban Forms in the Age of Tourism*, edited by Nezar AlSayyad, 68–89. London: Routledge.

Guichard-Anguis, Sylvie. 2009. "Japanese Inns (*ryokan*) as Producers of Japanese Identity." In *Japanese Tourism and Travel Culture*, edited by Sylvie Guichard-Anguis and Okpyo Moon, 76–101. London: Routledge.

Harvey, David, and Timothy J. Wilkinson. 2019. "Landscape and Heritage: Emerging Landscapes of Heritage." In *The Routledge Companion to Landscape Studies*, 2nd ed., edited by Peter Howard, Ian Thompson, Emma Waterton, and Mick Atha, 176–191. London: Routledge.

Hobsbawm, Eric J., and Terence O. Ranger, eds. 1983. *The Invention of Tradition*. Cambridge: Cambridge University Press.

Howard, Peter. 2003. *Heritage. Management, Interpretation, Identity*. London: Continuum.

Jackson, Ben, and Robert Koehler. 2012. *Korean Architecture: Breathing with Nature*. Seoul: Seoul Selection.

Kangwŏndo Chibang Munhwajae Kwalliguk. 1976. *Ojukhŏn chŏnghwaji* [The purification of Ojukhŏn]. Ch'unch'ŏn: Kangwŏndoch'ŏng.

Kim, Ann Meejung. 2016. "Marketing the Past: Rhetorical Presentation of Bukchon in Tourist Literature." *Korea Journal* 56 (3) (Autumn): 136–172.

Kim, Chŏng-gi. 1972. "Korea's Traditional Architecture." *Korea Journal* 12 (7) (July): 17–23.

Kim, Hyon-sob. 2017. "Representing Korean Architecture in the Modern West: Two Korean Pavilions from 1960s International Expositions." *arq: Architectural Research Quarterly* 21 (2) (June): 155–170.

Kim Tong-hyŏn. 2011. "Pulguksa, Ch'ŏnmach'ong tŭng Kyŏngju palgul chosa wa hamkke han ch'uŏk." In Munhwajaech'ŏng, *Munhwajaech'ŏng 50 nyŏnsa. Charyop'yŏn* [The fifty-year history of the Cultural Heritage Administration. Materials], 797–801. Seoul: Munhwajaech'ŏng.

Kim, Yersu (Kim Yŏ-su). 1976. *Cultural Policy in the Republic of Korea*. Paris: UNESCO.

Krauss, Werner. 2008. "European Landscapes: Heritage, Participation and Local Communities." In *The Ashgate Research Companion to Heritage and Identity*, edited by Brian Graham and Peter Howard, 425–438. Burlington, VT: Ashgate.

Lee, Young-ho (Yi Yŏng-ho). 1972. "Modernization and Tradition: Korean Attitudes." *Korea Journal* 12 (10) (October): 12–17.

Moenig, Udo, and Kim Minho. 2016. "The Invention of Taekwondo Tradition, 1945–1972: When Mythology Becomes 'History.'" *Acta Koreana* 19.2 (December): 131–164.

Moon, Okpyo. 2010. "Dining Elegance and Authenticity: Archaeology of Royal Court Cuisine in Korea." *Korea Journal* 50 (1) (Spring): 36–59.

Moon, Seungsook. 2008. "Buddhist Temple Food in South Korea: Interests and Agency in the Reinvention of Tradition in the Age of Globalization." *Korea Journal* 48 (4) (Winter): 147–180.

Munhwa Kongbobu [Ministry of Culture and Information]. 1969. *Asan*

Hyŏnch'ungsa yŏnhyŏkchi [The history of Hyŏnch'ungsa in Asan]. Seoul: Munhwa Kongbobu.

———. 1970. *Haengju Sansŏng posu chŏnghwaji* [The repair and purification of Haengju Fortress]. Seoul: Munhwa Kongbobu Munhwajae Kwalliguk.

———. 1975. *Hyŏnch'ungsa yŏnhyŏkchi. Chŭngbop'an* [The history of Hyŏnch'ungsa, enl. ed.]. Seoul: Munhwa Kongbobu.

———. 1976. *Ch'ilbaek Ŭich'ong posu chŏnghwaji* [The repair and purification of Ch'ilbaek Ŭich'ong]. Seoul: Munhwa Kongbobu Munhwajae Kwalliguk.

Munhwajaech'ŏng. 2011a. *Munhwajaech'ŏng 50 nyŏnsa. Charyop'yŏn* [The fifty-year history of the Cultural Heritage Administration. Materials]. Seoul: Munhwajaech'ŏng.

———.2011b. *Munhwajaech'ŏng 50 nyŏnsa. Ponsap'yŏn* [The fifty-year history of the Cultural Heritage Administration. Its history]. Seoul: Munhwajaech'ŏng.

O'Keeffe, Tadhg. 2007. "Landscape and Memory: Historiography, Theory, Methodology." In *Heritage, Memory and the Politics of Identity. New Perspectives on the Cultural Landscape*, edited by Niamh Moore and Yvonne Whelan, 3–18. Burlington, VT: Ashgate.

Pai, Hyung Il. 2001. "The Creation of National Treasures and Monuments: The 1916 Japanese Laws on the Preservation of Korean Remains and Relics and Their Colonial Legacies." *Korean Studies* 25 (1): 72–95.

———.2013. *Heritage Management in Korea and Japan. The Politics of Antiquity and Identity*. Seattle: University of Washington Press.

Park, Chung Hee. 1962. *Our Nation's Path: Ideology of Social Reconstruction*. Seoul: Hollym Corporation.

———.1972. "1973 nyŏndo yesanan chech'ul e chŭŭm han sijŏng yŏnsŏlmun" [A rectification speech on the 1973 budget bill]. Accessed March 3, 2018. http://www.pa.go.kr/research/contents/speech/index.jsp?spMode=view&catid=c_pa02062&artid=1306344

———.1973. "1973 nyŏn yŏndu kija hoegyŏn" [1973 Beginning-of-the-year press conference]. Accessed April 14, 2018. http://pa.go.kr/research/contents/speech/index.jsp?spMode=view&artid=1306372&catid=c_pa02062

———. 1977. "1977 nyŏndo yesanan chech'ul e chŭŭm han sijŏng yŏnsŏlmun" [A rectification speech on the 1977 budget bill]. Accessed March 2, 2018. http://pa.go.kr/research/contents/speech/index.jsp?spMode=view&artid=1306529&catid=c_pa02062

Park, Saeyoung. 2010. "National Heroes and Monuments in South Korea: Patriotism, Modernization and Park Chung Hee's Remaking of Yi Sunsin's Shrine." *The Asia-Pacific Journal* 24 (3) 10 (June 14). Accessed June 21, 2017. https://apjjf.org/-Saeyoung-Park/3374/article.html

Saeji, CedarBough T. 2014. "Creating Regimes of Value through Curation at the National Museum of Korea." *Acta Koreana* 17 (2): 609–637.

Sîntionean, Codruṭa. 2015. "The Preservation of the Chŏnju Hanok Village: From Material Authenticity to the Themed Replica." *Future Anterior* 12 (1) (Summer): 56–75.

Stephenson, Janet. 2008. "The Cultural Values Model: An integrated Approach to Values in Landscapes." *Landscape and Urban Planning* 84 (2): 127–139.

Tangherlini, Timothy R. 2008. "Chosŏn Memories: Spectatorship, Ideology, and the Korean Folk Village." In *Sitings. Critical Approaches to Korean Geography*, edited by Timothy R. Tangherlini and Sallie Yea, 61–82. Honolulu: University of Hawai'i Press.

Ŭn Chŏng-t'ae. 2005. "Pak Chŏng-hŭi sidae sŏngyŏkhwa saŏp ŭi ch'ui wa sŏnggyŏk" [The development and character of sacralization projects during the Park Chung Hee era]. *Yŏksa munje yŏn'gu* 15 (December): 241–277.

Van Zile, Judy. 2011. "Blurring Tradition and Modernity. The Impact of Japanese Colonization and Ch'oe Sŭng-hŭi on Dance in South Korea Today." In *Consuming Korean Tradition in Early and Late Modernity. Commodification, Tourism, and Performance*, edited by Laurel Kendall, 169–194. Honolulu: University of Hawai'i Press.

Yi Kyŏng-hŭi. 2011. "Munhwa yusan p'aioniŏ–minjok chŏngch'esŏng ch'atki 50 nyŏn. 1. Chŏng Chae-hun chŏn Munhwajae Kwalligukchang" [Pioneers of cultural heritage–A fifty-year search for national identity. 1. Chŏng Chae-hun, former director of the Office of Cultural Properties]. Interview with Chŏng Chae-hun. *Chungang Ilbo*, May 10. Accessed August 18, 2017. http://news .joins.com/article/print/5466067

CHAPTER 11

Rematerializing the Political Past

The Annual Schoolchildren's March and North Korean Invented Traditions

ROBERT WINSTANLEY-CHESTERS

Whan that Apriil with his shoures soote
The droghte of March hath perced to the roote . . .
So priketh hem nature in hir corages;
Thanne longen folk to goon on pilgrimages

—Geoffrey Chaucer, *The Canterbury Tales*
(General Prologue 2005, 1387)

Geoffrey Chaucer's fourteenth-century narrative of pilgrims en route to Thomas à Beckett's shrine at Canterbury in England of course is a world away from contemporary North Korea. This chapter seeks to make no connection between the two other than to reconfirm the cultural importance across time and space of the practice of pilgrimage and other such journeys. While pilgrimage has not faded from the world's repertoire of cultural practice (Santiago di Compostella, Uman in the Ukraine, and the annual hajj to Mecca being particularly relevant contemporary examples), such practices are less familiar than in the past. Pilgrimage holds obvious advantages for the modern human—carving out time in busy human lives and creating shared and safe group experiences within a significant journey. But pilgrimage's key feature as transmitted in secular, contemporary forms, has been its utility as a vessel for the carrying, sustaining, and socialization of memory. New contemporary memories demand the creation of what Hobsbawm and Ranger (1983) declared invented traditions. These invented traditions support and underpin what Benedict Anderson named imagined communities (1983). Chaucer's pilgrims, hajjis the Islamic world over, and contemporary Irish visitors to the shrine of the Blessed Virgin Mary at Knock are very much part of imagined communities as Anderson understands them. These various communities pledge emotional fealty with their bodies and minds to community at its most loosely defined, to the *ummah*, to the fellowship of the faithful, to the ideologically sound. Together faith in the memory of something sacred and profound binds these communities together, constructing a framework of practice and praxis around those memories.

Invented Traditions and their imagined communities are not required to be either new products or of the deep past. This chapter does not suggest that Koreans as *minjok* (ethnic nation) are an imagined community. While disputes may rage as to the historical longevity or homogeneity of Koreans as an ethnic group, including any interruptions, ruptures, or breaks in either longevity or homogeneity, this chapter does not suggest imagination is required on this point. Both Korean nations now present on the Korean Peninsula have been subject to extraordinary historical and political forces in the last two centuries. Koreans have been forced to rethink what it means to be Korean in light of transformations in technology, capital, commerce, political and social organization, and notions of sovereignty. In more recent times Koreans have been required to imagine themselves anew once more. This time citizens on the Peninsula have had to define themselves as North Korean or South Korean, separated from family, brothers, sisters, and *minjok* by what Paik Nak-chung described as The Division System (2011). While in 2018 it appears there may be unexpected gaps, cracks, and fissures in the once monolithic separation, Koreans are still required to in some sense "other" each other by virtue of their location on the Peninsula. Much of that othering is undertaken through the function of a collection of new traditions, real or invented through which contemporary Korean sovereignty, statehood, and communities are imagined.

This chapter looks to North Korean traditions that while vitally important to Pyongyang's political structures, power, and centralized institutional memory, are physically sited far from the capital, deeply connected and embedded within the landscape of its northern terrains. Paektusan is enmeshed in the political memory and practice of North

Korea. Pyongyang refers to its political dynasty as the Paektusan Generals (Berthelier 2013) named after the memories of struggles in favor of socialism and Korean nationalism in the mid-1930s by a select group of guerrilla fighters (under the control of a Kim Il Sung, if not the Kim Il Sung), against Japanese and colonial forces, which is so vital to the framing of national history (Suh 1995). This group of political guerrillas would later emerge supreme over a number of other political factions in a young North Korea and would seal Kim Il Sung's legacy. These memories and legacies are themselves invented traditions but this chapter does not privilege the grand narratives focused on North Korea's leadership. Instead its focus is rather more prosaic traditions involving its un-garlanded citizenry. While it is virtually impossible to directly engage with North Korea's public *in situ*, the invented and imagined traditions that surround them, which they are supposed to engage with and which literature and public media from Pyongyang can focus on with some intensity are certainly accessible. In recent years some of these new traditions have become incorporated into the institutional structures and training practices of North Korean bureaucracy and important moments in the timetable of the country's school year. This chapter specifically focuses on the 250 Mile Schoolchildren's March, an event first seen in 2015, and the study visits of North Korean bureaucrats and civil servants to Paektusan, visits that have increased with such frequency in the last five years as to become important traditions themselves. The year 2015 appeared potentially particularly impactful for North Korea's developmental narrative given there were a number of important anniversaries that year that it would be vital to mark with new or renewed connections with the charismatic past.

THEORETICAL FRAMES

Aside from Hobsbawm and Ranger's (1983) notion of invented traditions that is vital to the structure of this edited volume, and its later intersection with Benedict Anderson's articulation of imagined communities (1983), this chapter holds a number of other elements in mind within its theoretical frame. Both invented traditions and imagined communities must function within a wider ecosystem of politics, history, and ideology.

This chapter explores invented traditions within North Korea's seemingly unique political framework. There are a huge variety of theories seeking to explain and explore the curiosities of North Korea's politics. From concepts of North Korea as a gangster state, international security threat, quasi-fascist ethno-blood nationalist, place of institutional insanity, or bureaucracy focused on muddling through, even a rational actor, every stripe of ideological analysis has been directed at Pyongyang. This particular author holds to Heonik Kwon and Byung-ho Chung's influential channeling of Max Weber and Clifford Geertz in their assertion that North Korea has all the hallmarks of a theater state (2012), in which performativity has a vital political function that might explain the longevity of its government and politics long after the collapse of the Soviet Bloc and similar ideological manifestations. Pyongyang's theatric sensibilities are powered by a Weberian sense of political charisma deployed on a national scale, breaking temporal boundaries and embedding itself within the nation's historical memory. As a human geography for the author of this chapter space, scale, boundaries, and bounding are all vital elements within analysis. In North Korea space and place for political performance and practice is equally vital. Theatric politics necessarily requires a stage for the performance or re-performance of its charisma, that stage is the landscapes of the nation itself. This author therefore twins theories and concepts from anthropology (Benedict Anderson, Heonik Kwon and Byung-ho Chung) and history (Hobsbawm), with geographic theories on the construction of symbolic, political, or social landscapes (Cosgrove 1984, 2004; Castree 2001).

Cosgrove determined that nations in the process of construction, literally build, generate, or reconfigure new landscapes that best fit both national narrative, religious and political ideologies, and cultural presumptions. Using the United States as an example Cosgrove suggests European settlers essentially rewrote the terrain of the future midwestern states such as Ohio, Indiana, and Illinois (among many), from what they saw as an unimproved, unorganized American landscape into a patchwork quilt of squares and rectangles reflecting European notions of property, gentility, and cartography (or the science of mapmaking). In small towns and cities in these emerging states, settler citizens and local bureaucracies would make certain to incorporate public parks and civilized amenities into new urban fabrics, attempting to bring the sensibilities of the old world into an at times hostile new world. Noel Castree's conception of political landscapes (2001), building on Cosgrove's work, suggested the direct embedding of political and economic ideologies into topographies and terrains. Utilizing the critical approaches to nature of scholars such as Neil Smith, Michael Watts, and David Harvey, as well as that of Cosgrove, Castree engages with Marxist dialectics, and in particular Engel's *Dialectic of Nature*, which was itself influential with those from whom North Korea would draw ideological inspiration (Winstanley-Chesters 2015). Castree's work would pave the way for contemporary geographic understandings of the overtly neo-liberal or economically conservative city with its predilections towards co-option and alienation of public space, and the privileging of spaces for consumption. Castree's analysis connects with the writing of Eric Swyngedouw on scale as political practice within landscape (1997, 2015), and the author's own on the application of such ideas in North Korea (2015). Swyngedouw's focus is the geography and hydrology of another particularly political territory, that of Franco's Falangist Spain, examining the embedding of the ideologies of fascist modernity into a reconfigured national hydrology. Scale and scaling may be unfamiliar terms to readers in this context, given that originally they derive from the field of cartography and seek to describe the relationships between physical maps and the terrains described by them. Swyngedouw reconfigures the terminology of scale for the context of political, social, and cultural geography, asserting that places represented or experienced by scaling are "the embodiment of social relations of empowerment and disempowerment and the arena through and in which they operate" (1997, 167). Building from Henri Lefebvre's conception that space and notions of spatiality themselves are products, social products, political products, this revisioning of scale is useful to articulate "how scale making is not only a rhetorical practice; its consequences are inscribed in and are the outcome of, both everyday life and macro-level social structures" (Marston 2000, 221), as well as these reconfigurations of notions of charisma and scale. A particular population's perception of the scale of their socially and politically constructed environment is not only shaped by their daily interactions with that environment—for example, commuting, working, and so on—it is shaped by official state policies and governmental control of maps and cartography and other markers of space in order to influence people's perceptions of their own environment. Government's both democratic and autocratic utilize practices of scale and scaling to project narrative and frame both debate and social/political possibility across categories of time and space.

Notions of scale and scaling are equally applicable to North Korea, and these notions are determined by the daily practices of North Korean citizens (going to school and work, obtaining food, engaging in leisure activity), but also by the political elites of Pyongyang in their attempt to control the population. In North Korea these processes of scale and scaling are very much rhetorical practices as much as they are about impacting politically on social relations and utilizing the charismatic energy described earlier through the work of Kwon and Chung across time as well as space. In addition therefore to the notions of the theater state and scale and scaling, there is one other vitally important theoretical concept that will help clarify the invented tradition of the Children's March. When it comes to scaling across time in North Korea and its invented traditions, these are best considered through the lens provided by Gilles Deleuze and Felix Guattari in *Anti-Oedipus: Capitalism and Schizophrenia* (1984). North Korean invented traditions and theatric energies are rescaled across time and space through the processes of what Deleuze and Guattari termed de-territorialization and reterritorialization (1984). These are essentially used to articulate the processes involved in the fracturing, collapse, or disintegration of situated social and cultural bonds between a physical terrain and the population or culture that inhabited it. Much of their analysis revolves around the impact of capitalism on such cultural bonds and the pressures that alienated communities from their territories and traditional homes. While these processes transform and sometimes deeply impact such cultures, they do not necessarily eradicate them and they can reform more powerfully or differently elsewhere. Deleuze and Guattari actually distinguish between absolute de-territorialization, in which the object of the process is completely destroyed or negated, and relative de-territorialization in which it reappears elsewhere or in a different moment reterritorialization (1987). Good examples of this when it comes to imagined communities include two Eastern European visions of nationalism. Livonia and its language of Livonian was an originally pagan territory of Balto-Finnic people roughly occupying what is now northern Latvia and southern Estonia. Once a powerful coastal trading nation who controlled the Daugava River, Livonia was devastated during the Livonian Crusade of 1198–1209 (the last campaign for mass conversion of a population in Europe), and never really recovered its position (Zajas 2013). Estonia was also the territory of another Balto-Finnic people long subsumed into more powerful nations such as Lithuania, Poland, Russia, and Sweden. Estonia's moment of independence before 1945 was also brief, nineteen years from 1920 to 1939. Estonia and the notion of being an Estonian was de-territorialized for many centuries under earlier rulers, and from 1939 to 1991 by Nazi Germany and the Soviet Union (according to Estonian historiography), yet in 2019 there is a vibrant and energetic Estonian state, a member of the European Union, famous for its tech-savvy democracy. Its de-territorialization was only relative (Peiker 2016). Livonia on the other hand would never rise again from underneath the memory or curtain of another state. Today only 250 residents of Latvia and 30 residents of Estonia claim to be Livonian and the last native speaker of the Livonian language, Grizelda Kristina died in Canada in 2013. Livonia and its culture's de-territorialization have certainly been absolute. An example rather closer to the geography of this chapter might be the attempt, as Korean nationalist historiography has it, of imperial Japan and its colonial institutions between 1910 and 1945 to absolutely de-territorialize Korean culture and national identity by eradicating the Korean language and demanding the adoption of a new imperial subjectivity by its colonial subjects. Relative de-territorialization is of most interest to this chapter and to the consideration of North Korean politics and practices connected to it.

Readers will have gathered by now that this chapter is focused on what I claim to be a new invented tradition of North Korea, a series of annual marches connected to important moments in the nation's history, in particular moments that were themselves journeys and crossings. Such journeys contain the charismatic political energy from which leadership and government of contemporary North Korea draw strength. This charisma is transmitted across time and into our and the North Korean present by not simply the processes of scale and scaling I have previously talked about in this section, but also through these relative processes of de- and re-territorialization familiar to Deleuze and Guattari reterritorialization (1984). The power of these journeys, crossings, and charismatic moments is de-territorialized, abstracted, and extracted from its original temporary and geographical context in the northern Korean Peninsula of the 1930s and re-territorialized in our and North Korea's present in the guise of the performative invented traditions described here. While Deleuze and Guattari did not originally include a temporal frame in their writing, doing so, so that such transformations also include de-temporalizations and re-temporalizations, allows for a more holistic consideration of the practices and implications of Pyongyang's new invented traditions.

Since these traditions and the mythologies behind them occur close to North Korea's border with the People's Republic of China, and though the nation on the other side did not exist during those moments that generate so much charismatic energy for Pyongyang, the border and practices of bordering must have theoretical attention applied to them. Bordering and border crossing as practices and processes have themselves been subject to extensive theoretical framing (Singer and Massey [1998] on Mexican border crossing and Grundy-Warr and Yin [2002] on Myanmar border crossing as examples). North Korean border crossing in particular is considered to demonstrate the institutional and ideological failure of Pyongyang's government. This is not the first time that border crossing has been problematic to institutional or national power on or near the north of the Korean Peninsula. Korea or the Chosŏn dynasty's northern border has, nationalist narrative aside, always been semi-porous and in places undefined. Qing dynasty and Chosŏn surveyors could not agree on the demarcation between the two in 1712 and from 1885 to 1887 (Song 2016, 2018). The diffuse nature of the boundary had not gone unnoticed and Korean settlers had problematically crossed the border and squatted on these debatable lands. Later this lack of definition would be used by imperial Russia and imperial Japan to problematize both Koreans in the border region and Korean sovereignty there at all (Song 2018). North Koreans crossing and re-crossing of the northern border are in contemporary times both problematized and idealized by Pyongyang's opponents. North Koreans both engage in border crossing to become problematic migrants in China or South Korea (Chung 2008), or as a strategy for individual or group survival through practices of exchange and interaction with guerrilla or informal markets (Byman and Lind 2010). Both are in a sense problematic for Pyongyang itself; however analysis has suggested that informal border practices provide something of an escape valve for a system and its institutions that can no longer service much of their governmental responsibilities (Smith 2015). North Korea's own historiography frames border crossers in the 1920s and 1930s as powerful actors and agents for national rehabilitation and re-creation. On the other hand, they were seen as extremely problematic to border and internal security by colonial and Japanese authorities (Haruki 1992). The reader will see how contemporary invented traditions from Pyongyang harness the energy of both of these conceptions of border crossing in the past.

Given the charismatic political construction manifest in North Korea, which utilizes as one of the core elements of its authority and legitimacy a physical engagement in terrain and space within historical memory, so avowedly temporalized, namely the guerrilla spaces of Paektu, generating, producing, and engineering through both performance, narrative, and assertion a constructed landscape, would it not stand to reason that such as social and politically constructed space could be iterated and transmitted by the processes of scale and scaling? North Korea's political and cultural cartography in a sense is operationalized by its bureaucracy and regime at the national level. It is theorized and de- or re-temporalized by this higher scale and it may be that in many circumstances it can be functionally useful in remaining at such an extensive and expansive scale. However, there are moments in which territorializing the charismatic spatial output of the wider, national production is a necessity in order to more realistically underpin or develop these narratives and their legitimating content. At such moments we witness the transfer of charismatic content from one scale, the national and the institutional, to another, the locally spatial and the locally encountered. In these instances rescaling of the charismatic social and political constructions allows and supports the embedding and embodying of the narrative and productions, not just simply within the abstract body politic of North Korea, but in the physical bodies of residents and participants and in the spaces and topographies in which that charisma is performed and enacted. These spaces, rescalings, and temporal enactments are at the core of this chapter's interest and to which it will now turn. To do so it will encounter three manifestations of such scalings and rescalings, considering in particular those vectors, signals, and processes by which they are operationalized.

THE DE-TERRITORIALIZATION
OF PYONGYANG'S SUN

Readers who are already particularly interested in or focused upon North Korea will be well aware of the ideologies surrounding its dynastic leadership, whose role within the nation's politics fully meets the definition of personality cult used in other instances of autocratic government. They might also be aware of some of the local distinctive peculiarities of North Korea's personality cult. Kim Il Sung for instance, the first president of the Democratic People's Republic of Korea (the official name for North Korea), is in fact the last president of the nation as he permanently holds that office, even though he died in 1994 (Yoon 2017). While forever having a dead president might seem unnecessarily odd or unusual, this extra-territorial, post-physical state of being in fact allows Kim Il Sung to serve more abstract and esoteric functions within North Korea's political structure.

The Great Leader (one of Kim Il Sung's many titles) serves as a vessel for memory and a carrier signal for the charismatic political authority generated as this chapter has already asserted, during the proto–North Korean guerrilla period of the mid-1930s. In a further abstraction of Kim Il Sung's physicality, one of the other titles ascribed to him is that of the "Sun" of the nation. As Pyongyang's "Sun," Kim Il Sung can permanently radiate beneficence, care, and inspiration upon North Korea's topography and territory, not subject to the impacts of time and aging (Suh 1995). His son Kim Jong Il and grandson Kim Jong Un, the current ruler of North Korea, as distinct and definite as they were as political figures, have also been abstracted a little by the impacts of this approach to both ideology and history. Kim Jong Il when younger and undergoing preparation or development for leadership in the 1970s was referred to in North Korean publications as "the party center" rather than by name (Shinn 1982). Kim Jong Il is also referred to as the Dear Leader among other names and can be represented along with his father by the image of one of the national flowers of the nation, the Kimjongilia and the Kimilsungia (Oh 1990). Kim Jong Un himself is less abstract, but when describing his activities on a day-to-day basis, North Korean media still make sure, rather than grounding him in the present, to place him within a continuum of memory that includes his father, grandfather, and a variety of events and moments within North Korea's memory (*Rodong Sinmun* 2018a).[1]

In order to concretize these abstractions of political power and to better ground the complex narratives of history and memory required to underpin Pyongyang's institutional power, constructed and invented traditions have been required. It is natural that a large number of these traditions revolve around the birthdays, moments of transition, triumph, or other important days in the lives of its dynastic leadership (Gabroussenko 2010). Another chapter could perhaps indeed focus on the invented traditions around the visits of one of the Kim family to factories, farms, hospitals, and other institutions or pieces of infrastructure, which lead to these places being named after the day on which either Kim Il Sung or Kim Jong Il first visited them (Winstanley-Chesters 2015). This chapter however focuses on invented traditions that do not focus on infrastructure, whether political, institutional, or military in nature, and not directly on the leadership of North Korea as it is now constituted. Instead this chapter considers invented traditions that directly attempt to include members of its wider population and bureaucratic classes. Citizens of North Korea, no matter how politically engaged or institutionally connected, unlike the imagined traditions of their leaders, live in concrete space and time. Citizens are therefore, regardless of how much effort the central government spends on propaganda and political messaging, potentially disconnected in vital ways (from a North Korean institutional perspective) from the source and font of national ideological, philosophic, or national inspiration. In order to bridge this disconnection Pyongyang has always sought to drive interest in the commemoration of important moments in the history of its leadership and charismatic political first family, or aspired to present an image of such interest where none might be actually present. A recent particular example of this tendency involved the 100th anniversary of the birth of Kim Il Sung's first wife, Kim Jong Suk, on December 24, 2017. Born in 1917, she is a figure somewhat distant to North Korea's contemporary population, even with her blood and filial connection to the Great and Dear Leaders. While Kim Jong Suk already has a number of places named after her (such as Pyongyang's Kim Jong Suk Textile Mill), December 2017 saw a large number of public events focused on both remembering her life, developing public interest in her narrative, and embedding it within the minds of future generations.

These events appeared to be a collaboration between the central government, the Socialist Women's Union of Korea, and the Korean Children's Union. Therefore, alongside the traditional wreath-laying ceremony at the Revolutionary Martyrs Cemetery (KCNA 2017a), the schoolchildren of Hoeryong (Hoeryŏng) watched and took part in a concert entitled "Eternal Sunray of Loyalty" at Hoeryong's Schoolchildren's Palace (2017b), KCNA asserting that interest in her and sites connected to her was "steadily increasing," with some 300,000 visitors to Hoeryong in 2017 alone (2017c).[2] North Korea's central bank printed gold and silver coinage with an image of her childhood home (KCNA 2017d), and the Ministry of Railways put a railway carriage and velocipede (a hand-powered railway vehicle), on display that Kim Jong Suk had used in 1945 (2017e). The crossings of Kim Il Sung this chapter considers in detail have also been matched with events of re-territorializing Kim Jong Suk's own moments of crossing. Important moments of historical memory essentially serve as North Korean "Saints Days," temporalizations and crystallizations of the supra-temporal and esoteric streams of narrative charisma. As well as a mythology such events also require a mythography on to which traditions and imagination can be implanted. While both the developing mythology of the North Korean political present has been considered by past academic work (Kwon 2013) and even the structural elements of the mythography on to which it is laid (Joinau 2014), what has not been addressed is the developing tendency for North Korea to provide opportunities and spaces for North Korea's own citizens to encounter the narrative and charismatic energies transmitted by these "de-territiorializings" and "de-temporalizings" for themselves, to walk theatrically in the footsteps of the nationalist past. In doing so these citizens become actors and agents within the process of new invented traditions that seek to revivify the political energy of the past, bringing it physically into the present.

Far from Pyongyang and the current centers of political power and energy in North Korea, as well as the monolithic, commemorative architectures of the city, the Tumen and Amnok rivers on the nation's northern boundary play a huge role in the way the rest of the world conceives of the nation. Gazing across the rivers from China, foreign eyes see a landscape of deprivation, barren nature, and failures in governmentality and development (Shim 2013). However, these river boundaries have an enormous place in North Korea's own self-perception. Long considered the boundary between Korean national territory and that of either China or Manchuria, the Tumen and the Amnok and their shores play a vital role in the histories of North Korea and Korean nationalism as transition spaces or zones of malleability (Winstanley-Chesters 2016). Travel through or interaction with these zones and spaces is in some Korean historical and mythological memories akin to crossings in sacred literatures of other rivers such as the Styx or the Jordan, crossings that transform and transfigure the crosser (Havrelock 2011). Another aspect of such zones and places are that they are seen within both mythologies, histories, and hagiographies as places in which "special" or significant things are more likely or possible to happen than in other more conventional territory (Barthes 1972). New Testament biblical texts even suggest that in such special places, a special temporal frame exists in which chronos, "chronological time" (χρόνος), is replaced by "kairos" (καιρός) or "special/significant" time (Smith 1969). Within North Korea's historiography the landscape of the Tumen and the Amnok is subject to an interesting historical dualism, in which the spaces of the rivers are both zones in which things that are significantly bad can happen and where events that are particularly positive can occur. In North Korea's historiography a number of key figures in the proto–North Korean nationalist guerrilla movements, such as Kim Il Sung and his first wife Kim Jong Suk, have important moments of crossing and re-crossing in their lives centered on these river zones (Winstanley-Chesters and Ten 2016). These important historical figures in North Korea's national story are forced by the circumstances of colonial rule to flee across the rivers to the less distinctly imperial space of Manchuria (later Manchukuo). They later return in a no less transformative moment, crossing back over the rivers to begin their campaigns of guerrilla harassment of colonial forces, campaigns that of course later become foundational to North Korea's notion of revolution and sense of national self (Suh 1995). In the process of crossing individuals such as Kim Il Sung and Kim Jong Suk not only support the transformation of the narrative of Korean or North Korean nationalism, but the transformation of their own selves. Connected via the transformative power of the de- and re-materializing process of crossing and re-crossing into special or significant places and times, these important characters in North Korea's history are transfigured from their child or precarious lives as colonial subjects, to powerful resistive, aggressive, political adults (Winstanley-Chesters and Ten 2016).

Kim Jong Suk in particular was completely transfigured by her crossing, leaving a slight child of oppressed and destitute sharecroppers and returning across the Tumen River a politically aware, energetic expert in military tactics and an excellent sniper (Winstanley-Chesters 2020).

Kim Il Sung's own particular moment of river crossing, according to current North Korean historiography, occurred in January 1925 over the frozen waters of the Amnok River (Suh 1995). It was this crossing that in North Korean mythology begins the period of guerrilla exile from which so much of his authority and charisma in Pyongyang's conceptual mind derives. The year 2015 would be the ninetieth anniversary of this moment so perhaps it should not be surprising that the anniversary was marked. *Rodong Sinmun* on January 23, 2015, reported: "A national meeting took place at the People's Palace of Culture Wednesday to mark the 90th anniversary of the 250-mile journey for national liberation made by President Kim Il Sung" (2015a). Neither was it surprising that the newspaper continued its report with a paragraph of assertions "On January 22, Juche [Chuch'e] 14 (1925) Kim Il Sung started the 250-mile journey for national liberation from his native village Mangyongdae (Man'gyŏngdae) to the northeastern area of China. During the journey he made up the firm will to save the country and the nation deprived by Japanese imperialism. New history of modern Korea began to advance along the unchangeable orbit of independence, Songun and socialism" (*Rodong Sinmun* 2015a).[3] As is common in North Korean media the text of the report attempts to include all three leaders produced by Pyongyang's political dynasty. Kim Jong Il, the Dear Leader's efforts to utilize this key source of nationalist power in 1975 through a commemorative march on its fiftieth anniversary, is also addressed by the text. Finally space is also made for some of Kim Jong Un's rather urgent and vociferous Paektusan-focused themes found within his 2015 New Year's Message: "Respected Marshal Kim Jong Un is wisely leading the work to ensure that the sacred tradition of the Korean revolution started and victoriously advanced by Kim Il Sung and Kim Jong Il is given steady continuity . . . calling on the school youth and children to hold them in high esteem as the eternal sun of Juche and carry forward the march to Mt. Paektu to the last" (*Rodong Sinmun* 2015a).

While repetition of past efforts and thoughts from North Korea's leadership might not be surprising in such a medium, the mention of the march is the first moment in which the invented tradition considered by this chapter appears. Observers and analysts of North Korean cultural and historical practice are familiar with many of the traditions connected to its political mythology. Many engage the audience and citizenry in worshipful, passive veneration of North Korea's political elite and their mythic past: standing in front of statues and monumental architectures, being shown sacred and important sites of memory, occasionally taking part in staged bouts of traditional dancing (*Rodong Sinmun* 2018d). So how would the school youth and children mentioned in the report from 2015 hold this "sacred tradition" in esteem, by passive participation at a meeting of the Workers' Party of Korea? Through the singing of songs and poems dedicated to moments of nationalist history recounted by the text? By appearing slightly overawed or afraid next to Kim Jong Un during a moment of on-the-spot guidance? In fact the answer would be none of these things, but something far more important, something that worked apart and aside from North Korea's more conventional commemorative traditions. Instead of abstraction and narrative opacity, there would instead be a period of de- and re-territorialization on the streets and paths of South Pyongan (P'yŏngan) Province, which itself would constitute a newly invented tradition. These schoolchildren would re-enact the crossing and journeys of Kim Il Sung in the 1930s, in the process using their own bodies as vessels and channels for the charismatic political energies rooted there for North Korean history. In short by this re-materialization of the political past, the children themselves become as Kim Il Sung and his small band of guerrillas.

There is a great deal missing in this first mention of this new tradition, much left out in the structure and conceptualization, but this is not uncommon for North Korean political practices and praxis, which often exclude content and coherence that might otherwise be expected. The process for the schoolchildren's selection, the nature of the institutions from which they came, or their ages, the number of children involved, even the exact length of the journey (as it is unclear whether the schoolchildren walk the entire distance), elements that might support a really convincing re-enactment process elsewhere in the world and tie into political themes and agendas, are never stated within the text of the *Rodong Sinmun* reporting of their enterprise. Yet the actual physicality and presence of their journey is clear and important to the narrative and the tradition. This physicality, common to pilgrimages elsewhere, perhaps even common to Chaucer's pilgrims mentioned at the very beginning of this chapter, in which breaks, pauses, and stops must be taken, presumably in this case to rest the children's tired legs after having "crossed one steep pass after another," is clear to the reader and a real element in the construction of this event (*Rodong Sinmun* 2015b). These are presented as real children of North Korea in 2015, not simply cyphers for the pre-Liberation, nationalist past, revitalized by the ideological connection and charismatic energies of the history they re-enact.

Simply conceiving of this journey or pilgrimage as yet another theatrical moment in North Korea's ceaseless flow of historiography and hagiography, however, would be to miss some of the important elements of the process and fail to draw out the greater and deeper levels of context and connection that underpin this new tradition. The theatric or performative potential of the event is clear. The children pass through, in North Korean tradition and practice, a well-prepared and well-trodden list of charismatic terrains, a list that is no doubt ideologically and narratologically entirely sound. Having left Mangyongdae, Kim Il Sung's home village according to *Rodong Sinmun*'s report, the children on the first march passed Kaechon (Kaech'ŏn, South P'yŏngan Province), Kujang and Hyangsan (both in North P'yŏngan Province), Huichon (Hŭich'ŏn), and Kanggye (Chagang), "along the historic road covered by the President with the lofty aim to save the destiny of the country and nation in the dark days when Korea was under the Japanese imperialists' colonial rule" (2015b).

Following Deleuze and Guattari's notion of de-territorialization, the spaces of relation and the practices of relation within the frame of the schoolchildren's journey are equally as important as its starting point, route, and destination, a fact held in common with much of the earlier narratives of North Korean journeying and crossing (Winstanley-Chesters 2015). Though within this newly invented tradition these children walk the route of the commemoration of what North Korea considers to be its period of national revolution and Liberation at this moment, temporally fixed in 2015, conceptually for those involved, however, it is supposed to be 1925. Whatever these North Korean children think in the quieter moments of their own particular every day (perhaps watching South Korean TV dramas on smuggled USB sticks, helping their parents engage in furtive transactions at semi-legal markets, or coping with the mixed ennui of resignation, exasperation, and desperation surely produced by daily interaction with Pyongyang's institutions), the social and personal context of those "dark days" in the late 1920s is activated and actualized by their every footstep. When they stopped for breaks they would hear the "impressions of the reminiscences of anti-Japanese guerrillas" and beginning their march again the schoolchildren, following the political power of those reminiscences, would become, represent, even channel, the affect, relation, and aspirations of those same guerrillas (*Rodong Sinmun* 2015b).

Following their departure from Pyongyang on January 22, 2015, these children arrived at their (and both Kim Il Sung and Kim Jong Il's) destination, Phophyong (P'op'yŏng) in Ryanggang Province around February 4 (*Rodong Sinmun* 2015c). Phophyong, according to North Korean historiography, is the actual site of Kim Il Sung's crossing of the Amnok River, the site where the young man would transition from subjugated Chōsen (colonial-period Korea) and the political frame of colonization, to resistance in the wild edges of Manchuria and new commitments and practices aiming for personal liberation and political and ideological struggle. This was the place and moment of Kim Il Sung's transformation and the foundational moment in this new invented tradition.

The North Korean historical narratives surrounding Kim Il Sung's first wife, Kim Jong Suk, also, as this chapter has suggested already, have her leaving her hometown of Hoeryong (North Hamgyŏng Province), and crossing the Amnok River in the early 1930s (Winstanley-Chesters 2020). The crossing itself is conceived of in a similar way to Kim Il Sung's as a moment of transformation, a harbinger of special times to come. It would not be surprising if other elements of this newly invented tradition of marching and re-materialization would be used to repurpose and reconnect with the charismatic energies of Kim Jong Suk's crossing (*Rodong Sinmun* 2014).

There have since 2015 been a wide variety of periods in which groups of children, workers, civil servants, and others within the institutional and political frameworks of North Korean society and bureaucracy engage in such walks, marches, and study tours (*Rodong Sinmun* 2018b). A number of these have marched and walked within some of the very same territory as the first march in 2015 (*Rodong Sinmun* 2018c). The Schoolchildren's March itself has been repeated in 2016 and 2017 following a similar route, but with additions and subtractions on each occasion. Some have sought to connect other places and spaces of political memory and power into the routes of their walks and marches, still others have included museums and commemorative spaces themselves within the itinerary. The marching visit of the Korean Children's Union to Mangyongdae and the Youth Movement Museum in June 2018 serves as a good example of such walks (*Rodong Sinmun* 2018d). It would be possible to frame these as more conventional acts of pilgrimage, if they were not deeply integrated into the ecosystems of North Korean politics. There have even been connections with the rich history of sacred spaces on and around Paektusan, in particular to the Secret Guerrilla Camp, the bivouacs, cooking spaces, and campsites of the guerrilla campaign and even to the extraordinary slogan trees (*Rodong Sinmun* 2018e). Paektusan's summit has not been excluded from these practices and there have been a number of instances of study tours and marches of civil servants and bureaucrats visiting the peak of the mountain as part of their activities (*Rodong Sinmun* 2018f). While surely visits and ideological pilgrimages to the sacred spaces of political memory in North Korea are not a new element in its conceptual repertoire of practice, there is something distinctly new about this category of invented tradition.

There has been little in the way of extra development of the actual Schoolchildren's March since 2015. Although 2020's iteration of the march appeared larger than the initial versions of the event in 2015 and 2016, *Rodong Sinmun*'s report of the start reads much the same (2020a). The Schoolchildren of 2020 began the march by holding a rally at Mangyongdae Revolutionary School in front of the statues of Kim Il Sung and Kim Jong Il (*Rodong Sinmun* 2020a). Choe Hwi, Vice Chair of the Workers' Party of Korea's Central Committee, was present to see them off, and the route is described as being "Kaechon [Kaech'ŏn, South P'yŏngan Province], Hyangsan [North P'yŏngan Province] and Kanggye [Chagang Province] to Phophyong" (*Rodong Sinmun* 2020a), much the same as in earlier years. On January 26 *Rodong Sinmun* reports that the schoolchildren have reached and passed Hyangsan, visiting Kujang Inn and Chongchongang [Ch'ŏngch'ŏngang, North P'yŏngan Province] Ferry Revolutionary Site and Tokgol Revolutionary Site along the way and engaging in what the newspaper records as "diverse political and cultural work including presentation on the reminiscences of anti-Japanese guerrillas and a question-and-answer study" (2020b). As in 2015 and other previous years they are met by party and local government officials at each point along the way and mark as many moments in the historical narratives of both Kim Il Sung's original march to Phophyong and Kim Jong Il's re-enactment of it (*Rodong Sinmun* 2020b). On February 1, 2020, *Rodong Sinmun* records the march's arrival in Kanggye (2020c), prior to which it had stopped at the Chongun and Pyolha inns and crossed the Myongmun and Kubong Passes [Chagang Province] (2020c). Finally on February 4, as in previous years, *Rodong Sinmun* records the Schoolchildren's March as having arrived in Phophyong to be greeted once more by Choe Hwi (2020d), and as always, unlike Kim Il Sung, to not cross the Amnok River.

While the Schoolchildren's March may not be greatly different in 2020 from its first contemporary iteration in 2015, the slogans, uniforms (even down to the blue and red jumpsuits worn by participants), being highly similar, what is different is the fact that far from being perhaps the only long-distance commemorative march or event at this time in the North Korean political year (after the oath-taking sessions traditionally following the New Year's Address, and in 2020 following the Fifth Plenary Meeting), many other study tours now share the pages of *Rodong Sinmun* and feature on North Korean television. Such study tours are not infrequent across Pyongyang's ideological calendar, but in 2020 in particular there have been a number of tours from organizations such as the Union of Agricultural Workers of Korea (*Rodong Sinmun* 2020e), the Kimilsungist-Kimjongilist Youth League (2020f), and even the "Commanding officers of the Korean People's Internal Security Forces" (2020g) to the politically important sites around Paektusan. The year 2019 even saw the Schoolchildren's March displaced for a year by a study tour and visit to the important sites of Kim Jong Il's life to mark his 77th birthday anniversary (*Rodong Sinmun* 2019). So in one sense there has been little change to the Schoolchildren's March in form, content, or geography when it appears. There have often been study tours and pedagogic political moments in North Korea's recent history, but the business of the current schedule of such events does seem to be new. Reiteration of all manner of political, historical, and ideological themes is perhaps at a premium toward the end of this first decade of Kim Jong Un's rule.

MARCHING AND RE-TERRITORIALIZING
IN 2015 AND BEYOND

In ending this chapter let me reiterate what in fact is distinct in the North Korean context when it comes to this newly invented tradition. Kim Jong Un assumed power in North Korea in 2011, one of several family members that could have taken power. North Korea's political system is rooted in and driven by political charisma, authority, and legitimacy projected into the present by various processes as I have discussed at the beginning of this chapter. Kim Jong Un as a young, seemingly untested man, the son of an arguably unimpressive Leader, who had led his nation through difficult struggles, profoundly lacked legitimacy at this moment and his authority was questionable. Much has been done to establish his legitimacy by North Korea's institutions and government since the death of his father. The prime way this has been done is to connect Kim Jong Un to the historical, charismatic lineage, doing so through the transformation of his physical resemblance and connections to his grandfather, repetition of important images and motifs (Chollima and white stallions in particular, as seen very recently on top of Paektusan), as well as an awareness of the unpopularity of Kim Jong Il, and the relative popularity of Kim Il Sung. The Schoolchildren's March (and perhaps other connected marches and organized political pilgrimages), which this chapter claims to be an invented tradition, is part of these efforts to connect to this deeper charismatic legacy, came just over a year after the violent purge of Jang Song Thaek, a reminder to both local North Koreans and the wider world of the factional struggles of Kim Il Sung and the brutality of the nation's autocratic politics and government. At the same time, of course, the march is part of these ongoing attempts to legitimize the grandson of Kim Il Sung and bestow some of North Korea's perceived historical charisma on him by further reiterating links to the legacy of the Paektusan Generals and Guerrilla dynasty.

The Schoolchildren's March of 2015 has been repeated in 2016, 2017, 2018, and has again occurred in 2020, so in the end was not simply a one-off re-enactment to connect to the particular energies generated by that year, or by the at-the-time impending 100th anniversary of Kim Il Sung's first wife Kim Jong Suk in 2017 who also engaged in river crossings and much journeying around the same time (which have themselves also been remembered through acts of re-territorialization and remembering in recent years). These marches are also not commemorating one particular moment in the history of Kim Il Sung's journeys and crossings; they do not follow a coherent or specific path of a single journey made by him. Instead as much as they re-territorialize collections of powerful moments, such as the crossings of the river, they are also assemblages of a number of different bits of historical narrative from the period within a geographical area generally considered to be charismatic within North Korea's political history. Essentially the march is a repertoire of important moments of historical memory connected together in such a way as to amplify the charismatic energies present within each moment.

However important and interesting as the Schoolchildren's March is, we should not only think about the specific event in 2015, but perhaps movement, crossing, and journeying, and their utility and usefulness in North Korea as processes of political scaling and rescaling. While such organized de- and re-territorializings (and intrinsic de- and re-temporalizings), are novel as newly invented traditions, Pyongyang's institutions have often harnessed the power of a particular sort of physical movement within its developmental and institutional strategies in order to underpin its goals or reconfigure the agenda. Analysts and watchers of North Korea will be familiar in recent years with the terms "shock brigades" (*ch'ungkyŏkyŏdan*) and "soldier builders" (*pyŏngsa kŏnch'ukŏpja*) (*Rodong Sinmun* 2018g). These categories of worker or operative are common to development or infrastructural projects in North Korea. They are deployed from an institutional network rooted in the Workers' Party of Korea or the Korean People's Army either at moments of crisis for a preexisting project or to undertake a key element of a new piece of strategy at an accelerated time scale. *Rodong Sinmun* and other North Korean media often report on the call for their usage or their later or finished work on the project. Often when these media do so they make sure to comment on the manner and speed of their journey to the site (*Rodong Sinmun* 2018h). It would not surprise the reader surely to hear that such journeys are often undertaken at considerable speed. The journeys of these "shock brigades" and "soldier builders" are themselves part of the theatric process of North Korean politics. In the terminology of geography, they are practical technologies of scale and scaling in which the political/social frames and praxis of the center are re-scaled out elsewhere in the nation's landscape and embedded in new terrains, reconfiguring provincial or peripheral political/social frames as they do so (Winstanley-Chesters 2015). As might be familiar to Erik Swyngedouw, such processes have most recently been seen within North Korea's hydrological and hydropower industries as the energy and authority of the state have been brought to bear on the river and reservoir systems of the country, embedding the logics and agenda of a particular form of politics in that terrain (Swyngedouw 2015). The invented traditions of the Schoolchildren's March and other marches or practices of journeying are themselves scalar processes in common with these preexisting traditions.

Beyond North Korea's more conventional and historically familiar efforts to scale and rescale its political energies across its territory, the journeys reconfigured within the newly invented traditions that this chapter encounters and explores are in themselves also acts of rescaling. However more than the practices and processes of aligning the agenda of the periphery, North Korea's more remote provinces such as Ryanggang and Chagang to the political aspirations of the center of power in Pyongyang, these traditions scale through and across time. Coupled with the processes of de- and re-territorialization and de- and re-temporalization the schoolchildren participants interact with the powerful political energies of North Korea's mythological or historiographic past, the charisma on which the authority and legitimacy (perceived) of Pyongyang's Paektusan Generals rests, rescaling it into the present day and our own temporal plane. These marches, processes, and journeys are themselves therefore scalar acts, as much as they are invented traditions. In the practice and process of these acts the participants are conceived of as not just re-enacting the journeys and travels of the past, cyphers and metaphorical vessels for them, but in some way they are transfigured into the physical realities of those who once, in North Korea's historical imaginary, trod the same paths and ground.

The importance of the Schoolchildren's March also lies beyond the march itself and the notions of space discussed in this chapter, to the practice of inventing traditions at particular salient moments of history of North Korea. The Schoolchildren's March therefore is certainly not a one-off invented tradition; there are a variety of other examples. The attempt at historicizing North Korea's foundational guerrilla tradition in order to legitimize the rule of Kim Il Sung (closely examined by Kwon and Chung among many others), might be considered a tradition of political amplification at least, if not one of complete invention. Thus a small group of Korean nationalists of a left-wing persuasion, though by no means committed to the ideological purity of Marxist-Leninism, who on occasion harassed Japanese border forces in the mid-1930s before disappearing, became foundational to North Korea's political memory and structures, memory that treated Kim Il Sung at times in messianic terms. Following the Korean War, captured materials from American forces in particular, such as the USS *Pueblo* assumed the position of relics of the conflict, manifestations of North Korea's claimed ability to overcome, and as it saw it, defeat the great imperialist. Later in North Korea's history and perhaps in competition with the developing commitment to conventional historiography and global reputation of its estranged southern neighbor and in spite of their earlier condemnation as vestiges of prerevolutionary feudalism and backwardness, folk traditions, royal heritages, and tomb archaeology were rediscovered. In particular, Pyongyang in 1994 rediscovered the tomb of King T'aejo (the king of Koryŏ between 918 and 943 CE), and other royal tombs at Kaesŏng, utilizing these reconstructed and reimagined pieces of national heritage in the service of a particularly North Korea–focused sense of material history, in which Koryŏ usurped Chosŏn as the most important prerevolutionary sovereign entity on the Peninsula. The invention and re-invention of such traditions serve a specific function, namely the revitalization of state authority at a moment the state chooses. These traditions in a sense share a lot in common with North Korea's ideological manifestations of Juche, Songun (*sŏn'gun*), and Byungjin (*pyŏngjin*)[4] (as just a few examples), aspirational rather than systematic, malleable and flexible, able to become whatever the state requires them to be at any moment.

The schoolchildren on the 250-mile march in 2015 and its iterations in later years, as well as other connected marches and "study tours" that sought to connect to the history and memory of Kim Il Sung and Kim Jong Suk are thus powerful, and as is the case with North Korea's varied ideologies, capable of many things, from serving as potentially transformative and transfigurative for those involved, to establishing a repertoire of newly invented traditional practices that can be and have been deployed elsewhere in North Korea. While they are extremely powerful and the practices of both scaling and de- and re-territorialization at the heart of them can achieve much, there is one key thing that they and other invented or reimagined North Korean traditions cannot do. In 2015 it was intriguing to consider their geographical place at the edge of North Korea's sovereignty as in 1925 this area was also the edge of the Japanese colonial terrain. While later in the history of Japanese imperialism, Manchuria would be reconfigured as the puppet state of Manchukuo, in 1925 the other side of the Amnok River at this point was still nominally Chinese territory. The crossing itself of Kim Il Sung is vital to the narrative for North Korea. However, in 2015 and in years since then the schoolchildren arrive at Phophyong, the site of this famous existential passage from one form of territory to another . . . yet they do not cross. Perhaps in those days of difficult and strained relations between Beijing and Pyongyang, prior to the events of 2018, such charismatic commemorations could not be enacted on either side of the boundary of sovereignty. Perhaps given the importance for North Korea of ideological soundness, its schoolchildren never could in reality have crossed over into a different political space. Whatever the reason, the most important fact is that in this act of pilgrimage, this newly invented tradition focused on the re-materialization of powerful charismatic energies by those schoolchildren, at the moment and place of crossing, they cannot actually cross, which leaves both the narrative and the invented tradition with a distinct disconnect, a functional void at its heart. Whatever aspirations North Korea may have at this point for this set of invented traditions, ultimately it cannot fully engage in their re-materialization. This newly invented tradition is for the moment at least trapped in North Korea's political present.

GLOSSARY

Amnok 압록
Byungjin (*pyŏngjin*) 병진
Chagang 자강
Chongchongang
 (Ch'ŏngch'ŏngang) 청천강
Chungkyŏkyŏdan 충격 여단

Huichon (Hŭich'ŏn) 희천
Hyangsan 향산
Kaechon (Kaech'ŏn) 개천
Kanggye 강계
Kubong 구봉
Kujang 구장

Mangyongdae (Man'gyŏngdae) 만경대

Phophyong (P'op'yŏng) 포평

Pyolha (Pyŏlha) 별하

Pyongan (P'yŏngan) 병안

pyŏngsa kŏnch'ukŏpja 병사 건축업자

Ryanggang 량강

Songun (*sŏn'gun*) 선군

T'aejo 太祖

NOTES

Apart from the unconventional spelling and style of North Korean political figures the author of this chapter indicates the North Korean spelling of North Korean place-names. These places may be familiar to South Koreans, but they are culturally and conceptually different for North Koreans and thus essentially different places in the mind, thus it is appropriate to romanize them in the manner a North Korean would.

1. It must be acknowledged that due to North Korea's habit of wiping the database of *Rodong Sinmun* articles every year or two, the author cannot guarantee that articles from *Rodong Sinmun* will still be available at the web addresses given. The author however keeps a copy of each *Rodong Sinmun* article in a word document and would be happy to share any with interested readers. It is also worth acknowledging that these are the English language versions of the *Rodong Sinmun* articles, Korean language versions of course exist and the author has copies of all of these as well. Again the author would be willing to share these with interested readers.

2. Korean Central News Agency, North Korea's state news agency has several websites. In 2010 KCNA established a .kp address registered in North Korea, but this did not supersede the original www.kcna.co.jp address as this Japanese-registered version has a searchable database going back some eighteen years, whereas the North Korea site only has the current year's stories. Recently the www.kcna.co.jp site has been unavailable as it has been geoblocked so that only browsers and computers with a Japanese internet connection can access it (NorthKoreaTech has a report on this at https://www .northkoreatech.org/2015/08/09/kcna-japan-site-isnt-down-its-geo -blocked/). This was extremely frustrating to all that use it and enabled the commodification of the database through paywalled access sites such as kcnawatch. The fact that it should only be available from Japanese computers however is not a barrier to using it outside of Japan, so instead of paying to access these links, use a VPN like Tor, or install the Hola extension on Google Chrome and set it to spoof your internet connection so that

it looks as if you are browsing from Japan; www.kcna.co.jp will then be free and accessible to you anywhere in the world. Download Hola from www .hola.org; download Tor from www.torproject.org.

3. Emerging in the aftermath of Kim Il Sung's 1993 death, the ideological concept of Songun (*Sŏn'gun*) is generally translated as "military-first politics" and was deployed by North Korea's government during the period of extreme hardship (1994–1998), during which Kim Jong Il stressed the importance of the army over the party as the principal organizing state institution of the DPRK and sought to mobilize the entire national population and all resources available for military purposes (Park 2007).

4. Byungjin (*pyŏngjin*) was Kim Il Sung's 1960s policy to develop simultaneously the military and the economy.

REFERENCES

Anderson, Benedict. 1983. *Imagined Communities: Reflections on the Origins and Spread of Nationalism*. London: Verso.

Barthes, Roland. 1972. *Mythologies*. London: J. Cape.

Berthelier, Benoit. 2013. "Symbolic Truth: Epic Legends and the Making of the Baekdusan Generals." *Sino-NK*, May 17. https://sinonk.com/2013/05/17/symbolic-truth-epic-legends-and-the-making-of-the-baektusan-generals/

Byman, Daniel, and Jennifer Lind. 2010. "Pyongyang's Survival Strategy: Tools of Authoritarian Control in North Korea." *International Security* 35 (1): 44–74.

Castree, Noel. 2001. *Social Nature*. Malden, MA: Blackwell Publishing.

Chaucer, Geoffrey. 2005. *The Canterbury Tales*. London: Penguin Classics.

Chung, Byung-ho. 2008. "Between Defector and Migrant: Identities and Strategies of North Koreans in South Korea." *Korean Studies* 32:1–27.

Cosgrove, Denis. 1984. *Social Formation and Symbolic Landscape*. Madison: University of Wisconsin Press.

———. 2004. "Landscape and Landschaft." Paper presented at the "Spatial Turn in History" Symposium, German Historical Institute, Washington DC, February 19.

Deleuze, Gilles, and Felix Guattari. 1984. *Anti-Oedipus: Capitalism and Schizophrenia*. London: Athlone Press.

———. 1987. *A Thousand Plateaus: Capitalism and Schizophrenia*. Minneapolis: University of Minnesota Press.

Gabroussenko, Tatiana, 2010. *Soldiers on the Cultural Front: Developments in the Early History of North Korean Literature and Literary Policy*. Honolulu: University of Hawai'i Press.

Grundy-Warr, Carl and Elaine Wong Siew Yin. 2002. "Geographies of Displacement: The Karenni and Shan Across the Myanmar-Thailand Border." *Singapore Journal of Tropical Geography* 23 (1): 93–122.

Haruki Wada. 1992. *Kin nissei to manshū kōnichi sensō* [Kim II Sung and the Manchurian anti-Japanese War]. Tokyo: Heibonsha.

Havrelock, Richard. 2011. *River Jordan: The Mythology of a Dividing Line.* Chicago: University of Chicago Press.

Hobsbawm, Eric, and Terence Ranger. 1983. *The Invention of Tradition.* Cambridge: Cambridge University Press.

Joinau, Benjamin. 2014. "The Arrow and the Sun: A Topo-Myth Analysis of Pyongyang." *Sungkyun Journal of East Asian Studies* 14 (1): 65–92.

KCNA [Korean Central News Agency]. 2017a. "Wreaths Laid at Bust of Kim Jong Suk." December 24. Accessed January 25, 2018. www.kcna.co.jp/item/2017 /201712/news22/2017124-14ee.html

———.2017b. "Kim Jong Suk's Birth Anniversary Marked in Hoeryong." December 24. Accessed January 25, 2018. www.kcna.co.jp/item/2017/201712/news22 /2017122-12ee.html

———.2017c. "Kim Jong Suk, Outstanding Woman Revolutionary." December 23. Accessed January 25, 2018. www.kcna.co.jp/item/2017/201712/news23 /2017123-15ee.html

———.2017d. "Coins to be Minted in DPRK to Mark Kim Jong Suk's 100th Birthday." December 22. Accessed January 25, 2018. www.kcna.co.jp/item/2017/201712 /news22/2017122-20ee.html

———.2017e. "Mementoes Associated with Immortal Feats of Kim Jong Suk." December 22. Accessed January 25, 2018. www.kcna.co.jp/item/2017/201712 /news22/2017122-11ee.html

Kwon, Heonik. 2013. "North Korea's New Legacy Politics." *E-International Relations.* https://www.e-ir.info/2013/05/16/north-koreas-new-legacy-politics/

Kwon, Heonik, and Byung-ho Chung. 2012. *North Korea: Beyond Charismatic Politics.* Lanham, MD: Rowman and Littlefield.

Marston, Sallie. 2000. "The Social Construction of Scale." *Progress in Human Geography* (2): 219–241.

Oh, Kong Dan. 1990. "North Korea in 1989: Touched by Winds of Change?" *Asian Survey* 30 (1): 74–80.

Paik, Nak-chung. 2011. *The Division System in Crisis.* Berkeley: University of California Press.

Park, Han S. 2007. "Military-First Politics (Songun): Understanding Kim Jong-il's North Korea." *KEI Academic Paper Series* 2 (7): 1–9.

Peiker, Piret. 2016. "Estonian Nationalism through the Postcolonial Lens." *Journal of Baltic Studies* 47 (1): 113–132.

Rodong Sinmun. 2014. "Leading Party Officials Start Study Tour of Revolutionary Battle Sites on Mt Paektu." July 31. Accessed August 17, 2014. http://www.rodong.rep.kp/en/index.php?strPageID=SF01_02_0&newsID =2014-07-31-0006&chAction=S

———.2015a. "The 250 Mile Schoolchildren's March." January 23. Accessed January 25, 2018. http://www.rodong.rep.kp/en/index.php?strPageID=SF01_02 _01&newsID=2015-01-23-0004&chAction=S

———.2015b. "The Schoolchildren's March Reaches Kanggye." February 3. Accessed January 25, 2018. http://www.rodong.rep.kp/en/index.php?strPageID =SF01_02_01&newsID=2015-02-03-0004&chAction=S

———. 2015c. "The Schoolchildren's March Reaches Phophyong." February 5. Accessed January 25, 2018. http://www.rodong.rep.kp/en/index.php ?strPageID=SF01_02_01&newsID=2015-02-05-0007&chAction=S

———.2018a. "Dancing Parties of Youth and Students Held." April 18. Accessed February 4, 2019. http://rodong.rep.kp/en/index.php?strPageID=SF01_02 _01&newsID=2018-04-18-0012

———.2018b. "Schoolchildren's Study Tour Starts." March 17. Accessed February 4, 2019. http://rodong.rep.kp/en/index.php?strPageID=SF01_02_01 &newsID=2018-03-17-0003

———.2018c. "Schoolchildren Visit Mangyongdae." June 9. Accessed February 4, 2019. http://rodong.rep.kp/en/index.php?strPageID=SF01_02_01&newsID =2018-06-09-0004

———.2018d. "Youth and Students Make Study Tour of Revolutionary Battle Sites in Mt Paektu." June 26. Accessed February 4, 2019. http://rodong.rep.kp/en/index .php?strPageID=SF01_02_01&newsID=2018-06-26-0003

———.2018e. "Officials and Members of Agricultural Workers Union Tour Area of Mt Paektu." August 16. Accessed February 4, 2019. http://rodong.rep.kp/en /index.php?strPageID=SF01_02_01&newsID=2018-08-16-0020

———.2018f. "Pak Pong Ju Inspects Samjiyon County and Tanchon Power Station under Construction." August 11. Accessed February 4, 2019. http://rodong.rep .kp/en/index.php?strPageID=SF01_02_01&newsID=2018-08-11-0009

———.2018g. "Pak Pong Ju Inspects Construction Sites in Samjiyon County." April 4. Accessed February 4, 2019. http://rodong.rep.kp/en/index.php?strPageID =SF01_02_01&newsID=2018-04-04-0008

———.2018h. "Schoolchildren Visit Mangyondae." June 9. Accessed February 4, 2019. http://rodong.rep.kp/en/index.php?strPageID=SF01_02_01&newsID =2018-06-09-0004

———.2019. "School Youth and Children Start Study Tour of Chairman Kim Jong Il's Birthplace." February 2. Accessed February 20, 2020. http://rodong.rep.kp /en/index.php?strPageID=SF01_02_01&newsID=2019-02-02-0008

———.2020a. "Schoolchildren Start March along Course of 250-Mile Journey for National Liberation." January 23. Accessed February 20, 2020. http://rodong.rep .kp/en/index.php?strPageID=SF01_02_01&newsID=2020-01-23-0001

———.2020b. "Schoolchildren on Tour of 250-Mile Journey for National Liberation Pass Hyangsan." January 26. Accessed February 20, 2020. http://rodong .rep.kp/en/index.php?strPageID=SF01_02_01&newsID=2020-01-26-0004

———.2020c. "Schoolchildren on Expedition of 250-Mile Journey for National Liberation Arrives in Kanggye." February 1. Accessed February 20, 2020. http://rodong.rep.kp/en/index.php?strPageID=SF01_02_01&newsID =2020-02-01-0002

———.2020d. "Schoolchildren's Expedition Group Arrives in Phophyong." February 4. Accessed February 20, 2020. http://rodong.rep.kp/en/index.php?strPageID =SF01_02_01&newsID=2020-02-04-0009

———.2020e. "UAWK Officials Start Tour of Revolutionary Battle Sites in Area of Mt Paektu." January 28. Accessed February 20, 2020. http://rodong.rep.kp/en /index.php?strPageID=SF01_02_01&newsID=2020-01-28-0001

———.2020f. "Youth League Officials Start Expedition to Revolutionary Battle Sites in Area of Mt Paektu." February 16. Accessed February 20, 2020. http://rodong.rep.kp/en/index.php?strPageID=SF01_02_01&newsID =2020-02-16-0004

———.2020g. "Commanding Officers of KPISF Tour Revolutionary Battle Sites in Mt Paektu Area." February 8. Accessed February 20, 2020. http://rodong.rep.kp /en/index.php?strPageID=SF01_02_01&newsID=2020-02-08-0009

Shim, David. 2013. *Visual Politics and North Korea: Seeing is Believing.* London: Routledge.

Shinn, Rin-Sup. 1982. "North Korea in 1981: First Year for De Facto Successor Kim Jong Il." *Asian Survey* 22 (1): 99–106.

Singer, Audrey, and Douglas Massey. 1988. "The Social Process of Undocumented Border Crossing among Mexican Migrants." *The International Migration Review* 32 (3): 561–592.

Smith, Hazel. 2015. *North Korea: Markets and Military Rule.* Cambridge: Cambridge University Press.

Smith, John. 1969. "Time, Times, and the 'Right Time'; Chronos and Kairos." *The Monist* 53 (1): 1–13.

Song, Nianshen. 2016. "Imagined Territory: Paektusan in Late Chosŏn Maps and Writings." *Studies in the Histories of Gardens and Designed Landscapes* 37 (2): 157–173.

———.2018. *Making Borders in Modern East Asia: The Tumen River Demarcation, 1881–1919.* Cambridge: Cambridge University Press.

Suh, Dae-sook. 1995. *Kim Il Sung: The North Korean Leader*. New York: Columbia University Press.

Swyngedouw, Eric. 1997. "Excluding the Other: The Production of Scale and Scaled Politics." In *Geographies of Economies*, edited by R. Lee, and J. Wills, 167–176. London: Arnold.

———. 2015. *Liquid Power*. Cambridge, MA: MIT Press.

Winstanley-Chesters, Robert. 2015. "'Patriotism Begins with a Love of Courtyard': Rescaling Charismatic Landscapes in North Korea." *Tiempo Devorado [Consumed Time]* 2 (2): 116–138.

———. 2016. "Charisma in a Watery Frame: North Korean Narrative Topographies and the Tumen River." *Asian Perspective* 40 (3): 393–414.

———. 2020. *New Goddess at Mt. Paektu: Myth and Transformation in North Korean Landscape*. Leeds: Black Halo/Amazon KDP.

Winstanley-Chesters, Robert, and Victoria Ten. 2016. "New Goddesses at Mt Paektu: Two Contemporary Korean Myths." *S/N Korean Humanities* 2 (1): 151–179.

Yoon, Dae-Kyu. 2017. "The Constitution of North Korea: Its Changes and Implications." In *Public Law in East Asia*, edited by Albert H. Y. Chen and Tom Ginsburg, 59–75. London: Routledge.

Zajas, Krysztof. 2013. *Absent Culture: The Case of Polish Livonia*. Frankfurt: Peter Lang.

CONTRIBUTORS

Andrew David Jackson is currently associate professor of Korean Studies at Monash University, Melbourne, where he has worked since 2017. Prior to this, he taught Korean Studies at the University of Copenhagen, Denmark. He obtained his PhD in Korean history from the School of Oriental and African Studies, University of London in 2011, where he wrote a dissertation on the Musin rebellion of 1728. He is also interested in modern Korean history and society, as well as South and North Korean film.

Codruța Sîntionean is assistant professor at the Department of Asian Languages and Literatures at Babeș-Bolyai University in Cluj-Napoca, Romania. She has been in charge of the section of Korean Language and Literature since its creation in 2008. Her academic interests include Korean heritage management practices and Korean history.

Remco Breuker is professor of Korean Studies at Leiden University, the Netherlands. A historian, he has published extensively on Korean and Northeast Asian medieval history and is one of the editors of the Cambridge History of Korea's medieval history volume. Next to his work on historical Korea, he also works on contemporary North Korea, in particular on exile narratives, human rights issues, and DPRK overseas economic activities.

CedarBough Saeji has an MA in Korean Studies from Yonsei University, and a PhD in Culture and Performance from UCLA. Saeji has taught

Korean Studies at University of British Columbia, Korea University, Hankuk University of Foreign Studies, Indiana University, Bloomington and is assistant professor in Korean and East Asian Studies at Pusan National University. Publications have appeared in edited volumes on women in traditional performing arts, Korean screen cultures, theater in Asia, and intangible cultural heritage, and journals including *Journal of Korean Studies, Korea Journal, Acta Koreana, Pacific Affairs, Asia Theatre Journal,* and *Asia Pacific Journal.*

Andrew Logie is assistant professor of Korean Studies at the University of Helsinki. His research interests include historiography of early northern East Asia, comparative approaches to early Korea and mainland Southeast Asia, Korean new religion, and twentieth-century popular music history. A graduate of the School of Oriental and African Studies, University of London, he completed his doctoral studies at the University of Helsinki with a postdoctoral period spent at Leiden University.

Don Baker is professor of Korean Civilization in the Department of Asian Studies at the University of British Columbia. He has published widely on philosophy, religion, and traditional science during the Chosŏn dynasty as well as on Korea's contemporary religious culture. He is the author of *Korean Spirituality* (University of Hawai'i Press, 2008) and *Catholics and Anti-Catholicism in Chosŏn Dynasty Korea* (University of Hawai'i Press, 2017). He is currently completing a translation of a commentary on the Confucian Classic *Zhongyong* by Chŏng Yak-yong.

Eunseon Kim is lecturer and convenor of the Korean Language Program in the School of Culture, History and Language at Australian National University. Her research interests include language ideology, the history of linguistic thought, and metalinguistic discourses, with a particular emphasis on Korean linguistic etiquette. She explores how speakers shape the cultural values of language in society in order to project identity, to establish group membership, and to engage with political issues.

Andreas Schirmer is an assistant professor at the Department of East Asian Studies at Palacky University Olomouc (Czech Republic). Holding a PhD in Modern German Literature from the University of Vienna, he has also completed a PhD program in Korean Language and Literature at Seoul National University. His current research relates to the representation of matters of public debate in contemporary Korean literature, to translation studies, and to historical cases of interaction between Koreans and Central Europeans.

Laurel Kendall (PhD, Columbia University, 1979, with distinction) is chair of Anthropology at the American Museum of Natural History and curator of Asian Ethnographic Collections at the Museum. Kendall is the author of many books and articles about Korean shamans, popular religion, material religion, modernity, heritage, and craft. Her *Shamans, Nostalgias and the IMF: South Korean Popular Religion in Motion* (University of Hawai'i Press, 2009) was the first winner of the Korean Society for Anthropology's Yim Suk-jay prize as the best work of Korean ethnography by a foreign scholar.

Keith Howard is emeritus professor and Leverhulme fellow at SOAS, University of London. He was formerly professor and associate dean at the University of Sydney, and has held visiting professorships at Monash University, Ewha Womans University, Hankuk University of Foreign Studies, and Texas Tech University. He has written and edited over twenty books as well as numerous articles and book and music reviews. He served as editorial chair for the SOAS Musicology Series (Ashgate/Routledge) and founded and managed the SOASIS CD and DVD labels as well as OpenAir Radio.

Jan Creutzenberg, a theater scholar, is an assistant professor in the Department of German Language and Literature at Ewha Womans University, Seoul. His research focuses on contemporary performing arts in Korea, with a particular interest in international and cross-genre collaborations. He has published and presented on the singing-storytelling art *p'ansori*, Shakespeare and Brecht in Korea, overseas performances of traditional music, and contributed to the *Routledge Handbook of Asian Theatre* (2016). He tweets as @JanCreutzenberg and blogs about his research and other performative experiences at seoulstages.wordpress.com.

Maria Osetrova is an associate professor at Moscow State Linguistic University and also a researcher at the Center for Korean Studies (Institute of Far Eastern Studies, Russian Academy of Sciences). She received her PhD in Korean Studies from Yonsei University in 2016 with a dissertation entitled "National Food and Gastronationalism in Contemporary Korea." Her main research interests include contemporary Korean culture and society (both North and South), food anthropology, and past and present of Russian-Korean cultural relations.

Robert Winstanley-Chesters is a geographer and lecturer at the University of Leeds, Bath Spa University, and a Member of Wolfson College, Oxford, formerly of Birkbeck, University of London, Australian National University, and Cambridge University. He is also managing editor of the *European Journal of Korean Studies*. He is author of *Environment, Politics and Ideology in North Korea* (Lexington, 2014), *Fish, Fishing and Community in North Korea and Neighbours: Vibrant Matters* (Springer, 2019), and *New Goddess of Mt Paektu: Myth and Transformation in North Korean Landscape* (Black Halo/Amazon KDP). Robert is currently researching North Korean necro-mobilities and other difficult or unwelcome bodies and materials in Korean/East Asian historical geography.

INDEX

Amnok River, 379, 380, 381, 384, 386, 391

An Ho-sang, 79, 89, 95

An Kyŏng-jŏn, 77–78, 80, 89, 92, 95

An Suk-sŏn, 289, 293, 295

antiquarianism, 44, 162

architecture, 32, 339–340, 344–346, 351–359, 379, 382

authenticity, 157, 221–223, 231, 239, 296, 336, 341; architecture, 346, 349, 353–355; Chosŏn period tradition, 230, 248; contention, 9–11; controversies over taekwondo, 20; and creativity, 271; food traditions in Korea, 324–325; historical materials (sources), 46, 61, 67–68, 122, 153–155, 167; means to determine, 257; mythology, 104; narratives of nation, 49, 54–56; *Sopyonje* and *p'ansori*, 22–26

Buddhist temples. *See* temples

cheya sasŏ (amateur histories), 52

Ch'ilbaek Ŭich'ong, 351, 357, 363n14

Chinese characters, 61, 115, 122, 142–143. See also *hanmun*; *hantcha*

Ch'iu, 98–99, 104

Cho In-sŏng, 52, 61

Choe Hwi, 385–386

ch'oga chip (thatched-roofed houses), 353

Choi Hong Hi (General), 19

Chŏlla Province, 23, 230, 232, 238–239, 247, 269

Chŏnbugyŏng (Celestial amulet sutra), 62, 71n13, 122, 127, 129

Chŏng Chae-hun, 348, 351, 353, 362n6

Chŏng In-bo, 79, 80, 86, 91

Chŏng Nam-hŭi, 262–264

Chŏng Yak-yong, 108n15, 109n26, 126, 189, 211n50

chŏnghwa saŏp (purification project), 339–340, 348–353, 356–359

Chŏnju, 128, 269, 359

Chosŏn (dynasty), 352; architecture, 352–355, 359; border with Qing, 375; *Chosŏn wangjo sillok* (see *sillok*); comb making, 236, 239; forged sources, 59; hangul, 144–145; historical understandings of ancient Korean states, 86; historiographers of, 63–65, 103; internal alchemy practices and medical practices, 123–127, 131; Koryŏ transition, 30; in North Korean historiography, 390; Park Chung Hee's negative assessment of, 342–343; Park Chung Hee's use of, 13–14, 16, 336, 342–345, 347, 353, 361; propriety, 156–160, 161, 163–165; satires, 194–195; Sinitic influences, 48, 157; Tan'gun-Kija in histories, 85, 127; tea drinking, 320; T'oegye, 125–127. *See also* Kojosŏn

Chumong, 82, 84

Chŭngsando (millenarian cult), 77, 96

colonialism, 8–9, 13, 24, 29, 31, 47–49, 80, 142–143

Confucianism, 84, 89, 92, 119, 127, 131, 160–161, 164, 189, 256, 343

conservation, 192, 199, 202, 203, 348, 355

cuisine, 34n15, 231, 304–320, 356

Cultural Heritage Administration (CHA), 225, 339–340, 344–359, 361n1, 362n6, 326nn9–10, 363n15

HAWAI'I STUDIES ON KOREA